· IN THE SHADOW OF ·
OLYMPUS

IN THE SHADOW OF

· THE · EMERGENCE

Eugene N. Borza

OLYMPUS

OF · MACEDON

PRINCETON UNIVERSITY PRESS

PRINCETON, NEW JERSEY

Library of Congress Cataloging-in-Publication Data

Borza, Eugene N.
In the shadow of Olympus: the emergence of Macedon / Eugene N. Borza.
p.   cm.
Includes bibliographical references and index.
ISBN 0-691-05549-1—ISBN 0-691-00880-9 (pbk.)
1. Macedonia—History—To 168 B.C. I. Title.
DF261.M2B67   1992   938.1—dc20   92–7973

· FOR KATHLEEN ·

• CONTENTS •

viii CONTENTS

· ILLUSTRATIONS ·

· P R E F A C E ·

Wrangle HAT follows is an account of ancient Macedon down to the age of Philip and Alexander. It was prompted by an interest in the historical geography, historiography and emerging archaeology of Macedonia. Two factors intervened to prevent this book from extending its scope into the Hellenistic period. The first was the untimely death in 1981 of my collaborator, Harry J. Dell, who was to have undertaken the history of the Antigonids in Macedonia. Second, there have appeared recently a number of works that deal in part or in whole with Hellenistic Macedon, and the interested reader now has a variety of sound, up-to-date views to consider. Moreover, fresh archaeological evidence from the Hellenistic era, while welcome, has provided relatively fewer new insights into the period than have comparable discoveries for the fourth century B.C. And, with the continuing appearance of interpretative histories of Philip II and Alexander the Great, it has seemed best, for the moment, to concentrate on early Macedonia.

Part of this book is narrative and part is thematic. It attempts to be chronologically comprehensive down to the death of Philip II in 336 B.C. It deals with the age of Alexander the Great in limited fashion, only as part of the continuum of Macedonian institutions and cultural expressions. I hope to have shown that the emergence of Macedon as a great power in antiquity from the shadow of the Greek city-states is paralleled in our own day by an increasing appreciation of distinctive Macedonian institutions and material culture.

Inevitably this work will be compared—for better or worse—with parts of Nicholas Hammond et al., *A History of Macedonia* (3 vols., Oxford: 1972–88). One suspects that parts of *A History of Macedonia* will not need revision for decades. But the very value of Hammond as a *Handbuch* has made it nearly inaccessible for all but the specialists, with other readers using it mainly for consultation on particular points rather than for narrative (Griffith's sections of Philip II and parts of the third volume on the Hellenistic kings excepted). Moreover, the first two volumes of Hammond were largely written by 1974, and thus could not take into account the remarkable archaeological discoveries in Macedonia since 1977. If there were no other reason to produce an

up-to-date Macedonian history for the earlier period, the need to incorporate the results of recent excavations alone would suffice. I regret
that I have been able to do little more than note for bibliographical
purposes most work published after 1986.

It is a purpose of this volume to offer an accessible historical essay to
anyone interested in the emergence of Macedon. That I do not agree
with Hammond's interpretations on a number of points should not be
construed as a diminution of respect for his pioneering effort. Where
differences exist, they will be so indicated, and the reader is free to
pursue these matters and decide between our respective views. On
some issues I hope to have broken new ground, and such issues will be
presented in technical detail. On others I have attempted to synthesize
existing opinion without arguing each question afresh. This procedure
will be especially evident in those areas in which I am not qualified as
a specialist. For the obligation of the historian in such cases is to read
the technical literature of the specialists who tend to write mainly for
one another, and to summarize their conclusions accurately for the
readers of a wide-ranging general history. The last quarter of the twentieth century has been marked by fertile scholarship in Macedonian
studies, and the present work intends to reflect that.

The history of a people is never conclusively written, and this author
expects that in time the present work will become obsolete, especially
in light of the rapidly expanding archaeology of the Balkans. No
doubt I have permitted myself more latitude of interpretation than I
might have expressed in a technical journal. Even so, the reader will
find the analyses cautious, perhaps too much so for some tastes. It remains for those who follow to offer other interpretations based on a
more sophisticated understanding of the historical process, better historical method, and the new evidence that archaeology is certain to
provide. Thus, this work is offered to those who seek some understanding in light of present knowledge, and to those who will use it to
improve and refine what is set out here.

In the matter of transliteration of Greek proper names, I have, like
many others before me, tried for consistency and failed. One should
simply accept the injunction of two great travellers in Greece—Col.
W. M. Leake and Stuart Rossiter—who, a century and a half apart,
recognized that in this matter "it is impossible in any manner to avoid
inconsistency."

In order to forestall chaos I have adopted the following system to
make things more comfortable for the reader. I have kept in their English form a number of names so common that any alteration might

prove inconvenient or precious (e.g., Athens, Corinth, Alexander, Philip). Other ancient Greek names have been given in Latin forms recognizable in the Western world (e.g., Herodotus, Archelaus, Eurydice, Eordaea). Where the ancient place name is still in common use and widely known I have used its Latin form (e.g., Olympus, Boeotia, Euboea); where not so well known, a standard transliteration from the modern Greek form is employed (e.g., Axios, Thasos, Pangaion, Peneios). Modern Greek names that have little or no famous ancient heritage have been transliterated directly, preserving the pronunciation whenever possible (e.g., Veria, Kozani, Paiko, Vergina). Anomalies exist, and I hope that, like the author, the reader will not worry too much about them.

· ACKNOWLEDGMENTS ·

Iт is a pleasure to record my thanks to a number of fellow scholars who have, over the years, shared their insights and provided information and criticism from their various disciplines: W. Lindsay Adams, Beryl Barr-Sharrar, William Biers, Judith Binder, A. B. Bosworth, Stanley M. Burstein, the late Harry J. Dell, J. R. Ellis, Ernst A. Fredricksmeyer, Paul B. Harvey, Jr., Frank L. Holt, George Huxley, Stella G. Miller, and Nancy J. Serwint.

Without the cooperation of colleagues in Greece, much of the archaeological, topographical, epigraphical, and linguistic material incorporated into this work would not have emerged into print. My Greek friends have my gratitude for helping make this an international effort: Manolis Andronikos, Kostas Buraselis, Miltiades B. Hatzopoulos, Louisa Laourdas, Dimitris Pandermalis, Photios Petsas, Katerina Rhomiopoulou, Chrysoula Saatsoglou-Paliadeli, Maria Siganidou, Yiannis Touratsoglou, and Julia Vokotopoulou.

Some persons listed above do not share all of my views concerning the Macedonians, but our differences do not limit my gratitude for their friendship and assistance on matters great and small.

At various stages of preparation, I have been the recipient of grants from the American Philosophical Society, the American Council of Learned Societies, and the Research Office of the College of the Liberal Arts of the Pennsylvania State University. Their generosity has enabled me to visit nearly every part of the Balkans mentioned in this volume, and I acknowledge with pleasure the value of those autoptical experiences. Most of the writing was done in London and Athens during sabbatical leaves granted by the Pennsylvania State University. I owe much to three librarians: Anna Healey, Institute of Classical Studies, University of London, where this book began; and Nancy Winter and Anastasia Dinsmoor, American School of Classical Studies, Athens, where it was finished.

A special acknowledgment is due three eminent scholars. The first is the dean of American "Macedoniasts," the late Charles F. Edson, who counseled in 1970, when I complained that I was bored and frustrated by my work on Alexander the Great, that I should delve into Alexander's Macedonian background. Nicholas Hammond, many of whose views are challenged herein, has remained a lively and cherished companion who pointed the way in Macedonian studies. And Ernst Badian has, during twenty years of friendship and encouragement, continued to set the standards that have taught the value of severe criticism. I regret that those who first taught me ancient history, Sam L. Greenwood and Stewart I. Oost, are no longer alive to read—and criticize—my work.

The maps were prepared by Eric Janota and Tammy Mistrick at Deasy GeoGraphics Laboratory of the Pennsylvania State University, under grants provided by Penn State's Department of History and College of the Liberal Arts.

The sound advice, frequent encouragement, and remarkable patience shown by Joanna Hitchcock at Princeton University Press kept the project on track under sometimes difficult circumstances. Peter M. Green read the manuscript with unusual care, and my work profited from his great learning and excellent eye. The infelicities that remain stem from my own stubbornness and inattention.

The most important contribution was made by her to whom the book is dedicated—wife, companion, friend, and editor. She alone has known the full burden of it.

Boalsburg, Pennsylvania
September 1988

For the Paperback Edition

I am grateful to Princeton University Press for the opportunity to produce an updated edition of this work. This has enabled me both to correct lapses and alter some minor points in the original text, and to add a few pages describing recent developments in the historical/archaeological scholarship on Macedonia. My indebtedness to colleagues in this country and abroad will be described in detail in the new appendix.

Boalsburg, Pennsylvania
December 1991

· ABBREVIATIONS ·

AAA	*Athens Annals of Archaeology*
AHB	*Ancient History Bulletin*
AHGr	Great Britain Admiralty Handbook, *Greece*
AHR	*American Historical Review*
AJA	*American Journal of Archaeology*
AJAH	*American Journal of Ancient History*
AJP	*American Journal of Philology*
AM	*Archaia Makedonia*, Proceedings of the International Symposia on Ancient Macedonia
AncW	*Ancient World*
AnnPisa	*Annali della Scuola Normale Superiore di Pisa*
AR	*Archaeological Reports*
ArchDelt	*Archaiologikon Deltion*
ArchEph	*Archaiologiki Ephemeris*
ArchNews	*Archaeological News*
AthMitt	*Mitteilungen des Deutschen Archäologischen Instituts. Athenische Abteilung*
ATL	*The Athenian Tribute Lists*
BalkSt	*Balkan Studies*
BAR	*British Archaeological Reports*
BCH	*Bulletin de correspondance hellénique*
BICS	*Bulletin of the Institute of Classical Studies*
BSA	*Annual of the British School at Athens*
C&M	*Classica et Medievalia*
CAH	*Cambridge Ancient History*
CHI	*Cambridge History of Iran*
CJ	*Classical Journal*
Comm. Thuc.	A. W. Gomme et al., *A Historical Commentary on Thucydides*
CP	*Classical Philology*
CQ	*Classical Quarterly*
CR	*Classical Review*
FGrH	F. Jacoby, *Die Fragmente der griechischen Historiker*
G&R	*Greece & Rome*

GRBS	*Greek, Roman and Byzantine Studies*
HM	N.G.L. Hammond, G. T. Griffith, and F. W. Walbank, *A History of Macedonia*
HSCP	*Harvard Studies in Classical Philology*
IG	*Inscriptiones Graecae*
JAS	*Journal of Archaeological Science*
JFA	*Journal of Field Archaeology*
JHS	*Journal of Hellenic Studies*
LCM	*Liverpool Classical Monthly*
M-L *GHI*	R. Meiggs and D. Lewis, *A Selection of Greek Historical Inscriptions*
PAPS	*Proceedings of the American Philosophical Association*
PM	M. B. Hatzopoulos and L. D. Loukopoulos, *Philip of Macedon*
PMI	J. R. Ellis, *Philip II and Macedonian Imperialism*
PP	*La Parola del Passato*
PPS	*Proceedings of the Prehistoric Society*
RE	Pauly-Wissowa, *Realencyclopädie des classischen Altertumswissenschaft*
REA	*Revue des études anciennes*
REG	*Revue des études grecques*
RIDA	*Revue Internationale des Droits de l'Antiquité*
SEG	*Supplementum Epigraphicum Graecum*
SO	*Symbolae Osloenses*
TAPA	*Transactions of the American Philological Association*
Tod *GHI*	M. N. Tod, *A Selection of Greek Historical Inscriptions*
WA	*World Archaeology*

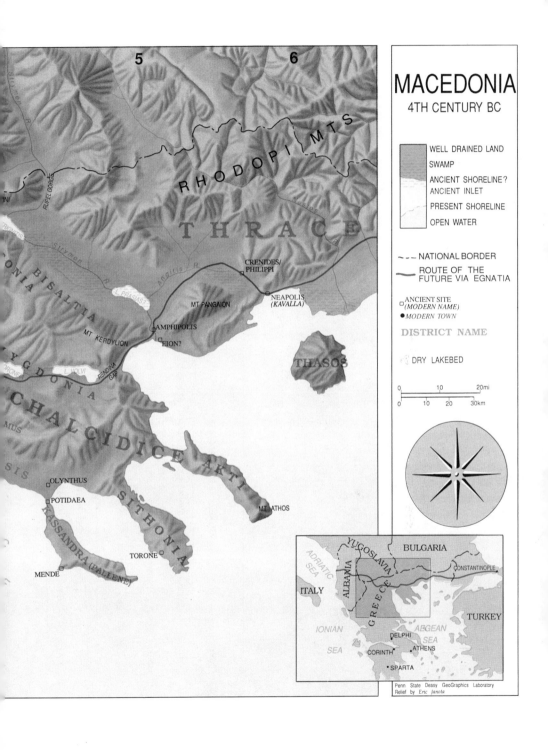

5   6

RHODOPI MTS

THRACE

MACEDONIA
4TH CENTURY BC

WELL DRAINED LAND
SWAMP
ANCIENT SHORELINE?
ANCIENT INLET
PRESENT SHORELINE
OPEN WATER

--- NATIONAL BORDER
ROUTE OF THE
FUTURE VIA EGNATIA

□ ANCIENT SITE
  (MODERN NAME)
● MODERN TOWN

DISTRICT NAME

DRY LAKEBED

0   10   20mi
0   10   20   30km

RUPEL GORGE

Strymon R.

Strymon R.

L. PRASIAS?

Angitis R.

CRENIDES/
PHILIPPI

MT PANGAION

NEAPOLIS
(KAVALLA)

AMPHIPOLIS

MT KERDYLION

EION?

L. VOLVI

RENDINA
GAP

THASOS

BISALTIA

YGDONIA

CHALCIDICE   AKTI

OLYNTHUS

POTIDAEA

KASSANDRA (PALLENE)

MENDE

SITHONIA

TORONE

MT ATHOS

YUGOSLAVIA   BULGARIA

ADRIATIC
SEA

ALBANIA

GREECE

CONSTANTINOPLE

ITALY

TURKEY

IONIAN
SEA

AEGEAN
SEA

DELPHI

CORINTH

ATHENS

SPARTA

Penn State Deasy GeoGraphics Laboratory
Relief by Eric Janota

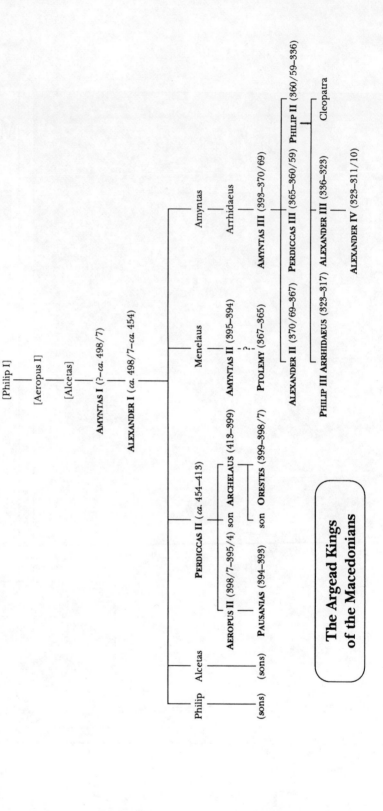

The Argead Kings of the Macedonians

[Perdiccas I]

[Argaeus]

[Philip I]

[Aeropus I]

[Alcetas]

AMYNTAS I (?–ca. 498/7)

ALEXANDER I (ca. 498/7–ca. 454)

Philip

Alcetas

(sons)

(sons)

AEROPUS II (398/7–395/4) son

PERDICCAS II (ca. 454–413)

PAUSANIAS (394–393)

ARCHELAUS (413–399)

son

ORESTES (399–398/7)

Menelaus

AMYNTAS II (395–394)

PTOLEMY (367–365)

Amyntas

Arrhidaeus

AMYNTAS III (393–370/69)

ALEXANDER II (370/69–867)

PHILIP III ARRHIDAEUS (323–317)

PERDICCAS III (365–360/59)

ALEXANDER III (336–323)

Cleopatra

PHILIP II (360/59–336)

ALEXANDER IV (323–311/10)

CHAPTER 1

Toward a History of Ancient Macedonia

THE frontiers of the Greek world have until recently received scant attention.[1] Scholarship—and indeed public interest—has been mainly focused on the great centers of Classical Greece: Athens, Corinth, Delphi, Olympia, and Sparta, to name a few; or on the popular archaeological sites of the Bronze Age: Knossos, Mycenae, Tiryns, and Santorini, among others. This phenomenon is due in part to the central themes of a rich ancient literature—much of it produced in Athens—and to the remarkable series of excavations conducted by Greek and foreign archaeologists in the central, southern, and Aegean regions of the country. It is also not a coincidence that the development of these archaeological sites corresponds with the growth of tourism (a major source of revenue for the modern Greek state) and that most of these sites lie within a few hours' journey from Athens by air, land, or sea.[2]

A perusal of the shelves of any well-stocked classics library reveals the enormous amount of space taken up by the excavation reports of the famous sites.[3] Taking into account the popular and scholarly general accounts of the Classical period, the often lavish and very beautiful picture books, and the guide books and histories, one could come away with the impression that ancient cultures in Greece existed mainly in such places. Barely noticed, tucked away midst these vol-

[1] Parts of this chapter, originally prepared for this volume, were presented as a paper to the symposium held in conjunction with the opening of the exhibition, "The Search for Alexander," at the National Gallery of Art, in Washington, D.C., in 1980. The paper was published, along with the others read at that symposium, in Barr-Sharrar and Borza, *Macedonia and Greece in Late Classical and Early Hellenistic Times.* I use the present opportunity to offer some altered views and new material.

[2] It may strike one as significant that Olynthus, Philippi, Dion, and Thasos, magnificent ancient sites, are relatively unknown to the visitor, while the remains of Corinth are among the two or three most popular tourist attractions in Greece. Corinth's popularity is due in part to its location, an hour and a half by road from Athens, en route to Mycenae, Epidaurus, Olympia, and other Peloponnesian sites.

[3] An informal shelf count reveals 32 separate volumes for Corinth, 34 (in 43 parts) for Delos, 32 for Delphi, 20 for the Athenian Agora, and 26 for Olympia.

umes, would be a few works with titles like *Epirus*, *Early Civilization in Thessaly*, *The Thracians*, *Archaia Makedonia*, and *Altthrakien*. These areas were the marches of the Greek world, peopled with "half-Greeks," as the late L. H. Jeffery called them. They are regions not much exploited archaeologically (the islands of Thasos and Samothrace and the fine inland site of Olynthus are among the exceptions). It is almost as if the northern and western regions of the Greek peninsula were to be forever relegated to the half-light of the barbarian world. It is to be regretted, for example, that we have as yet little internal evidence for two important and wealthy Chalcidic cities: Mende has not been systematically excavated, and the site of Torone has only recently been explored for the first time.

Yet it is an encouraging trend in classical scholarship that these remote areas are beginning to receive attention. Several factors account for this emergence. We may have nearly reached a stage of exhaustion in mining the traditional sources for Greek history. How much more historical material can be squeezed from Thucydides? What new authors will come to light? It is sobering to reflect that, a half dozen or so recent major finds excepted, virtually all the Greek literature we now possess has been known since the Italian Renaissance. Indeed, it may be the simple passage of time, during which we have worked carefully through the literary evidence from antiquity, that now forces us to seek fresh materials. As these seem not to be forthcoming for Classical Greece, we turn increasingly to non-Classical periods—note, for example, the recent surge of interest in the Dark Ages and Archaic period—and to regions heretofore thought to be outside the mainstream of Greek history.

Moreover, most of the important Classical sites in the south have been dug, and, while much remains to be excavated, increasing urbanization, industrial development, and large-scale agriculture will make it economically undesirable and technically difficult to explore virgin archaeological zones. Major Bronze Age excavation will probably continue apace. Interest in the period is high, many of the sites are located in sparsely populated areas, and the Greek government sees such regions as attractive to tourism. Thus, virtually by default, attention shifts to the peripheral areas, many of which are not yet densely peopled and industrialized, where one may still walk unhindered over field and slope, noting surface sherds and identifying natural landmarks. As we turn to less familiar and mainly unworked regions, we do so with a sound base of traditional Greek history and an increasing skill in the integration of literary evidence with material finds. We also have learned much from the social, behavioral, and physical sciences, which enable us to join to the critical core of humanistic endeavor the insights of economics, cultural, and physical anthropology, geology, and environmental studies. The final decades of this century are proving to be a new era of fulfillment for the study of Balkan regions hitherto relatively unknown. And this is no more true for any region than for ancient Macedonia.[4]

Ancient Macedonia: The Nineteenth-Century View

The course of Macedonian studies in the modern era has been fitful. Neglect of Macedonia has occurred partly for the reasons stated above: funds for excavation have usually been directed toward the more accessible, famous, and tourist-oriented sites in the southern lands and islands of Greece, places that have direct links with a literature and history that once formed the core of education in the West, and that continue to permeate the popular consciousness everywhere.

Ironically, the ancient Macedonians themselves are unwittingly partly responsible for their own relative obscurity. They produced a commander of unrivaled reputation whose career—part conquest and part romance—has overwhelmed the literature on Macedon, and has diverted our attention from the society from which he sprang. Moreover, in their own day both Alexander the Great and his father, Philip, incurred the enmity of the greatest of the Athenian orators. Demosthenes' castigations of the Macedonian kings have echoed through the centuries. Whatever one thinks of Macedon's conquest of Greece, Demosthenes has had his revenge, as the Demosthenic view of the Macedonians has affected our understanding of fourth-century Greek politics. That view produced a drama in which the "civilized" cities of Greece, led by Demosthenes and the Athenians, struggled against domination by the northern "barbarians," Philip and his Macedonian warriors.

Only recently have we begun to clarify these muddy waters by revealing the Demosthenic corpus for what it is: oratory designed to sway public opinion at Athens and thereby to formulate public policy. That elusive creature, Truth, is everywhere subordinate to its expressive servant, Rhetoric. Demosthenes' pronouncements are often no

---

[4] The sentiment of these last sentences was originally expressed in the summer of 1977 as part of my review-article of Ellis, *PMI*, entitled "Philip II and the Greeks" (239). In another part of the same essay (238) I wrote: "Few regions of modern Greece hold so much promise for excavation as Macedonia." Within three months M. Andronikos had uncovered the royal cemetery at Vergina (ancient Aegae), and within a year a number of important contributions to Macedonian studies, long in preparation, reached print.

6 **CHAPTER 1**

more an accurate recording of the events and personalities of the day than are the public statements of politicians in any age.[5] The Demosthenic view colored our reconstruction of events. Demosthenes' language and elegant style made him part of the Athenian literary traditions that have pervaded Western education and culture, appealing not only to our refined tastes but also to our patriotic feelings. Few persons spoke in behalf of the Macedonians in their day, and those who did were regarded as fools or traitors. Macedon spoke with its spears. But Macedonian arms, so effective against Demosthenes during his life, have been powerless against him since.

Moreover, the ancient Macedonians inhabited an area that was a hinterland of modern Greece. At the very moment when Heinrich Schliemann, Wilhelm Dörpfeld, and Arthur Evans were uncovering the riches of Bronze Age culture in the Peloponnesus and Crete, Macedonia still lay uneasily under Turkish overlordship. Most of ancient Macedonia was incorporated into the modern Greek state only in 1913 (see below, pp. 9–10), and it has been a politically sensitive region ever since, in its relationships both with the Athens-dominated government in the south and with its non-Hellenic neighbors to the north.

During World War I there was widespread internal opposition to the Greek government's policy of accommodation with the Central Powers. In 1916 a National Movement was formed under the leadership of Eleftherios Venizelos, who established an alternative provisional government at Salonica. By June 1917 the Salonica-based movement had succeeded in gaining the recognition of the Allies and overthrowing the regime at Athens. As late as the 1950s and 1960s there existed among right-wing politicians and military officers in Athens a deep suspicion of and hostility toward left-wing politicians and university students in Salonica. Fear of left-wing trends in the north contributed to the coup that produced the military dictatorship of 1967–74. The important strategic character of Macedonia is reflected in the current organization of the Greek government: Macedonia (including western Thrace) possesses its own cabinet-level minister, the Minister for Northern Greece. The only other region of the nation to claim its own ministry is the Aegean.

Comprehensive studies of Macedonia are thus a mark of recent twentieth-century scholarship. The nineteenth century saw Macedonia largely in terms of political biography and "missionary history." The

[5] This is made clear everywhere in Ellis, *PMI*. Of course, *everything* said by Demosthenes is part of the history of the period because it reveals Demosthenes' views and the politics of Athens.

"mission" was the notion prevalent in German scholarship
Philip and Alexander's destiny to propagate Hellenic u'
spread the higher culture of the Greeks among the more b&
peoples of the world. It was a civilizing mission. It had little to do wɪ.
Macedon or Macedonian history except insofar as that northern race
had produced two men whose historical impact was undeniable.
Philip, after all, was the conqueror and unifier of Greek city-states long
torn by internecine conflict. Thus freed from the burden of energies
dissipated in continual strife, the Greeks might at last release their
higher culture upon the world, with the Macedonians acting as the
vehicle for its spread. The impetuous, brilliant young Alexander, tutored by Aristotle, fond of Homer and Euripides, was the suitable instrument for the mission.

It was a dynamic idea in the minds of nineteenth-century scholars,
made no less important by the fact that many German intellectuals and
politicians felt witness to the same phenomenon in their own day: the
unification of the German states and the consequent spread of their
own *Kultur*. This vision remained a feature of German scholarship on
the subject—the emergence of the World Figure as a stabilizing force
and as the articulator of the potent energies of a creative people. Until
the Hohenzollern collapse, the modern analogy was the adoration of
the Prussian dynasty. In the twentieth century it was transformed into
a more generalized messianic *Führerprinzip*.[6] Whatever the value of this
concept as a reflection of contemporary moods in historiography and
political ideology, it has dealt mainly with the dramatic external features of Macedonian history, such as the conquests of famous kings.
Serious study of the infrastructure of Macedonian society and history
still lay in the shadow of ancient Argead imperialism and modern
Prussian diplomacy.

One of the inescapable dilemmas faced especially by German scholars was the recognition that Philip, the embodiment of national will
and the unifier of Greece, was also regarded as a threat to the higher
civilization of an Athens widely admired among educated persons in
the Western world. Even the staunchest advocates of Philip's apparent
single-minded resolve were forced to retreat before Demosthenes'
ringing cries for freedom from tyranny. Few saw through the rhetoric.
When the English historian-archaeologist D. G. Hogarth attempted in

[6] The phrase is Badian's, from his "Some Recent Interpretations of Alexander," 281.
Although dogmatic and polemical in its conclusions, Badian's essay is an excellent review of German attitudes toward Alexander, with special reference to the National Socialist and post-World War II periods. Other useful summaries are given by Green (*Alexander of Macedon*, 482ff.), and by Borza (in Wilcken, *Alexander the Great*, xii–xxi).

1897 to present a view of Philip that emphasized the king's *Macedonian* outlook, echoed Diodorus Siculus's (16.95.1–4) encomium to Philip's statesmanship, hinted at some duplicity in Demosthenes' activities, and questioned the orator's ethics, his book was greeted with mixed reviews.[7] Western philhellenism and pro-Athenian sentiment were too strong to permit a serious attempt to acquit Philip of the charge of threatening civilization by warring with Athens. Thus Hogarth's work had little effect on subsequent scholarship. Early twentieth-century historians continued occasionally to write political biographies of the pre-eminent fourth-century B.C. kings, and when they did consider Macedonian affairs they viewed them only as part of general Greek history.[8] What was required for a deeper understanding of Macedon and its kings were serious source studies and archaeology, but archaeological interest remained dormant for decades because twentieth-century interest in Macedonia sprang from modern politics rather than from the study of antiquity.

Macedonian Studies and the "Macedonian Question"

In modern times "Macedonia" has meant mainly *to Makedonikon zē-tēma*, the infamous "Macedonian Question." At least as early as the 1880s, both the Great Powers and local irredentists were anticipating the prospect of allocating portions of the decaying Ottoman Empire in Europe. No part of European Turkey was more complex than Macedonia, with its roiling mix of nationalities and its great prize, the port of Salonica (Thessaloniki), Aegean gateway to the Balkans. One visitor to Salonica could describe it thus: "There congregates a confusion of nationalities and of dirt unsurpassed at least in Europe . . . all around such a confusion of high-pitched voices as can only be fitly compared to the parrot-house in the Regent's Park." And another: "Salonica has the moral squalor of Europe with the physical squalor of

[7] Hogarth, *Philip and Alexander*. For more detail on Hogarth's place in Macedonian historiography, see Borza, "Philip II and the Greeks," 236–38, and "David George Hogarth," 97–101.

[8] Some examples of the former: Wilcken, "Philip II"; Momigliano, *Filippo il Macedone*; F. R. Wüst, *Philipp II*; Cloché, *Un fondateur d'empire* and *Histoire de la Macédoine*. Examples of the latter: a cursory survey of the influential modern histories of Greece (Beloch, Berve, Bengtson, Busolt, Holm, Bury, and the early editions of the *Cambridge Ancient History*) reveals only casual references to the Macedonians before the reign of Philip II. Even Hammond, *History of Greece*, 3rd ed.—mainly a reprint of the 1959 and 1967 editions—has rather little on early Macedonia. Only E. Curtius, in his *Griechische Geschichte*, 6th ed., deals with Macedonia at length in a separate section on northern lands. Curtius's regional organization has much merit.

the East."[9] Perhaps nowhere else in Europe had the centuries left such
a multiethnic residue as in Macedonia.[10] The region abounded in en-
claves and admixtures of Greeks, Bulgarians, Serbs, Jews, Turks, Albanians, Vlachs, other minority groups, those of mixed ancestry, and
those of uncertain or even capricious nationality (the salad "macédoine" is well named). The very definition of nationality was unsettled. Did one's ethnic identity depend upon language, religion, adherence to a local political faction, or loyalty to a foreign state? Not only
could the western European observers not agree, but in a region where
some Jews practiced Islam and some Bulgarian-speakers regarded
themselves as Greek, it was apparent that even many of the residents
were uncertain what the basis of nationality should be. In a land whose
villages were being ravaged by bands of terrorists representing national
liberation movements, the local inhabitants often resorted to whatever
languages or customs might enhance their chances of survival as the
raiders swept through their lives.

As Turkish authority in the region waned, new nations and allegiances emerged. Albania took form as a separate modern state. Serbs,
Bulgarians, and Greeks fought first against the Turks and then against
one another for control of Macedonia. The result of these two Balkan
Wars (1912–13) and the First World War was the success of the Serbian
claim to the northwestern regions of Macedonia, the cession to Greece
of Epirus, central and western Macedonia, and the eastern portions up
to the Nestos River (including Salonica and Kavalla), and the granting
to Bulgaria of much of the remainder of Ottoman lands in Europe.

Two significant historical movements may be observed in this period. One is the desire for the Ottoman overthrow and the reconciliation of Great Power interests with local independence movements.
The second is the attempt by Bulgaria, a state facing the Black Sea, to
gain a Mediterranean seaboard by establishing a claim along the Aegean in Macedonia and Thrace. Blocking Bulgarian aspirations was
Greece, which claimed both regions on the basis of a historical continuity going back to antiquity. The situation was exacerbated by the

---

[9] The first quotation is from Hogarth, "In Macedonia," 282; the second is from Brailsford, *Macedonia*, 83. The latter's sympathies were with the Bulgarians on the Macedonian question, while Hogarth's views were more balanced, if slightly prohellenic. Salonica's population in the late nineteenth century was estimated at 110,000, of whom about
70,000 were Sephardic Jews, descendants of the Jewish community forced to evacuate
Spain in the late fifteenth century. During World War II, most of Salonica's Jews were
deported by the Germans, and exterminated.

[10] For a colorful contemporary account of the rich ethnic mix of early nineteenth-
century Macedonia, see Cousinery, *Voyage*, ch. 1.

inextricable mixture of Greeks and Bulgarians in many of the disputed areas.[11] The Greeks seized Salonica early in the first Balkan war against the Turks. On 9 November 1912 a Greek army raced into the city just hours before the arrival of a Bulgarian force. Although frantic diplomatic efforts averted a military struggle for control of the city, the Bulgarians were outraged at having been deprived of their prize. Salonica has been Greek from that day, and the Bulgarians were deprived of their Thracian littoral by the Treaty of Lausanne (1923), which fixed the Greek-Turkish frontier at the Evros River, where it remains today. Bulgaria was thus shut out of the Aegean. The Bulgarian-Greek bitterness that smoldered in the region throughout the interwar period broke out openly during the Second World War when nearly all of eastern Macedonia was given by the Germans to Bulgaria to administer as occupied territory. The Bulgarians proceeded to incorporate the region into their state, thus temporarily regaining an Aegean outlet.[12] Moreover, the lure of Salonica for Balkan Slavs was still strong. There is evidence to suggest that Germany offered Salonica (at different moments) to *both* Yugoslavia and Bulgaria as an enticement to cooperate with German policy in the Balkans in 1940–41;[13] the ancient Slavic dream of an Aegean port was thus exploited by Germany with considerable effectiveness.

As the World War II Occupation was transformed into a prolonged period of civil strife inside Greece, the Yugoslav and Bulgarian socialist states continued to press the Macedonian Question, sometimes favoring the creation of a Greater Macedonia dominated by Slavs, at other times favoring the detachment of parts of Greek Macedonia, but always to the detriment of Greek territorial integrity. The communist insurrection in Greece eventually failed for a number of reasons fully described in the literature on the period.[14] One of the principal features of this civil war is that Greek communists were supported at various times by Yugoslavia, Bulgaria, and the U.S.S.R. But Yugoslav and

[11] In 1902 the Greek prime minister, Alexander Zaïmis, openly admitted that the chief threat to Hellenism in Macedonia came from the Bulgarians, not the Turks; see Bridge, *Austro-Hungarian Documents*, doc. #50 (report of the Austro-Hungarian legation in Athens).

[12] Discussed at length by Kofos, *Nationalism and Communism*, 100–110; this is an unusually objective and well-documented work, given its subject and the provenance of its publication.

[13] Ibid., 96–97, evidence cited. It is significant that the Germans, who permitted virtually all of the surrounding areas in Macedonia up to the Axios to be controlled by the Bulgarians, never relinquished authority over Salonica itself.

[14] E.g., the account of Woodhouse (*The Struggle for Greece, 1941–1949*), with full bibliography of secondary literature and sources from all sides.

Bulgarian interests in Macedonia were incompatible with the Hellenic ethnocentricity of most members of the Communist Party of Greece (KKE).[15] And when the Soviet Union eventually ordered the KKE to conform to Bulgaria's view of the Macedonian question, Greek communists and leftists found themselves in a precarious position, caught between official policy and their own Hellenic identity, the latter reinforced by ideological principles based on Lenin's doctrines about self-determination: Greek Macedonia was comprised largely of ethnic Greeks. When at one point the KKE announced its support for the detachment of Macedonia from Greece, an uproar was created at home.[16] The military defeat of the Greek communists in 1949 apparently settled the Macedonian Question from the Greek side. But it was clear that the Hellenic-Slav conflict over Macedonia would be joined by a Yugoslav-Bulgarian dispute over Slavic Macedonia, a hostility that has soured relations between the two states ever since.[17] Neither Yugoslav (meaning primarily the Macedonian federal republic of Yugoslavia) nor Bulgarian extraterritorial claims are clear even today, and as late as 1986 Greek newspapers and public opinion were convinced that both of their northern neighbors were engaged in anti-Hellenic propaganda on matters Macedonian. Only the passage of time will tell if the Macedonian Question will become another relic of Balkan history.

Against this modern backdrop it will be seen that studies of ancient Macedonia were subordinated not only to the intense interest in famous southern Bronze Age and Classical sites, but also to the continuing drama of contemporary Macedonian politics. Almost certainly the very precarious position of modern Macedonia has until recently discouraged intensive studies of the region. Once the political status of Macedonia had been determined by the treaties settling World War I, however, a period of relative stability settled on the countryside. The main issues for the region were the establishment of Greek administration and the settlement of large numbers of refugees, mostly from the population exchange that followed the birth of the modern Turkish state and collapse of Greek ambitions in Asia Minor.[18] This influx of Anatolian refugees resulted in the establishment of scores of new farm-

---

[15] Ibid., 7–11 and 188–89.

[16] Kofos, *Nationalism and Communism*, 128–53 and 179ff., with evidence cited.

[17] In outline, ibid., 188ff.

[18] The 1928 census put the population of Greek Macedonia at 1,412,477, of whom more than 638,000 were refugees; see Eddy, *Greece and the Greek Refugees*, 131 and 145. Eddy was chairman of the Greek Refugee Settlement Commission appointed by the League of Nations.

ing villages, the draining of marshes, the building of roads, and the conversion of an area that had often been described by early travellers as largely barren and depressed into what is today one of the richest agricultural regions of Greece. In the Mediterranean world one of the most common consequences of the human effort to alter the face of the landscape for economic development is to uncover (literally) the past. There is no way to measure the unanticipated discovery of antiquities in Macedonia except to gain some general impressions by scanning the annual reports issued by the Greek archaeological service and foreign journals. Archaeological "rescue" operations in the face of modern construction have become as commonplace in northern Greece as they have been for decades in the central and southern areas.

The Archaeology of Macedonia

Long under Ottoman rule, and beyond the sea lanes of the eastern Mediterranean, Macedonia was virtually unknown to the West beyond the reputation of its famous kings. It never attracted the dilettante visitors who came to Athens and the islands to gaze in awe at ruined temples and to meditate over battered sculpture. The European discovery of Macedonia instead was connected with military endeavors.

It was with France in mind that the British government dispatched Captain (later Lieutenant-Colonel) William Martin Leake in 1804, charging him with surveying the countryside to provide detailed information about topography, fortresses, and naval stations and reporting on "the political and military dispositions of the inhabitants." Leake was also required to render assistance to the Turks in the event of a French invasion.[19] In several journeys in 1805–10, Leake conducted his mission with such precision and competence that he not only was cited by his government and attracted the attention of Nelson, Wellington, and Byron, but himself noted enough detailed information about the countryside in the Peloponnesus and central and northern Greece that he was able during his years of retirement to publish a number of volumes recounting his journeys.[20] Leake made several visits to Macedonia and adjacent regions.[21] His keen eye for details, an-

[19] Leake's instructions from Lord Harrowly and other relevant documents from the Leake family papers can be found in Marsden, *A Brief Memoir*.

[20] Among others, *Topography of Athens, Travels in the Morea, Travels in Northern Greece*, supplements to the Athenian and Peloponnesian volumes, and one of the earliest systematic studies of Greek coins, *Numismata Hellenica*.

[21] Described in *Travels in Northern Greece*, vol. 1 (chs. 6–9) and vol. 3 (chs. 24–28 and 30–31).

tiquities, customs, and topography made his life's work a historical handbook for Greek archaeology, and provides the modern historian with one of the sharpest available pictures of early nineteenth-century Greece. Rarely has Greece enjoyed such a traveller.

In 1861 the French observer Léon Heuzey was dispatched to northern Greece under an imperial commission of Napoleon III, the purpose of which was to commence a study of the remains of antiquity. Heuzey's lavish report[22] describes in detail the region around Philippi in eastern Macedonia, the Hellenistic palace complex near Palatitsia (near modern Vergina), other central Macedonian sites, and an archaeological reconnaissance in western Macedonia and along the Albanian coast. But even with the work of Leake, Heuzey, and others, Macedonia remained remote from the European consciousness. One eminent German classical scholar even neglected to include Macedonia in his otherwise comprehensive geographical survey of Greece.[23] As late as 1912, the British scholar A.J.B. Wace would write, ". . . the whole region [upper Macedonia] is still archaeologically a *terra incognita* and since the existing literary sources give us little information about its geography we must look to archaeology for the solution of some existing problems."[24] And the most authoritative early twentieth-century military handbook described Macedonia as "a region which has been for the last forty years less traversed by Western Europeans than any other part of Europe south of the Arctic regions."[25]

In fact, the opening of Macedonia was due largely to Wace and others associated with the British School at Athens. Early in its history the School had expressed an interest in northern Greece by publishing an article on contemporary folk customs.[26] Wace himself made several journeys into the region in the period from 1906 to 1912, and pub-

[22] Léon Heuzey and H. Daumet, *Mission Archéologique de Macédoine*.

[23] Bursian, *Geographie von Griechenland*. Although Bursian included Epirus, for him Greece ended at the northern border of Thessaly, thereby excluding Macedonia and Thrace. In one of the standard modern handbooks (*The Geographic Background of Greek and Roman History*), Cary included Macedonia and Thrace (290–91 and 302–5) in the sections on the Balkans, not Greece.

[24] Wace and Woodward, "Inscriptions from Upper Macedonia," 167, based on the authors' 1911 and 1912 journeys in the region.

[25] Great Britain Admiralty, Naval Intelligence Division, Geographical Section, *A Handbook of Macedonia and Surrounding Territories*, 19.

[26] Triantaphyllides, "Macedonian Customs," 207–14. In an editorial note, the School's director, Cecil Smith, offered a hope that modern Greek customs and folklore would "usefully occupy the attention of the foreign schools at Athens." Unfortunately, Smith's wish has gone largely unfulfilled, a victim of the School's success in archaeology.

lished continuously in the *Annual* of the school on what he had observed there.[27] In 1912 he wrote, "Now that [Macedonia's] political status has been changed only recently it would be premature to attempt here any full discussion of its ancient geography, since we may expect fresh discoveries."[28] Wace himself would help create interest in "fresh discoveries." Among the most interesting relics of antiquity were the large tumuli that dotted the central Macedonian plain and adjacent slopes. Leake had commented on them, and in 1914 Wace described some seventy tumuli and associated pottery,[29] many of which subsequently were found to contain prehistoric remains.

The First World War proved to be an unanticipated boon for Macedonian studies. Macedonia was occupied by British and French armies (reinforced by Serbian and Greek units) in 1915–18 so as to hold an Allied Balkan front against the enemy. The front was mainly static (the British having pushed their lines forward only 20–30 miles in the period 1916–18), the fighting desultory, and malaria rampant. Although strategically important to protect Salonica and to thwart the ambitions of Bulgaria and the Central Powers in the area, the Allied zone served mainly as a buffer between disputing Greek factions until its single great northern offensive in 1918.

Among the British officers were former members of the British School at Athens, and the French army had attached to it a *service archéologique*. For two years during the lull in military engagements, reports were gathered on prehistoric tumuli and historical sites, material finds were conserved and studied, archaeological survey maps were drawn, and plans were formulated for postwar excavation and museum construction. In a happy display of Anglo-Gallic cooperation, these studies were coordinated and published in British and French journals in the immediate postwar period.[30]

[27] "North Greek Festivals"; "The Mounds of Macedonia"; and "The Site of Olynthus."

[28] "Inscriptions from Upper Macedonia," 167.

[29] Leake, *Travels in Northern Greece*, 3: 260; Wace, "The Mounds of Macedonia."

[30] Summaries by Picard, "Les recherches archéologiques"; Casson, "Note on Ancient Sites"; and Mendel, "Les travaux du Service archéologique." The main reports (with excellent maps) are Rey, "Observations sur les sites préhistoriques et protohistoriques de la Macédoine"; Observations sur les premiers habitats de la Macédoine"; and Gardner and Casson, "Macedonia. II. Antiquities Found in the British Zone." A considerable space in *BSA* 23 (1918–19) was given over to reports of the British Salonika Force that described special matters, e.g., prehistory, pottery, inscriptions, tumuli, etc. At least a dozen British School members saw Macedonian military service: among them were E. A. Gardner, M. N. Tod, A. M. Woodward, M. S. Thompson, S. Casson, and A. W. Gomme.

This wartime research may have produced more enthusiasm and interest than new knowledge. One of the leading British scholar-soldiers recognized the mixed results of the military survey: On the vexed question of town sites, he states, "From the various discoveries of Greek and Roman date above described no very coherent idea of Macedonia in historical times emerges." Yet he notes: "The exigencies of war rendered methodical exploration for the most part impossible, but from the occasional discoveries made it has been possible to piece together a certain limited idea of classical culture in that part of Macedonia occupied by troops of the British Salonika Force."[31]

Perhaps the most important result of the wartime activity was its direct influence on Macedonian archaeology in the 1920s. For their part, the French, whose interest in the area dated from Heuzey's time, began to excavate along the eastern Macedonian littoral. Their exploratory prewar and wartime surveys gave way to systematic excavation at Thasos and Philippi.[32] But it was the British, having demonstrated a commitment to Macedonian studies before the war, and having collected a great deal of information during their military occupation of north-central Macedonia, who opened the region to archaeology. In 1915, Wace, who had already written on the subject, identified and explored the site of the great Chalcidic Greek center at Olynthus. This was a preliminary survey; he expressed hope that "the British School at Athens will before long be able to begin excavation here."[33] But it was not to be, at least not for Wace and the British. For in 1920, Wace, now director of the School, was called south to begin those remarkable excavations at Mycenae which revealed so much of the language and culture of Bronze Age Greece. Olynthus would have to await the spade of an American, David M. Robinson, who uncovered it in a series of campaigns from 1928 to 1938, during which he recovered a large amount of material illuminating the culture of northern Greece before the city's destruction by Philip of Macedon in 348 B.C.[34]

Wace's Macedonian efforts, however, found worthy successors. Stanley Casson, who had been active with the British Salonika Force, dug at Chauchitsa in the middle Axios valley in 1921–22. In 1926 Casson published his *Macedonia, Thrace and Illyria*, based on the archaeo-

[31] Casson, in Gardner and Casson, "Macedonia. II. Antiquities Found in the British Zone," 40–41.

[32] See *Études Thasiennes, Guide de Thasos*, and Collart, *Philippes, ville de Macédoine*, all published under the auspices of the École Française d'Athènes. Preliminary excavation reports can be read at large in *BCH*.

[33] Wace, "The Site of Olynthus," 11–12.

[34] Robinson et al., *Excavations at Olynthus*.

logical fieldwork of the British School and on a number of his own journeys into these areas in the period 1913–15. It was the first systematic attempt to reconstruct the early history of the northern regions down to the time of Philip II. A pioneering work, it suffered from the fact that scientific archaeology was in its infancy in Macedonia and Thrace, and Illyria was as yet virtually unknown archaeologically.

About the time that Casson's book appeared, another member of the British School, W. A. Heurtley, was commencing a series of studies of tumuli that would establish him as the father of Macedonian prehistory. Although the main activities of the British School were elsewhere, a small Macedonian Exploration Fund was available to Heurtley. Throughout the 1920s Heurtley excavated judiciously at several sites in central and western Macedonia, slowly establishing a chronology and describing the connection between early Macedonia and Greece. In 1931, however, the British School was given an opportunity to excavate at Ithaca, and Heurtley, like Wace before him, was called away from Macedonia, the lure of Homer being irresistible. Because of the Ithacan campaigns and other interruptions, Heurtley did not produce his valuable *Prehistoric Macedonia* until the eve of the Second World War.

In December 1929 Heurtley led some young British School students, fresh from Cambridge, on a walk up the Haliacmon Gorge, and then taught them something of Macedonian pottery. One of the students, Nicholas Hammond, embarked on a series of walks in 1930 upon which was based a study of the passes over the Pindus Mountains from Epirus into Macedonia and Thessaly.[35] The pioneering effort to explore by foot a hitherto largely unknown region continued up to 1939. Hammond spent part of World War II as a British liaison officer with the Greek Resistance in Thessaly and Macedonia, and came to know parts of the country thoroughly.[36] This autoptical experience, joined by considerable postwar research, resulted in the publication in 1967 of Hammond's *Epirus*, the most comprehensive Greek regional study done up to that time. Its thorough review of geography, historical topography, and antiquities established a model for such studies, and would be matched later by Hammond's *A History of Macedonia*. The latter work, encyclopedic in scope, has attempted to include virtually everything known about Macedonia in antiquity. Hammond laid heavy emphasis on geographical factors as historical determinants;

[35] Hammond, "Prehistoric Epirus and the Dorian Invasion."

[36] Hammond's wartime activities are chronicled in his *Venture into Greece with the Guerrillas, 1943–44.*

the soundness of this method will appeal to anyone with experience in Greece.

The unique aspect of Hammond's history, however, lay in its attempt to synthesize the work of Bulgarian, Albanian, Yugoslav, and Greek archaeologists on the prehistory of the region (heretofore they might as well have been excavating on different planets).[37] Moreover, Hammond unified topography, archaeology, and history based on literary sources in a grand manner that few generalists and no specialists would have attempted. It is a highly personal work because of the nature of its evidence-gathering procedures. Some of its methods and conclusions have not satisfied many readers, especially on matters of prehistoric and protohistoric migrations. But, taken together with *Epirus*, it serves as a useful model for the development of regional studies for other parts of the southern Balkans.

The Second World War and continuing internal strife virtually halted archaeological investigation in Greece except for some small-scale German and French excavations. With the renewal of scientific activity in the 1950s, the foreign institutions of archaeology, in particular the British, American, French, and German schools, continued to dominate the excavation of most major classical and some Bronze Age sites. With a few exceptions, most of these were located in the central, southern, and Aegean regions of Greece. The Greeks themselves, though often skillful and enthusiastic, lacked funds and had not appeared to match the foreigners in producing major results. The rudimentary level of Macedonian archaeology had produced only Heurtley's basic prehistoric classifications, the excavations of a few major sites and individual monuments (mainly Greek and Roman), some exploratory investigations, and a general understanding of topography. Pella had barely been touched, Edessa only slightly so, Veria was hardly known, and the sites of many famous ancient places were either unexcavated or not yet identified: Mende, Acanthus, Torone, Methone, Dion, and Pydna, to mention a few.

Two developments characterize Macedonian archaeology since 1950. The first is the increasing intensity with which the countryside is being examined. Many famous sites have been identified and surveyed, and the excavation of others has begun. Second, most of this archaeological activity has been in Greek hands. The prewar period saw some Greek work, notably by Pelikides and Romaios, but the postwar era is dominated by the excavations sponsored by the Greek Archaeological Service, the Archaeological Society of Athens, and

---

[37] The phrase is Hammond's: *HM* I: viii.

Greek universities. A short list would include Amphipolis, Derveni, Dion, Edessa, Kavalla, Kozani, Lefkadia, Naousa, Pella, Potidaea, Servia, Torone, Vergina, and Veria. M. Andronikos, G. Bakalakis, K. Despinis, D. Lazarides, Ch. I. Makaronas, D. Pandermalis, Ph. Petsas, K. Rhomiopoulou, M. Siganidou, I. Vokotopoulou, and their colleagues have until recently labored in relative obscurity in the north. But their accomplishments have contributed to the reconstruction of a Macedonian history. Parts of Philip and Alexander's capital at Pella have been unearthed; at Derveni and near Lefkadia, a series of fine tombs from the fourth century B.C. and later show something of the material wealth and artistic sophistication of the Macedonian gentry; and Hellenistic, Roman, and Byzantine materials have been uncovered at Veria. Moreover, the fortifications of ancient Edessa are coming to light, a continuous occupation from the Bronze Age to Roman times has been revealed at Kozani, the Naousa region has been identified with ancient Mieza, and extensive prehistoric sites have been studied at Servia and Nea Nikomedeia. The rich Chalcidian city of Torone has been identified and excavation begun, an extensive Roman city at Dion both surprises us in its own right and promises exciting earlier levels, and what appears to be a royal cemetery has been discovered at Vergina.[38]

The obscurity of Macedonia has ended. There has been revealed a culture more sophisticated in the later periods than we had heretofore suspected. A few methodological problems remain (see below, Chapter 4), and some procedural matters continue to dog scientific advance, in particular the continuing lack of coordination among Greek, Albanian, Yugoslav, and Bulgarian scholars (twentieth-century history and habitual uneasiness die hard).[39] But we stand on the brink of understanding for the first time the history of one of the most important nations of antiquity.

The Writing of Macedonian History

If archaeology was one of the factors wanting for the production of a Macedonian history, research based on literary sources was the other. We have already seen that nineteenth-century historical scholarship had produced some general accounts of Greek history in which Macedonia was mentioned only as an area peripheral to the mainstream of Greek events until the time of Philip II and Alexander the Great. Some

[38] For bibliography, see Appendix A below, pp. 283–84.
[39] See Appendix A below, p. 284.

biographical studies of both Philip and Alexander emerged from the intense interest in Philip's quarrels with Athens, his conquest of Greece, and the spread of Hellenism resulting from Alexander's conquests. In nearly every respect these events were seen as external to the Macedonian national experience, itself a concept not yet formulated in the modern mind. That is, the Macedonians were viewed as an adjunct to Greek history. It may not go too far to suggest that Macedon seemed important only insofar as it catalyzed certain movements among the Greeks, and later resisted the expansion of Rome.

To the slight extent that there was anything like an independent Macedonian history, it was part of the general *Hellenismus*, that broad conception of Greek culture framed by J. G. Droysen (its fullest expression is found in his *Geschichte des Hellenismus*) and others in the mid-nineteenth century. *Hellenismus* described the culture of the Greek city-states, Ptolemaic Egypt, and the Seleucid areas of western Asia. Macedon and its sister kingdoms were described mainly as the decayed Hellenistic residue of Classical Greek culture ripe for the Roman conquest.[40] It is true that even today in most English-speaking universities, virtually no Hellenistic history is taught for the period between Alexander's death and the Roman conquest of the East. Some independent Hellenistic histories appeared early in the twentieth century, notably of the Ptolemaic and Seleucid monarchies for which material finds (especially papyrus documents from Egypt) became available.[41] But it is indicative of the state of Macedonian studies that Macedonia's history on a large scale had to wait seventy years more for the pen of Hammond.

That is not to say that scholarship on Macedonia has been lacking, only that it has taken the form of monographs and journal articles on limited subjects. A veritable cottage industry on Alexander the Great has arisen in the modern period. The biographies of Macedon's most famous king alone number in the scores, and a whole volume has appeared devoted entirely to a modern bibliography on the subject.[42] Studies of Philip II have not been so numerous, and until recently have

---

[40] Some exceptions to the trend: Kaerst, *Geschichte des Hellenismus*, vol. 1 (3rd ed.), vol. 2 (2nd ed.); and Bengtson, *Die Strategie in der hellenistischen Zeit*; plus a number of recent works on Hellenistic culture.

[41] Bevan, *The House of Seleucus*; Bouché-Leclerq, *Histoire des Séleucides* and *Histoire des Lagides*.

[42] Seibert, *Alex. der Grosse*. Useful shorter bibliographies have been compiled by Lauffer, *Alex. der Grosse*; Hornblower, *The Greek World*; Badian, "Alexander the Great, 1948–1967"; and in the most useful and comprehensive of modern biographies, Peter Green's *Alexander of Macedon*. A provocative discussion of some modern trends in Alexander historiography is Badian's "Some Recent Interpretations of Alexander."

been mainly the products of German scholarship. The guidelines laid down in the nineteenth century for the study of these preeminent Macedonian monarchs continued almost without exception to dominate twentieth-century studies. Students of Philip were still required to reconcile their sympathies for the unifier of Greece with their misgivings about the man who ended the independence of Athens. Whatever the resolution, it was usually the Greek context that prevailed. Only recently has a more balanced view emerged, one that would probably have pleased David George Hogarth.[43] As for Alexander, manifold interpretations have been offered concerning motives, designs for good or evil, degree of civility or barbarism, and military competence—interpretations as often as not reflecting the psychological predilections of the authors themselves. Whatever personal ideologies and systems of source analysis lay under these portraits of Alexander, nearly all have shared the late nineteenth-century conception of a world figure writ larger than life. The minimalist position has not been popular.

Some biographical studies of Macedonian kings of the Hellenistic period have appeared, along with accounts of special periods and topics, and collections and commentaries on several categories of evidence.[44] The great general histories of Greece barely touched Macedonia before the eve of Philip II's rise to power. Any survey of several such early twentieth-century histories and of the *Cambridge Ancient History* will reveal scant attention paid to Macedonian affairs in volumes focused on the development and activities of the Greek city-states. This is not to condemn the general-history approach; there are horrendous problems associated with any attempt to organize the materials of large-scale history,[45] and the peripheral areas will always seem to suffer in favor of the mainstream. The unintended result is to fragment and thereby diminish the history of a region or a people. Such has been the case of Macedonia.

We have seen that several factors have hindered the development of a synthetic Macedonian history: intense interest in the literature and archaeology of Classical Greece, the remoteness and political upheavals of the Balkans in modern times, the fragmentation of Macedonian scholarship into studies of limited subject matter (especially the biog-

---

[43] Review of earlier scholarship on Philip by Borza, "Philip II and the Greeks." The break came with the publication in 1976 of Ellis's *Philip II and Macedonian Imperialism*, written as a piece of *Macedonian* history. This was soon followed by Cawkwell, *Philip of Macedon*, Griffith's section on Philip in *HM* vol. 2, and a series of essays by various authors in Hatzopoulos and Loukopoulos, *Philip of Macedon*.

[44] See Appendix A below, pp. 284–86.

[45] The historian's age-old bane; see Diod. 1.3.5–8, 5.1.4, 16.1.1–3, and 17.1.2.

raphies of kings), and the delayed development of Macedonian archaeology. To these must be added an additional burden. In attempting to
construct a framework for a national history of Macedonia, the historian is faced with the uninviting prospect of writing about a people
who are virtually silent about themselves. Egyptians, Jews, Sumeri-
ans, Assyrians, Athenians, Romans, and others have left rich legacies
of literature, folk epic, architecture, inscriptions, and other material
finds. But the Macedonians remain one of the mute peoples of antiquity, joining the Spartans, Etruscans, and Carthaginians. This would
appear to be a cruel fate for a people who shielded Greece from barbarian invasions,[46] who produced the most famous conqueror of all
time, and whose power was one of the few major obstacles to the for-
eign-policy objectives of the Roman Republic.

A reconstruction of Macedonian history rests on three main categories of evidence. The first is our general knowledge of historical topography in the southern Balkans, with special reference to the movement of peoples, the effects of climate, and the relationship between
human beings and the lands they inhabit. The second is the growing
body of material finds from the historical period, including tombs,
grave goods, coins, and inscriptions. Although archaeological excavation is now intense, the publication and analysis of these discoveries
is slow. The third category, and for the traditional historian the most
comfortable material with which to work, is the body of literary evidence. But a formidable obstacle to the writing of Macedonian history
is the fact that we have no truly Macedonian source. Few persons who
visited the region in antiquity ever wrote about it, and only a handful
of authors were even marginally contemporary with the Macedonian
events they describe.

What survives from the early period are fifth- and fourth-century
writers whose attitudes about Macedonia range from the mildly curious (e.g., Thucydides 2.99 is written as if describing a tribe living in
some Asian or African limbo) to the contemptuous. Some writers, like
Isocrates and Aeschines, avoided the prevalent hostility, but their
views are as shaded as those of Demosthenes. Our best narrative account of Philip II was written by Diodorus three centuries after the
king's death, and was based mainly on non-Macedonian sources.[47]
Likewise the evidence for Alexander's career is late and derivative.[48] It

[46] Edson, "Early Macedonia," 17–18; and Dell, "The Western Frontier of the Macedonian Monarchy," 115–16.

[47] Hammond, "The Sources of Diodorus Siculus XVI," now brought up to date in his
Three Historians of Alexander the Great, 32–51.

[48] See my introduction to Wilcken, *Alexander*.

is the continuing occupation of those interested in Alexander to recover the earliest and most contemporaneous sources underlying these
late histories, and there is reason to believe that some internal Macedonian materials may survive, however encrusted, in these later accounts. Most of what we know about Macedonia in the Hellenistic era
comes from fragments scattered through a dozen later writers, from
Polybius's narrative account of Roman imperialism, and from the
traditions imbedded in and expressed by Rome's national historian,
Livy. It is clear that many of these sources are biased, making one hope
that historical geography and archaeology will come to the historian's
aid, speaking as they often do (to paraphrase Mommsen quoting Tacitus) without love or hate.

The Land of Macedonia

ABOUT every two hours an Olympic Airways plane leaves Athens for Salonica. Flying almost due north out of Attica, the plane crosses the Euripus at Chalcis, shuddering slightly as the currents sweeping up from the Euboean mountains play upon the wing surfaces. The mass of Mt. Dirphys suddenly looms and then falls away abruptly into the sea. Within minutes we are over the tree-studded northern Sporades, among the least visited and most beautiful Aegean islands. The aircraft changes course slightly to the northwest and begins a gradual descent as it enters the Thermaic Gulf, flying its length right up to Salonica. To the right lies the odd three-fingered peninsula called Chalcidice, rich in grains and vines today as it was in antiquity.

But it is the view to the left—the west—that commands attention. Until the triumph of modern apathy, the seats on this side of the aircraft were considered most desirable, for the passengers (mainly Greeks) hoped to gain a glimpse of Mt. Olympus. Although Olympus's nearly 10,000-foot summits lie a mere twelve miles from the sea, they are often invisible from within their crown of cloud. If the view is unobstructed, however, the fortunate traveller is treated to a spectacular panorama of Olympus's rocky heights, presenting an eastern face that is one of the most imposing mountain walls in Europe.

As we continue northward, the lesser ranges of the Olympus massif, the Pierian Mountains, trail off to the north, descending into a great plain, well watered and tilled. In the distance we see that the plain is enclosed by mountains except for the sea side. If the day is free from haze (an increasingly rare event in modern Greece), we perceive in the distant west several parallel north-south ranges culminating in the high Pindus, like some gigantic geological corduroy.

As the aircraft banks toward its final approach we note that the plain's northern boundary is not so abrupt, giving way gradually to individual hills and small ranges until finally it disappears in the higher elevations along the Yugoslav frontier. A number of rivers cross the plain from several directions, all converging where the throat of the plain meets the sea near the head of the Thermaic Gulf. Three of these streams have their natural and man-made mouths within a few miles of one another in a featureless marsh of silt and reeds, and the discharge of their muddy waters reaches nearly across the head of the gulf, staining the blue sea with bands of yellow and brown. The area lies so low that the seafarer finds it virtually impossible to pick out the coastline, and the *Mediterranean Pilot* warns of accidents caused by the constant mirages over this shore.

At the very end of the Thermaic Gulf, where the rivers enter, is a smaller bay that extends eastward for a few miles. At its head lies the ancient city of Thessaloniki—Salonica (or Saloniki) in common parlance. The second city of modern Greece, and the most important settlement in this part of the Balkans since the third century B.C., Salonica marks the eastern end of the great Macedonian plain. Less than an hour from Athens, the aircraft lands at Salonica's modest international airport, situated some ten miles south of the city center among the disappearing fields and encroaching suburbs of northwest Chalcidice. We are in Macedonia.

During the final few minutes of the flight from Athens one can observe a few landmarks that shaped the course of much of the history of northern Greece. For Macedonia—caught between the barrier ranges of the Yugoslav-Bulgarian frontier and the huge obstacle of the Olympus massif bordering Thessaly—is the transition between Greece and the main part of the Balkans. The Balkans are, cartographically speaking, the easternmost of the three great southern European peninsulas.[1] The northern boundary of the Balkan peninsula can be marked roughly by a line between the head of the Adriatic and the Danube's mouth. This peninsula is largely mountainous, with major barrier ranges running northwest-southeast along the Adriatic coast, bisecting Albania and Greece clear to the tips of the Peloponnesus. Two transverse ridges, the Haemus (Balkan) and the Rhodopi, split the northeastern part of the peninsula, the latter separating the Bulgarian lowland from the Aegean coast, the former bisecting the heart of Bulgaria along an east-west axis. A series of complex river systems originate in the Balkans and flow into the Black, Adriatic, and Aegean seas. Upland plateaux and coastal alluvial plains complete the region. The area may be further divided into two distinct historical areas: the Balkans and Greece.

[1] For Balkan geography, the works of Cvijić (*La péninsule balkanique*) and Carter (*Hist. Geography*) are especially useful.

Climate

When dealing with a region as geographically complex as the Balkans, it is difficult to generalize about climate, since climate is the product of a number of variable factors: latitude, altitude, proximity to the sea, condition of the sea, prevailing winds, local winds, and topography. I hold that, given the climatologic data and archaeological evidence, the general climatic conditions in Greece in modern times are virtually the same as they were in antiquity. Some temperature data recorded in the Admiralty handbooks of the early twentieth century, however, are a more reliable guide to the traditional Mediterranean climate than are some contemporary readings, as modern population and industrial centers such as Salonica and Athens have produced masses of smog that have elevated local temperatures. The nearly omnipresent rural haze that results from construction, motorways, and mechanized agriculture has also contributed to a slight alteration in the climate. The discussion that follows takes into account these modern variables.

Two quite distinct climate zones characterize the Balkan peninsula.[2] The "Continental" climate is marked by cold winters and hot summers, while the annual range of mean monthly rainfall totals is relatively narrow. The range of mean monthly temperatures is wide. The "Mediterranean" climate is characterized by much more variation in mean monthly rainfall, that is, very distinct rainy and dry seasons, and by a much narrower annual range of mean monthly temperatures, producing a generally warmer and more moderate climate.

For example, the average of the monthly mean temperatures for Continental Sofia and Belgrade is 49 degrees, while that of Mediterranean Athens is 64. What is more important is that the mean range of temperatures at Sofia between its coldest (27) and warmest (69) months is 42 degrees, while at Athens, where monthly mean temperatures vary between 49 and 81, the annual temperature range is only 32 degrees.

The pattern of rainfall is equally revealing. The annual rainfall at Sofia is 26 inches, at Athens only 15.6. The wettest month (May: 3.44 inches) at Sofia sees 2½ times as much rain as the driest month (De-

---

[2] The climatological data that follow are taken from the handbook by the Great Britain Admiralty, Naval Staff, Geographical Section, *Notes on Climate*, ch. 1; *AHGr* 1: 41–51; and Turrill, *Plant-life*, 57–68. In some cases the figures have been rounded off to the nearest degree Fahrenheit. I am indebted to S. Lindaros of the Greek National Meteorological Service, Athens, for providing me with otherwise unpublished climate information for western Macedonian sites, some of which has been collected over the past 30 to 50 years.

cember: 1.44 inches), whereas at Athens there is more than 10 times as
much rain in November (2.92 inches) as there is in July (.28 inches).
Athens is also typically Mediterranean in its distribution of rainfall,
with almost half the annual rainfall occurring in November through
January (which is the driest period at Sofia), and only trace amounts in
mid-summer, whereas Sofia enjoys its heaviest rain in May through
July. The distribution and quantity of rainfall of the Mediterranean climate, together with relatively mild winters, has determined the pattern of agriculture since prehistoric times: Cereal grains are sown in
autumn and harvested in spring.

Although latitude influences general temperature ranges, it plays a
less significant role in local climate than do a number of other factors,
including altitude and proximity to the sea.[3] To the extent that a gen-
eralization is possible, it may be said that the Mediterranean climate is
mainly a coastal phenomenon, including both the Adriatic littoral of
the Balkans and the Adriatic/Aegean coasts of Greece. The interior
parts of Greece vary considerably. Those under the influence of the sea
are truly Mediterranean, while others, including the high mountains
and plains of Thessaly and Boeotia, are more subject to the Continental extremes—thus Hesiod's comment about his Boeotian home town,
Ascra: "bad in winter, difficult in summer, good at no time" (*Works
and Days* 640).

One is tempted to say that a useful definition of a Mediterranean
climate is "a region where the olive grows." However we attempt to
explain the Mediterranean climate in geographical and meteorological
terms, a fundamental truth emerges, and that is that the olive thrives
in this kind of mild climate with its short, rainy winters and long, dry
summers. The olive is sensitive to cold and to altitude, and prefers the
moderating influence of coastal regions.[4] Areas marked by the typical
Mediterranean climate include the low-lying and coastal regions of
Greece, Yugoslavia, Italy, France, Spain, and the Asian rim of the
Mediterranean, as well as those parts of Chile, Mexico, California,
Australia, and South Africa that are similar.

It is impossible to describe Macedonia's climate as conforming
strictly to either the Mediterranean or the Continental model, not only

[3] Mediterranean and Continental climates are often only marginally affected by latitude. For example, London lies at the same latitude as Calgary and Kiev, Athens as
Washington, and Rome as Boston. The moderating influences of the Gulf Stream and
the Mediterranean give London, Athens, and Rome less extreme climates than their
counterparts.

[4] Pliny *NH* 15.1.1, quoting Theophrastus, says that the olive will grow only within
forty miles of the sea.

because the variations within the region are so great, but also because Macedonia is a zone of transition between the Balkans proper and Greece. Indeed, we would not be in error to conceive of Macedonia as the Greek-Balkan frontier, as meteorological data from three representative places suggest.[5] Monastir (modern Bitola), on the northwest march of ancient Macedonia, and representative of the remote interior, has relatively high rainfall year-round, except for a dry period in late summer. Salonica stands on the eastern edge of the great central plain, and experiences wet seasons in early winter and late spring. Kavalla, an eastern Macedonian coastal site on the Thracian frontier, enjoys a quantity of rainfall as high as inland Balkan Sofia's, but with a Mediterranean distribution pattern. All three sites follow similar temperature curves, with Kavalla and Salonica nearly identical. Bitola differs only in that its overall temperatures are lower and marked by a wider range (like that of Sofia), as one might expect for an inland Balkan site. The higher average and narrower range of temperatures at Salonica and Kavalla are comparable to those of Athens.

When one adds data from stations at Florina (about 20 miles south of Bitola), Kozani (in the southwestern highlands), and Edessa (on the terrace-land of Mt. Vermion above the western edge of the central plain), it becomes clear that, climatically speaking, there are two zones in Macedonia: western Macedonia and the Aegean littoral, although even in these regions consistency is illusive.[6]

Although Macedonia is Balkan in its mountainous western interior, large parts of it—including the plains and coastal regions—are marginally Mediterranean in three respects: mild winter temperatures, narrow annual temperature range, and mild annual average temperatures. Only in the amount of rainfall and in the extreme temperatures of its

[5] *Contra* Hammond, *HM* 1: 4–5, who gives Macedonia, including Salonica, a Continental climate, while I see it as variable and transitional between the Balkans and the Aegean. In Broekhuizen's *Agro-Ecological Atlas of Cereal Growing in Europe*, nearly all of Greek Macedonia, including most of Chalcidice, is shown as a distinct, near-Mediterranean climate zone. The exceptional areas are the northwestern region around Florina, shown as more Continental, and the Strymon River plain, shown as more Mediterranean. All the statistical material can be confirmed visually with a glance at the maps in Knoch, *Klima-Karten von Europa*. Cvijić, *La péninsule balkanique*, ch. 4, shows a Mediterranean climate for all but the northwestern mountains and the Strymon plain.

[6] For example, Edessa has temperatures virtually identical to those of Salonica and Kavalla. Edessa is like Salonica with respect to rainfall distribution, but has heavier amounts, more like Kozani and Florina. The latter sites share the general Macedonian temperature curve, but with mean temperatures 5–7 degrees cooler at any point on the curve. The rainfall patterns at Kozani, Florina, and Bitola differ from one another, being more influenced by local factors than by any general condition.

mountainous areas does Macedonia seem more Balkan. Macedonia is the transition from the Balkans to the Mediterranean, but it lies on the fringe of the Mediterranean world. In general, Macedonia is not suitable for the olive.

General Geography

Hammond described Macedonia as a geographical, not political, entity: ". . . Macedonia is best defined as the territory which is drained by the two great rivers, the Haliacmon and the Vardar [Axios], and their tributaries."[7] This is a narrow definition, even geographically. Aware of the danger of a more inclusive description, Hammond argued correctly that "to define Macedonia along political lines, we shall be chasing a chameleon through the centuries." It is not proposed here to chase a Macedonian chameleon through all those centuries, including the medieval Bulgarian empires, the period of Ottoman rule, the collapse of Turkish overlordship, the political division of ancient Macedonia among modern nation-states (see Chapter 1 above), and the continuing Macedonian Question. My present objective is somewhat more limited. As this work is focused on the Argead monarchy, and is not a comprehensive regional study, a different definition of Macedonia may be offered. Macedonia is the territory so called both by the Macedonians themselves (insofar as we have any information about this) and by those who wrote about them in antiquity.

To accept this view inevitably leads to a political definition that is useful only so long as we limit ourselves to a study of the ancient Macedonians down to the time of the Roman conquest. Unlike Hammond's unyielding Haliacmon-Axios axis, our definition of Macedonia will have changed in antiquity in relation to the shifting fortunes of the Macedonians themselves and of the people who were, at various times, part of the Macedonian dominion. That is, once we have dealt with the historical geography and prehistory of the territory of Macedonia, we shall concern ourselves with the kingdom of Macedon. Hammond's definition reflects a northwestern orientation. This follows not unexpectedly from his personal experiences in the area, his work on Epirus, and his view of Macedonia as part of the Balkan land mass rather than as part of Greece. The present work lays somewhat less emphasis on these remote mountain regions, and correspondingly more on the central areas and on the region east of the Axios, which were eventually incorporated into the Macedonian kingdom.

[7] HM 1: 3–5.

Macedonia's political boundaries (that is, those of the kingdom of Macedon) fluctuated in antiquity, as have the borders of several European nations in modern times. The Macedonian *ethnos* in antiquity depended in part upon the inclusion of several different populations at various times under the general overlordship of the king and his retinue.[8] A purely geographical definition is too limited to account for these political fluctuations. For example, the true Macedonian heartland may be said to be the area along the southern border of the central (Emathian) plain, the original home of the historical *Makedones*. Yet the power of these people spread throughout the plain, into the western mountains, across the Axios and the Strymon to the region around Philippi and Mt. Pangaion. At its zenith Macedonian influence prevailed in an area that includes virtually all of modern Greek Macedonia and much of Yugoslav Macedonia, including territory not drained by the Haliacmon–Axios. Macedon must then be defined as the Balkan region where Macedonians ruled. Like the ancient Greeks, we must understand that a state should be defined according to where men's loyalties (whether voluntary or coerced) lie.[9] This is a social condition enforced politically.

To sum up: "Macedonia" is a geographical term, and Hammond's conception of Macedonia as being the territory of the Haliacmon–Axios watershed will be enlarged to include areas further east and south. For present purposes "Macedon" will mean the area within that geographical entity that was ruled directly and traditionally by Macedonian kings, but not including Greece, Asia, and Balkan imperial acquisitions. The definition of Macedon will enlarge along with the territory ruled by its monarchy, so that the concept of a "greater Macedon" will emerge as the Macedonians establish themselves as the Balkans' major power. This larger Macedon included lands from the crest

[8] I am of course referring only to old Macedonia. In the fourth century B.C. Philip II would make wide-ranging treaty arrangements with Greek states, and Alexander would add through conquest a huge Asian empire. At no time, however, was either Greece or Asia to be considered as part of *Macedon*, even while under the control of Macedonian kings. The same may be said of the imperial extension of third-century Macedonian monarchs.

[9] Thuc. 7.77.7: *andres gar polis*, a common aphorism in antiquity, especially with reference to the defense of towns, e.g., Plut. *Lyc.* 19.4; Dem. 18.299; Soph. *OT* 56. The point is the same, be it city-state, tribal state, or nation-state. The concept is sociopolitical, not geographical. Unfortunately, we are unable to make a case for defining Macedonia as where Macedonians *lived*. There is, in every period, insufficient information about settlements, as well as an ongoing controversy about the meaning of "Macedonian" as both an ethnic term and a description of rights and privileges. E.g., see Anson, "The Meaning of the Term *Makedones*."

of the Pindus range to the plain of Philippi and the Nestos River. Its northern border lay along a line formed by Pelagonia, the middle Axios valley and the western Rhodopi massif. Its southern border was the Haliacmon basin, the Olympus range and the Aegean, with the Chalcidic peninsula as peripheral.

Regional Geography

For the purpose of historical narrative Macedonia may be divided into three regions:

1. *Western (Upper)*[10] *Macedonia*: the mainly mountainous area west and southwest of the Emathian plain, stretching to the Pindus, and corresponding roughly to the region drained by the middle and upper Haliacmon River. These mountains are broken by two north-south corridors and several east-west passes.

2. *Central (Lower) Macedonia*: the region of the great central plain, including the plain itself, Almopia, the Pierian piedmont and coastal plain, and the lower Axios up to the highlands above Salonica.

3. *Eastern Macedonia*: an area of varying topography from the highlands of the Gallikos-Strymon divide eastward to the Nestos River, including the plains drained by the Strymon and its tributaries and the regions around Philippi, Kavalla, and Mt. Pangaion. The area is bordered by the Rhodopi Mountains on the north and the Aegean on the south.

Chalcidice was not strictly part of Macedonian antiquity, as its history and products were more closely associated with the Aegean and the Greek world in the south than with the Macedonian hinterland.[11] It is peripheral to Macedonia proper, but it would eventually become an integral part of the history of Macedonian expansion and Macedonian relations with the Greek world.

We thus have a conception of Macedonia both more and less extensive than Hammond's—less in that it reduces emphasis on the northwestern lands that lie today within the Yugoslav state, but more in that it takes into greater account the territory east of the Axios. It is a definition based on the political development of the Macedonian state over

[10] The concept of "upper" (*anō*) and "lower" (*katō*) is Herodotean: e.g., 7.173.1, 4; 7.128.1; 8.137.1.

[11] Hammond, *HM* I: 192.

a long period of time, incorporating the territory drained by three rivers, adding the Strymon to the Haliacmon and Axios.[12]

Mediterranean rivers flow, and sometimes flood, in rainy months, and are either dry or a trickle in summer. The three great Macedonian rivers, however, are of the Continental type, with considerable flow year-round, befitting their origins in the high northern mountains and the continuing supply of rain run-off throughout the year. The major river plains—the Emathian formed by the Haliacmon, Axios, and Loudias (now artificially altered and controlled), and the Strymonic and Philippic formed by the Strymon and its tributaries—are alluvial and marshy. The higher elevations adjacent to these plains have supported human settlement since prehistoric times.

Two major Balkan routes intersect in Macedonia. The main north-south route from the Danube to the Aegean follows the Morava River east of Belgrade, runs across the Morava-Vardar divide near Skopje, and accompanies the Vardar south through the defiles of Yugoslav Macedonia to the Greek frontier. From there it runs 45 miles to the Thermaic Gulf just west of Salonica. The main land route from the Adriatic to the Aegean (see end map) runs from the port of Durrës (ancient Dyrrhachium) in Albania, across the Yugoslav frontier in the region of Lake Ohrid to Bitola, south into Greek Macedonia near Florina, east to Edessa on the terraces of Mt. Vermion, and thence across the northern fringe of the Emathian plain to Salonica. From Salonica it continues across eastern Macedonia and Thrace to its terminus at Constantinople. This was the route of the great Via Egnatia of Roman times. The north-south and east-west routes cross about 15 miles north of the Axios's mouth at the eastern edge of the Emathian plain. It is no wonder that Salonica, located on a fine natural inlet of the Thermaic Gulf nearby, emerged as the gateway between the Aegean and the Balkans.

Western (Upper) Macedonia

Western Macedonia comprises the mountainous land embraced by the drainage basin of the Haliacmon River and the upper Axios (Vardar) tributary, the Crna (anc. Erigon) (Map I). Extending in a fan shape west from the Emathian Plain to the high Pindus and the barrier mountains along the Albanian frontier, the area reaches north into the territory around Skopje. It is a rough corduroy of mountain ranges and plateaux running along a generally north-south axis. Between the

---

[12] Casson's discussion on this point is useful; see *Macedonia*, 3–25.

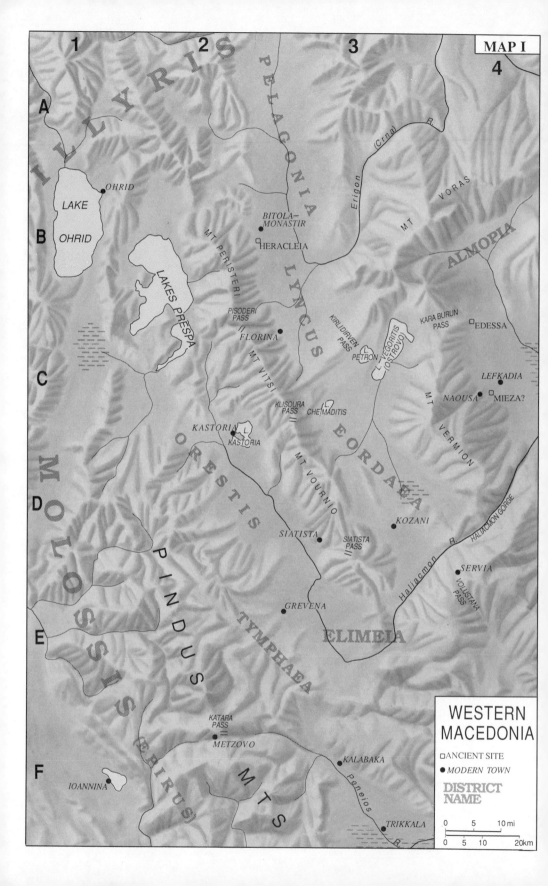

MAP I

1 2 3 4

A

ILLYRIS

PELAGONIA

Erigon (Crna) R.

VORAS

LAKE OHRID

OHRID

B

MT PERISTERI

BITOLA–MONASTIR

HERACLEIA

MT

ALMOPIA

LAKES PRESPA

LYNCUS

PISODERI PASS

FLORINA

KIRLIDIRVEN PASS

L. VEGORITIS OSTROVO

KARA BURUN PASS

EDESSA

MT VITSI

L. PETRON

C

MOLOSSIS

ORESTIS

KLISOURA PASS

CHEIMADITIS

EORDAEA

MT

NAOUSA

LEFKADIA

MIEZA?

VERMION

KASTORIA L.

KASTORIA

MT VOURNIO

D

PINDUS

SIATISTA

SIATISTA PASS

KOZANI

Haliacmon R.

HALIACMON GORGE

SERVIA

VOLUSTANA PASS

E

TYMPHAEA

GREVENA

ELIMEIA

MTS

KATARA PASS

METZOVO

KALABAKA

F

IOANNINA

(EPIRUS)

Peneios

WESTERN MACEDONIA

□ ANCIENT SITE
● MODERN TOWN

DISTRICT NAME

0   5   10 mi

0   5   10   20km

TRIKKALA

parallel ranges are two main north-south corridors connected by some east-west passes that since earliest times have provided the means of access through these formidable mountains from the Adriatic hinterland to the Aegean basin.[13]

THE HALIACMON CORRIDOR

The westernmost corridor is that of the Haliacmon River, whose sources lie in the high peaks east of the Prespa lakes.[14] The Haliacmon is a geologically active river, still cutting its course backward, with the effect of draining an increasingly larger area of northwestern Greece. Eventually it will drain Lake Prespa itself.[15] Leaving its sources above Kastoria, the river flows for about 65 miles in a southeasterly direction, winding through hill and plateau country past Grevena, where it makes a great bend of about 15 miles to the east. Turning again, the river runs about 45 miles to the northeast through its own deep gorge, and suddenly enters the central plain near Veria. Another 25 miles across the southern part of the Emathian plain brings the Haliacmon to the sea.

The Haliacmon corridor running from Lake Prespa to the river's great bend gives access to an easy watershed connecting the Haliacmon valley and the tributaries of the Peneios River to the south, running down past Kalabaka and Trikkala into the Thessalian plain. This is one of the major routes from northern into central Greece, used by the Germans in an important attack in 1941. The Haliacmon corridor is not densely populated outside the towns of Kastoria and Grevena, which lie across transverse routes. The area may not have been thickly settled in antiquity.[16] The tillable land is planted mainly in cereal grains and vineyards, and the neighboring slopes are forested in oak, pine, and beech. In general, the region is remote, because its northern end terminates in the high mountain country around Lake Prespa.

[13] Hammond's detailed account of this region (*HM* 1: 19–123) is a mine of information about local historical geography. I prefer, however, the overall geographical scheme laid out in *AHGr* vol. 3, ch. 5; in what follows I offer a version of that, confirmed and modified by my own observations in the field.

[14] There are two Lakes Prespa. Little Prespa lies wholly within Greece, except for a small Albanian inlet, while its larger neighbor, separated from it by only a narrow strip of land, is shared by Greece, Albania, and Yugoslavia. Geographically the two lakes form a single entity, and will be so considered herein.

[15] *AHGr* 3: 92.

[16] The distribution of inscriptions from the area as published in Rizakis and Touratsoglou's end map (in *Epigraphes Anō Makedonias*) suggests light settlement, although one should be cautious about drawing any firm conclusions from such a small statistical sample and variable factors of survivability.

The northern part of the Haliacmon corridor and its adjacent slopes correspond to the ancient canton of Orestis, and the southern part to Tymphaea and Elimeia.[17] Orestis was one of the most important tribal states of upper Macedonia, mentioned as early as Hecataeus (frag. 107), who regarded the Orestae as a Molossian (Epirote)—not Macedonian—tribe. Whatever their stock, their affiliation with the Macedonian state is a later development, certainly post-Thucydidean.[18] The Orestian-Tymphaean border is not precisely known, but probably lies a few miles northwest of modern Grevena.[19] From there Tymphaea and western Elimeia comprise the southern part of the Haliacmon corridor, including the region between the great bend of the Haliacmon and the headwaters of the Peneios River in Thessaly. Located within these cantons is the route over the watershed from the Haliacmon to the Peneios, the way into Thessaly. Moreover, the southern border of Tymphaea ran near the traditional route that connected Epirus (Molossis) with Thessaly and upper Macedonia, roughly corresponding to the spectacular modern road that crosses the high Pindus from Epirotic Ioannina to Thessalian Kalabaka through the Katara Pass above the alpine village of Metsovo. Thus the Tymphaean district is part of a junction for the major routes between mountainous western Greece and the eastern lowlands, and between upper Macedonia and the Thessalian plain.

Paralleling the Haliacmon corridor on the east is a range of mountains whose northern reaches near Skopje—the Sar Planina, which includes some of Yugoslavia's highest peaks—form one of the sources of the Axios (Vardar) River. The southern extension of this range ends only at the Thessalian plain east of Trikkala. Many of its summits are above 6000 ft., and in the north a few are between 7000 and 8500 ft. This difficult barrier is pierced in a number of places. The most northerly of these passages is also the easiest, a low wooded pass north of Mt. Peristeri between Lakes Ohrid and Prespa and the town of Bitola (Monastir)—the route of the Via Egnatia. Some 20 miles south lies the high Pisoderi Pass between little Lake Prespa and the town of Florina at the southern end of the Pelagonian plain. This wild and beautiful pass, over 5000 ft. high, is cloaked in great forests (lumbering is an important industry) and is liable to be blocked by as much as six feet of snow anytime from December through March.[20] The Pisoderi Pass

[17] For details, see *HM* I: 110–17.
[18] Ibid., 111.
[19] See Appendix B below, p. 287.
[20] Constant maintenance is necessary to keep the modern road open; *AHGr* 2: 328. I have seen drifts several feet thick as late as April.

is also the place where the Haliacmon and Axios nearly touch. The headwaters of the Haliacmon can be found above the summit of the pass on the western slope, while a few hundred meters to the east, below the crest on that side, is the source of the Crna (ancient Erigon) River, one of the major tributaries of the Vardar/Axios. The waters of these cascading mountain streams, which derive from a common origin in the melting snows and rainstorms of the peaks above the Pisoderi Pass, will be in proximity again only at the head of the Thermaic Gulf, having meanwhile described separate great arcs as they grow into the full rivers that embrace most of western and central Macedonia.

The Klisoura Pass (*ca.* 3800 ft.) lies 17 miles to the south, below Mt. Vitsi (*ca.* 7000 ft.), and leads from the heart of Orestis near Kastoria to the Bitola-Kozani corridor. There is an easy pass below Siatista, which today links Grevena with Kozani, and a minor pass a few miles south. Even further south, the mass of Mt. Vourino interposes and is breached only by the great bend of the Haliacmon, itself not an accessible route. No other major pass exists in this range before its descent into the plain of Thessaly. These western mountains form the boundary between the ancient cantons of Orestis on the west and Lyncus and Eordaea on the east. The Siatista Pass may have been the northern boundary of Elimeia,[21] whose western and southern boundaries are described by the great bend of the Haliacmon River. The southern part of the range down to the Thessalian plain is within the canton of Perrhaebia (see Map II).

THE BITOLA-KOZANI CORRIDOR

The Bitola-Kozani corridor begins in the Pelagonian plain (1800–2500 ft.), which runs north from Florina about 55 miles. The plain, a fertile region of mixed farming today, is drained by the Crna (Erigon) River, which flows northeast through high mountains to join the Vardar below Titov-Veles. Crossing a rocky threshhold south of Florina, one enters the plain of Eordaea, the northern part of which contains the "lake district" of Western Macedonia. The largest of these, Lake Ostrovo (Vegoritis), is a true deep mountain lake, but several others, including Petron and Cheimaditis, are residual, caused by the inadequate drainage of this mountain basin. Marshes abound, and until recently the area suffered badly from malaria.[22] The plain continues southward for 26 miles, and varies in width from 6 to 12 miles. A low ridge inter-

---

[21] Hammond, *HM* 1: 116–17 and map 11.
[22] *AHGr* 3: 95.

venes above Kozani, from which the corridor slopes gently for 9 miles to the Haliacmon, 1200 ft. below.

Continuing south across the Haliacmon the ground rises steeply toward the main gate between Macedonia and Thessaly—the Volustana Pass (Stena Sarandaporou). Until the completion of the modern sea-level highway along the Thermaic Gulf and through the Vale of Tempe, the main road from central Macedonia into central Greece ran through the Emathian plain to Veria, up along the flank of the Haliacmon Gorge, down to Kozani, then across the Haliacmon and up into the Volustana Pass. The pass drops into a great basin separating the Kamvouni range from the broad southwestern slopes of Olympus. From the head of this basin there are easy routes into the Thessalian plain. The military value of this route was confirmed during campaigns in 1897, 1912, and 1941. From antiquity until the mid-twentieth century it was perhaps the most important route from Macedonia into Thessaly and central Greece.

The Bitola-Kozani corridor comprises the whole or parts of several ancient cantons. The northern part is the open Pelagonian plain that gave access to Stobi on the Vardar/Axios River, probably the route of the Roman road from Heracleia to Stobi.[23] It is difficult to fix the frontier between Pelagonia and Lyncus, although it lay somewhere just north of the modern Yugoslav-Greek border. Diodorus (16.8.1) tells us that the territory of Lyncus was extended when Philip II captured the region between Bitola and Lake Ohrid. The major ancient town of the area, Heracleia, would continue to bear both Lyncestian and Pelagonian attributions for centuries after Philip's conquest. To the south, Lyncus was a small and vital canton.[24] Possessing no ancient towns of consequence, it nevertheless was well watered with good pasture and timberland, and was a vigorous tribal state. It was enclosed on the west by Mt. Peristeri and on the east by the foothills of the Voras Mountains. Its southern boundary was a low ridge through which the Kirli Dirven Pass, just west of Lake Petron, led south into Eordaea's lake country. This was the route followed by the Via Egnatia as it wound its way east from the Pelagonian plain. The whole of Lyncus measured barely 20 by 15 miles, but its importance rested on its position astride important routes, as the relatively high number of inscriptions already discovered there testifies.[25]

[23] For the general historical geography of Pelagonia, see HM I: 59ff.
[24] For details, ibid., 102–5.
[25] Rizakis and Touratsoglou, *Epigraphes Anō Makedonias*, end map, though with the caution expressed above, note 16.

To the southeast lay Eordaea,[26] a large canton that ran about 45 miles from Mt. Voras south to the ridge overlooking Kozani and the Haliacmon. To the west lay the Lyncestian watershed and the mountain frontier of Orestis; the eastern border was dominated by the mass of Mt. Vermion. As a canton straddling communications routes, Eordaea had unrivaled importance. The Via Egnatia route entered Eordaea from the Pelagonian plain and Lyncus through the Kirli Dirven Pass in the north, wound around Lakes Petron and Ostrovo, and exited east at Edessa, where it dropped into the central plain. Further south, the Klisoura Pass led west across the mountains to Lake Kastoria and the heart of Orestis. Another way ran south eventually to join the Grevena-Kozani-Veria route connecting Macedonia with Thessaly. The Eordi themselves were a tribal state, the original inhabitants perhaps having been replaced by repopulating Macedonians.[27]

The remainder of the Bitola-Kozani corridor contained the eastern part of Elimeia, with its crossing of the Haliacmon, and the mountainous region of Perrhaebia. The Elimeian-Perrhaebian frontier may have run along the Pierian ridge overlooking the Haliacmon, near the Volustana Pass, which led into Thessaly.

To return to the northern part of the corridor, the jumble of mountains forming the eastern border of the Pelagonian plain are isolated from central and western Macedonia by the high, impassable massif of Mt. Voras. This tremendous barrier extends from above Lake Ostrovo to the Axios gap some 50 miles east, and forms the western section of the great 300-mile-long mountain wall separating Greek Macedonia from the north. No road pierces the Voras today, and we may assume that in ancient times anyone who desired to move into Macedonia from the upper reaches of the Axios was forced either to follow the gap in the wall created by the Axios itself, or to detour west to the Pelagonian plain and the Bitola-Kozani corridor, thence to follow the route of the Via Egnatia. This latter route lay in a pass, Kara Burun, between the Voras and Vermion ranges, at the eastern opening of which lay Edessa. South of Kara Burun lies the mass of Mt. Vermion, 12 miles wide, up to 6700 ft. in elevation, and yielding no passage through it until one reaches the Haliacmon Gorge crossing 30 miles to the south. The Haliacmon Gorge itself is impassable, although a route exists high on the shoulder of Vermion overlooking the gorge, the modern Veria-Kozani highway, which was until recent times the main road from the Macedonian plain to Thessaly. Rising steeply from the

---

[26] There is some dispute over the name; see Hammond, *HM* I: 106–10.
[27] Thuc. 2.99.5, and Hammond, *HM* I: 109.

opposite side of the Haliacmon Gorge is the Pierian range, an extension of the Olympus massif, forming a formidable mountain obstacle
between Macedonia and Thessaly. Though topographically a section
of the great western Macedonian longitudinal ranges, the slopes of
both Mt. Vermion and the Pierian Mountains are part of the history of
central Macedonia.

Central Macedonia

We come now to the Macedonian heartland—the central plain and its
adjacent slopes.[28] The plain is formed from the alluvial deposits of four
rivers: Haliacmon, Axios, Loudias, and Gallikos (Map II and end
map). The plain's southern limit is marked by the Pierian Mountains,
its western by the long ridges of Mt. Vermion, its northern by Mt.
Paiko (an extension of the Voras frontier mountains), which juts into
the plain, and on the east by the uplands of the left bank of the lower
Axios valley. It measures about 30 miles from the Axios to its western
boundary, and 20–25 miles in its north-south dimension. In the southeast corner the plain opens into the upper Thermaic Gulf in a marshy
area where the four rivers have mouths within the space of only 15
miles, and where the Haliacmon and Axios meet the sea only 7 miles
apart. The center of the plain was not permanently inhabited until recently, being poorly drained and subject to inland flooding. No prehistoric remains have been found in the plain,[29] and no town existed
there until modern times, when land reclamation and flood-control
programs made the place habitable. In antiquity, five known settlements overlooked the plain: Aegae (Vergina), Beroea (Veria), Mieza
(near Naousa), Edessa, and Pella, all on high ground at the plain's
edge.

The Haliacmon enters the plain at its southwestern corner through
a gap between Mt. Vermion and the Pierian range. The latter is part of
a series of mountains, including Olympus, that forms the barrier between Macedonia and Thessaly. The mountains of Pieria, heavily forested in beech and oak, occupy most of the territory between the Haliacmon Gorge and the sea.[30] Along the Thermaic Gulf runs a narrow
coastal strip separating the Pierian and Olympus Mountains from the
Aegean. Much of it is marshy from the constant run-off of the high

[28] In detail, Hammond, *HM* 1: 142–75.

[29] See the site-distribution map in French, *Index of Prehistoric Sites in Central Macedonia*,
now reproduced as an end map in Crossland and Birchall, *Bronze Age Migrations*.

[30] For a sympathetic description of the Pierian Mountains based on considerable first-
hand experience, see Hammond, *HM* 1: 123–25.

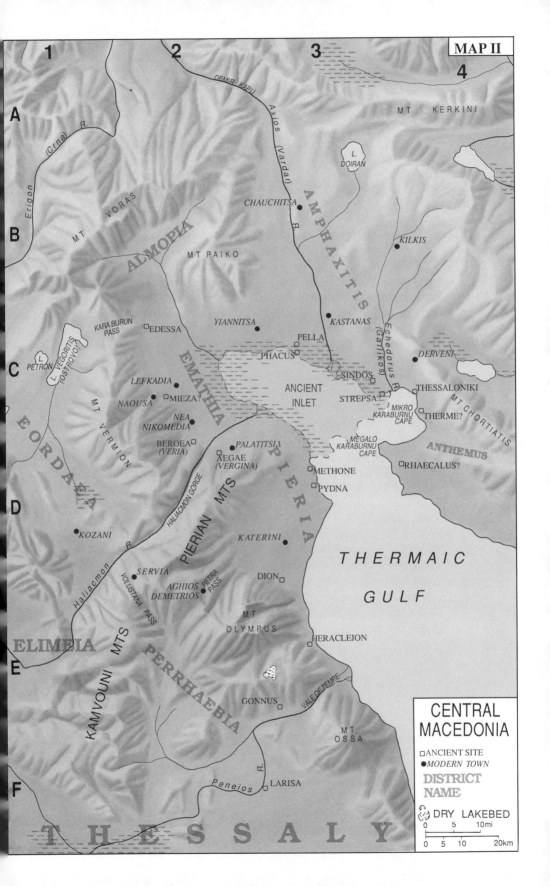

MAP II

1 **2** **3** **4**

DEMIR KAPU

Erigon (Crna) R.

Axios (Vardar)

MT KERKINI

A

MT VORAS

L. DOIRAN

ALMOPIA

AMPHAXITIS

CHAUCHITSA

B

MT PAIKO

KILKIS

KARA BURUN PASS

EDESSA

YIANNITSA

KASTANAS

Echedorus (Gallikos)

PELLA

DERVENI

PHACUS

L. PETRON

L. VEGORITIS (OSTROVO)

EMATHIA

SINDOS

C

LEFKADIA

MIEZA?

ANCIENT INLET

STREPSA

THESSALONIKI

MT VERMION

NAOUSA

MT CHORTIATIS

NEA NIKOMEDIA

I MIKRO KARABURNU CAPE

THERME?

EORDAEA

BEROEA (VERIA)

PALATITSIA

ANTHEMUS

AEGAE (VERGINA)

MEGALO KARABURNU CAPE

RHAECALUS?

METHONE

HALIACMON GORGE

PIERIA

PYDNA

D

KOZANI

PIERIAN MTS

KATERINI

THERMAIC

Haliacmon R.

SERVIA

DION

GULF

VOLUSTANA PASS

AGHIOS DEMETRIOS

PETRA PASS

ELIMEIA

MT OLYMPUS

KAMVOUNI MTS

PERRHAEBIA

HERACLEION

E

GONNUS

VALE DE TEMPE

MT OSSA

Peneios R.

LARISA

F

T H E S S A L Y

CENTRAL MACEDONIA

□ ANCIENT SITE
● MODERN TOWN
DISTRICT NAME
🌀 DRY LAKEBED

0   5   10mi

0   5   10   20km

mountains. It is nearly harborless and was not heavily populated in antiquity. Its present population surge results from improved agricultural technology and a growing influx of tourists drawn to extensive sand beaches. Three cities existed there in antiquity: Dion, Methone, and Pydna.[31] The original inhabitants of coastal Pieria were either killed or sent east of the Strymon River (Hdt. 7.112; Thuc. 2.99.3), displaced by the spread of the early Macedonians.

To the northwest, where the foothills of the Pierian Mountains merge into the central Macedonian plain, is a piedmont that was the homeland of the historical Macedonians. This 15-mile-long terrace held numerous prehistoric settlements, and was chosen by the original Makedones to settle sometime after their migration out of the western mountains.[32] It was here, on a small plateau overlooking the Haliacmon just east of its entry into the plain, near the modern villages of Vergina and Palatitsia, that the Makedones eventually established their ancient center, Aegae. Nicholas Hammond has argued persuasively in favor of this location for Aegae, and there is no need to treat the matter anew.[33]

Along the western edge of the plain lies Mt. Vermion, its summit ridges snow-capped most of the year. Its lower slopes merge with the plain as a series of terraces running north nearly 30 miles from the entrance of the Haliacmon Gorge. These terraces are fertile and well watered by streams draining the eastern slopes of the mountain, and they support three prosperous hill towns: Veria, Naousa, and Edessa. Near the entrance to the Haliacmon Gorge lies Veria (615 ft.), commanding the route to Thessaly that runs along the shoulder of Mt. Vermion as it drops precipitously into the gorge. There was an ancient town here (Beroea) at least as early as the late fifth century B.C.,[34] although its importance in antiquity seems to have developed during Roman times. Naousa (*ca.* 1000 ft.) lies about halfway between Veria and Edessa well up on Vermion. It is a lively town noted in modern times for its silk and fruit, and which today gives its name to the excellent local red wines. The name may be a corruption of the Roman Nea Augousta. Nestled in a charming glen among the orchards on the slopes below Naousa is a Macedonian site that probably is Mieza, fa-

[31] For a detailed topography, see ibid.. 123–39.

[32] *HM* 1: 430–33, and below, pp. 78–80.

[33] See Appendix B below, pp. 287–88.

[34] *HM* 1: 158–59. I have not been able to incorporate the findings of A. B. Tataki's recent (1988) monograph, *Ancient Beroea*, which is a mine of testimonia about the history of the town and its population, and is based upon the author's exhaustive prosopographical analysis of hundreds of inscriptions.

mous for its Nymphaeum, where Aristotle tutored the adolescent Alexander the Great (Plut. *Alex.* 7.3).[35] Edessa's lofty site (1150 ft.) overlooks the plain, and sits astride the pass through which runs the route of the Via Egnatia. It was an important station on that east-west route in antiquity, and the place is marked by impressive walls and settlements from Classical, Hellenistic, and Roman times.

Northeast of Edessa, the Moglenitsas River enters the plain from a gap between Mt. Vermion and Mt. Paiko, whereupon it joins the Loudias River system (see end map). The Moglenitsas drains a high plain hard up against the frontier Voras barrier range. This place is the Almopia of antiquity.[36] It is one of the most fertile places in Greece, capable of supporting several prosperous towns. At an early stage the Macedonians drove out the Almopes and repopulated it themselves (Thuc. 2.99.5). This remote 80-sq.-mile basin is surrounded by well-forested, high peaks—a Macedonian Shangri-la. Today it is difficult to imagine that this alpine cul-de-sac, with its clear air and sparkling streams guarded by imposing snowy summits, was a bitterly contested killing ground during the Greek civil war of 1944–49. The main exit from Almopia is the Moglenitsas river gap. There also exists a pass at its north end that runs between Mt. Paiko and the main ridges of the Voras range. This difficult route winds its way through heavy woods and hilly country before opening onto the broad Axios valley 20 miles to the east. From observation, it appears to be infrequently used and largely uninhabited.

Mt. Paiko itself intrudes far into the Emathian plain, its lower slopes providing the same support to towns as do the terraces of Pieria opposite and of Vermion to the west. The largest of the Macedonian towns in classical times, Pella, was constructed on a low plateau where Mt. Paiko merges with the marshland of the central plain, and where the route of the Via Egnatia hugged the northern edge of the swamps. Pella might also have been (or had) a seaport, as the head of the Thermaic Gulf extended some distance into the plain in those days.[37] Pella's strategic position lying across the main east-west route near the west

35 Ibid., 163; Petsas, *O Taphos tōn Lefkadiōn*, 5–14; and Touratsoglou, *Lefkadia*. Also see Appendix B below, p. 288.

36 Details in *AHGr* 3: 111–13, and *HM* 1: 166–67.

37 For evidence and discussion, see *HM* 1: 145–49, and Edson, "Strepsa," 176. On the matter of the Thermaic Gulf extending well into what is now the plain, I follow Bintliff, "The Plain of Western Macedonia," and Carter, *Hist. Geography*, ch. 3. For synthesis and analysis of the evidence, see Borza, "Some Observations on Malaria," 114–15, and "Natural Resources," 16–19.

bank of the Axios gave it an importance surpassed only by Salonica at a later time.

A few miles east of Pella flows the Axios, draining much of the central Balkans. The hilly region across the Axios was called Amphaxitis in antiquity.[38] It is a rich agricultural area today, and is marked by a large number of prehistoric mounds. This arable land, drained by the Axios and neighboring Gallikos (ancient Echedorus) Rivers, was one of the most prosperous areas of prehistoric Macedonia, owing to its fertility and to its location close by the Axios route into the Balkans. An important German excavation at Kastanas on the east bank of the Axios about midway between the Yugoslav border and the river's mouth has revealed a settlement that flourished over a period of several centuries.[39] The lower Axios plain is, one suspects, a potentially rich site for the archaeological exploration of the prehistoric and early historical periods. At the head of the Thermaic Gulf, and dominating the eastern shore of its own inlet, is Salonica (Thessaloniki), founded as Thessalonikeia by the Macedonian ruler Cassander in 315 B.C. It is a city whose past is manifest, with its impressive Roman, Byzantine, and Turkish monuments built in a natural amphitheatre sloping from huge ancient ramparts down to the sea. A clear winter's day provides a spectacle unsurpassed in modern Greece—a view of the snowy mass of Mt. Olympus looming out of the Thermaic Gulf some 55 miles to the southwest. Salonica's situation on the most favorable natural harbor of northern Greece and near the crossroads of the Axios valley and the main east-west route has given it an historical vitality over two millennia unmatched in the Balkans by any city except Constantinople.

We may now turn to the plain itself.[40] As stated previously, the central plain was formed by the alluvia of four rivers. The region lying north of the Haliacmon was called Bottia (or Bottiaea) in Herodotus's day (7.123.3), but by the time of the Roman Empire it seems to have acquired the name Emathia, a term that we shall use for the plain as a whole.[41] The plain has been poorly drained from ancient times to modern. Heavy silting at the rivers' mouths not only created a con-

[38] Discussed in *HM* I: 176–79.

[39] The major publication by several authors is under the general editorship of Bernhard Hansel, *Kastanas*. Periodic reports from the excavation appear elsewhere, e.g., H. Kroll, "Bronze Age and Iron Age Agriculture in Kastanas, Macedonia." There is a useful display of materials from Kastanas in the Archaeological Museum of Thessaloniki.

[40] Details in *HM* I: 142–62.

[41] For evidence, see ibid., 153–54.

stantly shifting coastline and changes in the streams' courses, but also caused inland flooding to the extent that from time to time lakes were formed, most notably Lake Loudias (Lake Yiannitsa in the nineteenth century).

To trace the geological history of river peregrinations and lake generation in this region is difficult in the extreme. One must depend heavily upon the notices in ancient authors about the configuration of landmarks, and compare these with modern observations about the landscape and with geological measurements. Apparently a western arm of the Thermaic Gulf extended quite far inland (as it still does eastward toward Salonica), perhaps nearly to the site of Pella (Hdt. 7.123.3). In 432 B.C. the Athenians were forced to march as far west as Veria in order to round this inlet (Thuc. 1.62.4; 2.99.4). In time, the heavy silting of the rivers closed the inlet, causing the rivers to seek new channels and, because of poor drainage, form an inland lake. When this blockage occurred is not known precisely: Herodotus (7.127.1) fails to mention it in his description of the region.[42] Whatever the date of the silt blockage, until the early to mid-fourth century B.C. Pella could be reached by ship.[43]

By Strabo's time, alluvia from the Haliacmon, Loudias, and Axios had all but closed the entrance of the sea inlet, thereby creating an inland lake. This lake, fed by the upper Loudias and other streams descending from Vermion and Paiko, was drained to the sea by the lower Loudias, and dominated the lower part of the Emathian plain. Hammond argues correctly that the Axios and the Haliacmon silted up the inlet, and that the consequent blockage caused the Loudias and Haliacmon to seek new channels to the sea. But one may have difficulty accepting his view (HM 1:148–49) that the new lake was replenished by a newly formed arm of the Axios. Eventually an arm of the Axios may have cut a new channel through these marshes to join the lake already formed—a lake formed by the inlet blockage and the consequent flooding of the river Loudias, which was its original source.[44]

The shifting configurations of this region have continued into modern times. It is virtually certain that the silting of these rivers, if permitted to continued unchecked, would eventually have deposited enough material to block the narrow entrance to the Bay of Salonica

[42] Ibid., 145–48, although it is difficult to believe on general grounds that the lower Emathian plain was transformed in less than a century (ca. 450–350 B.C.) from an ocean inlet deep enough to permit ship passage into a lake-river system.

[43] Evidence in HM 1: 148–49.

[44] See Bintliff's account of the alluviation ("The Plain of Western Macedonia," esp. 238, fig. 10), which I prefer to Hammond's.

as well. Man's hand, however, has stayed nature's efforts. In an endeavor at flood and malaria control and land reclamation, the lower course of the Axios was altered in 1925, Lake Loudias was drained in 1927–36, a joint Axios-Haliacmon irrigation project was undertaken in 1953–63, and the Haliacmon was controlled by the recent completion of a dam below Servia, which has created a lovely 30-mile-long artificial lake in the Haliacmon Gorge. All such natural and man-made alterations of the plain have occurred with respect to a virtually constant sea level in the region.[45]

It is thus impossible to discuss with precision the topography of the ancient Emathian plain, both because of a lack of exact information and also because the shape of the main features—lakes, rivers and marshes—has not remained fixed. Yet the following general picture emerges: Lake Loudias has varied in size and shape, and its periphery has been a vast marshland.[46] There were no prehistoric or historical-era settlements, and the present lowland towns exist only as the result of twentieth-century drainage and land reclamation. In classical antiquity much of the plain was waterlogged, uncultivated, and uninhabitable.[47] It was only on the well-watered terraces above the plain—the piedmont of the Pierian range, Vermion, and Paiko—that human settlement took hold, and can be regarded as the core of the Macedonian state.

Eastern Macedonia

Eastern Macedonia comprises the hilly divide separating the Axios valley from the Strymon plain, the Strymon valley itself (including its offshoot, the plain of Philippi), and the adjacent region of Mt. Pangaion (Map III).[48] It is difficult to establish with precision the Thracian-Macedonian frontier, as there were Thracians living in many places east of the Axios in the mid-fifth century B.C., and neither Herodotus nor Thucydides is clear about such a boundary. In antiquity it may be said that, at various times from the sixth to the fourth centuries, Macedonia merged with Thrace at the Axios, at the Strymon, and at the

[45] *Contra* Hammond (*HM* 1: 145), who states that the sea level in the Mediterranean has risen some five feet since antiquity. See Appendix B below, pp. 288–89.

[46] See Appendix B below, p. 289.

[47] *Contra* Hammond, *HM* 1: 160. For more detailed discussion of cultivation, see Borza, "Natural Resources," 12–19.

[48] Discussions of these regions can be found in *HM*, vol. 1, ch. 5; *AHGr* 3: 118–42; and Samsaris, *Istoriki Geographia*. Part of what follows is based on these works and part on personal experience in the area.

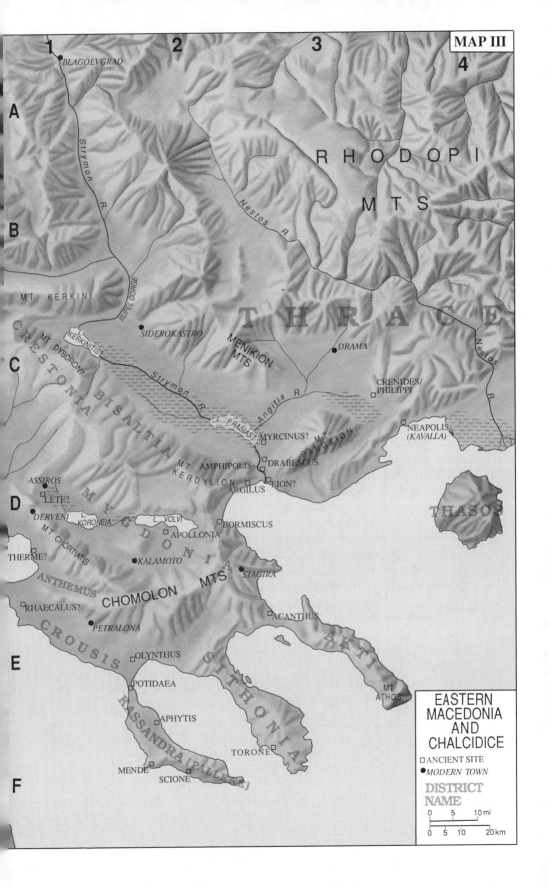

MAP III

1　　　2　　　3　　　4

BLAGOEVGRAD

A

Strymon R.

R H O D O P I

B

Nestos R.

M T S

MT KERKINI

RUPEL GORGE

T H R A C E

CRESTONIA

BISALTIA

MT DYSORON?

L. KERKINITIS?

SIDEROKASTRO

MENIKION
MTS

DRAMA

C

Strymon R.

Angitis R.

CRENIDES/
PHILIPPI

L. PRASIAS?

MYRCINUS?

MT
PANGAION

NEAPOLIS
(KAVALLA)

MT
KERDYLION

AMPHIPOLIS

DRABESCUS

Nestos R.

ASSIROS

ARGILUS

EION?

THASOS

LETE?

MYGDONIA

D

DERVENI

L.
KORONEIA

L. VOLVI

BORMISCUS

MT CHORTIATIS

APOLLONIA

THERME?

KALAMOTO

ANTHEMUS

CHOMOLON　MTS

STAGIRA

AKTI

RHAECALUS?

ACANTHUS

CROUSIS

PETRALONA

SITHONIA

OLYNTHUS

E

POTIDAEA

MT
ATHOS

EASTERN
MACEDONIA
AND
CHALCIDICE

KASSANDRA (PALLENE)

APHYTIS

□ ANCIENT SITE
● MODERN TOWN

TORONE

DISTRICT
NAME

MENDE

SCIONE

F

0　　5　　10mi

0　5　10　　20km

Nestos, the latter being the modern administrative boundary. The expansion of Macedon to the east was at the expense of Thracian territory.

We have seen that the fertile strip directly east of the lower Axios and paralleling it was called Amphaxitis in antiquity. Separating Amphaxitis from the Strymon is a large expanse of high hills running northwest to southeast from the Kerkini range along the Bulgarian border toward the Lake Corridor (see below) and the Strymon Gulf. Bearing no common name, but extending from Mt. Dysoron in the north to Mt. Kerdylion in the south, this belt measures about 55 miles in length with a width of about 18 miles. It contains a few summits as high as 3000–3500 feet. It was well forested in antiquity with pine and perhaps with oak and chestnut as well; today only a few high ridges are heavily wooded. Except for the Gallikos basin in the northwestern corner, the Dysoron-Kerdylion hills are not well suited to agriculture owing to the failure of the underlying rock to hold soil and water. Consequently the streams are dry in summer and the region is covered with maquis (scrub), the villages being located in a few watered hollows where marginal farming activity is possible. The Mediterranean appearance of its interior probably results from the landscape's inability to recover from centuries of human exploitation.

The western part of this hilly region was the canton of Crestonia, including the sources of the Gallikos River (ancient Echedorus; Hdt. 7.124, 127.2) and the uplands to the southeast, centered in the relatively prosperous agricultural region around Kilkis. The area was early under Macedonian control (Thuc. 2.99.6), although the inhabitants were not expelled. Along the Dysoron-Kerdylion divide lay the frontier of Bisaltia (Hdt. 8.116.1), which in Xerxes' day included the eastern slope of the divide leading to the lowlands in the Strymon plain itself.[49] By Roman times Bisaltia seems to have included as well most of the lower Strymon valley from the site of Amphipolis near the river's mouth up to the Rupel Gorge. When the Macedonians conquered Bisaltia (Thuc. 2.99.6), the inhabitants, a well-organized Thracian people called the Edoni, were driven across the Strymon (Hdt. 7.110 and 114.1).[50] Bisaltia was richer than Crestonia, and the Edoni were among the first of the northern peoples to coin money; both silver and rich forests were close by.

Two corridors connect the Axios hinterland with the valley of the Strymon. In the north, a corridor runs from the region of Lake Doiran

[49] For ancient evidence, see *HM* 1: 181–82.
[50] For details, see ibid., 192–93, and Chapter 5 below.

and the upper Gallikos basin to the head of the Strymon plain. This corridor, a deep, narrow valley, lies between Mt. Dysoron and the nearly vertical, unbroken ridge of the Kerkini range along the Bulgarian frontier. It is the short route into central Macedonia for anyone in the middle or upper Strymon plain, or for anyone wishing to avoid the narrow and defensible Rendina gap in the southern Lake Corridor. This "short way" may have been Darius's route to the west (Hdt. 5.15–17), and Alexander's to the east (Arr. 1.11.3).[51]

At the southern end of the divide is a low-lying "Lake Corridor," running between the heads of the Bay of Salonica and the Strymon Gulf. It is narrow—2 to 6 miles in width—and closed off at the west by the northwest ridges of Mt. Chortiatis behind Salonica. The eastern access is a narrow, wooded, near-sea-level ravine at Rendina (see end map). The corridor is enclosed on the north by the Dysoron-Kerdylion divide and on the south by the mountains of Chalcidice. This 40-mile-long corridor is mostly taken up with Lakes Volvi and Koroneia. Although cultivation and a few villages exist mainly on a narrow plain that lies between the lakes and the Chalcidic hills above, the corridor has seen little settlement, the region having been highly malarious. The route of the Via Egnatia followed the plain south of the lakes, as does the modern highway. It is only the existence of high ground at the west and the present relative sea level that keeps this corridor from being flooded, and Chalcidice from being an island. The Lake Corridor and its adjacent slopes to the north formed the canton of Mygdonia (Hdt. 7.123.3), which also included the area west to the Axios below Amphaxitis.

Along the northern frontier of modern Greece, only two gaps appear in the unbroken 300-mile-long mountain wall. Between the Pelagonian plain in the west and the eastern terminus of the Rhodopi Mountains near the Turkish border, two rivers, the Axios and the Strymon, have cut their way back through the barrier ranges. The steep faces of the Rhodopi massif have blocked access from the Aegean coast to the Balkan interior. There is no easy Aegean-Balkan passage east of the Axios valley until one reaches European Turkey and the Dardanelles. This fact accounts in part for the historical importance of Salonica and Constantinople.

Unlike the Axios gap, the valley of the Strymon was not a major route through the mountains in antiquity, its hinterland being less ac-

---

[51] On this point and several others concerning the historical geography of the Strymon-Philippi region, I differ from Hammond. My views are laid out in detail in "Some Toponym Problems."

48 CHAPTER 2

cessible than that of the Axios. The Strymon is born in the high mountains between Sofia and the Yugoslav border, threads an impressive canyon in southwestern Bulgaria below Blagoevgrad, and enters Greece through the Rupel defile. Thence it opens onto a broad river plain that points toward the sea some 50 miles to the southeast. The alluvial Strymon plain is about 12 miles wide, and runs between two parallel mountain chains, the Dysoron-Kerdylion on the west and the Menikion on the east. Drainage is poor, as the lower end of the plain is blocked by the mass of Mt. Pangaion and a low coastal ridge. The river reaches the sea through a gap between Pangaion and Kerdylion, the site of the Athenian outpost of Amphipolis. In modern times the Strymon's course has been altered through extensive flood- and malaria-control programs. In antiquity one or two lakes may have occupied the plain. The lower of two modern lakes, near Mt. Pangaion, has been drained, and the upper controlled by floodworks.[52] The exact course of the river in ancient times is impossible to determine (except for its lower path past Amphipolis), and thereby the frontier between Bisaltia and the Paeonian tribes to the east is also uncertain. Like the Emathian plain, the plain of the Strymon seems not to have seen much human settlement, most towns being confined to adjacent slopes. Until the Persian and Macedonian advances in the sixth and fifth centuries B.C., the Strymon was inhabited by Paeonians and Thracian tribes.[53]

Mt. Pangaion (6260 ft.) is a huge, isolated, complex peak that nearly fills the lower Strymon plain. About 15 miles north of the Strymon's mouth, a gap appears between Mt. Pangaion and the Menikion range, through which flows the Angitis River. East of this gap, the Angitis drains a large, formerly marshy plain measuring about 25 by 10 miles, which runs parallel to the Strymon plain but is separated from it by the Pangaion and Menikion Mountains. This plain is blocked from the sea by a narrow, low ridge on whose coastal slopes today lies the important agricultural and shipping center of Kavalla. The plain is the tobacco-producing basin of Drama and the old plain of Philippi. The ancient site of Crenides, originally a mining colony of Thasos, was taken over by Philip II, who renamed it after himself, and who is said to have reclaimed the marshes.[54] It achieved further prominence as an important station guarding the route of the Via Egnatia and is, of

[52] The nomenclature of these lakes in antiquity is a problem. It is possible (*contra* Hammond et al.) that the lower lake was named Prasias and the upper Kerkinitis. Details in Borza, "Some Toponym Problems," 60–61.

[53] *HM* 1: 193–94 and 197–98, and Chapter 5 below.

[54] Theoph. *de Caus. Plant.* 5.14.6.

course, the site of the renowned battles of 42 B.C. that saw Julius Caesar's assassins yield to the resolve of the Second Triumvirate.

The Strymon plain and its periphery were more productive in antiquity than was Emathia. Mt. Pangaion was one of the major sources of gold in the lower Balkans, substantial amounts of silver were exploited throughout the region, the nearby mountains provided a rich supply of timber, and several routes passed through the area. The Strymon plain's prosperity declined only in recent times, largely because of political instability and land mismanagement, reaching its nadir in the late nineteenth and early twentieth centuries. It has more than recovered to become one of Europe's richest agricultural districts. East of the Strymon lies an impenetrable mountain region with few roads even today, and not much known archaeologically. The Nestos River runs through this wilderness, but it is not navigable, and its course through the Rhodopi and coastal mountains provides little access into the interior. Its huge delta, reaching out toward the island of Thasos, is rich in agriculture, but this is a modern phenomenon. Once we reach the Nestos we are in the world of the Thracians.

The three-fingered peninsula of Chalcidice is not part of Macedonia proper.[55] Its Aegean seafaring tradition and settlement by Greek colonists made it look seaward and southward. It was, especially on the extended peninsulas, part of the world of the Greek city-states. Except for a few campaigns staged there during the early part of the Peloponnesian War, Chalcidice remained rather isolated from Macedonian affairs until its cities were organized in a fourth-century league powerful enough to challenge Macedonian interests east of the Axios.[56] Chalcidice comprises two distinct regions: its three-pronged peninsulas, and a mountainous interior.

The interior of Chalcidice is a mass of rugged, heavily wooded hills. Although cut off from Macedonia proper by the Cholomon Mountains, the region offers both flora and settlements more Continental than Mediterranean. The area is relatively unknown archaeologically, and is generally remote. As one approaches the Aegean coast, however, a remarkable transformation occurs in the landscape. At the crest of the Cholomon transverse ridges, the deciduous and pine forests of the interior suddenly give way to olive trees. Within a few hundred yards, the Balkans have become Mediterranean. A long slope down to

[55] Following Hammond, *HM* I: 92. A useful guide to the historical and touristic sites of Chalcidice is now available: Papangelos, *Chalkidiki*.

[56] Only two Chalcidic areas, the western coastal strip known as Crousis, and Anthemus, the rich valley opening onto the coastal plain below Salonica, were part of Macedonian history; see *HM* I: 186–87.

the sea was rich in olives and grains, which accounts in part for the
wealth of Olynthus, its dominant city in antiquity.

Once islands in the distant geological past, the three fingers of the
Chalcidice have only tenuous connections with the mainland. In the
case of Kassandra, the link is a sandspit, virtually at sea level. Sithonia's
is a 300-foot hill, and the isthmus of Akti is low, although some 45 feet
higher today than when Xerxes cut his canal through it in 482 B.C.

The peninsulas were active and prosperous in antiquity: Mende, Torone, Aphytis, Potidaea, and Acanthus were among their main Greek
towns. Since ancient times, however, the peninsulas have been backward and isolated. Kassandra (ancient Pallene) is the most fertile and
least rugged, and recently its fine beaches have been exploited to help
satisfy Europe's insatiable quest for the sea and sun. Sithonia's mountains rise to about 2600 feet. It is enjoying a revival of its famous ancient wine industry. Seismologically active Akti is remote and difficult
of access. Akti is better known as Aghion Oros, the Holy Mountain,
a semiautonomous region of reviving monasteries, where the Ortho-
dox Middle Ages live on. The peninsula culminates in the spectacular
pyramidal peak of Athos, rising nearly 6700 feet directly from the sea.
Famous for its storms, and mercifully saved from an ancient legendary
plan to carve a colossal portrait of Alexander the Great into its face,
Mt. Athos survives as one of the most impressive natural wonders of
the northern Aegean.

Natural Resources

Macedonia was, by Greek standards, well endowed by nature with resources.[57] Abundant rainfall, flowing rivers, arable land, extensive forests, and precious-metal reserves made the Macedonians self-sufficient. And with modest needs until the time of Philip II, there was little
in the way of material goods or foodstuffs from the outside world that
Macedon would regard as necessary. The enormous disposable wealth
attested to not only by the grave goods in the tombs of the gentry but
also by the commitment of resources to military activity in a huge land
suggests something of the wealth upon which the king could depend.
The Macedonian kingdom was rich because its inhabitants learned to
marshal human resources to exploit natural ones. The most vivid testimony is the account of the vast riches of Macedon that so impressed
the Romans in 167 B.C. (Livy 45.40.1–3), accumulated in barely three

[57] The evidence and detailed discussion for what follows can be found in Borza,
"Some Observations on Malaria," esp. 112–15; "Natural Resources," 3–20; and "Timber
and Politics."

decades following the humiliation of their greatest Hellenistic king, Philip V.

Our survey of the Macedonian landscape suggests a land well suited to pastoral and agricultural activities. With their basins and meadows, Macedonian mountains are ideal for the transhumance of flocks, that widely practiced Balkan custom of alternating pasturage between summer highlands and winter lowlands. Not only did the flocks produce wool, meat, and milk, but they fertilized their own grazing grounds. Animal manure could be left to rot and enrich the soil, as there was an abundant supply of wood in many areas. The need to use dung cakes as fuel—a practice that has contributed to the continuing cycle of poverty in some parts of the world—was absent in much of Macedonia.

The pollen-analysis techniques that have provided information about ancient agriculture in other regions have not been extensively utilized in Macedonia. General reasoning based on land-use models and a survey of containers found in excavations are helpful, and provide a picture of agricultural activity. As one might expect, agriculture was to be found wherever arable, watered land was available, and in this respect Macedonia was fortunate. The Haliacmon corridor, the Bitola-Kozani corridor, and the low transverse mountain passes are all moderately fertile. The piedmont areas of central Macedonia—that is, the lower slopes of the Pierian range, Mt. Vermion, and Mt. Paiko— are all quite fertile, as were those parts of the Axios basin that were elevated above heavy marshland. The Pierian coastal plain is fertile today, but it may have been wooded in antiquity, unlike most of the central plain. In eastern Macedonia the piedmont above the plains of Philippi, Drama, and the Strymon was also good farmland, as were the coastal areas of Chalcidice. We would expect these regions to produce grain and vegetables in sufficient quantity. That Philip II drained the marshland around Philippi shortly after he took the area in 356 B.C. suggests that there was some need for additional land. This need may also have prompted Philip's interest in Chalcidice, both for agricultural use and for the raising of horses.

The vine flourishes today in many parts of Macedonia, but we can only make estimates about the type, quantity, and locations of Macedonian vineyards in antiquity. Some things, however, are apparent.[58] The Macedonians were, by Greek standards, notorious drinkers. It was not merely a matter of soldiers' rough drinking habits, but the fact

[58] For what follows, details in Borza, "The Symposium at Alexander's Court," 48–49.

that they often drank their wine *akratos*—unmixed—as opposed to the Greeks, who mixed wine with water. It is significant for an understanding of wine-drinking habits among the Macedonians that the krater, a rather common Greek vessel-type used for the mixing of wine and water, is rare in Macedonian burials (see Chapter 11). Only a few have been recovered among the plethora of wine vessels, and some are works of decorative art, not practical implements.

The vine, which is sturdy enough to survive winter frosts, needs well-drained soil, spring rains, and sunshine just before harvest. Many areas of Macedonia provide these conditions. Col. Leake praised the wines of western Macedonia, and the terraces around Naousa today produce some of the best red wines of the Balkans. Although there is no direct evidence about local wine production, it is fair to suggest that this enormous thirst for the fermented juice of grapes could not be satisfied by the importation of wine alone.[59] There was probably a considerable local production, supplemented by the importation of wines by a gentry with the wealth and taste to do so.

Macedonia is not as kind to the olive, however. One of the longest-lived and sturdiest trees, which thrives under conditions that doom other plants, the olive cannot tolerate extreme cold for extended periods.[60] Some of the terrace-land above the Emathian plain supports olive trees, where they can avoid frost by catching sea breezes from the Thermaic Gulf. There are olives along the seaside of the Pierian coastal plain, in parts of the plain of Philippi, and along the Strymon Gulf. But one must reach the Mediterranean slopes of Chalcidice before entering the Greek world of the olive grove. Further archaeology may reveal the extent to which the Macedonians imported oil; the source may have been Chalcidice, which had oil in abundance, or the Greek cities to the south, which may have provided oil in exchange for Macedonian timber. Recent excavations have shown that some of the early inhabitants of the Axios valley produced flax, which, either ground or pressed into linseed oil, is a tolerable alternative to the olive.[61] We also

[59] There is no study of Macedonian wine imports, although the evidence in the form of stamped amphora handles found at Pella provides some evidence about the foreign origin of some wines. My own survey of the photo archives of the Pella amphorae revealed that wines were imported from Chalcidice and from Thasos. Some of the wines produced in Chalcidice today are arguably among the finest in Greece.

[60] Details and bibliography in Borza, "Natural Resources," 14–15. There is a single olive tree planted in the courtyard of the Archaeological Museum of Thessaloniki. It survives only because it is protected from the chill "Vardar" winter winds, and the present director of the museum, Julia Vokotopoulou, informs me that, in her memory, it has never produced fruit.

[61] H. Kroll, "Bronze Age and Iron Age Agriculture in Kastanas, Macedonia."

must not discount the possibility that a well-forested country with abundant game may have yielded animal fat to an extent greater than in the Greek world, and that the Macedonians' oil needs consequently were not importunate.

Macedonia's precious-metal resources were renowned.[62] There is hardly a part of the country in which mining for metal has not been an activity, although the resources of western and central Macedonia seem not to have been much exploited in antiquity. It was eastern Macedonia that emerged as the center of mineral wealth. Many of the streams flowing out of the Rhodopi Mountains are auriferous. When the gold-bearing sands are heated, the metal coagulates; the slag thereby produced is the archaeologist's clue. The same streams produced some magnetite iron-bearing sands, but it is unknown whether these were worked in antiquity. Silver existed in abundance in several places, but Macedonia had no native resources for the manufacture of its bronze, and the region lay outside the main tin route from Britain to the Mediterranean.

The early inhabitants of the region seem to have been herders and farmers, and their graves do not yield the quantities of gold found in burials further north in the Balkans. But a major change occurred in the late sixth century B.C. The recent excavation of hundreds of graves near the village of Sindos along the lower Gallikos River has turned up considerable quantities of objects well wrought from gold, iron, and bronze.[63] It has yet to be determined if the sources of the precious metals are local. By the fifth century, however, there was no doubt about the renown of Macedonian metals, and several parts of the region east of the Axios commenced being exploited on a larger scale.

There were three main centers of mining activity. The first was the upper Gallikos basin, where both gold and silver were extracted. Nearby was Mt. Dysoron, so rich, according to Herodotus (5.17), that it produced a talent of silver a day for Alexander I. The precise location of ancient Mt. Dysoron is not known. The modern peak of that name is located at the very northern part of the Dysoron-Kerkylion divide. It is possible, however, that in antiquity, the whole range bordering the Strymon valley might have been given that name. If so, and if ancient Lake Prasias were the lower of the two Strymon lakes, the famous silver mines were further south, closer to the site of Amphipolis and nearby Mt. Pangaion.[64]

---

[62] Full discussion, with bibliography, in Borza, "Natural Resources," 8–12.

[63] See the catalog of the exhibition of Sindos materials in the Archaeological Museum of Thessaloniki, Vokotopoulou et al., *Sindos*.

[64] See Borza, "Natural Resources," 10, and "Some Toponym Problems," 60–61.

A major center of mining activity was located in the region of Philippi and Mt. Pangaion. The Thasians founded an outpost at Crenides in the sixth century, an extension of mining activity already established on their island. After Philip II's conquest of the area—and the renaming of Crenides after himself—the exploitation of its mineral riches continued. Pangaion had been worked for silver since perhaps as early as the seventh century. Together these areas produced sufficient metals to enable the local Thracian tribes to issue an abundant silver coinage of good quality. The output of Dysoron provided considerable silver for the superb coinage of Alexander I in the mid-fifth century. Diodorus's comment (16.8.6–7) that the mines of Pangaion were not significant until the time of Philip II must refer to the output of gold. Whereas silver had been extracted for more than a century and a half, it was Philip who exploited the gold-bearing potential of the mines. His is the first gold coinage, and the extensive use of gold in the burials at Vergina suggests something of the considerable supply of this metal. The mining of gold continued sporadically even through the temporary Roman closure of the mines in 167 B.C.[65]

A third mining center was located in the Cholomon Mountains of central Chalcidice, but it is not known whether these mines were open before the time of Philip II. Certainly they were heavily worked during the Hellenistic period, and were among those closed briefly by the Romans (Livy 45.29). Gold and silver were extracted, and the region of the eastern Cholomon hills, near Aristotle's birthplace at Stagira, offered a variety of other metals, many of which continued to be exploited in Turkish and modern times.

Mining technology was primitive. Most gold and silver was extracted from streams by placers. There is little archaeological evidence to suggest deep mining, although the breakthrough in gold production in Philip's reign may be attributed to some kind of administrative or technological improvement, if Arrian's summary (*Anab.* 7.9.3) of a speech of Alexander the Great can be trusted. Philip seems to have had strong interests in technology (e.g., the draining of swamps and building of roads), and perhaps he supervised the opening of safe shafts and galleries in the Pangaion region. Although we have no information about the organization of mining activity, it is possible that numerous small mines could be worked profitably under conditions considered impossible today. The economy of scale did not obtain in a culture in which labor, either slave or free, was cheap. It is also likely that the

[65] On Roman policy toward the mines, see Gruen, "Macedonia and the Settlement of 167 B.C."

output of the mines was under royal control, as was the case with Macedonia's most important other natural resource, timber.

"The best timber which comes into Greece for the carpenter's use is Macedonian. . . ." Thus Theophrastus (*Hist. Plant.* 5.2.1) evaluates Macedonia's most valuable resource, its great deciduous and evergreen forests.[66] Much of the Macedonian countryside above *ca.* 700 ft. is forested, and our best ancient source on these matters lists no fewer than 34 varieties of trees (Theoph. *Hist. Plant.* 3.3.1). Population pressures deforested much of Greece quite early on, so that by the Classical period many Greeks were forced to look elsewhere for the tall timbers necessary for building and ship construction. Because of suitable mountain slopes and fertile riverside land, Macedonian forests, even when exploited, were done so by a relatively small population and were able to regenerate themselves with the abundant rainfall. Thus the Greek world turned to the north as the closest supply of excellent timber for a variety of needs.

Virtually every mountainous area of Macedonia is well forested, but these wooded lands vary in the types and accessibility of trees for harvest. Western Macedonia is forested on its higher slopes, but the area is generally remote, and the timber gained from these mountains will have had only local use. Although this is not a factor in Macedonian foreign trade, the availability of wood for local use almost everywhere is an important component of the local economy.

There is evidence of major forests of tall timbers on the slopes of the Pierian-Olympus ranges (where today the processing of great evergreens can be seen from the National Highway running through the Pierian coastal plain), along Mt. Vermion, and on the Strymon slopes of the Dysoron-Kerdylion divide. Little information about the felling of trees and preparation of timber for export from Macedon has survived. There is, however, a general body of information about tree harvests in antiquity, and nothing to indicate that Macedonia was a special case.[67] Trees were felled by axemen, perhaps working in teams of three. Branches were stripped by axe, and the timber was crosscut with saws in preparation for transport to the sea. Timber slides, wagons, drag-hitches, and river flotation were used to move timber internally, and ordinary cargo or special timber ships provided overseas transport.

Pine was widely used, for both ship and building construction. It is

[66] What follows is taken from my two earlier studies of Macedonian timber, in "Natural Resources," 2–8, and (more extensively) "Timber and Politics," with full documentation.

[67] Indispensable as a survey of the ancient timber industry is Meiggs, *Trees and Timber*.

relatively light in weight, it can be hewn in long, straight pieces for masts and major beams, and its resinous character is an advantage for hull planking. Oak was valued for keels. The best oars were made from flexible young fir trees (Theoph. *Hist. Plant.* 5.1.7), each oar shaped from a single tree. The naval construction needs for Athens alone for the period 480–410 B.C. may have run to 1500 triremes and at least 300,000 oars.[68] Most of this timber came from Macedonia. As valuable as timber itself was pitch, necessary to seal ships' hulls. The amount required by Greek shipyards is incalculable.

As was likely the case with mines, the control of Macedonian forests rested in the hands of the king. We lack sufficient information to reconstruct the process whereby the king acquired these prerogatives, but all surviving treaties regulating commerce in timber between foreign states and Macedon were made with the king personally. This is more than the normal procedure of the king serving as the embodiment of the Macedonian state: the king also held as a royal prerogative the right to give gifts of timber as he pleased. Royal control over forests is well attested, most recently by a new interpretation of the summary of a royal decree of Alexander the Great,[69] in which the king prohibits the sale of timber from Dysoron. This is not to suggest that the king was in the timber business. He probably granted permissions to private individuals to harvest timber under the control of woodland commissioners, according to terms of contracts let with royal approval. By granting rights to harvest and export, and by levying fees on that export, the Macedonian king exploited forest products as a feature of foreign policy and as a source of revenue. Timber became a major factor in the relations between Macedon and the Greek city-states, as a number of those states attempted to gain access to timber and deny that access to their adversaries. Some Macedonian kings were able to exploit the timber needs of Greeks, whereas others found themselves struggling to preserve Macedonian national integrity against those who wished to insure a supply of timber through the use of force (see Chapters 5 and 6 below).

Macedon's natural resources, in particular its plentiful land, mineral wealth, and forest products, contributed to self-sufficiency, an unusual condition in the eastern Mediterranean. Its wealth supported the ambitions of many of its kings (especially when eastern Macedonia was under royal control), and made the region attractive to foreigners from

[68] Borza, "Timber and Politics," 34.

[69] The best text of the decree, which dates from 335 or 334 B.C., is by Missitzis, "A Royal Decree," with some emended readings and extended interpretations by Borza, "Some Toponym Problems," 62–66.

the sixth century B.C. on. In the hands of skillful monarchs capable of organizing human and natural resources, and bending them to some national purpose, it was probably inevitable that Macedon would emerge from the Balkan backwater to become a major force in the ancient Mediterranean world.

Prehistoric Macedonia

THE oldest known inhabitant of Macedonia may have been a woman. In 1960 a passerby stumbled into a cave near Petralona in northwest Chalcidice, and found himself staring at the fossilized skeleton of a human being. Originally thought to be a Neanderthal creature, recent analysis of the skull—the other remains may have been destroyed when the local villagers attempted to pry them loose from their encrusted stalagmitic formation—makes *archanthropos petraloniensis* at least 270,000 years old, the earliest evidence of humans in the southern Balkans. Further excavation of the cave has revealed evidence of human activity for at least half a million years.[1]

Neanderthal creatures roamed widely from Macedonia to Elis down to about 50,000–30,000 B.P, but these early protohumans were anticipated by a race whose existence goes back to about 100,000 years ago. Evidence of these pre-Neanderthal primates occurs in the form of a primitive stone hand-axe discovered in western Macedonia near Siatista: thus far it is the oldest paleolithic implement found in Greece.[2] Only by the most chauvinistic stretch of reason can one think of these primeval creatures as "Macedonian." In any case, the description of their tenuous existence is better left to the physical anthropologists with their special skills in recreating the patterns of human life from the strata of cave floors and detritus of gravel banks. What is clear is that, as far as we know, the northern regions of Greece supported the earliest protohumans in the southern Balkans.

To speak of "prehistoric Macedonians" in the context of a Macedonian history is to begin with the early Neolithic era, *ca.* 6000 B.C., and

---

[1] The skull was first published by Kokkoros and Kanellis, "Découverte d'un crâne d'homme paléolithique dans la péninsule chalcidique." Excellent plates of the skull and the Petralona cave are in *History of the Hellenic World*, 1: 44–45. For the considerable controversy over the date of the skull, see Poulianos, "Petrolona"; Stringer et al., "The Significance of the Fossil Hominid Skull"; and Liritzis, "A Critical Dating Re-evaluation," with extensive bibliography.

[2] Illustrated in *History of the Hellenic World*, 1: 43. For Neanderthal in Greece, see Weinberg, "The Stone Age in the Aegean," esp. 557–62.

to trace mankind's activity down to the end of the Late Bronze Age, *ca.* 1100 B.C. Everyone who has studied this period recognizes the serious difficulties implicit in generalizing about it. The era's remoteness in time and its lack of written records force one to depend entirely upon the evidence of material remains and upon analogies with other cultures in similar primitive stages of development. The archaeological record is often fragmentary, absolute chronology is tenuous, and one is sometimes required to draw conclusions for a whole region on the basis of a single developed site or a few scattered artifacts—a statistically precarious procedure at best. Other methodological problems abound. For example, must a change in pottery style necessarily reflect the influence of an external culture, such as the intrusion of new people or trade contacts with a foreign population, or can it equally indicate innovation in internal technology and taste? Do similarities in burials, pottery, implements, and use of materials between two separate cultures necessarily imply contact between them? Does one categorize and date objects found in Macedonia by a long-established Greek-Aegean chronology, or by some modification in a central European-Balkan system?

The level of our knowledge of prehistoric Macedonia is roughly akin to what was known about central and southern Greece at the beginning of the twentieth century. Macedonian prehistoric archaeology is in its infancy, but the possibility that some Macedonian equivalent of the Linear B tablets will be unearthed to promote a leap in learning is remote. What follows is a reconstruction of events that seems probable on the basis of an analysis of current information. But the reader should be aware that progress nowadays in these remote periods is often rapid and sometimes revolutionary, and occasionally one finds that yesterday's conclusion no longer appears warranted. We must be prepared to yield our notions to a new stroke of the archaeologist's pick, or to some esoteric technique of laboratory analysis. The historian can do little more than digest the most current literature and offer a reasonable interpretation of the inferences drawn by specialists from a number of fields.[3]

The most advanced Early Neolithic site known in Greece is at Nea Nikomedia, in the central Macedonian plain a few miles north of Veria. Located near a then-existing marsh or sea inlet, and dated to between *ca.* 6200-5300 B.C., this well-developed community yielded several multiroom houses (some with porches), hearths, storage bins

---

[3] See Appendix A below, pp. 283–84.

and pits, a central shrine, and numerous burials.[4] These were a settled people who grew crops and raised animals. In addition to their vessels and implements of clay and flint, they left small representations of a female fertility figure, and insights into contemporary local fauna: figurines of frogs, goats, boars, and bulls. The artifacts bear similiarities to the Neolithic proto-Sesklo culture of Thessaly. Perhaps the site originated as an offshoot of Thessalian settlement, as a group migrated north over the passes into Macedonia and followed the Pierian Mountains down to the central plain. Here, with well-watered and fertile land, and wildlife and timber close by, the village flourished, and in its later stages took on a number of independent cultural characteristics.

At Servia, near the Haliacmon crossing of the route between Kozani and the Volustana Pass into lower Thessaly, a Middle Neolithic (*ca.* 5000–4000 B.C.) settlement shows complex rectangular houses, postframed, with mud-plaster walls and pitched roofs supported by central posts.[5] Whatever the origin of the Servia village (Hammond makes it an offshoot of Thessalian Sesklo, an Anatolia-based group), its architectural features in the later Neolithic phases resemble those normally associated with central European and northern Balkan sites, including the Neolithic houses in Pelagonia.[6] That is, by the Late Neolithic period, at least western Macedonia was experiencing some movement of peoples who may have influenced one another.

By the Late Neolithic period (*ca.* 4000–2800 B.C.) these movements became more pronounced, and the western and central areas of Macedonia became more extensively settled. Both Pelagonia and Lyncus were well inhabited, as the rich mounds of the so-called "Porodin" culture have shown. In the southern and central areas, both Nea Nikomedia and Servia were resettled, perhaps by migrants from the northwestern regions. New sites appeared along the western edge of the central plain, but seem not to have moved east from there.[7] The settlements were mainly small and agricultural, and there is some reason to believe that they attracted traditional herdsmen during the winter season. Thus—if our interpretation is correct—the Late Neolithic

---

[4] The most widely accepted date of *ca.* 6000 B.C. (e.g., Rodden, "Excavations at Nea Nikomedeia," passim; Weinberg, "The Stone Age in the Aegean," 577–82; and Hammond, *HM* 1: 219) has now been challenged by Bintliff ("The Plain of Western Macedonia," 24), who down-dates the early levels to 5500–5300, based on a different method of organic analysis.

[5] The excavations were supervised by K. Rhomiopoulou; see *AR* (1971–72): 17, and (1972–73): 22; also *HM* 1: 219–20.

[6] In particular, the clay floor built over a log substructure such as found in the Porodin culture in Pelagonia; see *AR* (1971–72): 17, (1972–73): 22; and *HM* 1: 219–20.

[7] *HM* 1: 220–24, *contra* Heurtley.

period saw the Thessalian settlers at Servia and Nea Nikomedia displaced by northerners from Pelagonia or beyond, who themselves were yielding before a southward drift of people from the region of the middle Danube. The area east of the Vardar-Axios valley was settled by groups of Anatolian origin who had migrated through Thrace, and by middle Europeans who had followed the Axios south. At the end of the Neolithic period, Macedonia was peopled with Thessalians along the southern frontier, northerners in the Haliacmon valley, Lyncus, and the western edge of the central plain, and a mixture of Anatolians and Danubians in the Axios valley. We have no information about Pieria and Emathia.

With the opening of the Early Bronze Age about the beginning of the third millennium B.C., parts of Macedonia experienced some disruption. Intrusions from the east penetrated the Emathian plain into its western parts, driving the inhabitants into the upper cantons. The general turmoil seems to have affected regions as far away as Pelagonia.[8] The newcomers from the east, together with migrants following the Axios, seem to have possessed a less advanced culture than one would expect from the period, as evidenced by the scarcity of bronze artifacts and wheel-made pottery. They appear not to have been enterprising about trade, although it has been suggested that this period witnessed the introduction of the horse into central Macedonia.[9]

While these less-advanced populations continued to settle in central Macedonia, Eordaea, Lyncus, and Pelagonia, other groups were migrating from the north into the southern Balkans and Greece. The beginning of the Middle Bronze Age (*ca.* 1900 B.C.) is marked by the emergence of so-called Indo-Europeans, whose appearance in Greece eventually gave rise to the earliest known forms of the Greek language. Who these Indo-Europeans were and what language(s) they brought with them is a point of some contention.[10] Hammond, adhering to the traditional view, suggested that the reservoir for the Indo-European languages lay among the "Kurgan" peoples (so-called from their custom of burial beneath barrows, called *kurgan* in Russian) who inhabited

[8] Weinberg, "The Stone Age in the Aegean," 607–8; and *HM*, vol. 1, ch. 8.

[9] *HM* 1: 267.

[10] See *HM*, vol. 1, ch. 10, esp. 272–75; and Hammond, *Migrations*, 116–19, and "Grave Circles in Albania and Macedonia." A study of the several interesting papers in Crossland and Birchall, *Bronze Age Migrations*, is instructive about the unsettled state of scholarship on this period, especially with regard to basic method. For a synopsis of the difficulties, see the editors' summaries (323–47) and S. Diamant's review in *AJA* 79 (1975): 287–89. Along the same lines: *Acta of the Second International Symposium on Aegean Prehistory: The First Arrival of the Indo-Europeans in Greece.*

the area north and west of the Black Sea *ca*. 3000–2500 B.C. The Kurgan peoples migrated into the Danube basin, and by *ca*. 2600 B.C., during the Early Bronze Age, had moved into northwestern Greece, bringing with them not only their battle axes and horse-drawn vehicles, but also their proto-Greek language. In the period between *ca*. 2600 and the beginning of the Middle Bronze Age, *ca*. 1900, these people prospered in northwestern Greece (some penetrating as far as Servia and Vergina), while maintaining the tribal languages that were the origin of some Greek dialects. The memory of these early times may be preserved in a fragment of Hesiod: "From the warloving king Hellen sprang Dorus and Xouthus [father of Ion] and Aeolus who took delight in horses."[11] Speakers of these various Greek dialects settled different parts of Greece at different times during the Middle Bronze Age, with one group, the "northwest" Greeks, developing their own dialect and peopling central Epirus. This was the origin of the Molossian or Epirotic tribes. According to this view, the Mycenaean period resulted from the entrance into the Greek peninsula of Greek-speakers already possessing dialects. These settlers bypassed central and southern Macedonia for a route through western Greece.

The most vigorous challenge to the traditional theory summarized above has been led in recent years by John Chadwick.[12] Chadwick argues that there is no evidence to show that Greek existed as a distinct language before the Indo-Europeans were established in Greece. What we call the Greek language developed rather as the result of the interaction between the Indo-European-speakers and the indigenous populations during the latter part of the Middle Bronze Age and throughout the Late Bronze Age.

Clearly the issue of the Greeks' origin (if by "Greek" we mean a Greek-speaker) is not yet settled. And the continuing argument affects at least one aspect of Macedonian history, Hammond's claim that ". . . the Macedones [were], like the Molossian group, a collateral branch of the Greek-speaking peoples in the northern mountainous part of Pieria in the centuries *c*. 1900–1600 B.C. . . ."[13] The geographical reference is based on a Hesiodic fragment that relates that Deucalion's daughter, Thyia, bore to Zeus "two sons, Magnes and Macedon, rejoicing in

[11] Hesiod *Cat. Gyn.*, frag. 4 (Loeb edition), also at Plut. *Quaest. conviv.* 747F. See Appendix C below, p. 292, for further commentary.

[12] E.g., *CAH*, 3rd. ed., vol. 2, pt. 2, 812–19, and forcefully in *The Mycenaean World*, 2–3. An analysis of the paradigms used to define the relationship between linguistic science and the archaeological record has been explored anew in a challenging manner by Colin Renfrew in *Archaeology and Language*.

[13] *HM* 1: 276.

horses, who dwell around Pieria and Olympus."[14] The medieval commentator on this passage says that the district Macedonia was called after Macedon, and elsewhere (Hdt. 7.131) Pieria is called the region of the "Macedonian mountain." There is no reason to deny that the ancients themselves associated the region of the northern Olympus-Pierian ranges with some kind of Macedonian heartland. Whether one can ascribe *Greek* characteristics to these early inhabitants, however, is problematic. The archaeological record is scanty, the linguistic theory is in dispute, and it is always risky to attempt to assign dates to early folk traditions.[15]

What seems certain is that, whatever the character of the populations who inhabited the Pierian region in the Bronze Age, they were different peoples from the Mycenaean cultures that flowered in the south beginning shortly after *ca.* 1600 B.C. There are few Mycenaean finds in Macedonia proper, whereas Thessaly was fully Mycenaean at the beginning of the Late Helladic period (*ca.* 1570 B.C.).[16] By *ca.* 1350 B.C. the coastal areas of the Thermaic Gulf begin to show Mycenaean pottery, but there is no indication that Mycenaeans settled there. For the next two centuries Mycenaean ware continues to appear in east-central Macedonia, but most are local, wheel-made imitations. The Axios valley-Thermaic Gulf area also shows local regional pottery with some types stylistically similar to those found in Bulgaria and Romania. The territory at the head of the Thermaic Gulf and east of the Axios was thus culturally independent from, even while showing contact with, the Mycenaean world.

Southwestern Macedonia, in particular the region around Kozani, has yielded a few Mycenaean objects from the Late Bronze Age. These may have been imported from Thessaly into the middle Haliacmon valley through the Volustana Pass, although the small incidence of settlements and objects suggests that that was not a heavily used route. But the picture is subject to change. Excavations in 1985–86 revealed a

---

[14] *Cat. Gyn.* frag. 3 (Loeb ed.), in Const. Porphy., *de Them.* 2.48b.

[15] The literary evidence relating to the origin of the Macedonians is collected in Kalléris, *Les anciens Macédoniens*, 1: 1–4, and in Daskalakis, *Hellenism*, 11–12. One must use both of these works with caution, however, since the question of the Macedonians' Hellenism is a matter that has prompted some authors to write *cum ira et studio* (see Chapter 4 below).

[16] Following the chronology of Hankey and Warren, "Absolute Chronology," 152. For the evidence of pottery and other artifacts, see Wardle, "The Northern Frontier of Mycenaean Greece," and *HM* 1: 290–300. Feuer, *The Northern Mycenaean Border*, 85–87, provides the most recent full account of the connections between Thessaly and Macedonia in the Late Bronze Age, excluding, of course, the 1985–86 discovery of a Mycenaean cemetery in the Petra Pass (see below; *AR* [1986–87]: 34).

Mycenaean cemetery at Aghios Demetrios, high in the Petra Pass north of Mt. Olympus. The Petra is the major link between the Volustana Pass and the Pierian coastal plain near Katerini and Dion. It may have been the route used by Xerxes in 480 B.C. to bypass the Vale of Tempe and enter Thessaly from behind Mt. Olympus. The existence of a Late Bronze Age Mycenaean settlement in the Petra not only confirms its importance as a route from an early period, but also extends the limits of Mycenaean settlement to the Macedonian frontier.

Moreover, if one can show that there was Mycenaean movement as far as the Volustana Pass, the possibility arises that Mycenaeans might have pushed even further north, perhaps into western Macedonia through the north-south corridors. Needless to say, there is as yet no archaeological confirmation of Myceanaean settlement or extensive trade in western Macedonia, although the area is only now being surveyed and explored systematically.

Whether the Aghios Demetrios settlement in the Petra Pass is an isolated outpost of Mycenaean Thessaly or the harbinger of other such communities awaits further investigation. As yet there is no evidence of Mycenaean settlement near the Vale of Tempe or along the adjacent coastal plain of Pieria. It would seem that the main Mycenaean communication with central Macedonia, where most Mycenaean ware is found, was by sea. There was virtually no contact between central and southwestern Macedonia, both of which had external links with the Mycenaean world, the former by sea and the latter by land, as we have seen. Southwestern Macedonia was most heavily influenced by Epirus and Albania, both in pottery and tumulus burials.

It is thus possible to trace three influences in Macedonia in the Late Bronze Age: small quantities of imported Mycenaean goods along the coast and the Thessalian border (but mainly locally produced imitation-ware in east-central Macedonia), influences from the lower Danube in the Axios valley, and western (from the region of Albania) affinities in the upper cantons. Much of central and parts of upper Macedonia were settled by the conservative non-Greek Paeones who had migrated earlier from the east. Similarities between some Late Bronze Age sites in central Macedonia—in particular a number of independent defensible citadels—and those in southern Greece do not imply a connection. In the absence of additional evidence linking the two regions, we must assume that such coincidences reflect similar local responses to similar local needs.

About 1200 B.C. a group of central Europeans of the "Lausitz" culture moved into the southern Balkans and Asia Minor. In Europe, they occupied central Albania, northern Epirus, and, by *ca.* 1150, much of

Macedonia west of the Axios. Some migrated down the Vardar-Axios valley, and others arrived through the Pelagonian plain. These Bryges (or Brygi) are mentioned by Herodotus (7.73): "According to the Macedonians, the Phrygians were called Bryges as long as they dwelt in Europe, where they were neighbors [*synoikoi*] of the Macedonians, changing their name to Phrygian when they changed their home to Asia." Later, referring to the enlargement of the Macedonian homeland by Perdiccas I and his brothers, Herodotus (8.183) wrote that "[Perdiccas] came to another part of Macedonia and settled near the gardens named after Midas, son of Gordias . . . above the gardens rises the mountain called Bermion, unassailable in winter." What can be established, despite an extremely slight archaeological record[17] (especially along the slopes of Mt. Vermion), is that two streams of Lausitz peoples moved south in the later Bronze Age, one to settle in Hellespontine Phrygia, the other to occupy parts of western and central Macedonia. There is no record of conflict between the Bryges and the local population; they are described as *synoikoi* ("fellow inhabitants" or neighbors) of the Macedonians.

If one accepts that an already well-defined group of "Macedonians" already lived in the Pierian ranges (Hammond's view), then truly the Vermion Bryges and Pierian Macedonians were neighbors. But Herodotus (7.73) admits that he is repeating a Macedonian tradition, and it is difficult to know whether a precise geographical or ethnic connection is meant, or whether "Macedonian" is used only in the most general sense, since the Bryges inhabited many parts of what later became the land of the Macedonians. Sometime *ca.* 800 B.C., at least some of the Bryges abandoned Macedonia to seek a new home in Asia Minor, although it is impossible to tell how many were simply succeeded or absorbed by the Macedonians. When the Macedonians eventually moved into the central plain, it was the Bottiaeans (Thuc. 2.99.3), not the Bryges, who were dispossessed.

Few subjects in the early history of Greece have been so energetically debated in recent years as the "Dorian invasions." The theory of the Dorian invasions (based on Hdt. 9.26, followed by Thuc. 1.12) is largely an invention of nineteenth-century historiography, and is otherwise unsupported by either archaeological or linguistic evidence. Most archaeologists and many linguists have abandoned the belief that

[17] See Hammond, *CAH*, 3rd ed., vol. 2, pt. 2, 707–12; *HM* 1: 302–9; and *Migrations*, 140. For a discussion of the literary evidence and the effect of the Bryges-Phrygian traditions on Alexander the Great's activity at Gordium in 333 B.C., see Fredricksmeyer, "Alexander, Midas and the Oracle at Gordium."

Greek-speaking Dorians devastated Myceanean centers at the end of
the Bronze Age, for the following reasons:

   (1). It has always been difficult to understand how a presumably numerically and technologically inferior population could
bring ruination to powerful, well-organized, and massively defended Mycenaean citadel-states.

   (2). No archaeological evidence of the invaders has been found
in the context of late Mycenaean destruction levels, a phenomenon that some have explained by suggesting either that the Dorians were culturally indistinguishable from the Mycenaeans (if
true—and there is no evidence—why even bother with the Dorians?) or that, having ravaged the Mycenaean centers, the Dorians
immediately withdrew without a trace of their passage.

   (3). The depopulation of many parts of Greece in the wake of
the Mycenaean collapse cannot be explained satisfactorily by the
flight of refugees in the direction *from which the raiders appeared*, as
some have argued.

   (4). The archaeological evidence once thought to represent
post-Mycenaean Dorian culture (e.g., fibulae and swords of a particular type, cist graves, cremation burials) are now known to
have existed earlier at late Mycenaean sites. That is, the later Mycenaeans were eclectic in their expressions of culture, with individual community preferences sometimes co-existing with uni-
form patterns.

   (5). The origin of the historical Dorian dialect need not have
resulted from the incursion of a new population. It is difficult, if
not impossible, to connect changes in a material culture with linguistic events. That is, one looks in vain at the archaeological record for evidence of the origin of the Greeks and their dialects.
Only when a major population transfer has occurred (certainly
not the case of the "Dorians") are there likely to be major cultural
and linguistic changes.

   (6). The origin of the historical Dorian dialect lies somewhere
within Greece, whether as a form of Mycenaean that survived into
the Dark Ages or as a new dialect that arose during the post-Mycenaean period.[18]

---

[18] The main lines of the revisionist argument can be seen, for example, in Chadwick,
"Who Were the Dorians?"; Ruiperez, "The Mycenaean Dialects," 461–67; Renfrew,
"Problems in Correlation"; Snodgrass, "Metal-work as Evidence"; Tritsch, "The 'Sack-
ers of Cities' "; and the useful review of new work by Betancourt, "The End of the
Greek Bronze Age," with full bibliography.

The old view that Mycenaean civilization was destroyed by the incursions of new groups of Greek speakers—the Dorians—sometime after *ca.* 1100 B.C. has been largely discarded. There is no denying that the collapse of Mycenaean Greece was both violent and prolonged. Equally there is little doubt that at some later time cultural and language changes altered Greek society. To establish a connection between the two events, however, is impossible. It is beyond our present concern to deal with the collapse of Mycenaean civilzation. The causes probably are manifold and complex, and no general theory can account for the several local and regional manifestations of a general decline.[19]

The Dorians are invisible archaeologically. Northern Greece has yet to produce a single artifact that can be related to the Dorians.[20] Hammond suggested that the Bryges brought pressure upon the Greek-speaking northwesterners, who in turn migrated south in the late twelfth century B.C. along a route west of the Pindus, and eventually came into central Greece and the Peloponnesus. No evidence of this so-called Dorian migration exists in central and western Macedonia and northeastern Thessaly.[21] Chadwick expressed doubt both about the route of these intrusions and about the ability of the rugged mountain-land of northwest Greece to generate enough population to colonize southern Greece.[22] The problem is further complicated by Rhys Carpenter's suggestion that Mycenaean civilization fell victim to a periodic and temporary climate change that produced a diminution of rainfall, especially in the Peloponnesus. This drought would have been disastrous to a marginal agricultural economy, and the great palace centers were destroyed by local uprisings reflecting a general breakdown in the social and economic fabric of society. The "Dorian invasions," unconnected with the Mycenaean collapse, were in reality the return to the south of those who had migrated to the northwestern mountains two or three generations earlier to escape the Peloponnesian drought. Carpenter's views have been both vigorously attacked and supported.[23]

[19] One is attracted to a theory of internal collapse of the centralized bureaucratic institutions of the Mycenaean states (Betancourt, "The End of the Greek Bronze Age," 45), although to suggest this is to describe a process without positing its cause.

[20] Wardle, "The Northern Frontier of Mycenaean Greece," 207. And the excavator of Vergina discounts that any of the materials in the Late Bronze Age levels of the cemetery there are "Dorian"; see Andronikos, "Excavations at Vergina," 170–71.

[21] Hammond, *HM* I: 310 and 405–7, and *Migrations*, 140–49.

[22] "The Prehistory of the Greek Language," 813, and *The Mycenaean World*, 3.

[23] The thesis appears in Carpenter's 1965 lectures, published as *Discontinuity in Greek Civilization*, and challenged by Desborough (*The Greek Dark Ages*, 22–23), and Snod-

On balance, only the most exacting paleobotanical analysis—valley-by-valley, if necessary—could provide a detailed picture of the climate of the Late Bronze Age. Connections between local sites and the several microclimates of these mountainous regions might then offer an archaeologically based test of Carpenter's theory. The necessary analytical fieldwork is yet to be done.

With major debates on such fundamental methodological questions as what precisely in the archaeological record signifies a historical or linguistic event, prudence demands an admission of uncertainty about the reasons whereby the advanced civilization of Bronze Age Greece was converted into the relatively backward culture of the Dark Ages. All that is certain is that the Greek language survived in somewhat altered forms as an expression of culture that maintained some continuity with the past. There is no archaeological record of the Dorian movements, and the mythic arguments are largely conjectural, based on folk traditions about the Dorian home originally having been in northwest Greece. Even if the latter were true, the connection between the original home of the Dorians and the well-known Dorian dialect of later times is not clear. Surely, all "Dorian Greeks" of the Classical period cannot have descended from the scattered tribes of the northwest Greek mountains. That they were later called Dorians is no more evidence of Dorian descent in any ethnic sense than was the habit of nineteenth-century Greeks to call themselves *Romaioi*, and the country *Roumeli*, evidence of their Roman heritage, despite their Greek language and Slavic admixture.[24]

One further perspective is worth consideration, and that is that Mycenaean Greece used two concurrent dialects, the language of the Linear B tablets, employed for religious and administrative purposes, and a spoken proto-Doric dialect, the demotic of the population. After the catastrophe that destroyed the Mycenaean palatial centers, the emergence of a historical Doric dialect suggests not Dorian incursions, but rather the successful uprising of Doric-speaking inhabitants of southern Greece.[25] In the end it seems best to be cautious: there probably

---

grass ("Climatic Changes"). Carpenter received some support on climatological grounds from Bryson, Lamb, and Donley ("Drought and Decline"), who concluded that Carpenter's proposed climatic changes *ca.* 1200 B.C. were consistent with the scientific evidence. For further discussion, see Betancourt, "The End of the Greek Bronze Age," 41.

[24] On this last, long-tortured (Slavic) point, see Herrin, "Aspects of Hellenization."

[25] This view is fully described by Hooker, *Mycenaean Greece*, ch. 7, esp. 163–80 (who supports in part Carpenter's thesis that internal rebellion caused the destruction of most Mycenaean palaces), and by Chadwick, "Who Were the Dorians?"

were movements of Greek-speakers within the Greek peninsula *ca.*
1100–1000 B.C., at the time of general instability, but the extent to
which these produced new dialects and a cultural transformation must
remain for the moment problematic. Recent scholarship has retreated
from migration and diffusionist theories as a means of explaining cultural change and moved toward an analysis of internal cultural pro-
cesses.

The Dorians are herein considered because they may have had some
connection with the earliest Macedonians. Herodotus (1.56) gives us a
story about the early tribe from which the Classical Dorians claimed
descent. It had been expelled by the Cadmeians from the territory below Mts. Ossa and Olympus called Histiaeotis, and lived "in Pindus
and was called Makednon." At a later time the tribe moved into Dry-
opis, in central Greece, and from there into the Peloponnesus, where
it took the name Dorian, presumably from a common ancestor, Dorus, son of Hellen. In another passage (8.43), Herodotus confirms the
traditions when, in listing a number of Spartan allies of the same ethnic
stock, he describes them as *Dorikon te kai Makednon ethnos*, "Dorian
and Makednon stock," who had come from (among other places) Dry-
opis. The temporary Pindus home of the Dorians is also mentioned by
Pindar (*Pyth.* 1.65). These traditions seem to span the period of the
later Bronze Age down to *ca.* 1000 B.C., and to deal with the migrations of the tribe of "proto-Dorians."[26]

What emerges is a name, *Makednon*, meaning "tall" or "high," a reference to the Pindus uplands where these early tribes resided. No significance can be attached to the personal name *Makedon*, also mentioned in the old tales.[27] Like other ethnic groups, the later
Macedonians created mythical ancestors. Prominent among these was
Makedon, who is variously described as the son of Zeus and Thyia
(daughter of Deucalion), son of Aeolus, son of Hellen and brother of
Dorus, son of Aeacus, and son of Lycaon, father of Pindus.[28] There is
no way to sort out these varying traditions—indeed, there is probably
no historical basis for these ancestors. The aetiologizing process was
widespread; for example, Emathia was said to have come from Ema-
thion, son of Zeus and Electra, and Orestis from Orestes, son of Ag-

[26] A term I prefer to Hammond's "Dorians-to-be"; e.g., *HM* 1: 309 and 453. For the
most part I follow Hammond's views on the early genealogy of the Dorian-Makednon
link; ibid., 309–11, and "The End of Mycenaean Civilization and the Dark Age," 681–
86.

[27] On this point I differ from Hammond, *HM* 1: 276 and 430.

[28] For evidence, *s.v.* "Makedon (1)," *RE* 27 (1928): 636.

amemnon.[29] The names of these regions and their inhabitants have geographical meaning. Macedonia and Orestis mean respectively "upland" and "mountainous," and Emathia is "sandy." Thus the Makedones could be "uplanders" or "highlanders," not "descendants of Makedon."[30]

To review: There are only two arguments that adduce the existence of Makedones on the Pierian slopes in the Bronze Age. The first is linguistic, suggesting that the Makedones were a collateral branch of Greek-speakers (see pp. 62–63 above). Yet we have seen that serious challenges have been issued to the notion that Greek dialects were brought into Greece by the Indo-European speakers. Moreover, there is as yet no evidence about the languages or ethnic stock of the Pierians during the Middle and Late Bronze Age, and their links with the Epirotic northwest Greeks are unclear. The second argument is genealogical: Hesiod's reference to Zeus's son, Makedon, dwelling around Pieria and Olympus. But tales that are the product of ancestor-creation are suspect as historical evidence, both on general grounds and in the particular case of the multiple traditions concerning Makedon. If one discounts both the conjectural linguistic view and the genealogical theory, the Bronze Age Pierian Makedones disappear.[31]

It remains to consider the proto-Dorian/Makednon link in the Pindus and middle Haliacmon basin. In Herodotus's time there was a strong tradition connecting the Makednon tribe with the Pindus and with the progenitors of the Dorians. Our knowledge of the languages spoken in this region *ca.* 1100, however, is so limited that any suggestion that the land was called *Makednia* and the people *Makedones* is conjecture based either on very late sources or on the hypothetical restoration of Bronze Age forms from known Classical words.[32]

What then might be the connection between the Dorians and the Macedonians? If one interprets Herodotus's story about the proto-Dorians being expelled by the Cadmeians as a reflection of the instability of the later Mycenaean period (the Cadmeians, too, are said by tradi-

[29] For evidence, *s.v.* "Makedon (2)," ibid., 636, and *HM* 1: 310–11. Hammond discounts any connection between Orestes and the Orestae.

[30] See, however, the intriguing suggestion of Andriotes, "History of the Name 'Macedonia,'" 143–44, that *Makedones* denotes a physical characteristic—"tallness"—like *Pygmaioi* ("fist-sized"), *Makrokephaloi* ("long-heads"), etc. (Note an incorrect citation [144] to the *Suda*, which has no heading for *Makedonia*.) In a burst of national pride, and without evidence, Daskalakis (*Hellenism*, 12) gave the Makedones a "tall, robust appearance."

[31] Herodotus's allusion (7.131) to the Pierian *Makedonikon oros* is, of course, a solid historical reference, and has nothing to do with the prehistoric period.

[32] As in *HM* 1: 309–10.

tion to have migrated to the northwest), we have a reason for a tribal movement into the Pindus. Carpenter suggested that there was a general migration of some Mycenaeans toward the northwest, that part of Greece always having more abundant rainfall than the south. After a period of time, some returned to their central and southern Greek lands, speaking the same basic dialect—which later became known as Dorian—the dialect spoken in the south during the Late Bronze Age, if Hooker and Chadwick are correct (see note 25 above). There is little linguistic or archaeological record of these migrations because they were not by aliens, but rather were temporary shifts among nonliterate Greek-speakers during a period of turmoil. The name *Makednon* became linked with these proto-Dorians only because some of this stock—who were to become the early historical Macedonians—migrated at a later time out of the Pindus/middle Haliacmon region down toward Pieria.[33] A memory was preserved of the early connection between those who would become Macedonians and those who would return to their southern lands and would become Dorians. The concept of "return" was later embodied in the tradition of the Return of the Heracleidae. We may note in passing that one of the Macedonian royal family's progenitors was said to have been Temenus, a descendant of Heracles—and Heracles is a major Dorian hero. Those who later came to inhabit the fine terrace-land above the Haliacmon River along the lower Pierian slopes eventually were recognized as *Makedones*, the "highlanders," perhaps because of their high west-country origin and their new homeland in the Pierian piedmont. These events culminated in the establishment and early expansion of the Makedones along the fringe of the Emathian plain in the early seventh century B.C.

This explanation for the connection between the Dorians and the Macedonians may be more ingenious than convincing, resting uncomfortably on myth and conjecture. We lack sufficient linguistic and archaeological evidence to substantiate it. But it is an attempt to reconcile some of the Classical Greek traditions about these matters with some current trends in scholarship. This is not to say that the Macedonians are of Doric origin, as some have tried to prove. It is to suggest rather that the ancestors of both the historical Macedonians and those who later were called Dorians may have co-existed along the slopes of the Pindus in the middle Haliacmon basin during the transition from the Bronze to the Dark Age.

[33] Now that the Petra Pass is confirmed as a route from the Volustana Pass and the middle Haliacmon in an earlier period, we must be prepared to accept the possibility that it served as an entry into the Pierian coastal plain.

One hopes that the prehistory of the Macedonians will emerge from the shroud that legend and ignorance have cast over it. Among the most important aspects of our awakening to this remote period is the recognition that continental and Balkan influences were at least as strong as those of the Aegean in forming culture in northern Greece. For more than a century, scholarship on the subject has been dominated by those who have seen human development in the Greek peninsula as a feature of the "Aegean-as-the-cradle-of-civilization" concept. We may now, however, begin to recognize the importance of eastern Europe and the Balkans as sources of innovation through the migrations of tribes and the growth of trade.

Indeed, Macedonia and Thrace seem to have been well advanced in the Neolithic period, perhaps more so than central and southern Greece. The temperate northern climate, with its abundant rainfall, forests, arable and fertile land, mineral wealth, and access to major land routes, promoted relatively progressive prehistoric settlements, while most of Greece, largely isolated at the tip of the Balkans, was a backwater. The emergence of more sophisticated cultures in the Greek mainland in the third and second millennia B.C. occurred because technological advances in sea travel put southern Greece into contact with the older civilizations of the eastern Mediterranean. Greece, struggling out of its Late Neolithic and Early Bronze Age phases, was gradually affected by Aegean influences, and those of Anatolia and Crete. Eventually the Bronze Age Greeks, under the steady stimulation of foreign contacts, progressed at a rate exceeding that of their land-bound northern neighbors, compared with whom they had seemed so backward for so long.

Macedonia and its inhabitants apparently were not part of the emerging culture of the Mycenaean Bronze Age, as known from sites in central Greece and the Peloponnesus. Whereas the Mycenaeans in the south developed a social and economic system centered on the massive fortified citadels necessary to marshal and protect the meagre agricultural resources of their countryside, the dwellers in Macedonia continued to live in scattered unwalled villages, content—as far as we know—to exploit on a local level the rich natural resources of their hills and plains. They remained largely unaffected by the vigorous expression of culture that flourished in the Greek south.[34]

[34] For a review of Greek-Macedonian connections in the Late Bronze Age, see Bouzek, "Macedonia and Thrace," 123–24, who shows that both coastal and piedmont Pieria were influenced by a multiplicity of Greek and non-Greek Balkan traditions in the sub-Mycenaean and early Iron Age periods. Bouzek, however, fails to draw adequate

Moving from the second to the first millennium B.C., we may re-
mind ourselves that much of what is known about the culture of the
peoples who inhabited northern Greece in these early periods derives
from a study of grave goods, and that these graves contain, for the
most part, the possessions of ruling groups.[35] Most of the population,
largely farmers and herdsmen, left little, and are nearly invisible to
us.[36] Except for a few excavated village sites, which are themselves
problematic, one can only guess at their material culture and ethnic
stock. As Hammond suggested, they are probably descended from
those many races who had settled in Macedonia over the centuries, and
one assumes that they were a mixed lot ethnically. Power, however,
lay with the owners of horses and weapons, whose fine burials provide
the meagre evidence we possess of the constant changes of ruling
groups in early Macedonia. And we are left with an unresolved methodological problem, namely the extent to which the changes that occur in the archaeological record indicate either the movements into an
area of new ruling groups or changes in the ethnic stock of a whole
population.

The importance of the early Iron Age (ca. 1050–650 B.C.) in Macedonia is that it probably saw the establishment of the basic ethnic pool
from which the historical Macedonians and their neighbors were derived. A number of important early Iron Age sites have been excavated, most prominently at Vergina, but also at Kozani, in Eordaea,
along the middle Haliacmon valley, near Dion, at Assiros, and in the
lower Axios valley.[37] These sites have produced an abundance of materials revealing something of the continuing pattern of outside influences, partly through trade and exchange, but mainly through migrations. A number of settlements have shown a remarkable continuity

distinctions among what in Macedonia was truly Mycenaean, what was imported, and
what were locally produced imitations of Myceanean pottery.

[35] On this point, see *HM* 1: 570.

[36] Modern archaeology is beginning to lift the veil of ignorance. For example, the
German excavators at the Bronze-to-Iron Age site at Kastanas in the lower Axios valley
have learned that there was a continuity of agricultural products produced from the second into the first millennium B.C.: cereal grains, figs, vines, and flax and poppies, the
latter crops grown to yield vegetable oil. See H. Kroll, "Bronze Age and Iron Age Agriculture in Kastanas, Macedonia."

[37] A survey of the finds from these numerous sites can be found in *HM*, vol. 1, ch. 13,
with references to the excavation reports. A 1986 excavation near Dion, along the lower
Pierian slopes of Mt. Olympus, revealed a highly developed Iron Age culture, as measured by its finely wrought imported and locally made pottery and metals. I am grateful
to Prof. D. Pandermalis, under whose supervision the excavation was conducted, for
showing me some of the materials from this otherwise unpublished site.

through the late Bronze and early Iron Age periods, suggesting no major disruptive invasions.[38] We have already seen that the Bryges were established in western and central Macedonia from Pelagonia to Vergina, along the slopes of Mt. Vermion, and in the Axios valley *ca.* 1150 B.C. By about 1050, they seem to have lost their lands east of the Axios, but their influence remained viable in the other areas until about 800 B.C.[39] With major centers at Edessa and perhaps Vergina, the Bryges were skilled metalworkers and active traders across the route of the Via Egnatia from the Adriatic to the Aegean. For reasons unknown to us, the Bryges abandoned their Balkan lands and migrated to Asia Minor to establish a powerful (Phrygian) kingdom there (Hdt. 7.73). During the period of the Bryges's dominance, other peoples continued to live among them: for example, the Eordi, who survived as a separate group following the Brygian withdrawal; the western Greek peoples (with affinities to the Epirotic tribes) in Orestis, Lyncus, and parts of Pelagonia; the Thracians in coastal Pieria; and the Paeonians east of the Axios.[40] Much of this reconstruction is inferential. Greater certainty awaits the excavation of more rich Iron Age cemeteries like those at Vergina and near Dion.

In the early ninth century there commenced an expansion of peoples in the Balkans originating in central Yugoslavia; this population is known historically as "Illyrian."[41] In a movement that lasted until *ca.* 650 B.C., the well-armed Illyrians pushed through the Vardar-Axios valley, displaced many Paeonians (some of whom re-established themselves in the Strymon basin), occupied sites along the Emathian piedmont, and penetrated not only the upper cantons, but also the area west of the Pindus to the Albanian coast. Whether this Illyrian expansion caused or resulted from the withdrawal of the Bryges from Macedonia can only be guessed at. There are numerous traditions attesting to the strong tribal adhesion of the Illyrians, but their influence was ephemeral—a warrior race come and gone—with only their graves to mark their passage in Macedonia. They eventually settled along the

[38] The increasing body of evidence appears to confirm the notion of continuity from the prehistoric into the historical periods; e.g., the excavations at Assiros, a few miles above lakes Koroneia and Volvi, supervised by K. A. Wardle. See *AR* (1977–78): 44–47; Wardle, "Assiros Toumba," 251; and, more fully, Wardle, "Assiros: A Macedonian Settlement of the Late Bronze Age and Early Iron Age."

[39] How pervasive this Brygian influence was is a matter of some contention; see *HM* 1: 410 and n. 2.

[40] Following Hammond, *HM* 1: 407–19, although some of this is conjecture. There is, for example, very little archaeological evidence for the Paeonians, the main body of information being early literary traditions.

[41] After *HM* 1: 420–27.

Adriatic coast and in the region northwest of the Pindus ranges, where they would continue to exercise power by threatening first the Macedonian and then the Roman hegemonies in the Balkan interior and along the Adriatic coast. In general, the prehistory and protohistory of the Illyrians remain to be written, a task made difficult by a meagre archaeological record, modern language barriers, and modern conflicting claims in the western Balkans over the Illyrian homeland.[42]

Other forces were at work. The Greeks, stirring from their Dark Age lethargy, began tentatively to send explorers and traders into foreign waters. These first commercial activities were little felt in Macedonia; Macedonian sites, for example, are poor in imported Greek proto-Geometric and Geometric pottery. In the middle of the eighth century, however, at least some Greeks had awakened to the potential exploitation of the northern fringes of the Aegean. Eretrians established three colonies along the Thermaic Gulf by *ca.* 730 B.C.: Methone in the northernmost part of coastal Pieria, Dicaea across the gulf (perhaps on the Crousian coast), and Mende on the southwestern coast of Kassandra (Pallene), the western prong of Chalcidice. Like most Greek colonies, these were probably founded as agricultural settlements, although in time commerce became paramount: certainly wine in the case of Mende, and perhaps Pierian timber at Methone.[43] About 710 Chalcis founded a colony at Torone, and *ca.* 700 the Achaeans established Scione, both in Chalcidice. We are not yet able to measure the effect of this eighth-century Greek influence on the inhabitants of Macedonia. For the moment it would appear that it was confined largely to the immediate hinterland of the new colonial foundations.

The Thracians may have been active in coastal Pieria from the later Bronze Age down to *ca.* 650 B.C., and, of course, they had long dominated the territory east of the Strymon. The Thracian tribes took advantage of the collapse of Illyrian power and the lightning raids of Cimmerians from the east to push west of the Strymon. By *ca.* 650, Thracian influence was dominant in the region east of the Axios (as shown by the recent excavations at Sindos), with a number of prominent tribes having settled in the area: Edones, Mygdones, Sithones, Bistones, and Odomantes. Some presumably non-Thracian Paeonians held on to local pockets of rule, as in the Strymon basin and the middle

---

[42] E.g., Stipčević (*The Illyrians*) shows almost no knowledge of English-language scholarship on Balkan prehistory. Still useful is the unpublished dissertation of Dell, "The Illyrian Frontier to 229 B.C."

[43] The fact that very early foundation legends preserved in later sources place both Methone and Dicaea in "Thrace" supports the view that these areas were not under the control of the Macedonians; evidence in *HM* I: 425–26.

Vardar valley. West of the Axios, the central Macedonian plain was occupied by the Bottiaeans (of uncertain origin)[44] and probably the ethnically mixed residue of the long-term Brygian settlement along the Vermion piedmont. This was the situation on the eve of the emergence of the Makedones in the mid-seventh century B.C.

[44] Hammond, *HM* I: 153, 368, 393–94, and elsewhere (following the unreliable Strabo), makes the Bottiaeans of Minoan Cretan origin, but this suggestion is not convincing to me.

Who Were the Macedonians?

OUR understanding of the Mace-
donians' emergence as a people with a distinct identity is confounded
by several factors. First, there is as yet a very limited Iron Age-early
Archaic Era archaeological record for central Macedonia, and the interpretation of what little material does exist rests upon some questionable assumptions. For example, to determine the date and path of
Macedonian intrusions into Pieria and Emathia requires the identification of objects or burial methods that are clearly "Macedonian," that
is, different from the artifacts left by non-Macedonian local populations. We are entirely dependent upon grave goods: virtually no settlements have yet been discovered. Recent revisionist tendencies in the
archaeological analysis of the late Greek Bronze Age and the "Dorian
invasions" have been instructive; we are less likely now to draw facile
conclusions from statistically small and materially limited samples.
Morever, the Macedonians of the late Classical and early Hellenistic
periods have proven to be so eclectic in the material expressions of their
culture (like many late Bronze Age Greeks) that one must be prudent
in defining what was properly "Macedonian" in every period.

It is tempting, for example, to take hope from the 1986 discovery of
a rich Iron Age cemetery located on the lowest slopes of the Mt.
Olympus range near Dion. The cemetery is not far from where the
Petra Pass opens onto the Pierian coastal plain. As it is now established
that the Petra was a route known as early as *ca.* 1200 B.C.—thanks to a
recent excavation of a late Mycenaean settlement there (see Chapter 3
above)—the pass is a feasible candidate for the route used by the Macedonians in their migrations from the western mountains into Pieria.
But one must be wary, for until the material from the Iron Age cemetery is studied, published, and compared with that from other settlements of the same period, such as the one at Vergina, it would be premature to make any but the most tentative suggestions about the dates
and sequence of Macedonian settlements in this region in this early
period.

The literary evidence—both the fragmentary "mythic" tradition and

the accounts of the ancient writers of "history"—provides little information and no more certainty. There are, in fact, two quite separate
features of these early traditions. One tells of the migration and establishment of the Macedonians as an ethnic group. Yet we have noted
above the difficulty of confirming such movements archaeologically
because of the paucity of Iron Age sites. And if the folk traditions
about early Macedonian migrations are invalid, there is no archaeological record, as those who became the historical Macedonians, like the
Dorians before them, were virtually indistinguishable from the general
population. The other feature of the literary tradition describes the
Greek origins of the Macedonian ruling house. The movement of a
foreign royal family into the region would probably have left no archaeological record. Thus we may look in vain for the archaeological
confirmation of the origins of both the royal family and perhaps even
of the Macedonian population itself.

The reconstruction that follows is tentative in the extreme, and the
reader is cautioned to be wary. Since the archaeological record is
scanty, this account of early Macedonian history is based on the most
sceptical analysis of literary traditions. We have seen (Chapter 3) that
the "Makedones" or "highlanders" of mountainous western Macedonia may have been derived from northwest Greek stock. That is,
northwest Greece provided a pool of Indo-European speakers of
proto-Greek from which emerged the tribes who were later known by
different names as they established their regional identities in separate
parts of the country. Thus the Macedonians may have been related to
those peoples who at an earlier time migrated south to become the
historical Dorians, and to other Pindus tribes who were the ancestors
of the Epirotes or Molossians. If it were known that Macedonian was
a proper dialect of Greek, like the dialects spoken by Dorians and Molossians, we would be on much firmer ground in this hypothesis. But,
as we shall see, the matter of identifying the Macedonian language is
far from settled. Thus one of the possible links connecting the Macedonians to other Greek tribes remains to be established, although,
given the nature of the evidence, it is doubtful that such a connection
can ever be proven or denied conclusively.

Sometime *ca.* 700 B.C. a group migrated out of the eastern Pindus
watershed, leaving what may have been its home in the upper and middle Haliacmon basin, to settle in the Pierian coastal plain and the Pierian piedmont of the central (Emathian) plain. The route of this migration cannot be established. Although it would have been possible
for a population to follow the Haliacmon valley itself for some distance
in its middle region, the river runs through a precipitous gorge just

before entering the Emathian plain between Veria and Vergina.[1] To reach central Macedonia from the middle Haliacmon, one must move to high ground, following the route on the river's left bank taken by the spectacular modern highway that hugs the Haliacmon Gorge before descending steeply to Veria. Although there is no archaeological evidence to suggest that this route was much used in early times, the importance of the site of Veria might equally be attributed to its place as a terminus for this inland route as well as to its location commanding the crossing of the Haliacmon.[2]

Alternatively, one may cross the Haliacmon near modern Servia and climb into the Volustana Pass leading toward Thessaly. Near the crest of the pass, a route deviates toward the northeast and becomes the Petra Pass, which separates the Pierian and Olympus ranges, before winding down into coastal Pieria. Both the highland Haliacmon route and the Petra route offer sufficient grazing ground in adjacent mountain meadows. Both are possible routes for the entrance of the Makedones into Pieria/Emathia. The Petra is more attractive: not only is there archaeological confirmation that the pass was used at an early time, but there is an Iron Age settlement in the coastal plain near the opening of the pass, about the same distance from the Petra as the Iron Age settlement at Vergina is from the Haliacmon route. Moreover, Thucydides' account (2.99) of the spread of the early Macedonians could be construed as a movement out of Pieria toward the north and west.[3] If one accepts that coastal Pieria below the Petra Pass was the starting point for Macedonian expansion, geographical necessity (the Emathian plain was still largely a sea inlet and swamp) dictated a movement north to the plain and then west and north again along its piedmont. If, however, Thucydides' account is rejected on chronological or geographical grounds, the Haliacmon route is still feasible. It means that the Makedones emerged into the lowland somewhere around Veria and expanded east along the Pierian piedmont—establishing a center at Aegae along the way—toward the Pierian coastal plain and north along the slopes of Mt. Vermion as well. It is clear that certainty is impossible without a fuller archaeological record.

What prompted such a migration can only be guessed; it may well have been that population pressure precipitated the movement of a hill people in search of better pastures or land for permanent settlement.

---

[1] Hammond, *HM* 1: 430 n. 2.

[2] For a useful description of the highland route above the Haliacmon Gorge, see ibid., 158–59.

[3] Hammond, *HM* 1: 436–38, offers an ingenious reconstruction of Thuc. 2.99, not entirely convincing, but worthy of the reader's consideration.

This process—well known thoughout the Balkans—is part of the transition from a way of life dependent on herding and hunting (which can support relatively few people in a fixed area of static resources) to a search for more and better land and the consequent settlement into agriculture. Virtually any moderately fertile area under cultivation can support a larger population than if it were given over to herding and hunting. These migrants were "Makedones" or "highlanders," and those who emerged—by whatever route—into the lowlands were to be distinguished from the Makedones who remained in the mountain cantons by the name Argeadae, "descendants of Argeas."[4] In their Pierian settlements they had access both to fertile land below and to pasturage and game above, a suitable environment that, we must conclude, enabled the Makedones to prosper and, eventually, under the direction of their kings, to spread their rule throughout central Macedonia.

The Macedonian Royal House

The ancestry of the Macedonian royal house is nearly as obscure as the origin of the Macedonian population. There was a persistent, well-attested tradition in antiquity that told of a group of Greeks from Argos—descendants of Temenus, kinsman of Heracles—who came to Macedonia and established their rule over the Makedones, unifying them and providing a royal house. The kings of this dynasty would guide Macedonian fortunes until the end of the fourth century B.C. There is no doubt that this tradition of a superimposed Greek house was widely believed by the Macedonians, and it was probably through them that Herodotus, during his journey to Macedonia *ca.* 460 B.C., heard the story that he related in his history (8.137–39). It is the earliest full version of the Argive origin of the Macedonian royal house, and it is told as a digression providing context for the Macedonian king Alexander I's pro-Athenian stance during the Persian Wars.[5] A paraphrase follows:

Alexander was seventh in descent from Perdiccas who, together with his brothers Gauanes and Aeropus—all descended from Temenus—had been banished from Argos. They spent some time in Il-

---

[4] Here following Edson, "Early Macedonia," 20–21; Hammond, *HM* 1: 309–11, 431–32, and 2: 24–29 (the latter on the Argeadae, but not the Temenidae); and Anson, "The Meaning of the Term *Makedones*," who (*contra* Hammond) argues that *Makedones* had both a regional and ethnic—but not juridical—connotation in the pre-Hellenistic period.

[5] For details, see Borza, "Athenians, Macedonians, and the Macedonian Royal House," now modified somewhat (below, pp. 112–13).

lyria whence they crossed into upper (*anō*) Macedonia to the town of Lebaea[?], where they served at menial tasks in the local ruler's house. As they prepared to depart, the ruler refused their due wages, offering them only the sunlight that shone down the smoke vent into the house. Whereupon Perdiccas accepted the proposal, and, with his knife, drew a line on the floor around the sunlight and gathered the light up into his garment. (One wonders if this story were the inspiration for the Macedonians' adoption of the radiate sun [or star] as a national symbol.) The three brothers went on their way with the local ruler's men in pursuit. The Temenidae crossed a river, which then flooded so as to halt their pursuers, and they came to "another part of Macedonia," where they settled near the Gardens of Midas, son of Gordias, above which rises Mt. Vermion. After acquiring possession of this land, they subdued the rest of Macedonia. There follows the royal lineage of fathers and sons: Perdiccas, Argaeus, Philip, Aeropus, Alcetas, Amyntas, and Alexander. According to Herodotus, this was the manner by which the descendants of the Argive Temenus of Heracles' house gained the rule of Macedonia.

It is risky to press the story on its historicity. The Argive context draws suspicion, as it was fashionable in the fifth century B.C. to lay at the door of the venerable Argive state all manner of heroic and mythical deeds.[6] Moreover, much of the story is recounted by Herodotus without much critical understanding of its meaning, as if he were repeating indiscriminately what he had heard. A few geographical details are plausible: the reference to Illyria and *anō* (upper) Macedonia,[7] the possibility that the river is the Haliacmon, and the reference to the Gardens of Midas under Mt. Vermion, which could be the lush region around Mieza (modern Kopanos/Lefkadia, below Naousa).[8] But nowhere does Herodotus specifically say that these Temenidae imposed their rule on the *Makedones*, only that they came to claim *Makedonia*, a geographical term that does not necessarily mean the land of the Macedonians at this early time. This royal house did in fact eventually emerge as the ruling family of the Macedonians, but, as we are unable

[6] Aeschylus (*Supplices*, 249–59) has a Dark Age Argos ruling everything as far as the Strymon River; Aeschylus also used Argos as the setting for the *Oresteia*. For this Classical predilection to inflate the importance of early Argos, see Kelly, *History of Argos*, 43–46, 84–86, and 105–6, with whose conclusions I agree. Argos was not only venerable but also politically useful to fifth-century writers and politicians; see below, pp. 121–22.

[7] Consistent with Hdt. 7.173, where the author preserves the distinctions between lower (*katō*) Macedonia, here meaning the Pierian coastal plain, and upper (*anō*) Macedonia, meaning the Perrhaebian hill country to the west.

[8] The mention of Midas and Gordias recalls the link between this region and the Phrygians. See Fredricksmeyer, "Alexander, Midas and the Oracle at Gordium," and Hammond, *HM* 1: 410–13.

to date either the reign of Perdiccas or the beginning of the expansion of the Makedones, it is impossible to know from Herodotus when and by what means this Greek family came to lead the Macedonians.

We are further confounded by the geographical discrepancy between the Mt. Vermion association of Perdiccas and the possibility that the Makedones settled first in coastal Pieria. We may suggest—and it is only a hypothesis based on no ancient evidence—that the westward movement of the Pierian Makedones eventually reached the piedmont of Mt. Vermion near Veria or Mieza, and that there they fell under some sort of chieftain through a process we cannot hope to know. If so, this would mean that the Macedonians had commenced their expansion along the Pierian piedmont before the imposition of Argead overlordship. If, however, the Makedones emerged into the lowlands from the Haliacmon, and not from Pieria, their migration into the central plain near Veria may be part of the same process that produced the ruling house in that very region. Accepting this, one would still need to explain why the eventual center of royal power developed at Aegae, whose location is about halfway between Mieza (Gardens of Midas) and coastal Pieria.

It is clear that the analysis of our earliest—and sole—source cannot produce a consistent and satisfactory sequence of events. My own view is that there is some underlying veracity to the Mt. Vermion reference (as evidenced by the Phrygian connections), that among the Makedones a family of Vermion background emerged as pre-eminent, but that the Argive context is mythic, perhaps a bit of fifth-century B.C. propaganda (as I argue in the next chapter). To deny such fables and attribute them to contemporary Macedonian propaganda may appear minimalistic But given the historical milieu in which such stories were spawned and then adorned, the denial of myth seems prudent. The Temenidae in Macedon are an invention of the Macedonians themselves, intended in part to give credence to Alexander I's claims of Hellenic ancestry, attached to and modifying some half-buried progenitor stories that had for a long time existed among the Macedonians concerning their own origins. The revised version was transmitted without criticism or comment by Herodotus. Thucydides (2.99.3; 5.80.2) acquired the Argive lineage tale from Herodotus, or from Macedonian-influenced sources, and transmitted it. His is not an independent version.[9] What emerged in the fifth century is a Macedonian-inspired tale of Argive origins for the Argead house, an account

[9] There is no hard evidence (pace Hammond, HM 1: 4) that Thucydides ever visited Macedonia, but it makes no difference; Thucydides is reflecting the official version of things.

that can probably be traced to its source, Alexander I (for which see Chapter 5 below).[10] The Temenidae must disappear from history, making superfluous all discussion of them as historical figures. Hereinafter the Macedonian royal house will be called the Argeadae.

There were further embellishments to the myth of the early royal family. In the last decade of the fifth century B.C. Euripides came to reside in Macedon at the court of King Archelaus, thereby contributing a new stage to the evolution of the Macedonian creation-myth. Euripides' play honoring his patron, *Archelaus*, probably adorned the basic story, replacing Perdiccas with an Archelaus as the descendant of Temenus—no doubt to the delight of his royal host.[11] Delphic oracles were introduced, and the founder's tale was extended by the introduction of Caranus (Doric for "head" or "ruler"). In the early fourth century, new early kings were added during the political rivalry among three branches of the Argeadae following the death of King Archelaus in 399, another example of the Macedonian predilection to rewrite history to support a contemporary political necessity.[12] The story continued to be passed through the hands of local Macedonian historians in the fourth century B.C., and by Roman times it was widely known in a number of versions.[13] Nothing in this later period can be traced back earlier than Euripides' revision of the Herodotean tradition. The notion that Alexander I or one of his predecessors obtained a Delphic oracle to confirm the Macedonian tie with Argos has no evidence to support it.[14] Had such an oracle existed we can be confident that Alexander, eager to confirm his Hellenic heritage, would have exploited it, and that Herodotus, who delighted in oracles, would have mentioned it. In the end what is important is not whether Argive Greeks founded the Macedonian royal house but that at least some Macedonian kings wanted it so.

[10] There is a huge literature on this problem. Two advocates of the Argos-Macedon link are Hammond, *HM*, vol. 2, ch. 1, and Daskalakis, *Hellenism*, pt. 3, both of whom support the notion of a Temenid origin for the Macedonian royal house.

[11] Full discussion in Hammond, *HM* 2: 5–14. For an excellent analysis of the growth of the foundation myths, see Harder, *Euripides' Kresphontes and Archelaos*, 131–37, who (288–90) accepts the possibility that Euripides may have also written a *Temenos* or *Temenidai*. Also see Chapter 7 below.

[12] See Greenwalt, "The Introduction of Caranus."

[13] E.g., Diod. 7.16; Eusebius, *Chronica* 1.277; Clem. Alex., *Protrepticus* 2.11; Just. 7.1.7–12. Full citations in Hammond, *HM* 2: 7–14 and 31–39, the latter an especially useful discussion. One modern compilation of ancient testimonia shows a pre-Perdiccas king list that gives thirteen names, clear back to Heracles. This is only a handful fewer than the number of historical kings from Perdiccas down through the reign of Alexander the Great! See Hatzopoulos and Loukopoulos, *PM*, 18.

[14] Argued in detail in Borza, "Athens, Macedonians, and the Macedonian Royal House," 12.

It is unnecessary for those who need to ascribe Hellenic ancestry to the Macedonians for their own reasons to do so by accepting the propaganda of ancient Macedonian kings. The Macedonians themselves may have originated from the same population pool that produced other Greek peoples. The fact that their fifth-century B.C. kings found it desirable to impose a southern Greek overlay through the adoption of Argive lineage in no way alters the picture, beyond suggesting that fifth-century Macedonians were less certain about their Hellenic origins than are some modern writers.

There is no reason to deny the Macedonians' own tradition about their early kings and the migrations of the Makedones. We have already suggested that a branch of these highlanders, the Argeadae, may have migrated out of the Haliacmon basin into the piedmont of northern Pieria.[15] It is impossible to assign a date to this migration, but if we allow for a royal lineage going back from Alexander I, and recognize that the Argeadae ruled central Macedonia after the disappearance of the Bryges and the Illyrians, we have a date of about 650 B.C. or somewhat earlier.[16] The Herodotean tradition of the three brothers may reflect the patronymics of three tribes or clan groups; one thinks of the Agiads and Eurypontids at Sparta. The evidence does not permit a sophisticated analysis, but the story may reflect the establishment of Gauanes' rule in Elimeia, Aeropus's among the Lyncestians (where such a royal name appears later), and of course Perdiccas's in central Macedonia. Thus, by this hypothesis, at least three related branches of the Makedones could trace their genealogy and kinship back to the seventh-century movement, with the Argead descent best remembered among the house of Perdiccas.[17] The basic story as provided by Herodotus and Thucydides, minus the interpolation of the Temenid connection, undoubtedly reflects the Macedonians' own traditions about their early history.

Expansion of the Macedonians

There was nothing peaceful about the expansion of the Makedones in central Macedonia. Neither Herodotus (8.138.3) nor Thucydides (2.99) leaves any doubt about the Makedones' (henceforth "Macedonians") forceful settlement of this region. Whatever the route taken out

---

[15] On the Argead Macedonians (but not the Temenidae) I follow Hammond, *HM* 2: 26-31.

[16] For details, see ibid., 4 and n. 2.

[17] Thuc. 2.99.2 and 9.83.1 include the Lyncestians and Elimiotes among the Macedonians.

of the mountainous west into the central plain and adjacent piedmont, a defensible site was established at Aegae (modern Vergina). From Aegae the earliest Macedonian dominion ran east along the Pierian piedmont to the northern opening of the rich Pierian plain below Mt. Olympus, an area from which the Pieres, a Thracian people, were expelled to resettle themselves in eastern Macedonia near Mt. Pangaion. To the west of Aegae, across the Haliacmon, lay the rich, well-watered slopes of Mt. Vermion, running from Veria to Edessa. The Macedonian settlement of this area is the only region mentioned specifically by Herodotus.

We now turn to Thucydides' account (2.99):

> For the race of Macedonians includes as well the Lyncestians, the Elimiotes, and the other peoples of the upper country, who, although allied with the nearer Macedonians and subject to them, have their own kings. But the country along the sea which is now called Macedonia, was first acquired and made a kingdom by Alexander [I], father of Perdiccas [II] and his forefathers, who were originally Temenidae from Argos.
>
> They defeated and expelled from Pieria the Pierians, who later came to reside at Phagres and other places at the foot of Mount Pangaion beyond the Strymon (and even now this area at the foot of Pangaion toward the sea is called the Pierian valley). And also [were expelled] the Bottiaeans from Bottiaea, who now dwell on the borders of the Chalcidians; they acquired as well a narrow strip of Paeonia extending along the Axios River from the interior to Pella and the sea. Beyond the Axios they possess the territory as far as the Strymon called Mygdonia, having driven out the Edoni. Moreover, they expelled from the district now called Eordaea the Eordi, most of whom were destroyed, but a small portion is settled in the neighborhood of Physca. [They also expelled] the Almopians from Almopia.
>
> These Macedonians also made themselves rulers of certain places, which they still control, belonging to other peoples, namely of Anthemus, Grestonia [Crestonia], Bisaltia, and a large part of Macedonia proper. But the whole region is now called Macedonia, and Perdiccas, son of Alexander, was king when Sitalces invaded it.

Thucydides' account of this early expansion, upon which most of our information depends, may not be chronologically arranged, but is rather a geographically organized description of the Macedonian kingdom at the time of the Thracian king Sitalces' invasion in 429 B.C. As

86   **CHAPTER 4**

we have seen, it is difficult to determine whether coastal Pieria or the
Vermion piedmont was settled first, although one is inclined to follow
Herodotus, both because he seems to have acquired his story directly
from Macedonian sources, and because the conquest of the Vermion
foothills, which lie within easy sight and access, seems a more natural
consequence of a settlement near Vergina than does the geographically
awkward swing around northern Pieria into the coastal plain.[18] Moreover, there is nothing to prove that Thucydides' reference to the Macedonians' conquest of Pieria refers necessarily to the Pierian coastal
plain rather than to the Pierian piedmont above the central plain. Some
support is lent by Thucydides at 2.100.4, where he describes Sitalces'
inability to penetrate beyond Pella into "Bottiaea and Pieria." It is unlikely that Sitalces (or anyone else) would strike south directly across
the water from Pella toward coastal Pieria. But if one follows the natural land route west from Pella around the central swampland, one
eventually comes to northern Pieria after passing by Bottiaea and Mt.
Vermion. No more precision is possible about any distinction Thucydides might have made between coastal Pieria and the Pierian piedmont that may have been the Macedonian heartland. It is thus impossible to say when the Pierian coastal plain fell to the Macedonians.[19]

If we accept that Thucydides' description is not chronologically arranged, it is possible to proceed on grounds that make more sense topographically. Setting aside the problem of when coastal Pieria was settled, the Macedonians moved onto the Mt. Vermion piedmont and
eventually took the ancient Brygian stronghold at Edessa, strategically
important since it guards the site where the route through the western
mountains issues onto the Emathian plain. Now in control of the hills
bordering the central plain, the Macedonians moved to secure their
position and acquire more land. They took the northern fringe of the
plain, ancient Bottiaea, which runs eastward to the valley of the Axios,
and also the fertile mountain-ringed Almopian plain north of Edessa.
The expansion thus represented the securing of the fertile C-shaped
piedmont above the waterlogged central plain and the control of the
main routes into the plain: from the west at Edessa, the southwest at
Veria, and the south at the Pierian coastal plain. Two adjacent regions
were taken: coastal Pieria below Olympus, and Almopia. This early

[18] *Contra* Edson, "Early Macedonia," 21, who seems to take Thucydides' description
as chronological. Also Hammond, *HM* 1: 434, although he reconsidered the matter in
HM 2: 30, perhaps not only in light of his detailed analysis of Thuc. 2.99 (*HM* 1: 435–
38), but also because of his recognition that the hitherto unknown site of the Macedonian
center at Aegae is now thought to be at modern Vergina.
[19] There is additional discussion in Hammond, *HM* 1: 153–54.

Argead kingdom emerged as an integral geographical unit, open only to the east beyond the Axios River, a region destined to excite Macedonian interest in due course.

It is clear from Thucydides' account that this first stage of Macedonian expansion is marked by destruction and deportation: the Pierians to resettle in the lower Strymon basin, the Bottiaeans to the region around Olynthus in Chalcidice, the Eordi to Physca in Mygdonia, and the Almopes to an unknown fate. The expulsion of peoples may not have been wholesale and complete; perhaps some remained as subject peoples in a conquered land.[20] This first stage in the Macedonian expansion took about a century, and by *ca.* 550 B.C. the Argeadae stood ready to secure still-exposed frontiers. About 520 B.C. they moved into Eordaea, west of Mt. Vermion.[21] This was certainly a strategic maneuver, as Eordaea sits astride several important routes, including the Monastir-Kozani corridor and the main east-west route (the Via Egnatia in Roman times) as it crossed from Pelagonia and Lyncus to the central plain. Moreover, the Klisoura Pass led westward from Eordaea to Lake Kastoria and the heart of Orestis. Heretofore, the Macedonian expansion could be seen mainly as an attempt to secure contiguous fertile land—thus the expansion along slopes adjacent to the central plain and into the fertile plains of Almopia and coastal Pieria. But Eordaea's attraction could not have been its mediocre fertility, and one suspects that, perhaps for the first time, the Argeads were taking a strategic initiative. It is also interesting to note that Thucydides (2.99.5) makes an unusual reference to most of the Eordi having been killed. Resistance to the Argead Macedonians must have been strong in the struggle for control over this valuable canton.

Along the open eastern frontier lay the possessions of the Paeonians, and beyond them the Thracian tribes. In the last half of the sixth century the Paeonians, whose ethnic stock is unknown, had expanded from the Axios and Strymon hinterland to occupy some sections of coastal Macedonia, including the coastal strip by Pella, Amphaxitis, and the lower Strymon basin.[22] They were a major power in eastern Macedonia and an obstacle to the westward march of Persian authority. About 511 B.C. the Persians, having established a presence in Thrace, moved against the Paeonians and, with the assistance of Thracian allies, succeeded in breaking up the Paeonian hegemony. Most of

[20] Ellis, *PMI*, 36.

[21] Following Hammond's chronology (*HM* 2: 62–64), though not necessarily for the same reasons. Unlike Hammond, I do not put much faith in Strabo as a source for these matters. See Appendix C below, pp. 292–93.

[22] Thuc. 2.99.4; Strabo 7, frag. 11; Hammond, *HM* 2: 55–59.

the Paeonian territory was occupied by Thracian tribes, but the Macedonians were quick to take advantage of the Paeonian dissolution and occupy the remainder of the central plain, the trans-Axios district of Amphaxitis up to the Crestonian highlands and the coastal plain on the eastern side of the bay of Salonica, including the rich valley of Anthemus.

The preceding reconstruction of events is Hammond's, resting on fragmentary archaeological and literary evidence.[23] In 1980 an archaeological discovery of enormous potential importance was made near the village of Sindos, about halfway between Salonica and the Axios River. During the course of some military construction, earth-moving machinery uncovered a large late Archaic and early Classical cemetery.[24] The multiplicity of graves and, especially, the considerable variety of imported and local goods, will shed much light on what must be considered the Macedonian frontier in the late sixth century B.C. Any interpretation of the historical significance of the Sindos finds must await the formal publication of the materials from the site, a work under preparation by the excavator, Aikaterini Despinis. Nonetheless, a few preliminary observations may be in order, based on an examination of the materials exhibited and described.

In general, the grave goods are unlike virtually anything found west of the Axios in the late Archaic period. A large number of objects are influenced by the east: Thrace, East Greece, or Asia, in some cases, Persia. The abundance of small bronze and iron miniatures—wagons, tables, chairs, and spits—suggests Near Eastern and Egyptian parallels. The use of gold in abundance in the form of death masks and clothing ornaments, as well as the superbly intricate granulated gold jewelry, tells of a society that, at least among some of its gentry, possessed disposable wealth and expressed its material substance in rich grave goods, and hints at some connections with the mines of Thrace. Moreover, there are sufficient helmets and weapons to provide evidence of a warrior class.

Now the interesting historical question arising out of such an unusual assortment of goods is whether the inhabitants of this site in the late Archaic period were in fact Macedonians. For we are on the frontier of Argead Macedonia, that is, along the Axios, but we are uncer-

---

[23] *HM* 2: 53–58.

[24] A description of many of the grave goods from Sindos can be found in the superb catalog of the materials on exhibition at the Archaeological Museum of Thessaloniki, Vokotopoulou et al., *Sindos*. The site has now been identified as ancient Anchialos by Hatzopoulos, "Strepsa: A Reconsideration," 60 and 161. I am grateful to Dr. Hatzopoulos for sending me a copy of his work in time to mention its significance in this note.

tain where the boundaries of Macedonian lands actually lay during that period. Sindos may in fact have been a Paeonian or Thracian community. If so, Hammond's view that the Macedonians were across the Axios by the later sixth century will need to be modified at least to take in account that some non-Macedonian peoples persisted into the period of Macedonian control.

Alternatively, we may have at Sindos a late Archaic Macedonian site at which the abundance of grave goods, including some of extraordinary richness, foreshadowed the elaborate burials known from the fourth century, to which would be added the influence of Classical Greece. Especially significant are the striking differences in burial customs between these people and the Greeks, suggesting that at least in this expression of a material culture, the strongest influences were Balkan and Asian rather than mainland Greek. Unfortunately, insufficient archaeological evidence of late Archaic Macedonia prevents us from developing a complete Balkan cultural context for the materials from Sindos. We are left with a body of materials representing strong eastern influences, but without the knowledge of whether these materials are pre-Macedonian or part of late Archaic Macedonian life.

By the end of the sixth century this stage in Macedonian expansion was complete, the kingdom having now secured defensible borders on all sides. To the east lived a number of Thracian tribes, who were engaged in an uneasy alliance with the empire of the Persians, and controlled the rich metal resources of the lower Strymon valley. Chalcidice was peopled mainly with Greeks and some Bottiaeans, and the western cantons with upper Macedonians, Molossians, and others.

These early stages of the Macedonian expansion down to *ca.* 500 B.C. were directed first to the acquisition of fertile land, and second to the security of borders. The Argead-led conquest was direct, and even ruthless, characterized by the expulsion and occasional extermination of populations. Although it is impossible to be precise about the process of resettlement, it may be suggested that several thousand Macedonians established themselves in the conquered territory as farmers and herders, with a heartland in the piedmont surrounding the great central Emathian plain and a royal residence at Aegae.[25] As the Macedonians settled the region following the expulsion of existing peoples, they probably introduced their own customs and language(s); there is no evidence that they adopted any existing language, even though they were now in contact with neighboring populations who spoke a variety of Greek and non-Greek tongues.

[25] Ellis (*PMI*, 36) calls this early state the "Kingdom of Emathia."

The Ethnic Identity of the Macedonians

The question of the Macedonian language has emerged during the past half-century as a problem of enormous interest. No other single issue about which there is so little evidence has achieved such notoriety. Ancient Macedonian ethnicity is important because it has become linked with the issue of national identities in the modern Balkans. The reader is reminded that questions of ethnic identity are still fought over in Greece, Bulgaria, Yugoslavia, and Albania. Minorities of ethnic Turks, Greeks, Albanians, Bulgarians, Serbs, and others residing in several national states have provoked a wide—and often sad—range of political and military responses. The implicit assumption is that ethnic identity is characterized, and perhaps even determined, primarily by language, with concomitant cultural features, such as religious practices, educational prerogatives, maintenance of family customs, and a legal code. Continuing programs by some governments to prohibit education in minority languages and to force families to change names to conform to the national standard are, in effect, an attack on language as the central prop of ethnic identity. The notion of a vital pluralistic society has not been a feature of modern Balkan life, except perhaps in Yugoslavia, where in order to preserve the federation of southern Slavs, attempts have been made to recognize ethnic diversity.

There was perhaps no area of the Balkans characterized by more ethnic variety than modern Macedonia.[26] As the result of the political settlements of the twentieth century, much of the ancient Macedonian kingdom was incorporated into the modern Greek state. Most of the non-Hellenic inhabitants of the area, including Serbs, Turks, and Bulgarians, moved into more compatible neighboring nations, while Macedonia received in turn a heavy influx of refugee Greeks, not only from other Balkan areas but also from Asia Minor, following the Greek military debacle there in 1922. The emphasis on Greek resettlement of Macedonia in particular occurred not only because the region was large and fertile, but also because it was a tenet of Greek national policy to stamp a permanent Hellenic imprint on a land long torn by ethnic rivalries, and thought by Greeks to be part of their nation.

When seen against this background it becomes clear that any attempt to speak of the Hellenic ethnicity of the ancient Macedonians would appear as well to support a Hellenic claim on modern Macedonia, if historical precedent has any value in making territorial claims. Thus, long before there was sufficient ancient evidence to argue about

[26] See Chapter 1 above.

the ethnic identity—as revealed by language—of the ancient Macedonians, there emerged a "Greek" position claiming that the Macedonian language was Greek, and that thus the inhabitants were Greek. The question of the ancient Macedonian language became part of a larger modern political issue, although in fairness to many contemporary Greek scholars who believe that the ancient language was a dialect of Greek, many believe so as the result of scientific endeavors and not out of a strict adherence to national pride and ideology.[27]

The "Greek" position, put simply, is that the meagre literary and archaeological evidence—the latter represented by inscriptions—points to the use of the Greek language by Macedonians. Macedonian kings regarded themselves as descended from Greek Argos, they participated in panhellenic events, the court was highly hellenized, there was considerable Greek influence in art and customs, and both place names and personal names show a high degree of Greek influence.

For example, recent work describes the funerary stelae found in the tumulus covering the royal tombs at Vergina. These stelae date from the fourth and early third centuries, and the preponderance of names are Greek.[28] As many of the stones list patronymics of persons who were alive in the mid-fourth century, we thereby have the names of residents at Aegae dating from the late fifth century. The excavator of Vergina, Manolis Andronikos, in a useful summary of the epigraphic evidence, writes: "In the most unambivalent way this evidence confirms the opinion of those historians who maintain that the Macedonians were a Greek tribe, like all the others who lived on Greek territory, and shows that the theory that they were of Illyrian or Thracian descent and were hellenized by Philip and Alexander rests on no objective criteria."[29]

[27] The fullest statement of the "Greek" position, and also the most detailed study of the Macedonian language, is by Kalléris, *Les anciens Macédoniens*, esp. 2: 488–531, in which alleged Greek elements in the Macedonian language are examined exhaustively. A more chauvinistic (and less persuasive) point of view can be found in Daskalakis, *Hellenism*, esp. pts. 2 and 3. The most blatant account is that of Martis (*The Falsification of Macedonian History*). This book, written by a former Minister for Northern Greece, is an polemical anti-Yugoslav tract so full of historical errors and distortions that the prize awarded it by the Academy of Athens serves only to reduce confidence in the scientific judgment of that venerable society of scholars. The most sensible and scholarly Greek position is that laid out by Sakellariou, in *Macedonia*, 44–63. Lest it seem, however, that the "Greek" position is held only by modern Greeks, see Cawkwell, *Philip of Macedon*, 22: "The Macedonians were Greeks."

[28] See Saatsoglou-Paliadeli, *Ta epitaphia mnimeia*, esp. 269–86, for an onomastic catalog.

[29] *Vergina: The Royal Tombs*, 83–85. This argument is true enough only as far as it goes. It neglects that the hellenization of the Macedonians might have occurred earlier

How does one go about determining the ethnic identity of the historical Macedonians? First, the matter of language. There is no doubt
that standard Attic Greek was used by the court for personal matters
and by the king for official business from at least the time of Archelaus
at the end of the fifth century B.C. This use of Greek may be a result of
the process of hellenization. The main evidence for Macedonian existing as a *separate* language comes from a handful of late sources describing events in the train of Alexander the Great, where the Macedonian
tongue is mentioned specifically.[30] The evidence suggests that Macedonian was distinct from the ordinary Attic Greek used as the language
of the court and of diplomacy. Whether it was a rude patois that was
the dialect of farmers and hillsmen or a style of speaking (like "La-
conic") is impossible to know from this scant, late evidence.[31] In any
case we cannot tell if it was Greek. Hammond's "firm conclusion" that
the Macedonians spoke a distinctive dialect of Aeolic Greek is unconvincing to me, resting as it does on an interpretation of a bit of myth
quoted by Hellanicus, who made Aeolus the father of the legendary
progenitor Macedon.[32]

The science of linguistics provides another point of view and a different method.[33] One of the characteristics of all historical Greek dia-

---

than the age of Philip and Alexander, and cannot therefore serve as a means of proving
that the Macedonians were a Greek tribe.

[30] E.g., Plut. *Alex.* 51.4; Curt.6.9.35; Plut. *Eum.* 14.5; also Athen. 3.122A and Plut.
Ant. 27 for other indications of Macedonian separateness. Some of these passages are
examined in detail by Daskalakis, *Hellenism*, 66–76. A scrap of papyrus (*PSI* XII. 1284),
which may be a fragment of Arrian's lost *History of the Successors*, has Eumenes "sending
forth a man called Xennias who was Macedonian in speech [*Makedonisti*]" (see note 31
below) to negotiate with the army, perhaps the Macedonian army of Neoptolemus (321
B.C.); see Bosworth, "Eumenes, Neoptolemus and *PSI* XII. 1284." Bosworth (236) sees
the fragment as corroborative that the Macedonian language was "separate from and
akin to Greek."

[31] *Makedonisti* = "to speak in the Macedonian manner," Liddell-Scott-Jones, et al.,
eds., *A Greek-English Lexicon*, 9th ed., *q.v.* The context of the scene described in the
papyrus fragment (note 30 above), however, leads one to suspect that more than a style
of speaking is meant: the Macedonian-speaking Xennias was dispatched by Eumenes to
negotiate with a commander of Macedonian troops. Such a mission required fluency
that apparently an ordinary Greek-speaker did not have. Eumenes, secretary to Philip
and Alexander, would have been in a position to know these things.

[32] Hammond, *HM* 2: 47–49; for Hellanicus, see *FGrH* 4 F74. Hammond's earlier position (in a review of A. B. Daskalakis, *O Ellēnismos tēs archaias Makedonias*, in *CR* 12
[1962]: 271) that the Macedonians spoke a "patois which was not recognizable as a normal Doric Greek but may have been a north-west-Greek dialect of a primitive kind" is
preferable.

[33] The leading proponent of what follows is Crossland, in "Linguistic Problems of the

lects, as opposed to some other Indo-European languages, is that over time they undergo certain changes. The handful of surviving genuine Macedonian words—not loan words from Greek—do not show the changes expected from a Greek dialect. And even had they changed at some point it is unlikely that they would have reverted to their original form. In this respect Macedonian seems closer to Illyrian and Thracian than to the Greek dialects. This is not, however, to insist that Macedonian is Illyrian or Thracian. It is only to say that there is an insufficient sample of words to show exactly what the Macedonian language was. It must also be emphasized that this is not to say that it was not Greek; it is only to suggest that, from the linguists' point of view, it is as yet impossible to know.

Archaeology provides little assistance in recovering the language. Macedonian tombs are thus far virtually without inscriptions, and those few inscriptions that have been recovered are written in standard Greek, as befits the gentry that ordered their construction in the fourth and third centuries. The publication of the fourth- and early third-century inscriptions from the tumulus at Vergina (see note 28 above) revealed some tendencies toward Doric Greek. Recent unpublished surveys of epigraphical materials from the villages near Veria offer some examples of Aeolic Greek. Thus within an area of a few miles exist examples of standard Attic plus two other Greek dialects from the late Classical and early Hellenistic periods.

The systematic collection and publication of Macedonian inscriptions has been hindered by the region's geographical isolation, difficult terrain, turbulent modern history, and slow development of archaeological surveys and excavations. The deficiency of an organized assembly of the epigraphic evidence, however, is being corrected by a long-term project jointly sponsored by the Greek Ministry of Culture and the National Hellenic Research Foundation. The result will be a series of publications presenting the ancient inscriptions of Macedonia.[34] There is hope in some quarters that the accumulation and publication

---

Balkan Area," 834–49, and in a paper on the Macedonian language read at the Fourth International Symposium on Ancient Macedonia (1983).

[34] The first volume, covering the inscriptions of the upper Macedonian cantons of Elimeia, Eordaea, Orestis, Tymphaea, and southern Lyncus, has already appeared: Rizakis and Touratsoglou, eds., *Epigraphes Anō Makedonias* (see Appendix A below, p. 284). While nearly all of the 225 inscriptions are in Greek, the overwhelming number come from the Hellenistic and Roman periods, by which time standard Greek was in use for such formal purposes. No indigenous material from the early period appears in the corpus. The recent publication of Tataki's prosopographical study of the inscriptions from Beroea, *Ancient Beroea*, will eventually contribute to our understanding of ethnicity in this corner of central Macedonia.

of a large body of epigraphical material will provide more clues to the language in common use. Yet prudence in these matters demands recognition of the fact that such epigraphical evidence may not supply information about the local dialect, any more than Latin inscriptions from remote parts of Italy or from Gaul or Asia Minor tell us much about the local languages. Indeed, it may be that the native dialect was never written, and that the inscriptions that do exist are an artificial attempt to represent in the Greek writing system some sounds of native speech.

Archaeology has provided a useful Balkan parallel: in early 1986 a village vegetable plot in northwestern Bulgaria yielded a buried hoard of 165 Thracian silver vessels from the fifth and fourth centuries B.C. Sixteen of the vessels were inscribed with Thracian personal and places names *in Greek*. The Thracians were, as far as we know, a non-Greek people whose language—which continued to exist well into Roman times—never achieved written form. We may recall, moreover, the long-known coin issues of Thracian tribes from the early fifth century B.C. on which the names of the tribes, their kings and their titles are inscribed in Greek (see Chapter 5 below). The lesson is clear: the use of the Greek language as a form of written expression does not by itself identify the ethnicity of a culture.[35]

The problem is nowhere near solution. The more we learn about the Macedonians, the more we are impressed by the variety of their cultural expressions. This eclecticism may also describe their use of language. Macedonia is, in Greek terms, a huge and diverse country with a population that was not homogeneous, if their material remains are a valid indicator. It should not surprise us if a variety of dialects were used—with writing in standard dialects of Greek and some patois in a language or dialect the knowledge of which is beyond recovery. One can only speculate that that dialect declined with the rise in use of standard *koinē* Greek. The main language of formal discourse and official communication became Greek by the fourth century.[36] Whether the dialect(s) were eventually replaced by standard Greek, or were preserved as part of a two-tiered system of speech—one for official use, the other idiomatic for traditional ceremonies, rituals, or rough soldiers' talk—is problematic and requires more evidence and further study.

If language provides one indicator of the ethnic identity of a popu-

[35] The Thracian vessels are described by Fol et al., *The New Thracian Treasure*. Examples of the coins can be found, *inter alia*, in Price, *Coins*, nos. 9, 13, 14, and 16, and Kraay, *Archaic and Classical Greek Coins*, nos. 482 and 483.

[36] Hammond, *HM* 2: 46 (n. 1) and 54, is persuasive on this point.

lation, customs provide another. As in the case of language we have only the sketchiest information about Macedonian customs, but what evidence does exist points to much that is quite different from the Greek city-states. The most visible expression of material culture thus far recovered are fourth- and third-century tombs (see Chapter 11 below). The architectural form, decoration, and burial goods of these tombs, which now number between sixty and seventy, are unlike what is found in the Greek south, or even in the neighboring independent Greek cities of the north Aegean littoral (excepting Amphipolis). Macedonian burial habits suggest a different view of the afterlife from the Greeks', even while many of the same gods were worshipped. The main body of written evidence on the Macedonian pantheon comes from the age of Philip II and Alexander, and makes it appear that Macedonians shared the Greek gods. Yet many of the public expressions of worship may have been different. For example, there is an absence of major public religious monuments from Macedonian sites before the end of the fourth century (another difference from the Greeks). We are thus dependent upon literary evidence, and must be cautious both in attributing Greek forms of worship to the Macedonians and in using these forms of worship as a means of confirming Hellenic identity.[37]

One could review the whole parade of customs—e.g., political organization, social associations, economic structure (the discussion of which will be left for later)—and it would appear that there is much in Macedonian society that was assimilated from Greece; but there is also a great deal that seems to be indigenous and non-Hellenic. Some of the differences may result from strong Asian or Balkan influences on Macedonian life, and others from the stage of monarchical development that characterized the Macedonians, a form of political and social organization that nearly all Greeks had abandoned rather early on. In this sense, some aspects of Macedonian customs more nearly reflect those of Bronze Age Greeks than those of their Classical contemporaries. In brief, one must conclude that the similarity between some Macedonian and Greek customs and objects are not of themselves proof that the Macedonians were a Greek tribe, even though it is undeniable that on certain levels Greek cultural influences eventually became pervasive.

An assessment of contemporary perceptions shared by Greeks and Macedonians provides another means of judging the ethnicity of the Macedonians. That is, how were the Macedonians perceived in their

---

[37] Herodotus (5.7) attributes to the Thracians the worship of Greek gods; Greek writers often saw foreign religion from their own viewpoint. See Hoddinott, *The Thracians*, 169–70.

own time? Both Herodotus and Thucydides describe the Macedonians as foreigners, a distinct people living outside the frontiers of the Greek city-states. In a controversial and sometimes misunderstood essay on this question, E. Badian concluded that, whatever the ethnic origins and identity of the Macedonians, they were generally perceived in their own time *by Greeks and themselves* not to be Greek.[38] Badian shows that, until quite late, the Macedonians as a people were excluded from panhellenic festivals in which only Greeks were permitted to participate, that the attempts of their kings to participate met objections from the Greeks, that contemporary Greek literature offers numerous examples of Greek contempt for the Macedonians as barbarians, and that to the extent that Macedonian kings participated in panhellenic or bilateral arrangements with Greeks, they did so as individuals.

No single argument is conclusive, but the case builds in quality as it grows in quantity of evidence, and, in the end, is persuasive.[39] Despite the efforts of Philip II and Alexander the Great to bridge the gap between the two cultures, Greeks and Macedonians remained steadfastly antipathetic toward one another (with dislike of a different quality than the mutual long-term hostility shared by some Greek city-states) until well into the Hellenistic period, when both the culmination of Hellenic acculturation in the north and the rise of Rome made it clear that what these peoples shared took precedence over their historical enmities.

Who were the Macedonians? As an ethnic question it is best avoided, since the mainly modern political overtones tend to obscure the fact that it really is not a very important issue. That they may or may not have been Greek in whole or in part—while an interesting anthropological sidelight—is really not crucial to our understanding of their history. They made their mark not as a tribe of Greeks or other Balkan peoples, but as *Macedonians*. This was understood by foreign protagonists from the time of Darius and Xerxes to the age of Roman generals. Their adoption of some aspects of Hellenism over a long period of time is more important than the genetic structure of either the Macedonian population in general or their royal house in particular. Moreover, the

---

[38] "Greeks and Macedonians." In some quarters Badian's views were regarded as an attack on the Hellenic ethnicity of the Macedonians, despite the fact that the author specifically declined to deal with the ethnic/language issue beyond briefly alluding to it in his introductory comments in order to set it aside. Badian's purpose (33) was to analyze Greek and Macedonian perceptions of one another. The judgment that the Macedonians neither considered themselves Greek nor were so considered by their neighbors is shared by Hammond, *History of Greece*, 534–35.

[39] It is indicative of the strength of Badian's case that his critics have succeeded only in nit-picking: e.g., Sakellariou, *Macedonia*, 534–35 nn. 52–53.

necessity for Macedonian kings from Alexander I to Philip II to impress the Greek world with their own purported Hellenic origins tells much more about relations between Greeks and Macedonians than any attempt to show that the Macedonians were a remote Greek tribe.

Once freed from the constraints of modern Balkan political rhetoric, the issue of the ethnic identity of the ancient Macedonians and their royal house recedes into its proper historical significance: the bloodlines of ancient peoples are notoriously difficult to trace. What the Macedonians became and how they acted are more appropriate historical questions, the investigation of which may help determine the extent to which Macedonians shared in the general culture that we call "Greek." It is time to put the matter of the Macedonians' ethnic identity to rest.

CHAPTER 5

Alexander I

WE KNOW less about the first five kings of Macedon than we know about the ancient kings of Rome. Amyntas I, who died at the beginning of the fifth century B.C., is the earliest Macedonian king about whom we have any certain historical information. Herodotus mentions Amyntas's five Argead predecessors, but they are merely names: Perdiccas (the founder), Argaeus, Philip, Aeropus, and Alcetas. When Herodotus visited Macedonia, he was probably given a version of the official king list preserving the Argead lineage of fathers and sons.[1] The assignment of dates to these shadowy figures is quite arbitrary, although one cannot be far wrong to allow an average generation of about thirty years, which would put the founding of the royal house in the early seventh century.[2]

When Amyntas became king of the Macedonians sometime during the latter third of the sixth century, he controlled a territory that included the central Macedonian plain and its peripheral foothills, the Pierian coastal plain beneath Mt. Olympus, and perhaps the fertile, mountain-encircled plain of Almopia. To the south lay the Greeks of Thessaly. The western mountains were peopled by the Molossians (the western Greeks of Epirus), tribes of non-Argead Macedonians, and other populations.[3] Beyond them lay the fierce Illyrians, loosely or-

---

[1] Hdt. 8.139; Thuc. 2.100.2. Justin 7.1–2 provides additional information about the early kings, but his account is based on late sources already corrupted by the interpolation of additional kings into the list.

[2] The average reign of the three major fifth-century kings—Alexander I, Perdiccas II, and Archelaus—was nearly thirty-three years. See Hammond's discussion (*HM* 2: 3–5), where he gives the adult dates of the early kings: Perdiccas I *ca.* 653, Argaeus *ca.* 623, Philip I *ca.* 593, Aeropus I *ca.* 563, Alcetas *ca.* 533, Amyntas I *ca.* 503. Both Hammond and Errington (*Gesch. Make.*, 271) prudently resist the temptation to assign regnal dates to the kings before Alexander I. See Diod. 7.15.1 (Euseb. *Chron.* 1.227) for an ancient Macedonian king list developed after the end of the fifth century B.C.

[3] I follow Edson ("Early Macedonia," 26–27 [after Hdt. 7.185.2]) rather than Hammond (*HM* 2: 62–65) in placing the expansion of Argead control into Eordaea during the reign of Alexander I rather than attributing it to Amyntas. On the tribal life of the early Macedonians and their neighbors, see Hammond, *HM* 2: 22–31.

ganized as a tribal confederation and given to frontier raids against
their Molossian and Macedonian neighbors. East of the Axios lay a
mélange of Paeonian and Thracian tribes that made up the population
of the eastern Balkans.

The thinly populated Argead kingdom with its tiny center at Aegae
was weak by the standards of a latter-day Macedon, but its continued
survival in the seventh and sixth centuries suggests something both
about its relative internal stability (probably resting on allegiance to
the Argead house) and the absence of a serious external threat. No
Balkan tribe emerged to disturb the situation. And none of the tiny
city-states of the Greek world that were in the heyday of their colonization movement seemed interested in challenging Macedon. The
Greeks preferred to establish their colonial foundations peacefully, taking land in uninhabited or lightly settled areas. Unlike Greek settlement for strategic purposes at a later time, Greek foundations in this
earlier period were mainly agricultural outlets for excess and dissident
populations. Greek settlements were established over a wide area from
Chalcidice to the Bosporus and beyond, but nowhere in this region
did they provoke an existing power.[4] Only two Greek outposts appear
in Macedonian territory during this period: Methone and Pydna were
founded in Macedonian Pieria, and it is significant that the Argeadae
were either too weak or too uninterested to challenge this intrusion.

Unlike their western kinsmen, who were relatively isolated in
mountain valleys, the lowland Argead Macedonians were exposed to
the political, economic, and cultural currents of the Aegean world—in
particular, to the influence of the Greeks.[5] The lowland Argeadae had
no tribal name. They emerge simply as the "Macedonians" (Thuc.
2.99.6 and 4.124.1). Herodotus is the first to use the term "Macedonia." He is followed by Thucydides, who also refers to "present Macedonia by the sea." The comparatively late introduction of the term
explains why in the fifth century Athenians still referred to the region
as part of Thrace, so that Strepsa and Methone, coastal cities in Macedonia, appear in the Athenian imperial tribute lists as part of the Thra-

[4] For a study of the Greek outposts in the north, see Isaac, *Greek Settlements in Thrace*.
Isaac lists 72 Greek centers altogether, of which 26 were in Chalcidice and coastal
Thrace. He shows (p. 20) that relations between the Thracians and Greeks were generally not hostile, as long as the Greeks did not attempt to found major towns, but rather
confined their interests to the exploitation of mines and the conduct of trade and agriculture on a small scale.

[5] After Edson, "Early Macedonia," 22 and 28–29. Edson's essay, now archaeologically
out of date and in parts subject to correction, is in many other respects still a very useful
brief narrative introduction to early Macedonia.

cian *phoros*. It would take a long time—perhaps until the era of Philip II—before the upper Macedonians would become hellenized. The course by which Hellenism penetrated beyond the mountain rim of the central Macedonian plain is a cultural question to which archaeology may provide the answer. For example, the 1986 discovery of a proper "Macedonian" tomb dated to *ca.* 300 B.C. in Eordaea, near modern Ptolemais up against the western slopes of Mt. Vermion, suggests that by that time at least one aspect of the culture of central Macedonia had already crossed the mountains into the west.

The Persians in Thrace

But events originating far from the pleasant Pierian foothills— events uncontrolled and perhaps at first even unknown by Argead lords— were to impinge upon Macedonia and forever alter the balance of power among the Balkan peoples and their petty feudal princes. Toward the end of the sixth century, the inexorable movement of the Persian Empire toward the west had reached the frontier of the Aegean/Greek world. Persian forces crossed the Bosporus *ca.* 513. Eastern Thrace was subdued (although probably not organized into a satrapy), and Asian fleets were sent to secure the Danube and Scythia and, reaching further, to tighten a ring around the Black Sea.[6] King Darius returned to Asia, leaving Megabazus in command of a European expeditionary force that, in 512 or 511, marched westward into the Strymon basin. There the power of the Paeonians, who had lived intermingled with Thracians, was broken, and the Paeonian population was deported into Asia. Megabazus made peace with a number of the Thracians, and is reported to have soon sent an embassy to Amyntas, king of the Macedonians.

Amyntas may have taken advantage of the collapse of Paeonian power in Thrace to cross the Axios and establish his rule in Amphaxitis.[7] His kingdom was clearly the next entity in the path of the Persian westward thrust, and it is consistent with Persian practice elsewhere to offer an opportunity to make a peaceful settlement. Thus, *ca.* 510 B.C.,

[6] The Scythian and Thracian campaigns are described in Hdt. 4.93 and 5.1–17. A recent general account of this early conflict between Asia and Europe is Burn, "Persia and the Greeks." Balcer's attempt to revise the chronology of the Thracian invasion ("The Date of Herodotus IV.1," esp. 129–32) has now been retracted by the author; see Balcer, "Persian Occupied Thrace," 8 n. 26. On the matter of the Persian organization in Europe, see Appendix C below, p. 293.

[7] This suggestion is Hammond's, *HM* 2: 57–59, who describes the territorial gains of Amyntas in the aftermath of Megabazus's invasion of the Balkans, although see above, pp. 87–88.

according to Herodotus (5.17–21), a party of seven high-ranked Persian envoys made their way from the Strymon valley into Macedonia, intent on demanding earth and water for King Darius.[8] Herodotus fails to mention where the meeting took place, but the Macedonian capital at Aegae is likely, as the setting of a formal banquet and the appearance of Macedonian wives suggest an established court. The Hellenistic "palace" at Vergina has a series of rooms in which such entertainments might have been set up. This existing complex, of course, considerably postdates Amyntas's time (see Chapter 11 below); the royal quarters of the early Macedonian kings is yet to be discovered. We are told that Amyntas formally submitted to the Persian envoys and then invited his guests to dinner. After a splendid feast the party continued drinking, and the Persians requested the company of women—wives and concubines—according to their wont. Despite Amyntas's plea that this demand was at variance with Macedonian custom, he agreed to provide the women.

Flushed with wine, the envoys began to fondle and kiss their female companions. Amyntas's fear of the Persians stayed his wrath, but his enraged son, Alexander, asked his father to leave the scene and permit Alexander to handle matters. Amyntas warned his son not to act rashly, and departed. Turning to the envoys, Alexander suggested that the women retire briefly to refresh themselves.[9] Unfortunately, there is insufficient archaeological evidence from early fifth-century Macedon to know what the living arrangements were in ordinary houses, much less in a royal residence. At most, we can only conjecture about the relationship between the sexes on formal occasions: there was a women's apartment of some sort, Amyntas protested that women and men did not normally share such occasions, and, even when women were admitted into the Persians' presence, they sat across from the men until Amyntas was forced to require them to sit beside the envoys. Even if the story were made up (as will be argued below), the social setting and customs are probably genuine.

Alexander then substituted beardless youths attired as women, informing the Persians that these were Macedonian wives and sisters, a special gift to the envoys of the Great King from the "Greek man who rules Macedon" (*anēr Hellen Makedonōn hyparchos*). When the Persians

---

[8] On Darius's route into Macedonia, see Appendix B below, pp. 289–90.

[9] *Eis tēn gynaikeiēn,* "to the women's quarters" (5.20). In his commentary on the passage, Macan, *Herodotus: The Fourth, Fifth and Sixth Books,* implies that this is a harem. For a discussion of the architecture of men's and women's quarters in private Greek houses as a reflection of the general segregation of the sexes, see S. Walker, "Women and Housing in Classical Greece."

resumed their abuse of the "women," the disguised males killed them. Herodotus concludes the tale by recounting that the envoys' retainers and train were wiped out, and evidence of the slaughter was concealed. Justin (7.3) gives a similar, though somewhat abbreviated, version of the embassy's visit to the Macedonian court.

For nearly a century most scholars have rejected the veracity of this story,[10] and hardly any credence is put in it today. It has been doubted on the grounds of general probability: that the young prince of Macedon should have dismissed his father so rudely, and engineered such a drastic act. (A century and half later another Macedonian prince named Alexander would be sent into exile for insulting his father and interfering with policy.) While we know virtually nothing about Amyntas personally, it is hardly likely that he was so weak or foolhardy as to entrust this delicate situation to a son whose deviousness is a matter of historical fact. The story is designed specifically to elevate the role of Alexander. This may have been part of Alexander's own attempt to promote his cunning character (a trait much admired among Greeks ancient and modern) and anti-Persian/prohellenic image, for which Herodotus was the gullible transmitter. We shall return shortly to these themes, as they recur in Herodotus's account of Alexander. The story must be rejected either as a piece of Alexander's own propaganda, or as an attempt by Herodotus's Athenian sources, who needed Alexander's timber, to whitewash him by making the royal Macedonian medizer part of the Resistance during the Persian invasion.[11]

Other objections have been raised, but what is more important—and has been overlooked—is that in the end Amyntas's submission to the Persians was aborted, as the embassy was annihilated.[12] With the rejection of the embassy tale there disappears the only evidence that Macedon was a vassal-state under Persian domination in the time of Amyntas.[13] Only one part of Herodotus's story may be preserved: he recounts (5.21) that, not long after the destruction of the embassy, the Persians sent out a search party, but the clever Alexander neutralized their inquiry by paying a sum to the Persians, and by marrying his

[10] E.g., the commentaries of Macan (*Herodotus: The Fourth, Fifth and Sixth Books*) and How and Wells (*A Commentary on Herodotus*) on the passage, and, more recently, Hammond, *HM* 2: 99.

[11] The latter view is Burn's, "Persia and the Greeks," 303.

[12] Errington seems to have been the first to have noticed this point; see "Alexander the Philhellene and Persia," 140.

[13] Hammond is correct (*HM* 2: 99) in suggesting that there is no evidence that Macedon rebelled from Persian vassalage. But this is not, as Hammond suggests, because the Macedonians remained loyal subjects. It is rather because, until Mardonius's campaign in 492, Macedon was not under Persian control.

sister Gygaea to the investigators' Persian commander, Bubares. The marriage is certain: Bubares appears later as one of the superintendents of Xerxes' Athos canal project, and his connection with the Macedonian royal house through marriage is one of the reasons Herodotus gives for Mardonius sending Alexander to Athens as a Persian envoy in 480/79 B.C.[14]

The marriage of Gygaea and Bubares is unlikely to have happened for the reasons given by Herodotus in the period shortly after the Persian embassy *ca.* 510. Alexander as prince of the realm was not empowered to give away his sister in an important foreign marriage. Either Amyntas himself arranged the marriage as part of negotiations with the Persians in the late sixth century, or the marriage was part of Alexander's policy after his succession to the throne *ca.* 498.[15] In either case, the marriage signifies alliance (or at least the recognition of a nonhostile relationship), but not necessarily vassalage. As we shall see, the practice of Argead men and women marrying foreigners for political/diplomatic goals would become common enough. But the existence of such a union is not—without additional information—alone sufficient evidence of determining which party, Macedonian or foreign, was subservient to the other.

There is no information about Macedonian policy during the rebellion of the Ionian Greeks against Persian authority (499–494 B.C.). Relations between Macedon and Persia may have remained friendly without the necessity of subjection, sealed by the marriage between Gygaea and Bubares. Bubares was called away from the Macedonian court perhaps at the time of the Ionian revolt, and a passage from Justin (7.4.1) that speaks of King Amyntas's death shortly after Bubares' departure is used to date the end of the Amyntas's reign and the beginning of Alexander's to 498 or 497.[16]

[14] Hdt. 7.22 and 8.136, in which the *son* of Bubares and Gygaea is named Amyntas, after his royal Macedonian grandfather.

[15] One clue might lie in Hdt. 8.136, where (in discussing events of 480 B.C.) Amyntas, the son of Bubares and Gygaea, is mentioned as having received from the Persian king as a dwelling place the Phrygian city of Alabanda. Setting aside some geographical difficulties (e.g., Alabanda is in Caria, not Phrygia; Hdt. 7.195), if Bubares and Gygaea's marriage had been arranged shortly after *ca.* 510 this would have been a gift to an adult Amyntas, who might have been 28 or 29 in 480. If, however, Gygaea's marriage occurred during the reign of Alexander at the time of Mardonius's invasion of 492, Amyntas would have been only a child in 480, and the gift seems less appropriate. I lean toward the earlier marriage, under Amyntas I.

[16] Hammond's attempt (*HM* 2: 60) to date Amyntas's death *ca.* 495, in part because of his belief that Alexander competed in the Olympic Games of 496 as a prince ("it is unlikely that Alexander competed as king of Macedon because the prestige of his kingdom

Shortly after his Scythian expedition, Darius had granted Histiaeus, tyrant of Miletus, a gift of Myrcinus, a district that controlled the crossing of the lower Strymon River, where Histiaeus proceeded to develop and fortify a city. He held the site until Darius recalled him to Susa.[17] This is the earliest clear evidence of interest in controlling a region that was rich in forest and mineral resources. But Megabazus's speech (Hdt. 5.23) persuading Darius to recall Histiaeus is replete with difficulties: Herodotus's assessment of the wealth of the place may be more a reflection of his own time that of the early fifth century; there is a reference to the number of Greeks living nearby (the closest Greeks were in Chalcidice), and there is an injunction that Histiaeus should never be permitted to return to "Greece." The region of Histiaeus's interest was Thrace (Hdt. 5.23, 126), not Greece. Seeing the turn of events in Asia against him late in the Ionian revolt, the rebel leader Aristagoras of Miletus led an expedition to Myrcinus, but he and his army were wiped out by the local Thracians (Hdt. 5.124–26). As far as we know, these events occurred outside Macedonian interests and territory.

In 492 a Persian expeditionary force under the command of Mardonius crossed into Europe with the intention of marching to Athens (Hdt. 6.42–45). It subdued the Thasians and next "added the Macedonians to the slaves they already had, as all the nations nearer to them had already been subjected to them before this time" (Hdt. 5.44). The most natural way to take this passage is to infer that until this time Macedonia had not been enslaved by the Persians. This is supported by the lack of evidence of a formal submission in Amyntas's time (see above), and by passages elsewhere in Herodotus and in a late chronographic tradition. Despite Hammond, who writes: "[Mardonius] *reasserted* [my emphasis] his authority over Macedonia,"[18] Herodotus explicitly says the opposite. Moreover, in his description of Xerxes' invasion in 480, Herodotus (7.108) reminds the reader that he has already shown that the whole country as far as Thessaly was under the Persian yoke due to the expeditions of Megabazus and Mardonius. The reference to Mardonius is a key: had Macedon—the last nation before Thessaly—been enslaved by Megabazus *ca.* 510, there would be no reason to mention Mardonius.

---

might have been involved"), is unconvincing. It rests on two questionable premises: that Alexander could not have competed as a king (for a persuasive rejoinder see Roos, "Alexander I in Olympia," 167–68), and that he participated in 496.

[17] Hdt. 5.11, 23–24, and 124.

[18] "The Extent of Persian Occupation in Thrace," 60.

Moreover, Syncellus states that Alexander gave water and earth,[19] although the date of Alexander's submission is uncertain. A line in this ninth-century Byzantine chronographer's work is a slim thread on which to hang the heavy historical burden of Alexander's surrender, were it not for its agreement with Herodotus. The evidence concerning the earliest Macedonian capitulation to the Persians thus points to the reign of Alexander I, probably at the time of Mardonius's invasion of 492. Whatever the nature of the Persian satrapal organization of the Balkans,[20] Macedon appears to have been outside it until 492 or later. Mardonius's expedition was less than completely successful. His fleet was wrecked attempting to round Athos, and he was attacked by the Bryges of Thrace, although he recovered sufficiently to subdue them before retiring into Asia. The next scene in the drama between Persia and the West would be played out two years later on the Attic plain of Marathon, far from the forests and rivers of the northern Aegean.

Alexander I and Xerxes' Invasion

With the accession of Xerxes to the Achaemenid throne in 486, events began building toward a more dramatic turn. By about 483 Bubares returned to superintend the construction of a canal through the narrow isthmus of Akti (Hdt. 7.22), and other preparations were underway for what was clearly planned as a major Persian effort in Europe. By 480 an enormous Persian force, supported by a heavy commitment of naval units, had crossed the Hellespont and advanced along the Thracian coast. Bubares's canal across the narrows of Akti was now open (traces of the canal are still visible), and the Asian fleet gained safe passage to Chalcidice. Advancing in three separate columns (Hdt. 7.121), Xerxes' army crossed the Nestos River and passed through the lower Strymon basin into eastern Chalcidice, where it paused briefly at the Akti canal before its drive toward Macedonia.

The fleet rounded the Chalcidic peninsulas of Sithonia and Kassandra (ancient Pallene) and headed north to the head of the Thermaic Gulf, where it put in along the coast between the Axios River and Therme to await Xerxes' arrival by land (Map IV).[21] The huge army

[19] Syncellus, p. 469 [Dindorf ed.]; p. 269, 10–11, in the Teubner edition of A. Mosshammer. For a favorable appraisal of Syncellus as a sound historical source, see Huxley, "On the Erudition of George the Synkellos," 207–17.

[20] On the Persian satrapy in Europe, see Appendix C, p. 293.

[21] The precise location of Therme is unknown, although it was undoubtedly on the northeast coast of the gulf that takes its name. Hammond (*HM* I: 150–51) puts it at the Cape Mikro Karaburnu, just south of Salonica, while Vickers, in a useful and fair review

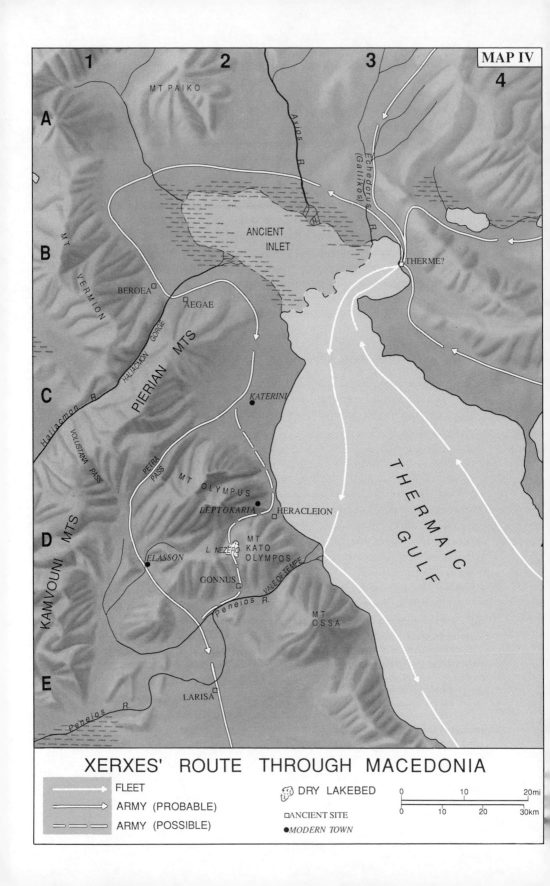

MAP IV

1   2   3

4

A

MT PAIKO

Axios R.

Echedorus (Galikos) R.

ANCIENT
INLET

B

MT VERMION

BEROEA

AEGAE

THERME?

HALIACMON GORGE

PIERIAN MTS

C

Haliacmon R.

VOLUSTANA PASS

KATERINI

THERMAIC

PETRA PASS

MT OLYMPUS

LEPTOKARIA

HERACLEION

D

KAMVOUNI MTS

ELASSON

L. NEZERO

MT KATO OLYMPOS

GONNUS

VALE OF TEMPE

GULF

Peneios R.

MT OSSA

E

LARISA

Peneios R.

XERXES' ROUTE THROUGH MACEDONIA

→ FLEET

→ ARMY (PROBABLE)

– – → ARMY (POSSIBLE)

🗺 DRY LAKEBED

☐ ANCIENT SITE

● MODERN TOWN

0   10   20mi

0   10   20   30km

encamped over a wide area on both sides of the Axios's mouth, and
Herodotus's comment (7.127) that they drank the Echedorus (modern
Gallikos) River dry may have its origin in the fact that the river yields
only a trickle of water in its streambed throughout most of the year.
Leaving his army at Therme, Xerxes sailed out into the gulf to scout
the Pierian coast and the pass through the Vale of Tempe. This narrow,
five-mile-long gorge, leading from the coast directly into the great
plain of Thessaly, splits the Olympus range from Mt. Ossa, and is
wide enough only for the Peneios River and a road. (The beds for the
modern road and railroad have in places been blasted into the cliffs on
either side of the river.) Xerxes had apparently already decided to bypass Tempe, perhaps (this is not clear in Herodotus 7.128, 130–31, and
173) on the grounds that it was more easily blocked than an alternative
route. Thus it may have been curiosity that drove the Great King to
peer from his ship into the gorge of Tempe, if indeed Herodotus's account is not simply a rhetorical device. Whatever the truth of it, Xerxes delayed in Pieria for many days, while his army pushed a road up
from the Pierian coastal plain, probably into the Petra Pass that bisects
the massif between Mt. Olympus and the Pierian range (the modern
road rises from the town of Katerini). Xerxes was thus able to pierce
the Olympus-Pierian range through an ancient route, and descend into
the Thessalian plain from behind Mt. Olympus and the Vale of
Tempe. The way into Greece was open.[22]

Herodotus is almost silent about the activities of the king of Macedon during Xerxes's passage through his country. Alexander is mentioned only in connection with Tempe: After introducing his account
of Xerxes' circumvention of the gorge (7.128–31), Herodotus makes
a long digression on Greek and Sicilian matters before returning to the
mainstream of his story. He renews his narrative by describing (7.172–
73) the Thessalian proposal to establish an allied defense of Tempe, led
by Spartan and Athenian commanders.[23] They were encamped only a
short time before messengers from Alexander appeared, persuading
them to depart before being overwhelmed by the huge Asian force.

---

of both ancient and Byzantine testimonia and modern scholarship ("Therme and Thessaloniki"), has Therme as the antecedent for Thessaloniki itself.

[22] For Xerxes' route bypassing Tempe, see Appendix B below, pp. 290–91.

[23] Some Thessalians, notably the Aleuadae of Larisa, had medized, but a number of
others were opposed to the Persian advance and had joined in the allied effort. For the
complexities of the situation, see Westlake, "The Medism of Thessaly," and Robertson,
"The Thessalian Expedition of 480 B.C.," who puts the Greek camp (116) at Heracleion
in the narrow coastal plain between Lower (Katō) Olympus and the sea, rather than in
the gorge of Tempe itself, a proposal energetically rejected by Pritchett, "Chimney Corner Topography."

Herodotus comments *post factum* that what really prompted the Greek withdrawal was knowledge that Tempe could be bypassed. Of the three passes from central Macedonia into Thessaly (including the Petra and the Volustana), Tempe is the most easily defended, but it can also be outflanked. Alexander's motive is unclear, whether he was acting as Xerxes' agent in getting rid of a potentially troublesome force, or whether, having advised Xerxes on how best to circumambulate Tempe, he was secretly playing the double agent by warning the Greeks of the Persian plan. He may, in fact, as a Persian subject/ally, have wished to avoid a confrontation with the Greeks, with some of whom he already had good relations. In any case, the way into Greece was now unrestricted, and Alexander disappears from our evidence until his mission to Athens during the following winter.

The message at Tempe was not Alexander's first contact with the Greeks. In the winter of 480/79, Mardonius would send the Macedonian as an envoy to Athens in an attempt to persuade the Athenians to make peace with the Great King (Hdt. 8.136, 140; Paus. 7.25.6). In the course of his speech Alexander personally advised the Athenians that Xerxes's power was enormous, and that Athens risked destruction. He reminded the Athenians of his goodwill toward them, for which there was precedent. Mardonius chose Alexander as the messenger partly because he was related to the Persians through his sister Gygaea's marriage to Bubares, and partly because he had learned that Alexander was already *proxenos* and *euergetēs* at Athens. These titles, for which there are no exact modern equivalents, may be translated as "patron" (or "public friend") and "benefactor." At Athens the titles were occasionally awarded to a foreigner as a honor for having performed a service that had benefited the city.[24]

Now, one wonders what service might have gained for the king of Macedon such honors among the Athenians. It is possible that the Athenians had offered these titles in recognition of Alexander's assistance several months earlier at the Vale of Tempe; one of the Greek commanders at Tempe was Themistocles, the architect of Athens's defense policy.[25] And at Athens, Alexander's expression of concern and his arguments about the size and power of the Persian force echo the message of his envoys at Tempe. Was Alexander's contact with the Greeks at Tempe (either acting on his own or as an agent of Mardo-

[24] For discussion, see M. B. Walbank, *Athenian Proxenies*, 2–9.

[25] Cole, "Alexander Philhellene and Themistocles," makes a case for a strong personal link between the two men, who saw in one another a kindred spirit and mutual political benefit.

nius) the reason for his Athenian honors, incidentally prompting Mardonius to send him on this second mission?

It is more likely that Alexander had been honored with this special status for some more grand service, akin to that which would be rendered by his grandson Archelaus, who would receive the same honors, some seventy years later: the provision of Macedonian timber to satisfy Athenian naval needs.[26] The Themistoclean naval program of 482–480 at Athens required timber of such quality and quantity as few places could provide. Macedon, renowned for the excellence of its wood and pitch, was well suited to supply the necessary materials. Recent views that Macedon, a vassal-state, could hardly have provided timber for Persia's enemies must be discounted.[27] Until Xerxes' invasion, Persian operations were confined to the coasts of Thrace and Chalcidice, regions outside Macedonian rule. The fact that the timber resources of the Strymon basin were under nominal Persian control is irrelevant, as the main source of timber for the Macedonians at this time would have been the Olympus-Pierian mountains above the Pierian coastal plain, rich in a variety of woods—a region that could have been harvested without Persian knowledge. Moreover, we have no evidence that Macedon's relationship with the Persians precluded the Macedonians from trading at will, although it does not seem likely that the Great King would approve the provision of timber to the city that had joined in the burning of Sardis, killed Persian envoys, and humiliated the Persian army at Marathon. This might explain Themistocles's ruse (Hdt. 7.144; Plut. *Them.* 4.1–2) in proposing a naval program for an Aeginetan, rather than Persian, war: it may have been as much an effort to deflect Persian suspicion as it was an attempt to persuade recalcitrant fellow citizens to build a fleet. Finally, it is possible that Macedon's status as a client-kingdom, which it had held since 492, had lapsed with the death of Darius and the accession of Xerxes, and was not reinstated until the time of Xerxes' invasion.[28] It is unlikely that Macedonian kings signed all treaties in perpetuity, and whatever the Persian attitude toward the permanence of their vassal-

[26] On the honors accorded Alexander I and Archelaus, see Walbank, *Athenian Proxenies*, nos. 1 and 90, and Tod *GHI*, no. 91 (Archelaus). For a description of fifth-century Athens's naval timber needs, see Borza, "Timber and Politics," 34–35.

[27] For the objections to Macedon as the source for Athenian timber, see Meiggs, *Trees and Timber*, 123–26.

[28] Following a suggestion proposed by Wallace, "Early Greek *Proxenoi*," 199–200, and more recently argued anew by Gerolymatos, "The *proxenia* of Alexandros I of Makedonia," who sees Alexander as sufficiently independent following Darius's death in 486 to provide timber and accept the honor of *proxenia*.

state relationships, the rulers of Macedon may have not seen it the same way. There are thus no major obstacles against the likelihood that, among Alexander's prohellenic and pro-Athenian services, his timber grants to help build the Athenian fleet in the late 480s may have contributed to his receipt of honors at Athens.

There is more. Herodotus tells of Alexander's activities on two other occasions. On the eve of the battle of Plataea (9.44–45), a lone horseman emerged from the darkness of no-man's-land, approached the Athenian sentries, and asked for an audience with their generals. The Athenian commanders arrived straightaway, and the visitor announced that his mission was secret and that he had risked coming over from the Persian lines for the sake of Greece, as he himself was by descent a Greek and did not wish to see Greece enslaved. He then provided information about Mardonius's plan to attack at dawn, and disappeared again into the night, identifying himself in parting as "Alexander the Macedonian." The Greeks took their counsel in light of Alexander's information and revised their own strategy.

The story is suspect on several grounds, including the common-sensical unlikelihood of the king of Macedon himself making his way across uncertain ground at night, the speech's Greek sentiments about patriotism and freedom, and the fact that there is no response from the Athenian side (the speech is a monologue). Moreover, the story does not square with the description of the opening of the battle (9.47–48): at dawn—at the very moment that Mardonius was supposed to attack—the Greeks began shifting battalions to different positions on the field, hardly a sound maneuver in the face of an imminent offensive. And, rather than attack the Greeks during this confusion (which any sensible commander would have done to his own advantage), Mardonius is said to have transferred some of his own troops as a response, causing the Greeks to move back into their original positions. The whole story is just short of absurd. However enigmatic these dawn maneuvers may be, the tale of Alexander seems separate, as if from a different, non-Athenian source. It is quite likely derived from Alexander himself.[29]

Following the improbable tale of Alexander's conspiracy to murder the Persian envoys (Hdt. 5.18–21; see above), Herodotus (5.22) adds an afterthought, that the Macedonian royal house is descended from Greeks, as "they themselves say," as he believes and will write more

[29] For Alexander at Plataea and at the Olympic Games, I have revised slightly my views expressed earlier in "Athenians, Macedonians, and the Macedonian Royal House," 9–11.

about later.[30] Continuing, Herodotus offers as evidence of Alexander's Hellenic monarchy the tale of the king's attempt to compete in the Olympic Games. When his fellow contestants objected to his presence as a competitor on the grounds that he was not Greek, he proved his Argive descent, and was permitted to enter, where he tied for first in the stade race.

Much has been written about this passage in recent years, with considerable attention focused on the date of Alexander's participation.[31] The stade race is a young man's event, and an earlier date (it has been assumed that in 496 Alexander would have been in his mid-thirties) suits the event better; even in his mid-thirties Alexander was at an advanced age for a sprinter.[32] Though the panhellenic fervor of the Games of 476 may suit the circumstances of admitting a foreign king on the grounds of his services in the recent anti-Persian effort, Alexander would in that year have been much too old for the stade race.

Other problems remain. For example, nothing certain is known about Alexander's age. Making him about thirty-five in 496 is pure guesswork. If one accepts the submission of Amyntas and the date of Gygaea and Bubares's marriage at *ca.* 510, putting Alexander in his mid-teens at this time, he would be in his late twenties in 496, a difficult, but not impossible, age for the stade race.[33] But if one regards the tale of the ill-fated Persian embassy as unhistorical, the whole basis for dating Alexander's participation in the Games on the criterion of age collapses. For example, Alexander might well have been no older than twenty at the time of his accession, nearly prime for competition in the stade race of 496 (the games of 492–480 being unlikely for political and military reasons). And in 476, at the age of about forty, he might have been honored with a special race as recognition of his prohellenic wartime service. If the latter were the case, however, the objections of the other athletes would likely not have arisen. Thus far, we have succeeded only in substituting one line of guesswork for another.

Herodotus's story is fraught with too many difficulties to make

[30] This is probably a reference to his description of the early Argeads at 8.137–39; see Chapter 4.

[31] E.g., Badian, "Greeks and Macedonians," 34–35 (476 B.C.) and Hammond, *HM* 2: 60 (496 B.C.). Hammond's effort to make Alexander compete in the pentathlon as well, based on an enigmatic passage in Justin (7.2.14) and a fragment of a Pindaric eulogy, is unconvincing to me.

[32] Roos, "Alexander I in Olympia," 167. Roos's article demonstrates clearly how many unanswered (and unanswerable) questions can be associated with Herodotus's tale.

[33] Hammond (*HM* 2: 60) makes Gygaea older than Alexander; I cannot find evidence to support this.

sense of it. For example, either (1) Alexander lost the run-off for his dead heat, which is why his name does not appear in the victor lists;[34] or (2) he won the run-off, although Herodotus does not tell us this; or (3) it remained a dead heat, which is implausible in light of Olympic practice; or (4) it was a special race, in which case it is unlikely that his fellow competitors would have protested Alexander's presence; or (5) Alexander never competed at Olympia. It is best to abandon this story, which belongs in the category of the tale of Alexander at Plataea. In their commentaries on these passages, Macan and How and Wells long ago recognized that the Olympic Games story was based on family legend (Hdt. 5.22: "as the descendants of Perdiccas themselves say [*autoi legousi*]"), weak proofs of their Hellenic descent. Moreover, the Olympic Games tale is twice removed: Herodotus heard from the Argeadae (perhaps from Alexander himself) that the king had told something to the judges, but we do not know what those proofs were.

The theme of the Olympic and Plataea incidents is the same: "I am Alexander, a Greek," which seems to be the main point. The more credible accounts of Alexander at Tempe and at Athens do not pursue this theme; they state Alexander's activities without embellishment or appeal to prohellenism. Morever, the insistence that Alexander is a Greek, and descended from Greeks, rubs against the spirit of Herodotus 7.130, who speaks of the Thessalians as the first Greeks to come under Persian submission—a perfect opportunity for Herodotus to point out that the Macedonians were a non-Greek race ruled over by Greek kings, something he nowhere mentions. In sum, it would appear that the Olympia and Plataea incidents—when taken together with the tale of the ill-fated Persian embassy to Amyntas's court in which Alexander proclaims the Greek descent of the royal house—are part of Alexander's own attempts to integrate himself into the Greek community during the postwar period. They should be discarded both because they are propaganda and because they invite suspicion on the general grounds outlined above. Herodotus transmitted some perfectly acceptable historical material concerning the activity of Alexander I during the Persian Wars, but the accounts of the king's message at Plataea, his participation at the Olympic Games, and the Hellenic lineage of his family are not among them.

One final observation following from this: The Macedonian royal house that in some respects would become quite highly hellenized by the time of Philip II and Alexander the Great found itself in the early to mid-fifth century having to plead with Greeks that it was

[34] Euseb. *Chron.* 1.203 (Schoene-Petermann ed.), and Moretti, *Olympionikai.*

of Greek descent. No Spartan or Athenian or Corinthian or Argive felt constrained to prove to the others that he and his family were Hellenes. But Macedonian kings seemed hard put to argue in behalf of their Hellenic ancestry in the fifth century B.C., and that circumstance is telling. Even if one were to accept that all the Herodotean stories about Alexander were true, why did the Greeks, who normally were knowledgeable about matters of ethnic kinship, not already know that the Macedonian monarchy was Greek? But—following Herodotus— the stade-race competitors at Olympia thought the Macedonian was a foreigner (Hdt. 5.22: *barbaros*). As we reject these stories, what becomes important is not whether the Macedonian royal family in fact were of Greek descent—and we have seen how tenuous is the evidence for this—but that the king of Macedon clearly wanted the Greek world to think so. One wonders why Alexander felt this was necessary, as he had already been honored at Athens while the war was still on, presumably for some friendly service such as supplying timber. The answer must lie with Alexander's postwar efforts to become more closely associated with some of his southern neighbors, perhaps as an effort to gain allies in the Macedonian competition against Athens for control of the territories east of the Strymon River. The result was a major change in Macedonian history, as the kingdom of the Argeads commenced a course of activity that would inextricably link Macedon with the history of the Greek city-states.

For his efforts on behalf of the Greek cause against the Persians Alexander is known to history as the "Philhellene." The earliest references to Alexander "the Philhellene" are quite late.[35] There is no contemporary evidence (e.g., Herodotus or his generation) for the use of the epithet, and it would be odd to call a Greek a "friend of Greece (or Greeks)." It is a title normally reserved for non-Greeks. The attempts of some modern writers to make "Philhellene" a synonym for "Hellene" have not been successful.

We may thus summarize Alexander's activities during the Persian advance into Europe as follows: Alexander submitted to Mardonius in 492. We do not know whether his vassalage survived the death of Darius in 486. He probably supplied timber to the Athenians in 482–480, for which he was awarded honors at Athens by 480. He was in submission to Xerxes in that year, either anew or as the result of continued vassalage since 492. He sent a message of warning to the Greeks at Tempe in 480, either as an agent of Xerxes or acting as a double agent.

[35] Evidence cited in Hammond, *HM* 2: 101 and n. 3; also see Badian, "Greeks and Macedonians," 46 n. 19.

During the winter of 480/79 he was sent by Mardonius as an envoy to plead with the Athenians to negotiate a peace with Xerxes. He fought as a Persian ally at Plataea. It is prudent to reject the stories of the ill-fated Persian embassy to Amyntas's court, Alexander's midnight ride at Plataea, and his participation in the Olympic Games as tales derived from Alexander himself (or from some official court version of things). All three stories are improbable on general grounds and all have a common thread: they are designed to create a Hellenic descent for Alexander, and probably originated during the postwar period, although it is impossible to be certain about their gestation (see below, p. 122) and the circumstances of their transmission to Herodotus.

After the death of Mardonius and the collapse of the Asian expeditionary force at Plataea, the Persians began their retreat from Europe. Herodotus is silent about Alexander's association with the Persians during their withdrawal through his kingdom. It may have been impossible for Alexander to have returned to Macedonia from Plataea in time make contact with the retiring Persian forces.[36] The remnants of the Persian army, led by Artabazus, wasted no time, and their flight from Thessaly through Macedonia towards Thrace followed the shortest inland route.[37] There is no evidence that any Asian troops remained in Macedonia, although some Persian sick appear to have been left behind during the withdrawal (Hdt. 8.115). It appears that the Thracian region was the Persian base (lending some support to the view that the Macedonian kingdom was not part of the Persian imperial system that included Thrace), and it was there that some Persian garrisons remained in strength for over a decade more.

The ambivalence of Alexander during the period of the Persian invasion is noteworthy. Technically a Persian subject/ally (probably since 492), he would have been pledged to uphold Persian interests in Europe. But by 482–480, he had already demonstrated his willingness to assist Athens in the matter of providing ship timber, an act contrary to Persian welfare. At Tempe his motives are unclear, although, as has been suggested above, he may have wished to avoid a military confrontation with the Greeks, some of whom were the very Athenians he had recently supplied with timber. At Plataea he could not avoid confrontation with the Athenians against whom he was arrayed (Hdt. 9.31), and the improbable story of his midnight ride may have been offered later to offset his role as a Persian military ally.

[36] Badian, "Greek and Macedonians," 44 n. 7.

[37] If Aeschy. *Persae* 494 is correct, this route followed the Lake Corridor into the lower Strymon basin and past Mt. Pangaion. See Appendix B below, pp. 289–90.

What lay behind Alexander's policy can only be guessed at. The study of history seeks order from events, and the historian is made uncomfortable by the lack of information concerning the king's motives. Setting aside as unedifying the possibility that Alexander's activities are completely irrational, one can only speculate that the king had already determined that the present and future of Macedon rested with some accommodation with the Greeks, although it would go too far to say that in the 480s he recognized in Athens a future greatness of which the Athenians themselves were not yet aware. Yet the realities of the present suggested a prudent accommodation with Persian hegemony in the north. The latter was acceptable: there is no evidence that Persian rule weighed heavily on Macedon. Indeed, Alexander seems to have operated rather freely, if not flamboyantly, as a Persian subject. And his relations with the Persians remained sound.[38] There is no evidence of hostility. Mardonius's willingness to entrust to the king the role of go-between in dealing with Greeks suggests as much a Persian ability to exploit Macedonian ambivalence as it does the Macedonian policy of coddling each side without antagonizing the other. Herodotus twice mentions Macedonians in the Persian army—once generally (7.185) and once specifically at Plataea (9.31)—and Macedonian agents were entrusted to oversee the loyalty of the Boeotian towns that had medized (Hdt. 8.34). The Macedonians were willing and useful Persian allies. The kingdom of Macedon lay in the crossfire between the Greek and Persian worlds. Macedonian kings—here Alexander, and later his son Perdiccas (who would himself be caught between Athenian and Spartan ambitions in the north)—learned to play both ends against the middle.

Conflict in the North

Part of the answer to the question of Alexander's ambivalence may lie in the area east of the Strymon, a region in which Greeks, Thracians, and Persians had already established their interests, and where mineral wealth might prove attractive to a manipulative, clever, and ambitious Macedonian king. This is not to say that Alexander had conceived a far-reaching plan for his eastern frontier. It is only to suggest that he acted so as neither to jeopardize his personal authority nor to destabilize his territorial claims, yet at the same time to allow for exploitation

[38] Justin's comment (7.4.1) that, shortly after Salamis, Xerxes granted Alexander the territory between the Olympus and Haemus ranges should be dismissed on the grounds of geographical, motivational, and chronological implausibility, not the least of which is that the king of the Macedonians already ruled over much of this territory.

of the continuing changes of circumstances in the northern Aegean. To understand this in context, we need to return to the first expressions of Greek interest in the north.

The widespread Greek colonization movement in the northern Aegean has been described elsewhere,[39] and was limited mainly to Thrace east of the Strymon. The evidence for these Greek settlements is largely archaeological. The literary references are occasional and unsystematic, primarily Herodotus and a handful of later sources. Until the recovery of a much fuller archaeological record from both the Greek and the Thracian sides, it will not be possible to write the history of Greek settlement in the region in the late Archaic and early Classical periods.[40] It is clear, however, that most Greek outposts, settled by both mainlanders and islanders (most notably the Parians at Thasos), were located in the coastal areas. There were at least three settlements in the lower Strymon. The river valley route itself seems not to have been much used, even though it provides adequate access into the interior of the Balkans through the passable Rupel gap in the Rhodopi Mountains. The Greeks apparently were not interested in the interior, both because of their natural inclination to settle in proximity to the sea and because the Thracian tribes who controlled the region resisted attempts to establish major towns beyond the coast.

It was into this setting that the Athenian tyrant Peisistratus emerged during his second exile from Athens, *ca.* 556–546 B.C. His political ambitions in Athens blocked by the opposition of clan coalitions, Peisistratus established himself in Macedonia at Rhaecalus on the eastern side of the Thermaic Gulf, which was as yet outside the Macedonian *imperium*.[41] Peisistratus's base in exile was Eretria, and his continued association with the Eretrians, who had founded Methone in Pieria (within sight of Rhaecalus across the Thermaic Gulf), may have whetted his interest in the north. No information survives about possible contacts between Peisistratus and the Macedonian king, and one can only speculate about the nature of an association that may have prompted King Amyntas to offer a grant of land to Peisistratus's son Hippias nearly half a century later (see below). Rhaecalus was probably

[39] See above, note 4.

[40] As made clear by Isaac in the introduction to the most current and comprehensive account of the movement, *Greek Settlements in Thrace*.

[41] Arist. *AP* 15.2. The exact location of Rhaecalus is not known, but it was probably close by Cape Megalo Karaburnu at the northern end of the Thermaic Gulf; see Charles F. Edson, "Notes on the Thracian *Phoros*," 88–91. Edson (91) suggests that this was "the first decisive intervention of the resources of the Macedonian area into the history of Athens."

not a *polis*, but a fortified outpost. Its history was brief, and it is not mentioned further, having served mainly as a temporary and secure refuge while Peisistratus plotted his next move. What may have seemed to the Eretrians and Methoneans a suitable site for a colony was probably of little attraction to an Athenian aristocrat determined to return to the political fray at home.[42]

Now sensing an opportunity to acquire the movable wealth necessary to finance his political ambitions in Athens, Peisistratus went east into the region around Mt. Pangaion. We do not know if Peisistratus settled anyone in the Pangaion–lower Strymon area. There is no evidence of conflict with Thracians or Greeks, but that may indicate only that his activity was not a threat to those who were already established. In the *Athenaion Politeia* Aristotle makes it clear that Peisistratus hired troops and became rich, then returned south in the eleventh year of his exile to the eventual establishment of his tyranny at Athens. Peisistratus's mercenaries were probably Thracian, and the money he acquired and would continue to earn even after his return (Hdt. 1.64) may have resulted from business interests, perhaps as a middle man in contact with local miners.[43] His success in the north likely drew Athenian attention for the first time to the rich north Aegean littoral,[44] and laid the basis for the eventual conflict between Athenians and Macedonians over the resources of the region.

The first known contact between the Argead monarchy and Athens occurred *ca.* 510 B.C., when the Peisistratids were expelled from Athens during the political competition that eventually brought Cleisthenes's faction to power. For reasons we can only guess at, King Amyntas offered to Hippias, son of Peisistratus, the region of Anthemus (Hdt. 5.94), a fertile valley and adjacent wooded slopes that run inland from the Thermaic Gulf in the northwesternmost part of Chalcidice.[45] The only certainty is that Anthemus was Amyntas's to offer,

[42] For Peisistratus in the north there are useful discussions in Hodlofski, "Macedonian Relations with Athens to 413 B.C.," 4–10; Cole, "Peisistratus on the Strymon"; and Dusing, "The Athenians and the North in Archaic Times," 57–68.

[43] After Best, *Thracian Peltasts*, 5–7, and Isaac, *Greek Settlements in Thrace*, 14–15. Dusing ("The Athenians and the North in Archaic Times," 60–64 and 68) argues not only that Peisistratus was actually involved in the mining operations and the continued importation of Thracian precious metals into Athens, but that the introduction of coinage into Athens was the result of his northern experiences.

[44] As tyrant, Peisistratus sent Miltiades north to establish a presence in the Thracian Chersonese (Hdt. 6.34–37), and thereby initiated a continuing Athenian interest in the region that would last for the next century and a half. There is a vast bibliography on the subject, but now see Isaac, *Greek Settlements in Thrace*, ch. 4.

[45] For details see Hammond, *HM* 1: 190–91. The district of Athemus seems to have

acquired rather recently among the earliest trans-Axios conquests, along with Mygdonia and parts of Crestonia (Thuc. 2.99.5–6). The proposal to the exiled Hippias may signify the renewal of an earlier association between Amyntas's predecessor and Peisistratus (Rhaecalus may have been located in coastal Anthemus), or it might mark an independent decision on Amyntas's part to establish for the first time a Macedonian link with a prominent Athenian. If the latter, Macedon's Athenian policy would undergo an abrupt reversal between Amyntas's offer to the exiled Peisistratid Hippias and King Alexander's assistance in the late 480s to an Athens that seemed obsessed with the fear of a Peisistratid return. It may thus be shown that Alexander's reign marked a new orientation in Macedonian foreign policy, characterized by a drift toward Athens, but without the shock of having to cut loose from Persian ties. Perhaps the death of Darius I and the accession of Xerxes in 486 enabled Alexander to take Macedonian policy in the new direction.

It is impossible to know what role the Persians, who supported the Peisistratids, played in the matter, although such a grant of land to Hippias would have met with no objection from the Persians, now ensconced in eastern Thrace. In the end, Hippias rejected the offer and settled at Sigeum, closer to his Persian base of support. A renewed Athenian interest in the Strymon may have occurred after the battle of Marathon. In 489 Miltiades had persuaded the Athenians to support an expedition of 70 ships to secure gold from some unnamed land (Hdt. 6.132). Although the expedition ended quickly after an unsuccessful siege of Paros, its object may have been the Strymon-Pangaion area, for which the attack on Paros was only preliminary.[46] If Miltiadess' goal was the north, it was a demonstration of renewed Athenian concern about mineral resources more than half a century after Peisistratus

---

been some sort of royal preserve at least down to the time of Philip II, who ceded it to the Olynthians (Dem. 6.20).

[46] Following Isaac (*Greek Settlements in Thrace*, 18–19), who revives an older argument that Miltiades' vague post-Marathon expedition to the Cyclades, which ended in failure at Paros, did not have the islands as the goal. The object was to secure gold, and the islands are geologically barren of gold. But Paros was the colonizer of Thasos, and perhaps a stage toward the ultimate goal, which was to seize the mines of Thrace. By the early fifth century, these mines had become a strong attraction to those who sought liquid wealth (see Ehrenberg, "Early Athenian Colonies," 141–42). The attempt by modern scholars to establish a link between Paros and the northern mines is tenuous at best, but one still wonders why Miltiades moved on metal-poor Paros if, as Herodotus says, his goal was gold; there might have been an unknown-to-us Parian-northern connection. If, however, gold was only an excuse to provide Miltiades with a command, the issue disappears.

first ventured there. Thus by the time of the Persian withdrawal into
Thrace a decade later, the Greeks, including the Athenians, had already
made clear their interest in the mineral resources of the northern Aegean lands.

The stage was now set for a competition among Greeks and between
Greeks and Macedonians in the lands east of the Strymon. It was a
rivalry made possible partly by the weakening of Thracian tribal authority during the Persian occupation, by the growth in the military
power of some Greek states, notably Athens, and by the ambitions of
the king of Macedon. The earliest manifestation of Alexander's policy
was along Macedon's eastern frontier. The boundary had been vague,
with Macedonian influence extending into Crestonia and parts of
Chalcidice. The Bisaltae, who inhabited Crestonia, the hilly region between the Axios plain and the Strymon valley, were among the Thracians who had refused to submit to Xerxes (Hdt. 8.116) and had fled
into the Rhodopi Mountains. Alexander took advantage of their dis-
persion and moved into their lands, thereby acquiring control over the
silver mines of Mt. Dysoron, said to have yielded him a talent a day.[47]
These Crestonian mines, along with those acquired later in the Pan-
gaion-Philippi region, produced silver and gold sufficient to sustain
fine local coinages, support the ambitions of Macedonian monarchs
from Alexander I to Perseus, and, of course, make the region attractive
to foreigners who recognized it as one of the most important precious-
metal resources of the eastern Mediterranean.

Thus far relations between Macedon and Athens had been friendly.
Athens had respected Macedonian hegemony in the Thermaic Gulf,
and Macedon's own interests in the northwestern periphery of Chalcidice were not in conflict with Greek colonization in the southern
parts of that peninsula. It was to be in the lower Strymon valley that
the problem would arise, both because of Athenian ambitions and because Alexander was expressing himself in an assertive manner that
would come to characterize many of his descendants on the throne of
the Argeadae. In 476 Cimon, son of Miltiades, led an Athenian expedition to seize Eion at the mouth of the Strymon.[48] Eion had been a
vital Persian supply base in the area, and one could see in this campaign

[47] Thuc. 2.99.4–6; Hdt. 5.17. Even under Macedonian control the Bisaltae retained
their ethnicity into Roman times; Livy 44.45.8; 45.29.7, 30.3. For the location of the
Dysoron mines, see Borza, "Natural Resources," 10 n. 21.

[48] Thuc. 1.98.1; Hdt. 7.107; Plut. *Cimon* 7.2–8.3; additional evidence in Isaac, *Greek
Settlements in Thrace*, 19, n. 92. For a description of Eion (which has never been excavated) and an account of its strategic importance, see Isaac, *Greek Settlements in Thrace*,
60–62.

an aspect of Athenian policy directed at clearing from the soil of Europe the remaining Persian bitter-enders. After a difficult siege, Eion fell. The local Thracians at Eion and in the nearby countryside perhaps as far as the site of Amphipolis three or four miles to the north were expelled, and the area was resettled with Athenians. The capture of and settlement at Eion generated enormous enthusiasm at Athens,[49] and it was clear that the reduction of Persian military power in the north was not the sole motivation for Athenian activity in the lower Strymon. Very soon Eion became an emporium and Athenian base.

Themistocles, the architect of Athens's defense against Xerxes' invasion, went into a political eclipse in Athens shortly after the Persian defeat, and the reasons for his collapse are not entirely clear. What is apparent is that in the immediate postwar period, Athenian politics reverted to their normal intense clan rivalry, and Themistocles, who sometimes was more slippery than usual for an Athenian politician, lost ground to the family of Miltiades and Cimon. Whether postwar policy in the north was an issue in the political competition cannot be said with certainty.[50] But Alexander, whose dealings with an Athens under Themistocles's influence had been mutually beneficial, was probably uneasy with Cimon's establishment of an Athenian outpost at the mouth of the Strymon. Moreover, now that Alexander's window into Athens was closing with the decline of Themistocles's influence, the king's relationship with Athens began to deteriorate. With Themistocles's exile from Athens *ca.* 471, there may have been no one to act on the Macedonian's behalf in matters that affected Athenian activity in the north.

It is unknown whether Alexander continued to supply timber for Athens's maritime needs. With the acquisition of the Dysoron mines, Macedon was no longer so dependent upon timber sales as a source of revenue. Both the excellent quality of Macedonian silver coinage from the mid-fifth century and Alexander's dedication of a gold statue of himself at Delphi testify to royal wealth.[51] Alexander's statue at Delphi represented something else: a celebration of his seizure of the Strymon crossing at Ennea Hodoi ("Nine Ways"), near the site of the future Amphipolis. Whether this action immediately preceded or followed Cimon's capture of Eion is a matter of debate, and the fourth-century protagonist of the source attributed to Demosthenes (12.21) argues that the Macedonians had historical priority in the settlement of the

---

[49] Isaac, *Greek Settlements in Thrace*, 20–21, for evidence.

[50] Cole, "Alexander Philhellene and Themistocles," 45–46, suggests that it may have been an important matter.

[51] Hdt. 8.121; Dem. 12.20.

area around Amphipolis.[52] It is a matter of some interest insofar as it indicates which of the two parties, Athens or Macedon, initiated post-war military action in the lower Strymon; one presumably would argue that the other's expedition in the area was thereby a justifiable and precautionary response. It has also been argued that both were rival attempts to control the exit of the Strymon basin.[53] Taken in this sense, a clash between the two powers would seem virtually inevitable.

Yet the rivalry that did in fact eventuate may not have been either premeditated or preordained. Alexander's actions in seizing the main crossing leading into his newly acquired frontier in Crestonia was sound strategy, the equivalent of taking control of the passes leading into Emathia at Edessa and Veria or into the lower Axios valley at the Demir Kapu gorges. Alexander showed no apparent interest in the sea, but real concern in securing the main inland route from the east. The Athenians, however, manifested abundant preoccupation with the sea, and spent much of the 470s in reducing Persian naval threats and in establishing a maritime defensive league. In the lower Strymon valley the powers' perhaps unrelated interests clashed, and policies that might have been initiated for separate reasons took on new meaning, leaving an impression among some of the sources that the ultimate object was no different from the original goal (e.g., Plut. *Cimon* 7). Only in the case of the Athenians, with their long economic involvement with the area, may the motives have been mixed.

By the early 460s the lines between Athens and Macedon were drawn. Themistocles, now in exile and on the run,[54] arrived in the north, where Alexander gave him sanctuary at Pydna (Thuc. 1.137.1–2; Plut. *Them.* 25–26), may have seen him at Aegae, and provided him with a ship to Asia. Cole has tried to show that Alexander and Themistocles had conspired to create a "third force" to counter Athens and Sparta, and that Themistocles had at one point persuaded Alexander

---

[52] E.g., Hammond, *HM* 2: 102, puts Alexander's capture of Ennea Hodoi between 478 and Cimon's campaign at Eion in 476/5, but his main argument seems to be that, had the Persians still held Ennea Hodoi in 476/5, they would have come to the relief of their commander, Boges, at Eion. There are other problems connected with the evidence for Alexander at Ennea Hodoi; see Cole, "Not Alexander But Perdikkas (Dem. 23.200 and 13.24)," although I am inclined to accept that Demosthenes made a slip by referring to Perdiccas's rather than Alexander's action against the Persians.

[53] As in Hammond, *HM* 2: 102.

[54] The dates of Themistocles' activities in exile are problematic, with a growing literature; e.g., Cole, "Alexander Philhellene and Themistocles," 45–47, with relevant bibliography and sources. Cole connects Themistocles' actions in the Peloponnese with Alexander's having provided refuge for a number of Mycenaeans, displaced by an Argive attack on their city (Paus. 7.25.6).

122   CHAPTER 5

to support the democratic faction in Argos. There is no proof, but the
suggestion raises the possibility that this may have been the origin of
Alexander's attempt to provide his family with a Greek Argive lineage.

It was all for nothing. Themistocles's career in Greece was finished,
and he was sent packing. Alexander faced problems of quite immediate
concern at his doorstep. For reasons unknown, Macedon had lost control of Ennea Hodoi to the Thracian Edoni, the original settlers before
the Persian occupation.[55] There seems to have been a Thracian revival
of sorts in the lower Strymon, and the reduction in the quality of Macedonian coins may suggest a more restricted access to Alexander's
sources of silver.[56] The Athenians, however, continued their pressure
in the north. About 465, Thasos rebelled from the Delian League, pro-
voking the commitment of a large Athenian force to the island. At
least part of the quarrel concerned commercial and mining interests on
the Thracian mainland (Diod. 11.70.1; Thuc. 1.100.2). At the same
time, and while the Athenian siege of Thasos was underway (it would
last for nearly three years), some 10,000 Athenian settlers were sent to
Ennea Hodoi. This was exactly the kind of major settlement of the area
that the Thracians, who had tolerated both Persian garrisons and Athenian emporia, traditionally resisted.

Ennea Hodoi was settled, but at Drabescus, further inland, the
Athenians (or some of them) were annihilated by a strong combined
Thracian force.[57] Cimon's siege of Thasos was successful, however,
and in 463, the Thasians surrendered. The Athenians took both the
city and the opposite mainland territory controlled by Thasos, including mines and emporia.[58] When Cimon returned home he was prose-
cuted for not following up on his victory by using the newly acquired
mainland territory as a base for an invasion of Macedonia. His failure
thus to cut off a great part of the Macedonian territory was laid to his
having been bribed by King Alexander (Plut. *Cimon* 14.2–3). Setting
aside that Alexander likely was perfectly capable of offering such a
bribe, the charge itself is a product of anti-Cimonian politics at home.

[55] Thuc. 1.100.3; Diod. 11.70.5.

[56] Price, *Coins* 19, and Hammond, *HM* 2: 114, but with the caution that the total
number of surviving examples of coins from all these remote periods is probably an
insufficient statistical base from which to draw conclusions on the evidence of coins
alone.

[57] This disaster has been much discussed. Main sources are Thuc. 1.100.3; Hdt. 9.75;
Diod. 11.70.5, 12.68.2; Paus. 1.29.4. Succinct discussion of main problems and relevant
bibliography in Isaac, *Greek Settlements in Thrace*, 24–30.

[58] Plut. *Cimon* 14.2 and Thuc. 1.100.2. The mines are probably those at Krenides and
at Skapte Hyle nearby, although the exact site of the latter is unknown.

The mainland territory acquired from Thasos was too far east to be a base for an invasion of the kingdom of Macedon. Between it and the Macedonian frontier along the Strymon lay those very powerful Thracian tribes that had just destroyed the Athenian settlements around Ennea Hodoi, the gateway into Macedon. If, indeed, it was part of the original Athenian plan to invade Macedon, Cimon's refusal must have resulted from the disaster at Ennea Hodoi, not from a failure to follow up from the mainland opposite Thasos. If that were the case, Cimon showed good strategic sense.

Yet the nature of the charge (even if bogus) against Cimon suggests something about public opinion in Athens. Why would Athenians now entertain the possibility of an invasion of Macedon, rather than merely a continuation of the rivalry in the Thracian territory east of the Macedonian frontier? If Athenian intentions reflected an economic imperialism in the region, the silver- and timber-rich Crestonian territory recently acquired by Alexander was sufficient motive. The economic imperative may have been intensified by Alexander's connection with the fugitive Themistocles, and at least one scholar has suggested a Macedonian involvement in the Thracian coalition that demolished the Athenian attempts to settle Ennea Hodoi and Drabescus.[59] Cimon was acquitted (just barely) of the capital charge, but was obligated to pay a fine of fifty talents.[60] Thus some Athenian ambitions in the region were frustrated by unexpected Thracian resistance and by Cimon's decision to return to Athens, although whether he was originally instructed to invade Macedon is obscured by the highly political nature of his trial. But Athens had gained its foothold in the mainland mining area opposite Thasos, it could trade through its emporia with Thracians and Macedonians for metals and timber, and its control over Eion gave it a gateway into the lower Strymon valley. Even though the Macedonians played only a slight role in these events, there can be no doubt that their king was apprehensive about future Athenian intentions along his eastern frontier.

Alexander's Macedonian Kingdom

One of the results of the confluence of activity in the north Aegean among Thracians, Persians, Greeks, and Macedonians was the emergence of Alexander's realm as the strongest state in the region. What

[59] Cole, "Alexander Philhellene and Themistocles," 48–49, and E. M. Walker, "The Confederacy of Delos," 58.

[60] Dem. 23.205; Plut. *Cimon* 15.1, *Per.* 10.5; Arist. *AP* 27.1. Also Raubitschek, "Theophrastos on Ostracism," 91 n. 7.

had been a backward feudal kingdom in the time of Amyntas had become under his son the most powerful monarchy in the Balkans. The
brief Persian hegemony in the Thraco-Macedonian mainland had cost
the Macedonians nothing beyond some troops furnished for the Persian military effort. Against that, Alexander may have profited from
the sale of timber to Athens and increased his wealth by exploiting the
turmoil in Thracian settlements caused by the Persian organization east
of the Strymon. Most notably, the Macedonians came to control the
mines of Crestonia abandoned by the Bisaltae after their refusal to submit to Persian rule.

Our sources, mainly concerned with Aegean affairs, provide little
information about events along the western frontier of the Macedonian
kingdom. At some point, perhaps in the period after the Persian withdrawal, Alexander fought against, defeated, and expelled the Eordi
from their land in the corridor west of Mt. Vermion.[61] The Argead
Macedonians were now in contact with some of the Macedonians of
the western mountains, who were forced to accept a vassalage with
which they never were comfortable. It is clear that these tribes retained
their own royal houses and considerable local autonomy. Their relationship with the lowlanders required them to sent levies of troops to
the Argeads when so called upon. But for at least the next century and
a half, the links between lower and upper Macedonians were tenuous
at best.[62] Despite the fact that Thucydides (2.99.3, 6) could now call
the whole area "Macedonia," the Argeads were not able to integrate
their highland kinsmen into the kingdom until the reign of Philip II,
and even then with only mixed success.

A stray piece of information assists us in understanding one aspect
of the relationship between the Argeadae and the mountain folk in the
west. A scholiast on Thucydides (1.57.3) mentions that the Elimiote
king Derdas was a cousin of Alexander I's sons, Perdiccas and Philip.
Elimeia, which lies south of Eordaea, and incorporates the great bend
of the Haliacmon and the routes south into Thessaly, was a natural
extension of Alexander's expansion into Eordaea. The evidence suggests a marriage connection between Alexander (or his sister) and the
royal family of Elimeia.[63] The use of marriage as a form of political
contract had begun (as far as we know) with the union of Alexander's

[61] Thuc. 2.99.5–6; 4.124.1. Here I follow Edson, "Early Macedonia," 27–28, with nn.
56 and 57, although I do not share his suggestion that Almopia was added at the same
time, preferring rather to attribute its annexation to an earlier expansion, perhaps under
Amyntas.
[62] For a detailed description of the ties between the Argeadae and the western Macedonians, see Bosworth, "Philip II and Upper Macedonia."
[63] Ibid., 100, and Hammond, HM 2: 18–19, with additional evidence cited.

sister Gygaea and the Persian Bubares. Now a connection was established with the ruling house of Elimeia, and marriages between Argeads and upper Macedonians, Greeks, and Balkan peoples would remain a feature of royal policy through the reign of Philip II. Whether Alexander's rule extended beyond the Bitola-Kozani corridor into the western Pindus ranges is not known, but it is clear that the kingdom of Emathia was now several times its original size as a result of the expansion into the western mountains and into the hills and plains east of the Axios River.

One assumes that Macedonian military power was up to the task of incorporating the new territories into the royal domain, but we are lacking in details. Indeed, we know almost nothing about the Macedonian army before the time of Philip. Most attempts to reconstruct the army of the fifth century B.C. are arguments back from Philip's time, and thereby risk anachronism. Without archaeology to provide examples or representations of weapons and armor, and without either archaeological or literary evidence sufficient to understand the social and political structure that supported an army, any attempt to assess the military organization of the early Macedonian kingdom is guesswork.

At Plataea—the earliest known engagement of Macedonian troops in Greece—the Macedonians were arrayed in the company of central and northern Greeks (Hdt. 9.31.2), who were probably lightly armed. But it is not clear whether Herodotus (or the Persians) arranged these allies geographically or by their weapons. Otherwise, except for garrison duty in Boeotian towns, the Macedonian army seems not to have been used by the Persians. We may fairly assume that Macedonian barons, like their kind in most European societies at an early stage of evolution, owned weapons that they were trained to use from horseback. These cavalry were later called *hetairoi*, or "companions" of the king, a social distinction as much as a description of how they fought. There is no evidence that there was a trained infantry, some equivalent of Thracian peltasts or Greek hoplites, both of whom were already noted for their skills in the early fifth century B.C. Macedonian foot soldiers may have been nothing more than a peasantry, armed with whatever weapons could be used effectively to hack at or bash the enemy, like their Homeric or medieval European counterparts. Recent attempts to make sense of a fragment of a fourth-century B.C. writer, Anaximenes of Lampsacus, who attributed to an "Alexander" the origin of the *pezetairoi* or "foot companions"—that is, trained infantry—have been disputatious.[64]

---

[64] E.g., Bosworth, "*ASTHETAIROI*," 245, who believes the reform must belong to

The division between foot and horse, or even which were considered the main strength of the army, is unknown. Evidence from the reign of King Perdiccas II later in the fifth century suggests that the Macedonians were not only deficient in trained infantry, but that the western Macedonians were supplying large contingents of cavalry both to the Argeadae and to their enemies.[65] Indeed, the mountain cantons would continue to be a major source of both cavalry and foot soldiers for Macedonian kings through the reign of Alexander the Great. One wonders if the military power of Argead kings existed mainly in proportion to their ability to maintain a satisfactory liaison with the Macedonians who lived in the west. Whatever the case, there is insufficient information to know whether the army of Alexander I, who was the first king tentatively to attempt an unification of the Macedonians, was reorganized along professional lines, or whether, as seems more likely, he continued to depend upon a baronial cavalry, untrained foot, and the occasional levies supplied by his western allies.

Clear evidence of the expression of new Macedonian power can be found in their coinage. The Macedonians' neighbors among the Chalcidic Greeks and the Thracians of the Strymon valley were among the first European peoples to issue coins.[66] A Lydian invention, the practice of stamping accurately weighed lumps of precious metal, spread to Ionia, and thence, by the middle of the sixth century B.C., to Thraco-Macedonia. Both the Greek cities of Chalcidice and the Thracian tribes began to produce coins, although it remains problematic whether the Chalcidic Greeks were inspired by the coin-issuing Euboeans who had established colonies in the region or by the nearby Thracians. The metallurgical skills and resources are probably local and Balkan. Among the Thracians some uniformity exists in the types and weights; whether the similarities stem from a monetary confed-

---

Alexander II (370–369/8); Brunt, "Anaximenes and King Alexander I of Macedon," who argues that Anaximenes incorrectly attributed the reform to Alexander I; and Hammond, *HM* 2: 705–13, who (in a thorough discussion) suggests that the honoring of the infantry as "foot companions" belonged to Alexander the Great. Hammond's account is the most persuasive on methodological and military grounds, even though conclusiveness is not possible. Also see the discussion of Philip II's military reforms, Chapter 9 below.

[65] Evidence gathered in Brunt, "Anaximenes and King Alexander I of Macedon," 151–52.

[66] What follows owes much to: Price, *Coins*, 2–19; Hammond, *HM* 2: 69–91 and 104–13; Kraay, *Archaic and Classical Greek Coins*, 139–43; and Price and Waggoner, *Archaic Greek Coinage*. My citation only of recent literature in no way diminishes the debt of all scholars to Svoronos (*L'hellénisme primitif*) and Raymond (*Macedonian Regal Coinage*; see Appendix A below, pp. 285–86), for their pioneering efforts to classify the northern coins.

eration, as some scholars have suggested, is uncertain.[67] As the sixth
century drew to a close the need to pay tribute to the Persians provided
an impetus for a standardization. And the unmistakable imprint of
Asian influence on the vessels recovered from excavations in Thrace
and as far west as Sindos suggests that trade with the East was not
negligible. Thus many coins adhere to an oriental standard, chosen to
facilitate contacts through the Persian Empire, within whose geographical frontiers so many of these coins have been recovered.

In addition to their utility as a medium of exchange, coins also serve
as a status symbol, although their use as propaganda devices in the
Greek world has probably been overemphasized in modern scholarship.[68] The design of coins could be enlarged and modified in keeping
with the political and cultural spirit of the times without affecting their
fundamental use, which was based on weight and purity of metal. The
earliest Thracian coins are small bits of electrum or silver stamped with
a rough square design made by the die punch. As coin designs became
more complex, these crude incuse squares became more sophisticated,
sometimes serving as borders for interior designs, sometimes taking
the form of swastikas, often subdivided diagonally or into four smaller
squares. The use of the incuse square on the reverse is a regular feature
of Thracian coins, while the obverse varies in accord with each tribe's
public symbols.

The earliest issues of Macedonian coins are problematic. Most numismatic opinion holds that the earliest Argead issues were struck *ca.*
490 B.C. as urban issues from Aegae, in the manner of the Thracian
town coins of Lete and Ichnae.[69] That the coins of Aegae are marked

[67] In favor of the existence of a monetary confederation are Price (*Coins* 3) and Raymond (*Macedonian Regal Coinage*, 47 and 59). Opposed is Hammond (*HM* 2: 81–82),
who argues that the idea of an alliance runs contrary to the historical evidence about the
relationships among the Thracian tribes, based on Thuc. 2.99, who paints a picture of
"war and deportation"; the coin resemblances are rather the result of cultural similarities.
One can only point out that the history of some fifth-century Greeks is also one of war
and deportation midst adherence to certain monetary standards. In the case of many
Greeks, both military alliances and monetary conformity existed, although the latter is
not necessarily a product of the former. Populations are perfectly capable of judging
what is in their own economic best interest without the requirement of a formal alliance:

[68] As has been persuasively argued recently by Martin, *Sovereignty and Coinage*; see
esp. 5–6 and 219ff. for summation of his thesis. Martin holds that the primary use of
coinage remained economic, and that the idea that they functioned primarily as political
symbols misrepresents their use. It is a matter of emphasis, and Martin's book, based
primarily on a study of Thessalian coinage of the fourth century B.C., is a salutary cor-
rective.

[69] E.g., Raymond (*Macedonian Regal Coinage*, 49), followed by Kraay (*Archaic and*

with a goat—etymologically (*aiges* = "goats") and mythologically associated with that town—has prompted most scholars to make this a coin from Aegae. Some of these coins have as an obverse device the symbol ⟳, taken as a retrograde abbreviation for Edessa. Raymond and Kraay held that Edessa was the old name for Aegae, but their work appeared before the archaeological discoveries at Vergina showed almost certainly that Aegae and Edessa were two different places.

Hammond, however, argues both that the oracles and the traditions (e.g., Just. 7.1.4–7) connecting goats with the founding of Aegae are later than the goat coins, and that the horse and the helmet, not the goat, are the marks typifying Alexander's coinage.[70] Hammond attributes all such goat/incuse square types to the Thracian Bisaltae, and has Alexander first issuing coins only after his seizure of the Bisaltic mines in the aftermath of Xerxes' withdrawal. Clearly one would be hard pressed to explain the Thracian incuse square on the reverse of a coin from distant Aegae. Yet Hammond's explanation for his assignment of these "goat staters" to the Bisaltae is not entirely satisfactory, and his views are compelling only if one assumes that Alexander did not replace a civic issue and local device with a national one celebrating his monarchy following the Persian Wars. Hammond's suggestion is not conclusive, but deserves consideration as an alternative to the conventional view. At present the question of whether the Macedonian king issued coinage before *ca.* 479 B.C. lies unresolved.

The links between the Thracians and Macedonians in the postwar period are somewhat clearer. Now in control of the Bisaltic mines of Mt. Dysoron, in the midst of a regional tradition of Thracian tribal issues, Alexander produced coins bearing the mark of their Thracian heritage and their present purpose. The incuse square was now a formal device around which Alexander, no longer a Persian subject, inscribed his name. The Thracians followed suit, with the coins of the Derrones, the Bisaltae, and the Orescii all suitably inscribed with their tribal names, in Greek letters. And in imitation of Alexander, one Thracian leader, known only from the coins, inscribed his incuse square with "Getas, king of the Edonians," in Greek.

This reconstruction represents a slight revision of the traditional view that the earliest Macedonian regnal issues were imitations of Thracian tribal coins. The discovery of the Asyut hoard in Egypt in 1969 added nearly 900 examples of late sixth- and early fifth-century

---

Classical Greek Coins, 141) and Price (*Coins* p. 9 and no. 17), a silver stater, incuse square on reverse, kneeling goat on obverse, also illustrated in *PM*, 44.

[70] *HM* 2: 81, 86, and 104–5. For the oracles, see my "Athenians, Macedonians, and the Macedonian Royal House," 12 and n. 23.

coins to the body available for study. Price and Waggoner have concluded that some of the Thracian coinages must now be downdated by
15–20 years.[71] If the new chronology holds, we must permit the possibility that the connection between the Thracian and Macedonian
coins was a two-way street. The impetus for coins and the adoption of
certain standards and types may have been Thracian in origin, but
would be imitated by Alexander in his civic issues from Aegae[72] and
by his regnal issues when he took control of the west bank of the Strymon in the wake of Xerxes' retreat. But in producing coins based on
Thracian models he took a step or two further, both by inscribing his
regnal signature on the incuse square and by providing an elaborately
designed obverse in accord with a high standard of Greek-influenced
workmanship. Although the Thracians continued to produce coins
well into the 470s and 460s, and although they adopted some of Alexander's innovations (such as inscriptions in Greek), the obverse designs
of their issues never achieved the quality of workmanship of their Macedonian counterparts. They remain "Thracian" in style, whereas the
Macedonian coinage is similar in its execution to the coins of the Greek
world.

The standards of these coinages, both Thracian and Macedonian, are
an enormously complex problem, perhaps the most difficult faced by
those who study the issues. We have already spoken of a uniformity in
weights and types, whether from a formal monetary confederation or
from an adherence to some cultural or economic imperative. Raymond
and Price saw the enormous variety of weights as an attempt to adhere
to both Asian and Greek standards, as well as to provide for local
needs. Hammond found this scheme unnecessary complex, and suggested that the early Macedonian coins represent a move away from an
Asian standard to conform to Greek ones.

It is a numismatists' dilemma, but in the end, the point is the same:
there is a recognition by these coin-issuing entities that the process of
exchange can be enhanced by adherence to some convenient standard.
Such exchange might include the payment of tribute to a distant Asian
king, or the trade of coins for some item of necessity or luxury. Most
coins of relative purity (some coins with a high content of base metal
were kept in local circulation) were used as bullion: it was their weight
in precious metal that counted. To inscribe such coins with the trappings of royalty and—by extension—nationhood was a gesture aimed

[71] Price and Waggoner, *Archaic Greek Coinage*, 28–29, 38–39, and 117–19.

[72] Ibid., 38–39; Price and Waggoner hold that some civic issues continued to be issued
from Aegae after the Persian Wars.

at the outside world. One of the king's most impressive issues, a huge silver octadrachm, portrays a mounted rider wearing the traditional Macedonian broad-brimmed hat (the *kausia*), holding spears, and sporting a cloth fillet, the distant precursor of the gilded diadem found in the fourth-century royal tomb at Vergina.[73] It is tempting in this issue to see a portrait of the king as hunter, one of the favorite themes of the Macedonian monarchy. Other coins of Alexander replaced the Thracian incuse square on the reverse with different devices: the head of a goat, a crested helmet, and the forepart of the lion.[74]

In addition to their economic value as a reliable currency, the well-crafted coins represent something else: decorated with a variety of Macedonian symbols and perhaps even a portrait of Alexander himself, they are clear evidence that the king of the Macedonians had assumed his place as a major figure in the eastern Mediterranean world. Indeed, this may help account for the existence of such large coins. Some of the great silver octadrachms of Alexander weigh nearly 30 grams, but no one has offered adequate economic reasons explaining why the Macedonians should issue such large coins. If these issues are correctly dated to the immediate post-Persian War period, there is no need for the coins as tribute, and there is insufficient evidence of trade that would require such heavy issues. We are forced to conclude that the significance of these monumental issues is related to their use as testimony to the self-proclaimed splendor of the Macedonian monarchy.

Moreover, it was to a Greek audience that Alexander intended to play. The prohellenic propaganda given to Herodotus was matched by Alexander dedicating a statue to himself at Delphi (or at Olympia, according to Solinus), thereby establishing a panhellenic link that would mark Macedonian royal policy into the era of Philip II and beyond. Pindar produced an encomium to Alexander in the mid-450s, and a late source hints at the king's patronage of writers as part

---

[73] Price, *Coins*, no. 18; Raymond, *Macedonian Regal Coinage*, nos. 109a and 110a; and a superbly illustrated example in *PM*, 29. For parallels from the Bisaltae and Edoni, see Price, *Coins*, nos. 14 and 16, and *PM*, 22. One curiosity: Alexander's great octadrachms clearly portray the central mounted figure as a hunter, yet the small dog that appears beneath the horse on some issues is a *melitaion*, similar to a modern Maltese. Dr. Linda Reilly, an expert in these matters, informs me that, in antiquity, this breed is normally shown playing with children or as a pet, but that the *melitaion* is not a hunting dog.

[74] The lion is often associated with Heracles, by now officially a progenitor of the royal house through Argos, and the helmet may be taken over from Thracian models; see Hammond, *HM* 2: 109–10. Examples in Raymond, *Macedonian Regal Coinage*, pls. 4–10, showing goats, helmets, and lions' heads as reverse devices.

of a developing court life.[75] And we have seen (above, note 54) that a number of refugees from Mycenae were resettled in Macedon.

There can be little doubt that Alexander hoped for acceptance into the Greek world, whether out of some personal philhellenic predilection or a pragmatic recognition of what was in Macedon's economic and political self-interest. He hoped to accomplish this by claiming Greek descent (which was quite likely untrue) and by adopting some aspects of Greek culture. It was the beginning of the hellenization of the Macedonian court. That the Greeks themselves down to the time of Demosthenes were not persuaded that the Macedonians were Greek does not alter the fact that the Macedonian kings very much wanted to be part of the Hellenic community. For in choosing a national orientation—Balkan, Greek, or Asian—Macedonian kings cast their lot with their Hellenic neighbors, and would remain very much part of Greek history until Philip II and Alexander the Great diverted their national effort in a new direction.

[75] Pindar, frag. 120, J. Sandys ed. (Loeb); Dio Chrysostomus, *Orationes* 2.33; Solin. 9.13.

 • CHAPTER 6 •

Perdiccas II

THE final years of Alexander's
reign are unrecorded. Herodotus's history, in which Macedonian
events are only peripheral to the main story, has come to an end. The
other sources are primarily concerned with Athenian matters, and
since these are for the moment diverted from Macedonia, we are left
in the dark. It has been suggested that Alexander fell upon hard times,
a view based upon a diminution in the quantity and quality of his coinage after *ca.* 465 B.C.,[1] but we have seen that the use of coins alone as
evidence can be both statistically biased and uninformative about the
underlying causes of events. There is no evidence that the kingdom
was in distress, and the silence of our sources about Macedon could be
more a reflection of their emphases than of any change in the condition
of the Macedonians.

The decade following Athens's intervention at Thasos and Eion in
the mid-460s saw a redirection of Athenian interests from the north
toward the south and west. It is impossible to say whether the Athenian abandonment of an active northern foreign policy was the result
of the mixed lot of success and failure in Thrace in the 460s, or whether
it represented an independent shift of priorities dictated by changes in
political direction at home and the perception of new threats from
abroad. It is safe to suggest that no major pressure from Greece proper
threatened to upset the balance among Macedonians, Thracians and
Greeks in the north during the last years of Alexander's reign.

In Athens, interest in Thrace and Macedonia seems to have abated
under the press of Peloponnesian events. When Athenian efforts in 464
to assist the Spartans against their rebellious helots were rebuffed at
Sparta, a political crisis mounted in Athens. Eventually, the party of
Cimon—whose family had been in the forefront of promoting an active policy in the north Aegean—was rejected, and Cimon himself was
ostracized in 461. An anti-Spartan policy led by the opposition under

[1] E.g., Price, *Coins*, 19. Hammond (*HM* 2: 115) suggests that the Bisaltic mines had
been lost and then regained by Alexander in 450s.

Ephialtes and Pericles was ascendant, and the Athenians became obsessed by their relations with Megara, Aegina, Corinth, Argos, and other Peloponnesian cities. Moreover, major expeditionary forces were sent to Egypt and Cyprus in continuing campaigns against the Persians, while the Athenians gradually extended their control over the maritime states of the Delian League.

Much of this activity required naval strength, and there can be no doubt about Athens's enduring need for ship timbers and pitch. Having failed to establish a northern outpost further inland than its base at Eion at the mouth of the Strymon, Athens continued to be dependent upon others to supply it with the required forest products. There is no hint in the ancient evidence that the Athenians developed an interest in Italian and Sicilian forests as reserves of ship timbers before the Peloponnesian War,[2] and it seems likely that they purchased their supplies from the Macedonians. Presumably such purchases had the approval of the king.

The Struggle for Succession

Both the date and the circumstances of Alexander I's death are uncertain. Only a single brief bit of information has survived about his demise, and, like so much else from this early period, it is controversial. The Roman biographer of Alexander the Great, Quintus Curtius (6.11.26), recounts a speech of the Macedonian commander Philotas, who, under torture for having been privy to a plot against the king, tells of a statement of one of the conspirators, Hegelochus. Hegelochus, it seems, had referred to revenge for the deaths of three earlier kings: (in order) Alexander, Archelaus and Perdiccas. As both Archelaus, and Perdiccas III died violently—respectively by assassination and in battle—it is suggested that Alexander I also met a similar end.[3] The assassination of a Macedonian king is not an improbable event, but the evidence of a disputed text of a comment attributed to Hegelochus as reported by Philotas—himself being tortured as punishment for conspiracy to murder a king—and recounted by a late and often rhetorical

---

[2] For a discussion of the importance of western timber to Athenian naval interests in the later fifth, fourth, and third centuries, see Meiggs (*Trees and Timber*, 124, 131, and 139).

[3] Efforts by some modern text editors to alter the order of the kings to Archelaus, Alexander II, and Perdiccas have not met with much approval. See the criticism of Edson, in a book review in *CP* 52 (1957): 280 n. 6 ("arbitrary" and "most unfortunate"), and a full review of the problem by Tripodi, "Sulla morte di Alessandro I," 1263–68. Were the emended order of kings acceptable, the only evidence for the circumstances of Alexander I's death would disappear.

source does not inspire confidence. In general, scholarship on the matter has not been sufficiently critical of the context of this reported statement, preferring instead to debate textual emendations. In short, by the normal rules of evidence, Curtius's passage relating to the death of Alexander I is highly problematic. That the royal succession following Alexander I's death was marked by disorder within the Argead family certainly suggests division, but the evidence for a death from violence or assassination is tenuous at best. Thus, for causes that can only be guessed at—including demise from old age—the first great Macedonian king, now about eighty, died ca. 454 B.C.[4]

The difficulty of ascertaining the precise date of Alexander's death contributes to an uncertainty about the succession of Perdiccas II. Moreover, there are wide discrepancies in the ancient writers concerning the length of Perdiccas's reign. Athenaenus (5.217d–e), in commenting on the controversy, recounts six ancient authorities who report from 23 to 41 years of rule, and other sources reflect the lack of agreement.[5] The unsettled nature of the issue may reflect a genuine historical controversy among ancient authors themselves, an uncertainty about the events immediately following the death of Alexander and the early years of Perdiccas's reign. Major challenges to Perdiccas's succession were raised by members of his family. The narrow range of dates for his reign may reflect only the period in which he ruled without internal opposition, while the broad range incorporates his whole reign from Alexander's death down to the accession of Archelaus. It is certain that he was king in 434 B.C. and that he still ruled in 414, whereas by 410 Archelaus was on the throne. For narrative purposes we can accept a reign from ca. 454 to ca. 413.[6]

Alexander had at least six children, of whom three sons had been given authority (archē) over some parts of the kingdom: Philip along the Axios (perhaps in Amphaxitis), and Alcetas and Perdiccas in areas

---

[4] For a study of Macedonian kings who "tended to die with their boots on," see Carney, "Regicide in Macedonia." Tripodi ("Sulla morte di Alessandro I," 1267) suggests that Alexander was about 80 years of age at his death, a reasonable estimate. Given the precarious evidence, I cannot share the confidence of Edson ("Early Macedonia," 34) and Hammond (*HM* 2: 103 and 115) about the king's violent end, whether by assassination or war. I accept a date of ca. 454, based upon a presumed date of accession of ca. 496 (see above, Chapter 5, note 16), as opposed to Hammond's proposal of ca. 452 (*HM* 2: 103–4).

[5] E.g., Diod. 7.15.2 (Eusebius); Syncellus, p. 469 (Dindorf ed.); and the Marmor Parium (*FGrH* 239 A58).

[6] Thuc. 1.57.2, 7.9.1; Diod. 13.49.1. For discussion, Cole, "Perdiccas and Athens," 55; Hammond, *HM* 2: 103–4; Geyer, "Makedonia," 704–705, and Gomme, *Comm. Thuc.* 1: 200–201.

unknown to us.[7] That Macedon should be divided into subordinate areas of administration under royal princes is certified by Thucydides, and probably reflects an attempt by Alexander to divide responsibility among the princes before his death, and not a description of a scramble for power following it.[8] There is no evidence to suggest that the designated successor was other than Perdiccas. Although an argument from silence, it places the burden of proof on those who would hold that other princes also had a legitimate claim. As we shall see, Philip challenged Perdiccas. Alcetas eventually lost his *archē* to Perdiccas by means not known, although mention of him in an inscription of the late 420s[9] as second in authority to Perdiccas suggests that the transition was peaceful. It is uncertain that Perdiccas was the eldest brother, but primogeniture may not have been binding on the succession, as we shall see (below, pp. 177, 189, 243–44).

Any system of shared responsibility designed to institute effective administration would have had to depend on a strong central authority. With Alexander's death, however, rivalries broke out among the princes and continued to plague the kingdom at least through the 440s, to be revived again occasionally with the intrusion of foreign assistance to one party or the other. It becomes clear that the Argeadae were notoriously quarrelsome, and that any unity that the Macedonian kingdom might possess would have to depend upon the strength that could be exercised from the throne. In the mid-fifth century, Perdiccas would eventually put down his rivals, and thereafter it is likely that only he actually held the throne.[10]

Athens and the Thracian Frontier

It may not be happenstance that Athens's renewed interest in the north coincided with the death of Alexander I. We are fortunate in having preserved a rare example of contemporary documentary evidence that sheds some light on Athenian activities in the north—the tribute lists

[7] Sources: Thuc. 1.57.3; Plato *Gorgias* 471a–b; Aelian *VH* 2.41. Discussion in Hammond, *HM* 2: 115, and Cole, "Perdiccas and Athens," 55–57. There is no evidence about a fourth son, Menelaus, and a fifth, Amyntas, is said to have lived as a private citizen (Syncellus, p. 500 [Dindorf ed.]).

[8] Following Cole, "Perdiccas and Athens," 55–57, rather than Hammond, *HM* 2: 115. Philip's hold on such an important area as the Axios makes it more likely that he received it from his father than from his brother; he held this region until Perdiccas eventually deprived him of it.

[9] The notorious *IG* I³.89, for which see below, pp. 153–54.

[10] E.g., all the coins of the period can be attributed to Perdiccas alone; see Raymond, *Macedonian Regal Coinage*, 148–65.

of the Athenian Empire. What had begun a quarter of a century earlier as an alliance designed ostensibly to protect the maritime Greek states of the Aegean from further Persian attack had, by the late 450s, become an empire exploited by Athens for its own economic and military well-being. The association of allies was being expanded and organized, and the tribute lists are the financial records of the assessments made against each member-state. An examination of these inscriptions provides some insight into Athenian policy along the Macedonian frontier.[11]

By the late 450s Athens was assessing settlements along the northern and eastern (but not the western, or Pierian) coasts of the Thermaic Gulf. Strepsa—whose precise location in the Gallikos-Axios delta is problematic—is included, and one wonders what kind of pressure Athens had brought to bear against the king of the Macedonians or what agreements had transpired between the two parties to permit the presence of an Athenian tributary state at such a strategic location within Macedonian territory. Setting aside the several tributary cities of Chalcidice as presently outside the Macedonian sphere of interest, the settlements of the Strymon command attention. Argilus, a town along the coast just west of the Strymon's mouth, is listed, as well as Berge, a community in the land of the Bisaltae some 25 miles upstream from Amphipolis.[12] Argilus may have provided an outlet for Strymon resources, but until its location is determined archaeologically along a coastline deficient in good harbors, rather little can be said with certainty. In any event, it will have been replaced as an outlet by the founding of Amphipolis in 437. Berge may be connected with Pericles having sent 1000 settlers to live among the Bisaltae.[13] The date is *ca.* 451, which is when Berge first appears on the tribute lists, and it is tempting to see the connection between the Athenian settlement at or near Berge and the emergence of Berge as a member-state. This event marks an extraordinary Athenian leap inland, which may be explained as part of a renewed Athenian policy to gain access to the timber resources of the area, and—if Hammond is correct—a desire on the part

[11] Basic corpus in *The Athenian Tribute Lists*, with relevant discussion in 3: 308–25. In what follows I depend upon the sensible analysis of Hammond, *HM* 2: 116–19, and the pioneering effort of Edson, "Notes on the Thracian *Phoros*," both with references to the views of the editors of *ATL* and other commentators. That all of the allies along the Macedonian coastline of the Thermaic Gulf should be included in the "Thracian" district for assessment purposes reminds us that the perception of "Macedonia" as distinct from "Thrace" is a relatively late fifth-century development.

[12] Evidence for Argilus, Berge, and Brea (see below) in Isaac, *Greek Settlements in Thrace*, 51–54 and 59.

[13] Plut. *Per.* 11.5.

of the Bisaltae to seek Athens's support against the neighboring Macedonians and Thracians. Moreover, an inland Thracian people probably had much less to fear from the excesses of Athenian imperialism
than did a coastal or island town.

A further step to secure the Strymon was taken *ca.* 446, when Athens established a colony at Brea. The exact status of the settlement is
as uncertain as its founding date and location, although it was probably
intended to be permanent and was located in Bisaltic country. "Brea"
is a Thracian word, suggesting an earlier local habitation, and the non-
tribute-paying Athenian settlement may have included a military
force.[14] The cleruchy seems to have been abandoned early during the
Peloponnesian War, perhaps because it was ineffective, or because the
foundation of Amphipolis made it no longer necessary. It is clear that
by the mid-440s Athens had not only incorporated its northern allies
into the imperial administration, but had also taken steps to establish a
presence in the Strymon basin. Moreover, the relative ease with which
the Athenians were able to extend their influence among the Thracians
in the Strymon basin suggests how weak was the authority of the Macedonians along their eastern frontier.

Had there been any lingering doubts concerning Athenian intentions in the north, they would have been erased by Athens's establishment of Amphipolis in 437/6 B.C.[15] The splendid site of the town, near
the Ennea Hodoi crossing of the Strymon, occupies part of a low hill
on the east bank of the Strymon at a gap just before the river opens
into its delta. At this point the Strymon describes an arc around the
base of the hill, thereby offering the city superb protection as well as
command over the stream itself. The location controls both the crossing of the river and the routes into the lower Strymon basin. Excavations by the Greek archaeological service have in recent years revealed
powerful walls and fortifications, a sanctuary, an athletic complex, and
private houses. The city's wealth in the fifth and fourth centuries has
left an impressive record in its ruins, with promises of further rich
finds from continuing investigation.

[14] *IG* I³.46 = M–L *GHI*, no. 49; and Isaac, *Greek Settlements in Thrace*, 51–52. Hammond (*HM* 2: 118 n. 2) makes it a cleruchy, as does Vartsos, "The Foundation of Brea,"
13–16.

[15] For which there is a considerable historical and archaeological bibliography, much
of which is gathered and cited in Isaac, *Greek Settlements in Thrace*, 35–48, and in Hill,
Meiggs, and Andrewes, *Sources*, 347 (esp. Thuc. 4.102.3, 103.3–4 and Diod. 12.32.3,
among the ancient sources). Important standard works include Papastavrou, *Amphipolis*;
Lazaridis, *Amphipolis kai Argilos* (with excellent maps); and Pritchett, "Amphipolis Restudied" (mainly on Brasidas's campaigns); plus the continuing excavation reports in
AAA, *Deltion*, *BCH*, and *AR*.

The obvious strategic advantage of the site was recognized by the Athenians as early as their ill-fated attempt to settle Ennea Hodoi in the 460s. A well-fortified, garrisoned city at the crossing was of greater military and economic advantage than the delta settlement at Eion. While Eion was successful as an emporium and naval base, it was nonetheless forced to trade with the interior. But Amphipolis was on the frontier of the interior and could maintain access to resources more effectively and cheaply, in particular the timber from the mountains bordering the Strymon basin. The importance of Amphipolis to the Athenians can be measured by the alarm felt in Athens at the time of its capture by the Spartan Brasidas in 424, as Thucydides (4.108.1) informs us. Eion's importance was linked to its use as an Athenian naval base, and its fortunes declined with both the commercial rise of Amphipolis and the eventual collapse of Athenian power in the north. But Amphipolis's strategic value was permanent. Today the visitor is dwarfed by the surviving monuments of Amphipolis, while the site of Eion has yet to be precisely located.

Amphipolis's population consisted of both Athenians and non-Athenians, the latter perhaps from among the Greeks who inhabited nearby outposts.[16] The city did not pay tribute. Its role was to protect and facilitate Athenian military and economic interests in the Strymon, the culmination of a preoccupation with the region that went back more than a century. What the Thracians had never before permitted in the area—the establishment of a large town—was now accomplished. As far as we know, the foundation of Amphipolis was unopposed, and we are left to speculate about what concessions Athens granted to the Thracians in return for their willingness to accept for the first time a major military and economic outpost on their frontier (see below).

There is no clear evidence about the Macedonian reaction to the foundation of Amphipolis,[17] nor indeed are we informed generally about Perdiccas's early relations with Athens. Following Pericles's suppression of a rebellion in Euboea in 446 or 445, a group of Euboean refugees from Hestiaea was given safe conduct for settlement in Macedonia.[18] Perdiccas is not mentioned in the sources, and there is no

[16] The status of the Athenians vis-à-vis the other Greeks of Amphipolis is much debated. For the literature, see Isaac, *Greek Settlements in Thrace*, 38–40.

[17] Hoffman, "Perdikkas," 366, suggests that Perdiccas was angered by the Amphipolis settlement and expressed "his hostility numismatically" by converting his coinage to non-Attic weights. Hoffman's argument is interesting, if not entirely persuasive.

[18] Thuc. 1.114.3; Theopompus, frag. 387 (*FGrH* no. 115). See Hammond, *HM* 2: 121–22, and Cole, "Perdiccas and Athens," 58.

other information about the negotiations between the Athenians and the Macedonians. Some modern commentators have been puzzled about the implications of this refugee settlement, but it seems self-evident that the acceptance of these refugees by Perdiccas points to a peaceful agreement with the Athenians over the disposition of the Hestiaeans. Moreover, there is no evidence in the tribute lists suggesting any Athenian aggression in the Thermaic Gulf. That is, the peaceful relations with Athens inherited by Perdiccas from his father appear to have lasted until at least 446/5.[19]

Perdiccas and Athens: Prelude to War

It is difficult to know whether the enmity between Perdiccas and Athens arose from a single cause or from a general deterioration of relations. Thucydides (1.57.3) is explicit: "[By 432] . . . though Perdiccas was formerly a friend and ally,[20] he had now become an enemy, because the Athenians had made an alliance with his brother Philip and with Derdas, who had joined forces against him."[21]

The Athenian decision to support the anti-Perdiccas coalition of his brother Philip and his cousin Derdas, king of Elimeia, must be set against a broader background. The establishment of an Athenian presence in the Strymon that might both threaten Macedon's eastern frontier and deprive it of access to mines and profits from the sale of timber provides additional sufficient cause for a breakdown in relations between Athens and Macedon. It was not that Athens could interdict Macedonian access to timber, as the main Macedonian forest resources were probably still those of the Olympus-Pierian ranges along the Pierian coast. But if Athens were to secure its own timber supply from the Strymon basin, Macedon would be deprived of a major customer for timber sales. Moreover, with Macedon's hold on the Bisaltic mines

---

[19] *ATL* 3.318–19, and Hoffman, "Perdikkas," 364–65.

[20] Unlike Hammond (*HM* 2: 122), I attach no significance to Thucydides' use of *symmachos* ("military ally") as indicative of a formal, perhaps treaty, relationship with Athens. While the use of *symmachos* might imply a decree of the Athenian demos, at 1.61.3 and 1.62.2 Thucydides uses forms of the same word to describe alliances that were makeshift and temporary, dictated by the pressures of a rapidly changing military situation in the north.

[21] Hammond (ibid.) accepts that a fragment of the alliance between Philip and the Athenians has survived: *IG* I².53, following Schweigert, "Epigraphical Notes," 170–71. Most editors since Schweigert, however, including Lewis at *IG* I³.67 (*q.v.* for bibliography), have followed Meritt's restorations to make this an Athenian decree concerning Mytilene, passed sometime before 427/6 B.C. Kagan, *The Outbreak of the Peloponnesian War*, 277 n. 14, puts the Athens-Derdas alliance as early as 435.

insecure both because of the growth of Thracian power and because Philip's rule in the Axios valley intervened between the central kingdom and the east, the economic threat to Perdiccas was manifest. Had Athens not intervened in the dynastic struggle in the Macedonian royal house, it might have continued to purchase timber from Macedonia without difficulty. But its attempt to establish by force its own outlet rather than depend upon a continuing relationship with the Macedonian monarchy—which, it must be admitted, could be capricious—created an unstable situation for the next several decades, ultimately preventing, rather than insuring, a dependable supply of timber.

The division within the Argead house apparently was not Athens's doing, but the Athenians were quick to exploit it. With the need for timber paramount (access to the mining resources of Thrace no longer appears to be a major issue for the Athenians, who by now had more than adequate revenues from imperial tribute), Athens developed a northern policy with two components: it would support Philip against Perdiccas—thereby contributing to a weakened Macedonian state—and it would plan a careful intrusion into the Strymon basin to acquire its own timber outlet. But the potential problem in the region remained the Thracians. Perhaps remembering the massacre of Athenians by Thracians at Ennea Hodoi, Athens moved cautiously, introducing a few settlers, establishing outposts, and finally, in 437/6, founding the powerful center at Amphipolis. It is clear that the Athenians could not have proceeded thus without having reached some accommodation with the Thracians.

Macedon was in no position to resist. Two decades of unrest in frontier areas had considerably weakened the kingdom. In the west, the Elimiote chieftain Derdas was allied with Philip, the Elimiote tie developed through marriage by Alexander (above, pp. 124–25) having been broken. In the east Perdiccas may have lost the Bisaltic mines as part of a general withdrawal in the face of the resurgent Thracians now cooperating with Athens. Indeed, the inability of Perdiccas to exercise Argead authority in the east may have been due in large part to Philip's control over the strategic east bank of the Axios, effectively interposing his *archē* between the Emathian heartland and the eastern marches. (One wonders if Archelaus's later shift of the capital from Aegae to Pella was in part an attempt to prevent this situation from recurring.) It may be said that the greater Macedonian kingdom was dangerously close to collapse.

Thus the enmity that broke out between Perdiccas and the Athenians might have had as much to do with Athenian strategic objectives in the north as with any overt anti-Athenian act of Perdiccas. Indeed,

Perdiccas's intention to preserve his territorial and monarchical birth-right as a legitimate aspiration of his kingship might have simply been at odds with Athenian policy in the region.[22] The rest of Perdiccas's career, spent in defense of the integrity of his kingdom against the vicissitudes of the Peloponnesian War, would seem to support such an interpretation. In short, Perdiccas's policy was defensive against the assertiveness of his Greek neighbors. The portrait of a "perfidious Perdiccas" is the result mainly of anti-Macedonian propaganda in contemporary Athens.[23] But what may have seemed crafty and unreliable in Perdiccas's character because it did not accord well with Athenian interests was, from the Macedonian point of view, a policy in behalf of the national interest by a king whose resources were sorely pressed. It is within such a context that we may examine the remainder of Perdiccas's reign.

Macedon, Athens, and the Thracians

By 432 Perdiccas and Athens were at odds, and their hostility produced the opening northern volleys of the Peloponnesian War. These events are described in Thucydides (1.57–65), an account that is not without chronological and contextual difficulties. Although the trend of the narrative is clear, Thucydides apparently knew only the general outline of the events leading up to the siege of Potidaea. Some of the details are problematic and probably beyond solution.[24] To counter an Athenian policy directed against his throne, Perdiccas, sensitive to events building in Greece, attempted to start a general war by involving Athens in hostilities against the Peloponnesians, Sparta in particu-

[22] Cole, "Perdiccas and Athens," 57–58, sees in Athens's support of Philip a means of encouraging someone who might, upon achieving the throne, be more receptive to Athenian policy. Cole's suggestion (61) that Athens may have begun its assessment of Methone and other Thermaic Gulf cities as early as 434, and that this was the cause of the Athens-Macedon split, is intriguing, but one should take note of Hammond's compelling argument (*HM* 2: 124–25) that Methone was outside the Athenian *imperium* until 432/1.

[23] E.g., Hermippus, *Phormophoroi*, frag. 63.8 (Edmonds ed., 1.304), who refers *ca.* 427 to the "shiploads of lies" imported from Perdiccas's country. The more sober—and probably more reliable—Thucydides, in describing the causes of the hostility (above), mentions no act of betrayal on Perdiccas's part, which he is likely to have done in a section in which the historian comments on Perdiccas's shifty nature (e.g., 1.61.1).

[24] Gomme, *Comm. Thuc.*, 1: 215. Two quite different modern analyses of Perdiccas's activities in the 430s and 420s can be found in Hammond, *HM* 2: 122–36 (emphasis on source commentary) and Cole, "Perdiccas and Athens," 60–72 (emphasis on larger strategic/political issues). *ATL* 3.308–25 gives an account of these same events utilizing the data from the assessment lists.

lar. He encouraged the Corinthians to support a revolt of their loyal
Chalcidic colony at Potidaea, which had been tributary to Athens since
at least 446/5, and he stirred up rebellion against Athens among the
Chalcidians and Bottiaeans. It was an aggressive foreign policy, and
one wonders how Perdiccas hoped to support it with force.

The Athenian response was quick. In early summer of 432, Athens
sent an expedition of 30 ships and 1000 hoplites north. Its primary
mission was to attack Perdiccas as a means of forestalling a serious
Chalcidic revolt (Thuc. 1.57.6, 59.2), but by the time it arrived the
rebellion was already underway. Prudently realizing that his force was
too weak to fight against both the Chalcidians and Perdiccas, the Athenian commander sent home a request for reinforcements, and then set
out to join the faction of Philip and Derdas, the latter of whose brothers attacked from a base in Elimeia.[25] This combined Athenian-Macedonian force seized Therme and endeavored to cut Perdiccas off from
his Chalcidic allies. As a defensive maneuver Perdiccas persuaded the
Chalcidians to abandon their coastal settlements where they were vul-
nerable to Athenian action, temporarily cultivate the king's land
around Lake Volvi (Thuc. 1.58.2) in Mygdonia, and regroup around
the protected site at Olynthus.[26]

Tribute-paying Olynthus, already settled by Greeks, was located on
a long mound commanding the southern Chalcidic plain as it sweeps
down to the sea. Rarely has there been a more favorable site for a town,
as it is easily defensible, has access to fertile land around, and is located
about three miles from the sea. About seven miles directly south lay
Potidaea, which sat astride the narrow isthmus connecting the peninsula of Pallene with the main body of Chalcidice. It is ironic that it was
a Macedonian king who, in attempting to initiate a Chalcidic confederation as a buffer against Athenian imperialism, unwittingly created
at Olynthus what would eventually become Macedon's most formidable antagonist in the north, a position the city would hold until its
annihilation by Philip II in 348. It will also be seen that Philip II's attempt to organize the Chalcidic Greeks within a Macedonian hegemony had its precedent with Perdiccas.

The Athenians turned from Therme and, in early summer 432, laid
siege to Pydna (Thuc. 1.61.2–3), where they were joined by reinforce-

[25] The relatively small size of this initial force either suggests a serious military mis-
calculation by the Athenians or indicates a well-founded assessment of the strength of
the Macedonians against whom it was sent to fight. Presumably, of course, it would
have been joined by the dissident Macedonians under Philip.

[26] The success of Perdiccas's strategy can be measured in part by the large number of
former tributary states absent from the assessment list of 432/1; *ATL* 3.322.

ments from Athens—another 40 ships and 2000 hoplites under the command of Callias. The siege not only brought pressure on coastal Pieria but also endangered the central Macedonian plain and Aegae, only a few hours' march away. Meanwhile the Corinthians, concerned about Athenian military pressure on its former colony at Potidaea, raised a private force of 2000 infantry under command of Aristeus, which arrived at Potidaea 40 days after the outbreak of the rebellion.[27] The arrival of the Peloponnesians caused the Athenians to abandon the siege of Pydna and seek a quick settlement with Perdiccas, as Thucydides (1.61.3) makes clear. Leaving Pydna, the Athenian forces moved toward Potidaea, reinforced along the way with some 600 horse under Philip and Derdas's brother Pausanias.[28] Perdiccas himself also arrived at Potidaea, commanding 200 horse, having left one Iolaus in charge at home. Thucydides (1.62.1), probably reflecting Perdiccas's unsavory reputation at Athens, tells us that the king had "again" abandoned the Athenian alliance, but with good reason, we might add, if the Athenians had themselves already broken the Pydna agreements and attacked Macedonian towns. Rarely can one find a clearer example of a settlement made in bad faith by both parties.

Thucydides's narrative (1.62–65) improves slightly in his description of the battles for Potidaea and Olynthus. In the end, superior Athenian force prevailed (Potidaea held out until the winter of 430/29), although the Peloponnesians under Aristeus got away by ship to continue raiding along the Chalcidic coast. One of the most interesting aspects of the campaign was that both sides depended upon allied Macedonian cavalry, which opposed one another before Olynthus, but broke off before engagement could occur. Whether the notion to pit these two forces was part of an Athenian strategy to weaken Macedon by promoting continued internal dissension, or whether their use was dictated by military necessity, is not known.[29] By the latter part of 432, the Athenians were continuing their campaign to suppress rebellion in Chalcidice, and Perdiccas had, one assumes, retired to Aegae to await the next turn of events.

This was not long in coming, for in the summer of 431 Perdiccas had again joined with the Athenians. How this came about is connected with the surge of Thracian power to the east and north of the Macedonian frontier. The Persian occupation of parts of Thrace had

[27] On the route and chronology of Aristeus's expedition, see Appendix C below, pp. 293–94.

[28] On the Athenian movement from Pydna to Potidaea, see Appendix C below, pp. 294–95.

[29] Cole, "Perdiccas and Athens," 63 and n. 32.

left a deep cultural and political impression.[30] The Thracians had not been weakened by the Persian advance into Europe. Indeed, the advantages of centralized power represented by the Persians probably became attractive to the Thracians, a tribal people who, though numerous and possessing wealth, heretofore had not been highly organized. Megabazus and Mardonius may have delegated considerable authority to the local chiefs, especially to the Odrysians, who had medized. By *ca.* 470, the Odrysians under King Teres had formed a state centered in southeastern Thrace that eventually grew to include much of the territory between the Danube and the Aegean.

By the late 430s Sitalces had succeeded Teres. Perhaps with an eye toward the expansionist schemes of Athens in the north Aegean, Sitalces moved to secure his southern flank. Recognizing the value of a powerful ally in the Balkans—one that seemed no overt threat to Athenian maritime interests—Athens responded in kind, and an Athenian-Thracian alliance was forged. It is difficult to trace the origins of this covenant, but by 437/6 the ground must have been prepared sufficiently to permit the foundation of Amphipolis in a region heretofore prohibited from major Greek settlement by Thracian tribes. By 431 Sitalces had married the sister of Nymphodorus of Abdera, a Greek.[31] The Athenians exploited this relationship to win over Sitalces, hoping for Thracian assistance in their campaigns against the Chalcidians and Perdiccas of Macedon. In the autumn of 431, Nymphodorus went to Athens, succeeded in establishing an alliance between the Athenians and Sitalces, was made *proxenos*, and even managed to gain Athenian citizenship for his son, Sadocus. These events mark the introduction of a Thracian subculture into Athenian life, culminating in 430 in the inauguration of an unprecedented cult and festival of a foreign deity, the Thracian Bendis.[32]

It was due to the intercession of Nymphodorus that Perdiccas was reconciled with Athens (Thuc. 2.29.5). The Athenians returned Therme to Perdiccas, and the king joined the Athenian army under Phormio to continue the war against the Chalcidians. It was an ar-

[30] See Hoddinott, *The Thracians*, 101–3.

[31] For what follows, Thuc. 2.29 and 2.67.2, and M. B. Walbank, *Athenian Proxenies,* no. 30.

[32] The so-called Bendideia; see Ferguson, "Orgeonika," esp. 157–63; and Hoddinott, in Fol et al., *The New Thracian Treasure,* 31–32. Plutarch (*Alc.* 1.2) and Plato (*Alc.* 1. 122D) mention the Thracian slave Zopyrus as tutor to Alcibiades. There had been a Scythian/Thracian contingent in Athens since they had been introduced as Peisistratus's bodyguards in the mid-sixth century (Best, *Thracian Peltasts,* 6–7); they continued to serve as police. There was, moreover, a considerable Thracian population in Piraeus.

rangement convenient for both parties: Athens had now gained the cooperation of the two Balkan powers for its campaigns to maintain authority over its northern empire and protect its timber sources, and Perdiccas had regained control of Therme. It would appear that Athens had abandoned Perdiccas's brother Philip, and thereby its policy of supporting dissension within the Argead house. Philip fled to the side of Sitalces, where he risked an uncertain refuge.

There remained the problem of establishing a mutually acceptable relationship between Sitalces and Perdiccas. Sitalces, through his Athenian connections, was a major force behind the reconciliation between Athens and Perdiccas, and he agreed to support Perdiccas's interests against the hapless Philip. What Perdiccas promised in return we do not know, and one wonders what the Macedonians had to offer Sitalces. Thucydides (2.95.2) is uninformative beyond indicating that Perdiccas did not keep his word, and modern commentators are reluctant even to hazard a guess. Thus in 429 Sitalces emerged from behind his Rhodopi mountain barrier and invaded Macedonia.[33]

Athens chose to support its Thracian ally, which has prompted some to suggest that the Athenians used the Thracian-sponsored reconciliation with Perdiccas eventually to subdue the Macedonian king by treachery.[34] For Sitalces had in his camp Amyntas, son of Philip, whom the Odrysian king intended to put on the throne of Macedon (Thuc. 2.95.3), and Hagnon of Amphipolis, who served as his advisor and commander of the Athenian allies. Sitalces led a great Thracian confederation south into Macedonia, including allies from most of the region between the Bosporus and the Strymon River and north to the Danube.[35]

Gomme once reflected that nowhere in our sources is a Thracian capital mentioned. The recent discovery of inscribed fifth- and fourth-century Thracian vessels suggests that the Odrysian kings had no capital, but rather moved among fortified residences (following a practice

---

[33] Gomme's comment (*Comm. Thuc.*, 1: 241) that Sitalces' invasion of Macedonia "is of very little importance" is true only insofar as its outcome did not produce a major geopolitical change. But its residual effect on both Macedon and Athens and its implication for understanding the fragile balance of power that existed along the northern Aegean littoral is telling. See Mihailov, "La Thrace et la Macédoine," 78–81, and pp. 146–49 and 160 below.

[34] Thus Hammond, *HM* 2: 123. For a suggestion that it was Perdiccas who initiated the new break with Athens, see below, pp. 146–47.

[35] The status of the Bisaltae and other tribes along the Strymon frontier of Macedon is unknown, although the mention of the Bisaltae, among others, as being part of Perdiccas's rule when Sitalces invaded Macedon (Thuc. 2.99.6) suggests that they were not part of the Odrysian confederation.

known elsewhere), carrying their royal authority with them.[36] The Thracian confederation could well afford an expedition, as the amount of tribute paid it annually by Greeks and others was about 400 talents worth of coined gold and silver, and an equal value in gifts.[37] For nothing, according to Thucydides (2.97.4) could be done among the Odrysae without the payment of gifts.

Entering Macedonia from the north, the huge Thracian army moved into the lower Axios.[38] The outnumbered Macedonians were forced to take refuge in their strongholds.[39] That the Macedonian army was somewhat undermanned (although in the end it would have made no difference against the gigantic Thracian force) may be due to Perdiccas's having dispatched 1000 troops to Acarnania to assist in a general uprising there favoring the Peloponnesians (Thuc. 2.80). Perdiccas had sent these soldiers without Athenian knowledge sometime shortly before Sitalces's invasion. They were joined by Molossian and Orestian contingents, and it has been suggested that their route leading through western Macedonia and Epirus into Acarnania was an attempt to demonstrate to the Peloponnesians that, once the Corinthian Gulf was crossed, troops could be be sent into Macedonia by a route that would avoid Thessaly.[40] Perdiccas's force arrived too late to do battle at Stratus, and there is no further mention of these troops as Peloponnesian allies. Clearly Perdiccas had decided to cast his lot with Peloponnesian policy in western Greece, and was perhaps attempting to impress the western Macedonians and Molossians with a military presence. But the secret was out: Perdiccas had supplied assistance to Athens's enemies, and we need look no further for a reason why the Athenian-Macedonian relationship foundered at the time of Sitalces' invasion,

[36] Gomme, *Comm. Thuc.*, 2: 243, and Fol et al., *The New Thracian Treasure*, 11–12.

[37] Thuc. 2.97.3, the figure paid under Sitalces' successor, Seuthes. See Hoddinott, *The Thracians*, 106, for a review of the types and quality of Attic and other Greek goods found in Thracian graves of the fifth century, and *ATL* 3.310 for a discussion of the tribute paid to the Thracians.

[38] Probably down the Axios valley, as reconstructed by Hammond, *HM* 1: 197, 200 and 2: 128–29, although Thucydides' account (2.99.1) is imprecise enough to make the route partly conjectural.

[39] The Macedonian fortifications were much improved later under King Archelaus, Thucydides informs us. The details of Sitalces' campaign in Macedonia are given in 2.100–101; the size of Sitalces' army is given at 100,000 foot and 50,000 horse (2.98.3; also Diod. 12.50.3), numbers that seem inflated.

[40] The Molossians were led by Sabylinthus, guardian of the boy-king Tharypas. Tharypas was the great-grandfather of Olympias, mother of Alexander the Great. See Gomme, *Comm. Thuc.*, 2: 214–15, and Beaumont, "Corinth, Ambracia, Appollonia," 64–65.

and what may have precipitated the Thracian intrusion into Macedonia.

Sitalces took some towns and, out of deference to Amyntas, son of Philip, spared others, probably in Amphaxitis. Reaching the marshlands of the Axios delta, the Thracians turned west to campaign near Pella, but did not round the central plain into Pieria. A cavalry force from western Macedonia (Perdiccas's Orestian allies now returned from the Acarnanian campaign?) arrived to support Perdiccas, and although they were excellent horsemen and were protected by mail, their numbers were insufficient and they withdrew. It may have been their appearance out of the west that prevented Sitalces from continuing his campaign in that direction. We do not know if the Thracian chief intended to strike a death blow at Aegae, or whether he planned only to take those eastern lands immediately bordering his own territory, for Sitalces returned to the Axios valley, crossed the river, and ravaged Mygdonia, Crestonia, and Anthemus.

Apparently there had been a plan for Sitalces to link with Athenian forces, but the promised Athenian fleet had not arrived. There is no evidence for Hammond's conjecture that the expected force was the Athenian army at that moment based at Methone. Thucydides (2.101.1) specifically mentions a fleet. It is possible that Athens's Methone force could have joined with the Thracians; the maneuver might have dealt the Macedonians a severe blow, as Hammond points out. But the arrival of a fleet was another matter. Events in the south in the main theatres of the Peloponnesian War almost certainly held up the dispatch of a major Athenian fleet; only envoys and gifts got through. The Athenians may have become wary about the potential threat their powerful ally represented to their economic interests in the north; by withholding support, the Athenians hoped that the Balkan kings would weaken one another.[41]

With or without Athenian allies, Sitalces' campaign had caused considerable trepidation among independent Thracians, Thessalians and central Greeks, and enemies of Athens everywhere. While Sitalces' awaited his Athenian allies, Perdiccas took the diplomatic initiative. He had secretly dealt with Sitalces' nephew, Seuthes,[42] promising him marriage to his sister, Stratonice, and a handsome dowry. Sitalces grew short of food and patience as winter approached. After a campaign of 30 days, eight of which were spent ravaging Chalcidice,

[41] *HM* 2: 129; Hoddinott, *The Thracians*, 105; Mihailov, "La Thrace et la Macédoine," 80.

[42] Seuthes was the son of Sparadocus, Sitalces' brother (Thuc. 2.101.5; 4.101.5); *pace* Hammond, *HM* 2: 129.

the Odrysian king agreed to the bargain struck by Seuthes and Perdiccas, and returned home in haste. Perdiccas kept his promise and gave
his sister to Seuthes in marriage.

Nothing more is heard of Sitalces, whose dream of a greater Thracian state ended in 424 with his death from battle or assassination during a fruitless campaign against the independent Triballi.[43] While there
would be slight resurgences of Thracian vitality under two of Sitalces'
successors, Seuthes I and Kotys I, the heyday of Thracian power had
come and gone. Had Sitalces followed up on his easy initial successes
in Macedonia, or joined with Perdiccas to form a greater Balkan coalition and invade Greece, the consequences for the subsequent history
of the Greek city-states would have been significant. As it was, Sitalces
retired from the Aegean world, and the Greeks would not have to face
a serious threat from the Balkans again until the rise of Philip II some
eighty years later.

The Peloponnesian War

One of the more remarkable traits of the Athenians was their ability to
remain alert to problems on several fronts during the first decade of
the Peloponnesian War. Despite real and immediate concerns in the
Peloponnese, the Corinthia, and the central Aegean part of its empire,
Athens seems not to have slackened interest in Macedonian affairs.
Sometime not long after the outbreak of the war in 431, Methone came
under Athenian control, although the date is disputed. Hammond
makes a plausible, though conjectural, argument that the Athenian object in besieging Pydna in the campaign of 432 (Thuc. 1.61.2) was to
establish a base in Pieria from which the heart of the Macedonian state
could be attacked.[44] Had Methone been part of the Athenian alliance
in that year there would have been no reason to waste an effort against
Pydna, as Methone was even better situated for a campaign into the
central Macedonian plain, if that is the point of the siege. In short, the
reason Methone was not attacked is that it was still in Perdiccas's hands
in 432, joining the Athenian alliance shortly after that, perhaps in 432/
1.

Athens's acquisition of Methone may have been part of a swap that
eventually restored control of Therme to Perdiccas. Perdiccas was in

---

[43] Thuc. 4. 101. 5; [Demos.] 12 *ad Epist. Phil.* 9. Mihailov, "La Thrace et la Macédoine,"
80, sees the hand of Perdiccas behind Sitalces' murder, based on the passage attributed
to Demosthenes (above). There is no proof, but if Perdiccas is the assassin referred to in
the passage, it answers the question *cui bono?* concerning Sitalces' death.

[44] *HM* 2: 124–25, and note 45 below.

no position to resist this first intrusion of the Athenian Empire into Macedonian territory. A Greek settlement of the seventh century, Methone had long been under Macedonian control, and was situated just south of the Haliacmon delta, where the Pierian coastal plain opens into the central Emathian plain. Whether the Athenians's motive was to establish a base to bring pressure upon the heartland of their sometime Macedonian allies, or whether Methone was thought to provide an outlet for the nearby timber resources of the Olympus-Pierian mountains, is a matter of speculation. If Methone were intended as a base for Athenian operations in central Macedonia, why did the Athenians not use it in autumn 429 to link up with Sitalces, who at that moment was holding the opposite side of the plain? Just such a combined Athenian-Thracian operation was what many northern and central Greeks feared, and it might have struck a devastating blow to Argead rule. Military pressures in the south may have prevented Athens from opening a major campaigning effort in the north, as suggested earlier, or the Athenians may have had second thoughts about the rapidly ascendant power of their Thracian allies.

Several Athenian decrees of the 420s dealing with Methone provide some insight into the matter,[45] for, whatever the initial Athenian impulse at Methone, the decrees are very much intended to insure that Perdiccas would not interfere with Methonian trade. Methone complained of being overassessed, its difficulty in paying tribute probably the result of Macedonian restrictions on its trade. Considerable diplomatic traffic is provided for, and one telling decree sends three envoys to Perdiccas asking him not to disturb Methone's freedom to trade by sea and with the interior (this can only refer to timber), and to refrain from taking Macedonian forces through Methone's territory without permission. It is clear that Perdiccas was bringing pressure against Methone, and the city complained to its patron. The concessions granted Methone by Athens may be indicative of the need to keep a trade in timber available to the Athenians. Athenian garrisons in Chalcidice were in position to observe that the conditions were met.

It would seem that some uneasy accommodation now existed between Perdiccas and the Athenians, provided that Athens took no further hostile action against the Argead throne or Macedonian cities and that the king of Macedon agreed to the status quo among Athens's

---

[45] There is a considerable bibliography and some disagreement on the date of Methone's first tribute assessment, and on the Athenian decrees concerning Methone that follow. For the texts and discussion, see M-L *GHI*, no. 65; Hammond *HM* 2: 124–28; Cole, "Perdiccas and Athens," 66; *ATL* 3.319 and 325; and Mattingly, "The Methone Decrees."

tributary cities. It was an arrangement that was not mutually beneficial except to allow each party an opportunity to concentrate on other matters for a time. But, as the editors of *The Athenian Tribute Lists* (3.325) put it, in one of the most telling understatements about Macedonian history: "Perdiccas was not an easy man to deal with."

During the 420s Perdiccas and the Spartans were in contact, as the latter were seeking alliances in many places.[46] By 424, a new threat to the fragile unity of Macedon appeared in upper Macedonia in the form of Arrhabaeus, king of the Lyncestians. The cause of the antipathy is not known, but apparently it was recent, as the Lyncestians were probably not hostile when Perdiccas's troops gathered allies in western Macedonia for the Acarnanian campaign in 429.[47] Perdiccas took the opportunity to exploit his continuing communications with the Spartans and join a number of Chalcidians to invite Sparta to send an army north. The Spartans were eager to have this diversion in the north, since they were, of late, under some military pressure closer to home. In fact, the Spartan Brasidas had already been preparing for an expedition to Thrace (4.70.1, 78.1). Thucydides (4.79.2) makes it clear that, although Perdiccas was willing to join the Chalcidian towns already in revolt from Athens on the basis of his old differences with the Athenians, his main goal was to seek military assistance against Arrhabaeus, with whom he had quarreled and whom he now wished to subdue. Once more Perdiccas had courted one major power and sacrificed a relationship with another to preserve the larger Macedonian kingdom. One suspects that he would have sold his soul to the devil to accomplish that, and there were probably those on several sides in the 430s and 420s who thought that he had.[48]

As a demonstration of good faith, Perdiccas contacted Niconidas, a Thessalian friend, and asked him to assist the force of 1700 hoplites under Brasidas with a safe passage through Thessaly. The Peloponnesians entered Macedonia, probably through the Petra Pass.[49] Upon hearing of their arrival, the Athenians broke their alliance with Perdiccas, and began sending reinforcements to Chalcidice. Perdiccas joined his forces with those of Brasidas and went off to make war against Arrhabaeus. Entering Eordaea through the pass above Edessa, the troops crossed that canton, which was loyal to the Argeadae, and ar-

[46] Thuc. 2.67.1 and 4.50.1.

[47] Gomme, *Comm. Thuc.*, 3: 546.

[48] E.g., the Athenians believed that Perdiccas had instigated Brasidas's campaigns in the north (Thuc. 4.82). For what follows, the narrative is Thuc. 4.78–84.

[49] Although see Appendix B below, p. 290, for the possibility of an alternative route.

rived at the Kirli Dirven Pass west of Lakes Petron and Ostrovo.[50] Here at the entrance to Lyncus, Brasidas suggested negotiating with Arrhabaeus, hoping to enlist him as a Peloponnesian ally, for the Lycestian king at this moment may have ruled an area stretching as far as Lake Ohrid. Indeed, Arrhabaeus was indicating a willingness to submit his dispute with Perdiccas to Brasidas's arbitration. Perdiccas greeted this turn of events by reminding Brasidas that he was paying half the expenses of the Peloponnesian force (presumably the Chalcidians were paying the other half), and that he had brought Brasidas to this place to destroy Perdiccas's enemies (whom he would point out), not to arbitrate. With an obstinacy matching Perdiccas's stubbornness, Brasidas continued to communicate with Arrhabaeus, and was persuaded to withdraw. The angry Perdiccas could do nothing but reduce his share of expenses to one-third—a gesture.

Brasidas moved off to the east to his (not Perdiccas's) priority, a campaign in Chalcidice and Thrace.[51] By the winter of 424/3 he had moved on Amphipolis with the aid of some Chalcidians. Perdiccas appears to be missing from the scene, although we are told that he helped instigate a revolt in Argilus, a town unhappy with its diminished role since the founding of nearby Amphipolis. Brasidas brought pressure against Amphipolis, and despite the hurried arrival of a small Athenian force from Thasos under the command of the historian Thucydides, the city surrendered to Brasidas. Thucydides installed himself in a defensible position at Eion at the mouth of the Strymon. Brasidas attempted to take Eion by assault from a fleet of river boats, but the Athenian base held. Not long after, Perdiccas arrived at Amphipolis to share in the success of his Spartan ally, and probably to determine how he might best exploit the situation. The loss of Amphipolis was greeted with alarm at Athens, for the city had supplied the Athenians with revenue from commerce and from its role as a collection agency for tribute from nearby towns. But its great value was as an outlet for ship timber. Brasidas could hardly have dealt the Athenian cause a more serious blow. The loss of Amphipolis after only a dozen years of Athenian rule would begin to alter Athenian policy in the north, and ultimately affect relations between Athens and Macedon.

During the remainder of the winter of 424/3, Brasidas contented himself with detaching additional Chalcidic cities from the Athenian alliance, an effort made easier now by the fall of Amphipolis. Defection from Athens seemed more attractive than ever. In spring 423, a

[50] See above Chapter 2, p. 37. Details in Hammond, *HM* 1: 103–5.
[51] Narrative in Thuc. 4. 102–8.

one-year truce was signed by Athens and Sparta (Thuc. 4.117), as the Athenians wanted to take stock, prevent further rebellion, and recover from the recent losses. Brasidas continued his Chalcidic policy of separating towns from the Athenian alliance, in contravention of the truce (4.122–23), and Athens prepared to send forces north to engage Brasidas at Mende, which had recently defected.

At this point Brasidas agreed to join forces again with Perdiccas in order to resume campaigning in western Macedonia (4.124.1). It is hard to understand Brasidas's decision to leave Chalcidice in the face of an imminent Athenian action there, unless Perdiccas had threatened to withdraw support. Perdiccas's own army was strengthened by hoplite reinforcements from nearby Greek towns.[52] Brasidas's had 3000 heavy-armed troops, the Chalcidian and Macedonian cavalry numbered 1000, and there was a large number of "barbarians," as well, to comprise what had become a formidable military force.[53] Retracing their route of the previous year, Brasidas and Perdiccas entered Lyncus to face their old adversary, Arrhabaeus. In the Pelagonian plain near the modern town of Bitola, Arrhabaeus's main force was defeated, but instead of following up immediately, Brasidas and Perdiccas decided to await the arrival of Perdiccas's Illyrian allies, a people noted for their ferocity in war. Another argument broke out between the Macedonian and the Spartan. Perdiccas wanted to carry the campaign against the Lyncestian villages, but Brasidas, nervous about the possibility of the Athenians arriving at Mende in his absence, opted for retreat.

While they thus wrangled, word arrived that the Illyrians had joined Arrhabaeus. Panic struck the Macedonian troops, who deserted the field during the night. At dawn Brasidas followed, but his retreat was under attack as the Illyrians took the Kirli Dirven Pass, the only exit from the Lyncestian plain. In a bold move, Brasidas seized the high ground at the pass and fought his way through into Perdiccas's territory at Arnisa.[54] The Illyrians did not pursue, and the Peloponnesians, now safe, vented their anger at the Macedonian desertion by looting Perdiccas's baggage train and slaughtering animals. The hostility was

[52] E.g., Strepsa and Pydna (Gomme, *Comm. Thuc.*, 3: 612). Thucydides' narrative of the second campaign against the Lyncestians is at 4.124–28.

[53] Thucydides' use of *barbaros* is problematic, although it would appear that he normally includes at least some of the Macedonians in the category. See 4.125.3 and Gomme, *Comm. Thuc.*, 3: 613, 615, and 616 on Thuc. 4.124.1, 126.3, and 126.5 respectively. For the topography of this second campaign, see Hammond, *HM* 1: 104–8.

[54] Perdiccas's country was Eordaea; Thucydides' comment (4.128.4) enables us to define the extent of Perdiccas's rule in 424/3 B.C. Arnisa was located just within Eordaea from Lyncus (Hammond, *HM* 1: 106), not at the site of modern Arnissa on the northeastern shore of Lake Ostrovo near the opening of the pass leading to Edessa.

mutual, and henceforth Perdiccas regarded Brasidas and the Peloponnesians as enemies, which, as Thucydides (4.128.5) points out, was an unusual attitude in someone who was a foe of Athens.

Perdiccas now made a characteristic decision. The attempt to add Lyncus to his domain having ended in failure, the king wished to be rid of Brasidas, at whom he was angry and who was no longer useful. Perdiccas contacted the Athenian generals in Chalcidice and proposed some agreements. The information was conveyed to Athens and a formal alliance ensued on terms that could only be regarded as attractive to the Athenians: timber and an alliance against the Peloponnesians. Fragments of a decree found on the Athenian acropolis are held to be portions of this very alliance, although the matter is one of the most hotly contested controversies in fifth-century Athenian-Macedonian history.[55] The document says that Perdiccas and the Athenians are to have the same friends and enemies and that Athens will have exclusive rights to take oars from Macedonia. A second decree on the same stone provides for friendship between Athens and the Lyncestian Arrhabaeus. The remaining lines cover the procedures for implementing the alliances and include a list of the Argead family members who took oaths to uphold the provisions of the covenant.

The stones of the inscription are fragmentary, and much of the text has been restored. Attempts to date the decree have depended upon epigraphical criteria (letter forms and length of the lines) and contextual grounds. The result has been a series of proposals ranging from *ca.* 435 to *ca.* 413.[56] The argument for a date of the mid-430s rests both upon the restoration of missing line lengths and upon Thucydides (1.57.2), who, we may recall, speaks of the break in relations between Athens and Perdiccas, who formerly had been in alliance. But we have seen (note 20 above) that Thucydides' language does not necessarily imply a formal alliance. As for letter forms and line lengths, there is honest disagreement among epigraphers. This is crucial, as the restored names of the Argeadae who took the oaths provide clues to the date, and the restoration of these names must conform to a proposed line length.

The poor condition of the text, however, precludes any decisive argument based on restored names in lines of uncertain or assumed length. That is, the epigraphical basis for dating these decrees is weak,

---

[55] Text of the inscription: *IG* I³.89, with pertinent bibliography.

[56] E.g., 436 B.C. (*ATL* 3.313 n. 61); 431 B.C. (Hoffman, "Perdikkas," 367–77); 423/2 B.C. (Gomme, *Comm. Thuc.*, 3: 621; Bengtson, *Die Straatsvertrage*, no. 186; Cole, "Perdiccas and Athens," 69); 417–413 B.C. (Lewis, *IG* I³.89); *ca.* 415 B.C. (Hammond, *HM* 2: 134–36); and *ca.* 413 B.C. (Edson, "Early Macedonia," 34).

and we are thus forced to seek the most reasonable historical context. While there is no certainty, this alliance would appear to fit best the situation of 423.[57] Perdiccas had by now abandoned his attempt to conquer Lyncus and was willing to accept a nonthreatening status quo there, as evidenced by the second decree in which Athens is pledged to reconcile Arrhabaeus and Perdiccas. This is not to suggest that Perdiccas initiated the idea of a peace with Arrhabaeus. It may be an Athenian inspiration, Athens wishing to avoid Brasidas's unproductive experience in western Macedonia. There was stability elsewhere in the kingdom. We have no information about the royal purse beyond the king's partial support of Brasidas's army. Whether revenues had become a serious problem we can only guess, and the coinage surviving from the last part of Perdiccas's reign provides no clues. To reach an agreement with Athens at this point would benefit Perdiccas in several ways. The western frontier would become stable, a powerful ally would be gained against Brasidas, whom Perdiccas (perhaps unfairly) disliked, and Athens would become a treaty-guaranteed market for Macedonian timber.

This last point needs emphasis, for Athens's main source of wood for ships had been lost with the fall of Amphipolis the previous year. And the decree is explicit on this point, that *oars* are to be supplied exclusively to Athens. The need for oars was critical during war and peace. Oars were frequently lost or broken, and the oar requirements for the Athenian navy in the fifth century numbered in the hundreds of thousands.[58] Each oar was shaped from a young fir tree, as Theophrastus (*HP* 5.1.7) informs us, and there was no substitute for the quantity and quality of the trees that Macedonia could provide. It may be assumed that the Athenians heretofore had acquired their timber on the open market, from Macedonia/Thrace and elsewhere. But the alliance of 423/2 was something new: a guaranteed supply, and the deprivation of oars to others. With Amphipolis recently lost to the Athenian *imperium*, the agreement with Perdiccas provides the most suitable context from the Athenian point of view.

In brief, Thucydides (4.128.5 and 132.1) informs us that in 423 Perdiccas initiated discussions leading to an alliance, and relates (5.6.2) that in the following year the Athenian Cleon asked Perdiccas for military assistance under terms of the alliance. At the outset Perdiccas

[57] On the date of the alliance see Appendix C below, p. 295.

[58] Borza, "Timber and Politics," 34: each trireme carried 170 oars plus 30 spares. Athens may have built as many as 1500 triremes between 480 and 410, that period alone accounting for 300,000 oars. At one point in the fourth century nearly 50,000 oars were kept in the Athenian arsenal for 253 triremes (Meiggs, *Trees and Timber*, 131).

demonstrated his good faith by persuading his friends in Thessaly to deny permission for Spartan reinforcements to march toward Macedonia through their country (4.132.2 and 5.13). There is sufficient cause why both parties should agree to an alliance: Athens to gain oars exclusively now that Amphipolis was lost, and Perdiccas to acquire an ally, stability, vengeance, and revenue. The fragmentary remains of the Athenian decree in question are consistent with both Thucydides' account and the need for a suitable context.

Perdiccas's alliance with Athens put Brasidas in jeopardy. The Athenian commander Cleon established a strong presence at Eion, and asked Perdiccas for military assistance—on the basis of their alliance—for an attack on Amphipolis, although there is no evidence that Perdiccas responded. Brasidas had meanwhile strengthened his defenses at Amphipolis through a union with the Thracian Edoni and by hiring other Thracians as mercenaries, but all his efforts came to naught as he fell during an engagement outside the city.

By 421 the first phase of the Peloponnesian War had ground wearily to a halt, and one is tempted to suggest that the Athenian loss of Amphipolis (despite the treaty with Perdiccas guaranteeing oars) may have contributed to Athens's willingness to accept a peace. In the arrangements embodied in the Peace of Nicias, Athens attempted to salvage the tatters of its northern empire, but the agreements reached with the Peloponnesians did not take into account the fact that many of the cities of Chalcidice and the old Thracian *phoros* had tasted autonomy and were unwilling to return to the Athenian fold, even under more liberal circumstances.[59] A considerable instability swept the Greek cities of the north, with hostilities continuing throughout much of the Peace, as these towns sought and received Peloponnesian alliances to support their individual interests.

For several years Perdiccas managed to remain aloof from these events and maintain his treaty with Athens. Although designated by the Peace to be returned to Athenian control, Amphipolis refused, thereby establishing an independence that would last until the time of Philip II. And the continuing local disorder in Chalcidice did not threaten Macedon so long as a major Athenian or Spartan force did not move north, something that was for the moment unlikely under terms of the Peace.

The situation changed, however, in 418/7, and Perdiccas was again drawn into the tangle of Greek affairs. In that year the Spartans and

---

[59] For a review of the Chalcidic situation in the aftermath of the Peace of Nicias, see Hammond, *HM* 2: 131–33, whom I follow.

Argives agreed to a fifty-year alliance (Thuc. 5.80.2), which in part involved support of some Chalcidic towns. Peloponnesian envoys were sent north in the spring of 417 to enroll Macedonians and additional Chalcidians. There is no doubt that this move was directed against Athens. Perdiccas had been an Athenian ally since the treaty of 423/2. He had abandoned Brasidas and thereby his former Chalcidian allies, and had looked to Athens for protection. As part of the arrangement Athens took control of towns that guarded entry into Macedonia at two critical points: Heracleion in Pieria near the pass at Tempe, and Bormiscus near the Rendina Pass leading from the Strymon into the corridor of Lakes Volvi and Koroneia. The tie with Athens in the period 423–417 was strong, and some have suggested that Macedon was in fact part of the Athenian empire.[60]

Perdiccas was persuaded to join the Argive-Spartan alliance, although he apparently was not yet prepared to desert Athens. What caused him to join the new coalition can only be guessed. Perhaps he was suspicious of renewed Athenian assertiveness in the north, as evidenced by Athens's addition of Heracleion and Bormiscus to its tribute-paying allies in the late 420s. Moreover, Brasidas was now gone, Perdiccas's anger has been dispelled, and Sparta was willing to relinquish Brasidas's gains in the north.[61] The invitation to join the alliance may have provided him an opportunity to resume the game at which he was already past master, of exploiting the constantly changing diplomatic circumstances, provided it was not too costly to Macedonian interests.

Since the moment the Spartan-Argive alliance had formed in 418, Athens had taken steps to counter it.[62] In the spring of 417, the Athenians were preparing to send an expedition to the north to challenge the Peloponnesian coalition and their Chalcidic allies, but Perdiccas's decision to join the coalition deprived the Athenians of their main ally

[60] See Appendix C below, pp. 295–96.

[61] Thus Andrewes (Gomme et al., *Comm. Thuc.*), 4: 146. Andrewes discounts Thucydides' comment (5.80.2) that Perdiccas joined the Argive alliance because he himself was of Argive descent. It is easy to agree with Andrewes's view that Argos was hardly relevant to Perdiccas's purposes, but one is, nonetheless, left wondering why Thucydides made such a comment. One also wonders if the Argives themselves used the purported Argos-Macedon link as a basis for their appeal to Perdiccas, and whether—whatever his real motives for joining the coalition—Perdiccas found it convenient to use the connection as a public justification for his new loyalty. Also Hammond, *HM* 2: 121 and 133, for the evidence of coins as an indication of an overtly pro-Argive Macedonian policy during this period.

[62] Evidence cited in Andrewes (Gomme et al., *Comm. Thuc.*), 4: 153–54, and Hammond, *HM* 2: 132.

in the region, and the fleet never sailed (Thuc. 5.83.4). The Athenians, of course, were furious at Perdiccas's betrayal, and, in the winter of 417/6, established a blockade of the Macedonian coast. The main purpose for such a blockade was almost certainly the interdiction of Macedon's timber trade. It is problematic how effective such a blockade could be, even though it would be made easier by the several Athenian bases in the area, at Heracleion, Methone, Potidaea, and Bormiscus. In the following winter (Thuc. 6.7.3) the Athenians landed an expeditionary force at Methone that went on to raid the Macedonian neighborhood.

But the punishment of Perdiccas and the deprivation of timber for his new allies was not a solution to Athens's continuing need for ship timbers. With Amphipolis now independent and their Macedonian suppliers hostile, the Athenians were forced to seek timber elsewhere, and it is clear that the forest resources of southern Italy and Sicily became a prime attraction for the Athenian expedition that sailed off to the west in 415 B.C.[63] That Athenian armada was probably outfitted largely with Macedonian wood, provided as the result of the treaties of 423/2 and the Peace of Nicias, and through private efforts.[64] What persuaded Perdiccas to abandon his Peloponnesian alliance and again join Athens is not known, but by 414 we find him serving with the Athenian commander Euetion and a force of Thracians in an attack on Amphipolis (Thuc. 7.9). Athens may have seen that the Sicilian expedition was not going well and offered inducements to Perdiccas for a renewal of relations that would guarantee the purchase of Macedonian timber. Moreover, a desultory Spartan policy in the north would have seemed to provide no profit for Macedon (the Spartans had been unable to persuade their Chalcidian allies to assist Perdiccas against Athenian raids in the winter of 416/5), and, as usual, Perdiccas followed what appeared to be his own best interest.[65] Nothing more is known of Perdiccas, and most modern authorities accept that he died in 413 B.C., to be succeeded by his son, Archelaus.[66]

[63] Thuc. 6.90.3 and 7.25.2, although it is difficult to distinguish between timber as a motivation for the Sicilian expedition and as a *post factum* justification. A need for timber is not part of the Athenian debates on sending the expedition (Thuc. 6.9–18). On the value of western timber for Athens, see Meiggs, *Trees and Timber*, 124, 131, and 139.

[64] See Borza, "Timber and Politics," 44 n. 52 (with citation of inscription corrected to *IG* I³.182).

[65] Hammond, *HM* 2: 133–34, sees Perdiccas as isolated and yielding to necessity, presumably reacting as a victim of circumstances rather than as an initiator of policy.

[66] Evidence for the date of Perdiccas's death is reviewed in Cole, "Perdiccas and Athens," 71, and Hammond, *HM* 2: 103–4.

We may now summarize Perdiccas's lively diplomatic relations with
Athens:

> **before the late 430s**: friend and ally of Athens;
>
> **by 432**: enemy of Athens, which was supporting P.'s brother;
> P. encourages Chalcidic rebellion against Athens;
>
> **432**: quick settlement with Athens during the siege of Pydna;
> Athens moves on Potidaea;
>
> **432**: shortly after, P. abandons the Athenians and joins the
> Chalcidians;
>
> **431**: reconciliation with Athens; Therme is returned to P. and
> Macedon joins Athens against the Chalcidians;
>
> **429**: enemy of Athens, P. supporting Peloponnesian policy in
> western Greece, Athens allied with Sitalces' invasion of Macedo-
> nia;
>
> **mid–420s**: uneasy accommodation with Athens; the period of
> the Methone decrees;
>
> **424**: enemy of Athens, allied with the Chalcidic revolt and with
> Brasidas in campaigns against Amphipolis and the Lyncestian Ar-
> rhabaeus;
>
> **423/2**: abandons Brasidas, P. seeks and receives alliance with
> Athens;
>
> **417**: joins Spartan-Argive alliance;
>
> **by 414**: allied with Athens in a campaign against Amphipolis.

It is an extraordinary record of mercurial behavior, and it certainly
contributed to the reputation of perfidy enjoyed by Perdiccas among
the Athenians. It is telling, however, that one Athenian with some actual experience in the north, the historian Thucydides, does not emphasize treachery as an unusual component of Perdiccas's career, and
we must admit, along with Hammond, that the Macedonian king's
duplicity was only equal to the standards of the day practiced by both
Athens and Sparta.[67]

Any assessment of Perdiccas must take into account that he did not
view himself or his kingdom as having to serve—like so many states—
the empire of Athens. Alexander I had established the independence of
Macedon, and Perdiccas seemed determined to preserve that integrity.
Unlike the tiny islands and coastal cities that could be forced to adhere
to Athenian policy, Macedon was too large and too far inland to submit easily to Athenian naval power. Morever, Macedon was distant
from the Greek world, and the Greeks were reluctant to commit sub-

---

[67] *HM* 2: 134. See also the sensible discussion by Cole, "Perdiccas and Athens," 71–
72, some of whose views I follow.

stantial forces for long-term campaigns in the north. Yet Perdiccas could not assert himself and enforce his will in traditional military terms, as Macedon lacked both a cohesive population and military organization. Thus unable to act aggressively in behalf of the national interest, Perdiccas was forced of necessity to be defensive, to react to the continually changing military and diplomatic circumstances dictated by the Greeks's internecine struggles.

Macedon's timber reserves, so vital to Greek (especially Athenian) navies, provided Perdiccas with an unusually potent diplomatic weapon that compensated for Macedon's meagre and fractured population and slim military resources. Barely able to survive the vicissitudes of internal discord—opposition from his brothers and the chieftains of western Macedonia (supported by Athens)—and unable to establish himself as a military power to rank with the Spartans and Athenians, Perdiccas was forced to exploit the general conflict among the Great Powers and their particular need for timber. Perdiccas's troops were never more than a minor ally of one side or the other in the struggles in the northern Aegean, and yet, through a shrewd diplomacy, Perdiccas was able not only to preserve Macedon's integrity against the encroachments of the Greeks, but also to establish his weak kingdom as a formidable factor in the events of the period.

Through a judicious and shrewd diplomacy that recognized no conventions beyond self-interest (his rage at Brasidas and consequent overtures toward the Athenians marking, perhaps, the single act of policy dictated by emotion), Perdiccas managed to contribute to the weakening of the Athenian empire in the northern Aegean, and yet prevent the Peloponnesians from establishing their own permanent influence there. His periodic encouragement of Chalcidian independence from Athenian rule severely reduced Athens's hegemony in the area, but the cost, which would be borne by his fourth-century successors, was the unwitting creation of a powerful Chalcidic federation under the leadership of Olynthus that would challenge Macedonian hegemony.

It is too much to suggest that all of this was part of a conscious plan. There is no evidence to suggest a strategic Macedonian policy beyond Perdiccas's desire to protect the integrity of his kingdom and his own royal prerogatives. But the lack of a conscious scheme in no way reduces the importance of Perdiccas's historical impact, nor does it diminish his place as a Macedonian monarch who, with but the slimmest of resources and at little cost in troops or territory, was able to maintain independent Argead rule in the kingdom.

Much might have been different. The most serious threat to Macedonian survival came from the federation of Thracians under Sitalces against which no wily timber diplomacy could be effective. It was only the limited ambition and impatience of Sitalces plus the failure of the Thracians to forge an effective military alliance with Athens that saved Macedon, and perhaps much of the rest of northern and central Greece as well. Moreover, had the Spartans not shortsightedly rejected the scheme to insure a permanent source of timber for themselves and their allies from Amphipolis or some other northern place, the Peloponnesian War might have ended years earlier.[68]

Finally, had the Athenians not been so overtly assertive in the north, establishing and attempting to maintain by force sources for timber, they might have retained their northern empire and insured a secure timber trade with Perdiccas. Such an arrangement would have required a long-term, mutually beneficial treaty of the type that was virtually unknown among the Greeks in this period.[69] Greeks used short-term treaties, limited force, and empires to provide access to necessary goods. Moreover, the practice of building stockpiles of vital commodities ran counter to the Greek economic outlook, which was not characterized by surpluses and long-range planning.[70] The evidence, such as it is, suggests that Macedonian kings were willing to engage in a peaceful trade in forest products, provided that no political threat emerged. From 423 until 417, when Perdiccas began to feel pressed by a renewal of Athenian power in the north and perhaps by a campaign against Amphipolis, Macedon apparently traded well and peacefully with Athens. And, as we shall see, Perdiccas's successor, Archelaus, maintained a healthy trade in timber (without the benefit of a treaty) with a late fifth-century Athens that had given up its ambitions along the Macedonian frontiers.

Perdiccas had no external ideological or political commitments during the Peloponnesian War, his primary concern being the security of his own kingdom against the ambitions of the Greeks and Thracians. Whether to effect his policies he was more or less exploitative than his Greek contemporaries is irrelevant. The kingdom his son, Archelaus, inherited was in many respects no worse off than that Perdiccas had received from Alexander. Perdiccas's successor would be free to effect policy without a major external threat, and the relative tranquility of Archelaus's reign may have resulted partly from the odd, four-decade-long exercise in survival managed by his predecessor.

[68] Thuc. 4.108.7 and Michell, *The Economics of Ancient Greece*, 281–82.
[69] Discussed in more detail in Borza, "Timber and Politics," 49–52.
[70] See Samuel, *From Athens to Alexandria*, and Borza, "Timber and Politics," 51.

CHAPTER 7

Archelaus

$\mathbf{I}$N THE *Gorgias* (471a–c), Plato tells a scathing story of how Archelaus, the bastard son of Perdiccas and of a female slave of Perdiccas's brother Alcetas, illegitimately took the Macedonian throne by murdering all the other claimants. The victims included Alcetas, Alcetas's son Alexander (a contemporary of Archelaus), and an unnamed seven-year-old son of Perdiccas. Thus an uncle, a cousin, and a younger step-brother perished in order to provide Archelaus his royal title.

The story was famous in antiquity,[1] but in modern times its veracity in whole and in part has been questioned.[2] Whether or not Archelaus was, as Perdiccas's eldest son, the rightful heir is a judgment based upon our interpretation of the role of primogeniture in the Macedonian succession. There is precious little evidence on the subject beyond the actual succession of kings, and the circumstances surrounding the elevation of some of them is murky due to the poor state of our sources. If one accepts that primogeniture was not the absolute rule (see below, pp. 177 and 179), it is possible that Perdiccas's brother Alcetas was the rightful successor.

This view is supported by the list of Macedonian notables in the treaty (*IG* I³.89) of 423/2 between the Athenians and the Macedonians. This list probably represents a ranked order: Alcetas's name follows Perdiccas's and immediately precedes Archelaus's. But the matter is confused by Perdiccas's appointment of Iolaus (Thuc. 1.62.2), not Alcetas, as acting ruler during the king's campaign at Potidaea in 432. We are thus left with some doubts about Alcetas's place in the succession. There is less question, however, about Archelaus's place as intended heir or regent. Not only does the treaty list put Archelaus before all others (after Alcetas), but one may suggest, based on the evidence of his eventual accomplishments as king, that Perdiccas, like Philip II, may have nominated his heir on the basis of merit. How much violence

[1] For its proverbial history, see Hammond, *HM* 2: 135.
[2] E.g., Geyer, *Makedonien*, 86, and Hammond's useful discussion of Archelaus's succession, *HM* 2: 133–37.

attended Archelaus's succession depends upon how much of Plato's story one accepts.[3]

The date of Archelaus's succession is not known precisely. Perdiccas was campaigning at Amphipolis in summer 414, and Archelaus was besieging Pydna in winter 411/10.[4] As Archelaus was killed in 399 (Diod. 14.37.5–6) and his reign is given as lasting 14 years, we may settle on 413 as the likely date of his succession, although the length of his reign is subject to the usual discrepancies among the ancient chronographers.[5]

Foreign Policy and Military Reform

The Greek world that greeted Archelaus's elevation to the throne had been marked by the collapse of Athenian ambitions in the west. The disaster suffered by Athens in Sicily was not only unrelieved in its human toll (Thuc. 7.87.6), but it provoked a series of military and political consequences as well. Athens's imperial designs in the west were abandoned. Its armada needed replacement, and with Italian and Sicilian timber now unavailable, and Amphipolis fiercely independent, the Athenians were forced to fall back on the forest resources of the Macedonians. Thus, when Archelaus commenced a policy of internal reorganization and strengthening, he found a ready ally in Athens. In 410 an Athenian fleet under command of Theramenes joined Archelaus in what had become a difficult siege of Pydna, whose independence as a Greek city in Macedonian territory the king was determined to end. The Athenian reinforcements turned the tide; Pydna was taken, moved inland some 2½ miles, and refounded as a Macedonian town.[6]

It is possible that the Athenian fleet at Pydna was constructed with Macedonian timber and pitch, as the Athenian response to their disastrous campaign in Sicily had been to rebuild naval forces as quickly as possible through both public and private resources (Thuc. 8.1.3). Ties were established with Macedon perhaps even before the siege of Pydna, individual Athenians were granted permission by the Mace-

---

[3] Against Geyer and Hammond's scepticism about parts of Plato's account is the judgment of Dodds, *Gorgias*, 241–42, who accepts it. And Peter Green suggests to me that one more dynastic bloodbath among the Macedonians is not only not improbable, but Plato, by providing a very detailed report only a few decades after the event, lends some credence to it. For the possible place of Plato's story in the larger context of anti-Archelaus propaganda in Athens, see below, p. 175–76.

[4] Thuc. 7.9.1; Diod. 13.49.1–2.

[5] Syncellus, pp. 482 and 500 (Dindorf ed.) (14 years), and Eusebius 1.227 (17 years).

[6] Diod. 13.49.1–2 and Hammond, *HM* 1: 128–29. For a review of the events of Archelaus's reign, see *HM* 2: 137–41.

donian king to export oars, and Athenian *probouloi* were assigned the task of procuring additional oars.[7] Shipwrights had probably long been at work in Macedonia by the time the Athenians passed a decree in 407/6 praising Archelaus for assistance in ship construction.[8] The decree honors Archelaus and his children with the status of *proxenos* and *euergetēs* for an astonishing series of specific services providing both materials and facilities in Macedonia for shipbuilding.[9]

It seems that Archelaus used his royal prerogatives to dispense forest products without the necessity of binding Macedon to a treaty, thereby insuring the technical neutrality he maintained to the end of the Peloponnesian War.[10] Although it was of little benefit in the end, Athens acquired naval equipment under circumstances far more favorable than it had enjoyed earlier through treaties and the use of force during the reign of Perdiccas. For his part, Archelaus, enjoying the unusual position of a Macedonian king dealing through advantage, pursued a policy of internal reorganization and revival, part of which must have been financed by the revenues of his timber and pitch sales to Athens. It was the most mutually beneficial relationship yet enjoyed by the Athenians and Macedonians.

Aside from his services to the Athenians, Archelaus seems to have refrained from further entanglement in the closing phases of the Peloponnesian War. Amphipolis continued on its independent path, and so long as the Macedonian, Chalcidic, and Thracian coasts were outside the struggles among Greeks, Macedon remained uninvolved. The perennially troubled western frontier, however, required continuing vigilance. Archelaus seems to have inherited his predecessor's struggles against the tribal kingdoms of western Macedonia and the Illyrians beyond. He continued Perdiccas's policy of military campaigns against the Lyncestian/Illyrian coalition, but sought to neutralize the Elimeans

---

[7] Andoc. 2.11. Sometime after 411, Andocides, on the basis of old family links with the Argeadae, was given permission by Archelaus to cut and sell Macedonian timber for Athenian oars; Ar. *Lysistrata* 421–23; also see Borza, "Timber and Politics," 44–45.

[8] M-L *GHI*, no. 91 (*IG* I³.117); M. B. Walbank, *Athenian Proxenies*, no. 90; and Meritt, "Archelaos and the Decelean War," 246–52.

[9] Meritt ("Archelaos and the Decelean War," 248 n. 8) suggested Heracleion in southern Pieria, or Bormiscus in northeastern Chalcidice, as the dockyard. The latter is unlikely, as the timber used at Bormiscus would need to be taken from the nearby slopes of the lower Strymon basin, an area now controlled by Amphipolis. A Pierian site for the dockyard is more suitable as being both close to Argead-controlled forests in the Olympus-Pierian mountains and more accessible to southern seas. One thinks of some place in northern Pieria, such as Methone or even Pydna, which might account for the joint Athenian-Macedonian effort against the latter town in 410.

[10] [Herodes] *Peri Politeias* 19.

through a marriage alliance. In order to strengthen his hand in a war against the Lyncestian Arrhabaeus II and the Illyrian Sirrhas (the son and son-in-law of Perdiccas's nemesis, Arrhabaeus), Archelaus gave his elder daughter in marriage to Derdas (son of Derdas, Perdiccas's old enemy), the king of Elimea.[11] Archelaus thereby retained through marriage the uneasy balance of power with some of the western Macedonian tribes that had been precariously managed by his predecessors, while serving notice on others that the Argeadae were willing to fight.

Along the eastern frontier, the king regained control over Bisaltia and its valuable mines. The absence of Athenian interest in the area, along with the reduction in Thracian power, may have provided Archelaus with an access to the east denied his father, and the revival of a fine silver coinage not seen since the reign of Alexander I may be testimony to the acquisition of these precious-metal resources.[12] Undoubtedly the revenues from the Bisaltic silver mines, along with the income from the timber trade, provided the funds needed for Archelaus's program of military and cultural reform.

The single foreign initiative of Archelaus seems to have been taken toward the end of his reign, when he was invited to intervene in Thessaly in support of the ruling oligarchs, the Aleuadae, against a more moderate faction. Thessaly, that great fertile mountain-ringed plain directly south of Macedonia, was undergoing a transformation from a traditional society ruled by horse-rearing, landed aristocrats to one in which towns and new political and economic groups were on the rise. The transition was marked by political struggles similar to those experienced by some Greek cities in the late seventh and early sixth centuries. Macedonian troops were sent to Larisa, Thessaly's leading town, where they were successful in supporting the local oligarchs, a Macedonian garrison was installed, Thessalian hostages were taken to Macedonia, and Archelaus may have been granted Larisan citizenship. In return for these services, Perrhaebia was ceded to Archelaus.[13]

The strategic importance of Perrhaebia is noteworthy, as both the Petra and Volustana passes from Macedonia join and move through Perrhaebia as they descend from the western slopes of the Olympus

[11] Arist. *Pol.* 1311b; Hammond (*HM* 2: 139) puts this marriage *ca.* 400 B.C.

[12] E.g., the silver staters illustrated in *PM*, no. 13, and Price, *Coins*, nos. 49 and 51.

[13] *HM* 2: 139 and 141. Hammond views the securing of his western Macedonian flank through marriage (see above) as a necessary precondition to the holding of Perrhaebia. For a general discussion of Archelaus in Thessaly, see Westlake, *Thessaly in the Fourth Century B.C.*, 51–59; Cloché, *Histoire de la Macédoine*, 87–90; and Hornblower, *The Greek World*, 82. On aristocratic rule in archaic and classical Thessaly, the account of Martin, *Sovereignty and Coinage*, 61–67, is useful.

range into Thessaly. The acquisition of these routes is consistent with Archelaus's policy of establishing defensible positions along the critical passes leading into Macedonia, although there is insufficient evidence to know whether the possibility of acquiring control over Perrhaebia was the motivation for Macedonian intervention in Thessalian affairs. In Thessaly, those opposing the Aleuadae and their Macedonian ally appealed to Lycophron of Pherae (a Thessalian town near modern Volos, along the Gulf of Pagasae) and to Sparta for assistance. The Spartans, attempting to exercise a wide hegemony in Greece in the period immediately following their victory in the Peloponnesian War, declared against Archelaus. Either Archelaus withdrew from Thessaly (to avoid a major war with Sparta) or his death soon thereafter prevented the outbreak of hostilities between Sparta and Macedon. Whether Thessaly was on the verge of becoming a province of Macedonia, as Westlake suggests, is problematic.[14] What is not problematic is the comment of Thrasymachus, who wrote an oration *On Behalf of the Larisaeans,* in which survives the comment: "Shall we, being Greeks, be slaves to Archelaus, a barbarian?"—a line attributed also to Euripides.[15]

We have seen that throughout the fifth century, Macedonian influence depended more on its kings' ability to exploit the kingdom's geographical location and natural resources than upon their skill in fielding armies to enforce its policy. The army was numerically small—a few cavalry (presumably those barons and king's men who could afford animals and equipment) and an inferior infantry. The kingdom may as yet have lacked sufficient manpower and organization of population resources to maintain either a citizen conscription or a permanent professional force. During the Peloponnesian War, Perdiccas fought as little as possible, and whenever he was constrained to engage in hostile action, he usually did so in the company of allies. Statistics are hard to come by, but it would appear that the Macedonians could not field an army of more than one to two thousand men. Moreover, there is no

[14] Westlake, *Thessaly in the Fourth Century B.C.,* 57. Much of Westlake's analysis of Archelaus's activities in Thessaly depends upon the acceptance of a late rhetorical source attributed incorrectly to Herodes Atticus, and supported indirectly by Arist. *Pol.* 1311b. Hammond (note 13 above) is more cautious than Westlake in accepting many of Pseudo-Herodes' details concerning Archelaus in Thessaly. See Westlake, *Thessaly in the Fourth Century B.C.,* 51–54; Hornblower, *The Greek World,* 305 n. 1; and Errington, *Gesch. Make.,* 232 n. 2.

[15] Frag. 2 (Diels ed., *Frag. Vorsokratiker,* 6th ed.) Daskalakis contended (*Hellenism,* 234) that Thrasymachus was not referring to barbarians in the usual sense. The passage, he argued, should be taken "in its rhetorical slant of a difference between advanced and backwards Greeks in an intellectual sense." This is strained and unconvincing.

evidence that these troops were trained according to high standards of conduct, as the allied campaign of Brasidas and Perdiccas against Arrhabaeus has shown. In brief, the Macedonian army before Archelaus may have been analogous to other Balkan armies, poorly trained and ill-equipped, men who fought for slaughter or loot or because they had been pressed into combat out of vassalage, and who were as dangerous to one another in the field as they were to their enemies.[16]

The reorganized army of Archelaus was part of a general scheme to strengthen the kingdom and add strategic areas such as Perrhaebia bordering Thessaly and (perhaps) Demir Kapu, the Axios River gorge that is the main gateway from the the inner Balkans to the Aegean littoral. And Archelaus's confidence in his forces was sufficient to prompt his intervention in Thessaly, although we cannot tell whether this was intended to be a temporary political expedient to gain Perrhaebia or was to be permanent, lapsing only under the threat of an engagement with the powerful Spartans. By the time Thucydides wrote (or revised) his second book (2.100.2) late in the fifth century, Archelaus had not only built fortresses in the countryside (presumably at the passes leading into Macedonia and in open towns), but had also made straight roads and improvements in the army.

In the passage mentioned above, Thucydides is explicit in saying that cavalry, hoplites, and other armaments became stronger, but his evaluation is limited to a comparison with Archelaus's eight predecessors. Nothing more is intended, and to make Archelaus a military genius is to read more into Thucydides than the source will allow. In fact, most of the information we have for the reorganization and development of the Macedonian army into a first-class fighting force comes from the period of Philip II and Alexander the Great. Whatever the nature of his reforms, Archelaus was probably the first Macedonian king to think strategically about Macedon's military potential. One wonders if, had he lived on, Archelaus might have anticipated Philip's attempt to make a permanent settlement with the Greeks.

Pella

Archelaus is usually credited with having moved the capital of the kingdom from Aegae to Pella.[17] Two problems are associated with this foundation. First, what is meant by "capital"? A capital suggests an

---

[16] On these matters, see Hammond, *HM* 2: 147–48.

[17] Ibid., 150. A general account of the history and archaeology of Pella, but not including the most recent excavations—most of which are as yet still unpublished—can be found in Petsas, *Pella*.

administrative center for a government more sophisticated than what may have actually existed in Macedon in the fifth and fourth centuries B.C. Indeed, one ancient state more complex and vast than Macedon had three "capitals." The Persian empire retained Susa as its administrative center and royal residence, Persepolis as the focal point of the annual renewal of fealty to the King of Kings by the subject nations, and Ecbatana as a summer abode. Moreover, Babylon remained a center for traditional religious practices.

We have also seen (pp. 145–46 above) that the Thracians had no capital, but rather a series of royal residences from which a peripatetic royal family could exercise its functions. It is thus to contemporary Asia or the Balkans rather than to the West in later times that one should look for analogies, as Macedonian practice appeared to be closer to Persian custom than to, say, that of Rome in the multiple use of towns.

If by "capital" we mean royal residence, it appears that Pella replaced Aegae about Archelaus's time. But the importance of Aegae as a burial site for Argead royalty was not diminished by the move to Pella. Moreover, the evidence of a theatre, an elaborate early Hellenistic palace, and festivals and celebrations at Aegae suggests that it remained a center for considerable royal activity. Dion, located in Pieria at the foot of the Olympus range, and discounted by Thucydides (4.78.6) as insignificant in Brasidas's day, had become a center of religious activity and festivals (Diod. 17.16.3–4) by Archelaus's time. Thus one can speak of Macedonian use of three centers: Dion and Aegae for ritual, festival, and burial purposes, and Pella as a royal residence and administrative/military center, to the extent that such matters were differentiated. One suspects that government was rather informal in those days, and that the center of the kingdom's activity lay near the doorway of the king's chamber, wherever that happened to be.

The second problem arises from the lack of information about the founding of Pella as the capital. The site had been occupied from early times, and it probably was Archelaus's contribution to move the royal residence and administration (such as it was) across the plain from Aegae. The administrative change is to be connected with Archelaus's military reforms and with a probable new Macedonian interest in the Vardar-Axios northern frontier. Now at peace with the Greek world, and free from the threats to the Thermaic Gulf, Chalcidice, and the Strymon Valley that had plagued his predecessors, Archelaus turned to the security of Macedon's landward frontiers. The main passage from the interior of the Balkans into central Macedonia followed the Vardar-Axios valley. About 25 miles above the modern Greek-Yugoslav border, the river pierces the barrier ranges in a narrow defile at

Demir Kapu, where remains of a major late fifth-century fortification suggest the establishment of a military garrison.[18] Lacking sufficient late fifth-century Macedonian parallels, we cannot with certainty date this fort to Archelaus's era. It is nevertheless tempting to permit the possibility—but no more than that—that the walls and tower at Demir Kapu are connected with Archelaus's reorganization. Thucydides (2.100.1) commended Archelaus for having improved the forts and strong places in the countryside after the Macedonians had used such places for refuge during the time of Sitalces's invasion from the north along a route paralleling the Axios narrows. Whether the fort was an attempt to guard the new capital at Pella, or the move to Pella is evidence of a Macedonian interest in the north—of which a fortified pass was an extension—cannot be known. Thus the connection between the Demir Kapu fort and Pella remains tenuous.

The evidence for Archelaus's move to Pella is indirect. A late source[19] tells of Archelaus's expenditure of a great deal of money on his palace, including the hiring of the famous painter Zeuxis, and the poet Agathon.[20] There is also considerable evidence to place the tragic playwright Euripides at Pella, where he produced at least *Bacchae* and *Archelaus*, and where he died *ca.* 406. The fourth-century *Periplus* of Scylax called Pella the capital (*basileion*), and Xenophon (*Hell.* 5.2.13) makes it the "largest city in Macedonia," although by Greek standards it was still a small town until the time of Philip II, who enlarged it (Strabo 7, frag. 20). The Athenian orators of Philip II's era all point to Pella as the center of official activity (and source of evil), and the town was the birthplace of Alexander the Great. Thus, although there is no certainty that Archelaus moved the royal residence—for that must be our definition of "capital"—the inferential evidence points to such a conclusion: there is no evidence of Pella's importance before the reign of Archelaus; there is evidence that Archelaus imported Greek artists into his court and that an expensive residence was built (location not stated); such a construction and adornment project is consistent with Archelaus's program and with no other monarch of the period; Euripides, patronized by Archelaus, worked at Pella; and within a generation Pella was the greatest of Macedonian cities. It remained so until its destruction by the Romans in 168/7 B.C.

Ultimately the problem of Pella's founding is capable only of an

[18] See Hammond, *HM* 1: 174 and 2: 146, with references to excavation reports.

[19] Aelian *VH* 14.17; the testimonia on Pella is collected in Papakonstantinou-Diamantourou, *Pella*, 101–47.

[20] On the poets assembled at Pella, see evidence collected by Hammond, *HM* 2: 149 n. 1, and Badian, "Greeks and Macedonians," 46 n. 18.

archaeological solution. The excavations carried out by the Greek archaeological service over the past three decades have revealed a huge Hellenistic site with abundant building foundations and decorated architectural fragments of the fourth to second centuries B.C., some of the earliest and finest existing pre-Roman mosaics, and a large number of small finds, including bronze ornaments, jewelry, coins, and terracotta figurines. Unfortunately, the site was thoroughly plundered by the Romans after the victory at Pydna that ended Macedonian independence, and in later centuries the ruins served as a quarry for nearby villages. It has thus been difficult to establish precise dates for much of what has been excavated, and the very size of the place has made excavation less systematic than at a smaller site. Given the huge expense and long time needed to excavate a site occupying hundreds of thousands of square meters, it will be many years before the archaeological answers to the question of Pella's founding will be forthcoming.

What has been recovered hints at a confirmation of the ancient writers' comments on Pella's splendors. Undoubtedly Archelaus's choice of the site reflected his recognition of the town's strategic location near the junction of the main east-west and north-south routes of the Balkans. A glance at a map will make clear the centrality of this location in strategic terms; that is, Archelaus may have realized the value of a site that would provide access to a wider area than just the central Macedonian plain. To reach the east by land from Aegae one had to describe a circuitous arc-shaped route that hugged the perimeter of the waterlogged Emathian plain. Events of the fifth century, in which Macedonian kings had found themselves frequently involved in regions east of the Axios, must have made the kings aware of the awkward location of the old capital. Pella was better suited than Aegae to administer and protect the routes that led westward toward western Macedonia, eastward across the Axios into Chalcidice and the Strymon, and northward into the heart of the Balkans.

Pella is located astride the modern highway that connects Salonica with Edessa and western Macedonia.[21] The modern road follows virtually the same course as the ancient route. To the south of the road is a gentle mound marking Phacus, Pella's port, a site that goes back to the Bronze Age. North of the road the ground rises gradually to a low ridge, the crest of which offers a sweeping panorama of the central plain, the head of the Thermaic Gulf, and the distant towering summits of the Olympus, Pierian, and Vermion ranges. The area known

---

[21] See Appendix C below, p. 296.

to encompass the ancient town measures more than 1½ square miles. The city was laid out on a grid plan, with blocks of *ca.* 50 m x 100 m, remarkably consistent in size throughout a vast area. Just north of the modern highway is a series of elaborate private houses, in which were discovered the well-wrought floor mosaics that are the centerpieces of the modest museum at the site. These large pebble mosaics, which formed the floors of rooms and passageways of Pella's villas, depict a variety of scenes, including Dionysus riding a panther, a lion hunt, an Amazonomachy, and a magnificent stag hunt signed by the artist, Gnosis. Many of the techniques of fine painting are here: foreshortening and other forms of perspective, shading, sculpture-like modeling of the human form, elaborate border designs, and harmonious composition. The mosaics speak of wealth and taste, and are an important, though not yet clearly understood, component in the development of Greek art in Macedonia.[22] North of the houses lies a highly developed agora, where fine shops and a sophisticated drainage system have been recovered.

On the higher ground to the northwest are the remains of what appears to be a huge palace complex. The absence of pottery and the poor condition of the remains—only foundations survive—have made the dating of the structure difficult. Dates ranging from the time of Philip II to the late fourth-century rule of Cassander have been proposed on the basis of the style of architectural fragments. If the former, it is an edifice worthy of the birthplace of Alexander the Great—covering about 60,000 m² (15 acres). An extensive veranda with a peristyle overlooking the town (a comparable large balcony exists also at the Hellenistic palace at Vergina), spacious courtyards, and the regular arrangement of rooms gives an axiality that not only lines up exactly on the city's grid plan but also makes one wonder if there is a duplicate structure lying in the unexcavated zone to the west. It is a building complex that could serve well as both a royal residence and a center of administration.

The palace of Archelaus has not been recovered, although it is unlikely that it lies under this great later fourth-century edifice. Perhaps it is located in the lower city, within an area of gates, houses, and cemeteries whose dating is yet a tangle. Nor has the theatre in which Euripides produced his plays been discovered (see below, p. 173), al-

[22] The antecedents of these early Hellenistic mosaics may have been a Macedonian invention of Archelaus's era. M. Robertson, "Early Greek Mosaic," suggests that late fifth-century Pella might have been the inspiration as well for the elaborate painted decoration and mosaics found somewhat later in houses in Olynthus and Athens. Also see Pollitt, *Art in the Hellenistic Age,* 40–41 and 210–16.

though we would be hard pressed to suggest what sort of structure one should look for, as there are no paradigms for late fifth-century theatres in Macedonian towns. That is, the Pella of Archelaus awaits identification amid the fragments of the later town. But there are sufficient architecture, sculpture, painting, and minor arts from the fourth century to hint not only at the wealth of Pella, but also at the high Greek style that Macedonian riches could graft onto native habits.

The move to Pella represented a new military and cultural orientation in the history of the Macedonian monarchy. Aegae, which had achieved its status for historical reasons, would not lose its significance as a ritual center and burial ground for Macedonian royalty. But the new showpiece of Macedon, designed to make a grand impression on the Greeks, and perhaps to compete with them in its architecture and cultural life, was part of the program of the first Argead to embrace Greece. It is unfortunate that as yet only bits and pieces of Pella, so thoroughly dismantled by Romans and later occupiers of the area, have yielded to the archaeologist's spade. Thus far we are still largely dependent upon literary sources for impressions of its grandeur.

Archelaus's Philhellenism

The creation of an impressive Macedonian center at Pella was, as we have seen, not only a political and military innovation, but also a cultural statement. The importation of Greek writers, artists, and architects as creators of and continuing participants in Macedonian court life gave the town a philhellenic cast unprecedented in Argead history. It was not that there had been no Greek influence in the kingdom prior to Archelaus; the Greeks who had lived in Macedon earlier, including those who served with Perdiccas, had, true to form, brought their culture with them, and some of it may have rubbed off on the Macedonians.[23] But Archelaus is the first Macedonian king for whom we have evidence of a conscious and public adoption of some aspects of Greek culture. The significance of this phenomenon has been much discussed in the modern literature. Some writers have suggested that Archelaus intended that Macedon enter into the Greek world as a Greek state. Hammond has quite sensibly rejected this view and pointed out that Macedon's important position in the Balkan-Aegean world resulted not from the adoption of some of the appurtenances of Greek culture,

[23] Hammond, *HM* 2: 148–49. Both Alexander I and Perdiccas II had entertained the occasional Greek writer at court.

but rather from the kingdom's "essential *difference* [my emphasis] in political structure, social layering, and economic development."[24]

But the question remains how "Greek" Archelaus and, by extension, Macedon really were. The external accessories of Greek culture must have been apparent in Pella, and it hardly seems likely that Euripides, who was in residence there, would have produced plays in Macedon that could not be understood by at least an elite audience. Indeed, the importation of Euripides can serve as a metaphor for an expression of admiration for the art and literature of Greece that marked the Macedonian ruling groups. In later times such devotion to foreign cultures would in similar fashion characterize the courts of Roman emperors and Russian czars. But, as Hammond shows, the significance of the Greek-Macedonian cultural conjunction was that the Macedonians adapted and exploited philhellenism for purposes that were uniquely Macedonian.[25] Indeed, one could add that the adoption of Greek adornments over the long run changed nothing fundamental in Macedonian society, so that many Macedonian elite may have talked like Greeks, dressed like Greeks, and imitated, imported, and admired Greek art, but they lived and acted like Macedonians, a people whose political and social system was alien to what most Greeks believed, wrote about, and practiced. It is thus not difficult to understand the implications of Thrasymachus's comment (above, p. 165).

The promotion of the legend proporting to show that the Argeadae were of Greek Argive descent is one of the most important examples of the extended philhellenism. We have seen (Chapters 4 and 5 above) that the tale of the Argive origin of the Argeads cannot be traced beyond Herodotus, who seems to have learned it from its probable inventor, Alexander I. As far as we know, the basic story remained unchanged until Euripides' arrival in Macedon.[26] Euripides' play *Archelaus* honored his patron by inventing a mythical Archelaus as a brave young man and descendant of Heracles who founded Aegae by command of Apollo. The playwright may have also produced a *Temenos* or *Temenidae* in which the progenitor Archelaus appears.[27] We

[24] Ibid., 149–50, with references to earlier work on the subject.

[25] E.g. (ibid., 150), Greek Pydna was refounded as a Macedonian city; the Greeks settled in the garrison at Demir Kapu were there to serve a Macedonian purpose; the festivals established at Dion and Aegae were dedicated to Macedonian expressions of worship; and the new Greek-looking capital at Pella was oriented to the continental, not Aegean, interests of Macedon.

[26] Thucydides' reference (2.100.2) to Archelaus's eight predecessors reflects the original king list that dates from the time of Alexander I.

[27] Harder, *Euripides' Kresphontes and Archelaos*, 129–37 and 288–90, whose work is now essential for an understanding of the problems associated with Euripides' work in

can date the revision of the foundation legend rather precisely, as Euripides arrived in Macedonia in 408 and died there in 406.[28] It is likely that the play was intended to celebrate Archelaus's Greek ancestry during a period in which both Archelaus and Athens were willing to encourage peaceful ties with one another. It is not possible to say where the play was produced. In Archelaus's time there was a festival at Dion (and a theatre was built somewhat later), and by the age of Philip II both a theatre and a festival were situated at Aegae. But as yet we have neither recovered a theatre nor found evidence of a festival at Pella.

Archelaus's coinage also reflects the Argive origin propaganda. With the recovery of the Bisaltic mines along the eastern frontier, the poor alloyed coinage of Perdiccas II gives way to good silver of weights designed to promote foreign trade, standards that would remain in effect until the reign of Philip II.[29] A number of obverse devices support the legendary apparatus: increasing use of the head of Heracles, the Temenid ancestor; use of a young male head, perhaps the mythical Archelaus or (later) Caranus; and the revival of the goat-head motif, connecting Archelaus with the founding of Aegae. While the best silver coinage was, as usual, reserved for foreign exchange—the object of its propaganda value—the first Macedonian issues of bronze coinage appear under Archelaus, suggesting an increasingly complex economic diversity requiring the use of coinage for local circulation. Finally, all Macedonian regal coins commencing with Archelaus's issues bear the king's name. The coins, therefore, provide evidence not only of Argead foundation legends, but also of the increasing status and power of the monarchy itself.

At Dion Archelaus instituted a festival to Zeus, including "Olympian games" and dramatic contests in honor of Zeus and the Muses.[30]

Macedon. Unlike Hatzopoulos ("Strepsa: A Reconsideration," 42), I do not hold that this link of the mythical Archelaus with Aegae supports a connection between the real Archelaus and Aegae as his capital. Euripides probably created the association because Aegae, as the original capital, was suitable for a founding myth.

[28] Harder (*Euripides' Kresphontes and Archelaos*, 125) puts the production of *Archelaus* in 408/7. By one tradition Euripides was torn apart at Pella by Archelaus's hunting dogs, by another he met the same fate from sheep dogs at Bormiscus (recounted in Steph. Byz. *s.v.* "Bormiskos," and accepted without comment by Hammond, *HM* 2: 139), and by a third at Arethousa (also accepted by Hammond, 1: 196 and 2: 160 and 162, wherein is also presented the testimonia for Euripides' burial in Macedonia). For the poet-dying-by-violence theme as a literary *topos*, see Lefkowitz, *Lives of Greek Poets*, 96–97.

[29] Kraay, *Archaic and Classical Greek Coins*, 119 and 144, and nos. 505, 507–8; Hammond, *HM* 2: 138; and *PM* 28 (illustration of an Archelaus goat stater). But it must be emphasized that the propaganda value of Archelaus's coinage, like Perdiccas's and Alexander's before him, is matched by its economic significance (see p. 127 above).

[30] Diod. 17.16.3–4 and Arr. 1.11.1. Arrian, perhaps mistakenly, puts the festival at

Dion, located in the Pierian coastal plain at the very foot of the mass of Mt. Olympus, would have presented a dramatic location for a festival to the Olympian Zeus. The Olympus-Pierian range rises abruptly from the narrow plain, providing a year-round backdrop of forested mountain outliers leading to craggy and snowy summits. Archaeology has yet to recover the site of the contests, but the excavation of this large city and sanctuary is just in its early stages, having produced impressive monuments from the Roman era, but only sporadic finds from earlier periods. Nonetheless, the quality of the epigraphical materials, bronzes, sculpture, and votive figures already recovered (though still mainly unpublished) from the period of the fourth century B.C. suggests that Dion may yet prove to be among the richest Macedonian sites, probably a major center of religious activity for the period commencing with the reign of Archelaus—a Macedonian Olympia.

Why Archelaus would wish to establish his own Olympian festival—or "counter-Olympics," as Badian has put it[31]—is a question that cuts to the core of the issue of philhellenism. It might be argued that he founded an Olympian festival as part of his general program of philhellenic embellishments in Macedon, with a peculiarly Macedonian character: a celebration honoring Zeus at a place called "Dion" (a form of the Greek word associated with divinity, and perhaps even Zeus) at the doorstep of the abode of the gods. But it does not seem likely that anyone interested in establishing himself as a Greek would risk antagonizing the Greeks by founding a competitor for the most famous of all panhellenic festivals. Not unless, of course, Archelaus, as a Macedonian, was not permitted to participate in the real Olympic Games, and was forced to initiate his own celebration in which Macedonians might compete. For it would appear that Greeks remained unpersuaded of the Greek descent of the Argeadae, who were thus prohibited from competing at the Olympic festival. It seems that no Macedonian king before Philip II participated in panhellenic games.[32] That

---

Aegae; here I follow Bosworth, "Errors in Arrian," 119–21, and *Hist. Comm. on Arrian*, 1: 97, rather than Hammond, *HM* 2: 150–51, and Hatzopoulos, "The Oleveni Inscription," 39–41. I do not, however, regard the matter as closed. The literary testimonia for Dion's importance as a religious sanctuary for Zeus is collected in Baege, *De Macedonium Sacris*, 10–12. An inscription (Tod *GHI*, no. 158, l. 9; see below, p. 217) describing an alliance between Philip II and the Chalcidians (356 B.C.) stipulates that the treaty shall be published in Dion at the sanctuary of Zeus, thereby testifying to the site's importance in the time of Philip.

[31] In a stimulating analysis of Archelaus's activity at Dion; see Badian, "Greeks and Macedonians," 35.

[32] Solinus 9.16 attests that Archelaus competed at Olympia and Delphi, winning the

Philip was able to do so may be testimony as much to his overwhelming political skills backed by formidable military power as to any acceptance by the Greeks of his Hellenic ancestry.

It may be possible to reconstruct Archelaus's policy of philhellenism from this fragmentary evidence. That he wished a closer relationship with the Greek world is beyond question. The sole surviving document from his reign—the inscription that attests to Archelaus supplying timber to Athens—attests to the peaceful and profitable link developed with that city. Whether his intervention in Thessaly was an attempt to demonstrate his ability to assume an equal station in the councils of Greek powers, or whether it was primarily a means of securing his southern frontier as a military necessity, is a matter of interpretation. His coinage and the adornment of the new capital at Pella testify both to his acceptance and exploitation of philhellenism, and to his self-proclaimed status as a strong monarch. The embellishment of the myth about the Argive origins of the Macedonian royal family is perhaps the clearest indication of Archelaus's desire to establish his Greek credentials. That is not to say that by Archelaus's time the Argeadae did not believe the story—almost certainly they did. But the Greeks did not.

Indeed, although Archelaus had been successful in luring some Greeks to contribute to the Hellenic imagery at Pella, and although he skillfully maintained a mutually beneficial diplomatic and economic relationship with Athens, he continued to suffer a poor reputation among many late fifth- and early fourth-century Athenians. Euripides and others had become Archelaus's clients in Macedon, as we have seen. Thucydides may have accepted the king's invitation,[33] but, according to Aristotle (*Rh.* 1398a.24), Socrates had refused. Aristophanes (*Frogs* 85) mocked one of those who had elected to join the banqueting in Macedon, and a tradition related by Athenaeus (345D) tells of the poet Choerilus, who spent on luxuries and food the large sums lavished on him by Archelaus.

Archelaus's patronage may have become a philosophical/literary issue in Athens: the foreign king who had murdered his way to the throne and was attempting to demonstrate his civility by buying notable Greeks to adorn his city and court. Probably there were those in

---

four-horse-chariot race, a source accepted by Hammond, *HM* 2: 150, without comment. Badian ("Greeks and Macedonians," 35 and 46 n. 16) has called attention to several extraordinary claims made by Solinus, and has argued persuasively for the rejection of this evidence. On Alexander I's alleged participation in the Games, see above, pp. 111–14.

[33] Following Wilamowitz, "Die Thukydideslegende," 353–56.

Athens who were jealous of the opportunities for personal advancement offered some of their contemporaries, but there was also a genuine underlying disgust at what Archelaus seemed to represent. The moralists had a field day. Archelaus emerged as the ideally bad man, as contrasted with the ideally good Socrates who had refused to become a client at the Macedonian court.[34] To emphasize the contrast between Socrates and those tied to Macedon, the sophist Gorgias, often cited as the antithesis of Socrates, was roundly criticized by the moralist Antisthenes for having taught the Thessalian Aleuadae, at that time friends of Archelaus.[35] And one wonders if the tradition that has Euripides killed by *Archelaus's* dogs (as opposed to anonymous canines; see note 28 above) is not an extension of the hostile tradition. One comes to appreciate even more Plato's withering account of Archelaus's accession (above, p. 161) when seen against the backdrop of such rhetorical enmity. Whether Archelaus knew of his evil reputation among some Athenians, or even cared about it, is a matter best left to speculation. But it is clear—his notoriety notwithstanding—that Archelaus was able to create a veneer of Greek culture by purchasing the services of some notable Athenians.

If the contemporary attitudes of Greeks mean anything—as measured, for example, by Thrasymachus's comment, the prohibition of Macedonian participation in panhellenic competition, and the attacks on those associated with Archelaus—many Greeks were not persuaded of Archelaus's Greek origins and did not welcome his attempts to introduce Hellenism into his court through the patronage of Greek artists, thinkers, and writers. What the Greek refusal meant to Archelaus is uncertain. One is tempted to speculate that Archelaus's intervention in Thessaly was a demonstration that, in the end, the Greek rejection of Macedon's Hellenism was irrelevant before the power of Macedonian arms. If true, Archelaus anticipates Philip II in this regard.

Hammond has rightly argued that there is no evidence to suggest that Archelaus intended that Macedon enter the larger world as a *Greek* power. One might add that all the symbols, the coinage, the importation of Greek culture, the Macedonian Olympic festival, the overtures to Athens, and the stories of the Argead's Hellenic ancestry are the signs not of one who exists in a fawning servitude before Greek culture, but of one who is independent, and does not wish to be rejected as yet another barbarian. It was not recognition as a Hellene that Ar-

[34] On this point see Dodds, *Gorgias*, 241. Socrates and Archelaus died in the same year (399), which cannot have gone unnoticed among those seeking parallels.
[35] Athen. 220D; Wade-Gery, "Kritias and Herodes," 25 n. 4.

chelaus wanted, but respect. Greek culture was perceived in the West as a standard by which civilized people measured their accomplishments. The adoption of that culture was one means of achieving respect. The other was force.

Archelaus's Death and the Struggle for Succession

Archelaus met his death in 399, accidentally killed by his lover Craterus during a hunting expedition, according to Diodorus.[36] The story might have been unquestioned were it not for another version found in Aristotle (*Pol.* 1311b.11–12), whose authority as one closer in time and place to these events must be given consideration. The context of Aristotle's comments about the incident is that some kings suffer as the result of their own shameful activities. He then proceeds to tell of intrigue among the young men of the court, culminating in the murder of Archelaus by Crataeus (Craterus in Diodorus's account; see note 36 above). A lover's quarrel and political ambitions play a role, and the episode is complicated by a hint of foreign conspiracy, as one of the schemers against the king is Hellanocrates of Larisa. Hellanocrates was also a lover of Archelaus; the king had promised, but failed, to restore him to his home, while continuing to exploit him physically.

For Aristotle—whose version is to be preferred—the assassination is triggered by both political and personal reasons.[37] There are elements in the story that recall other Macedonian plots—for example, the murder of Philip II and the conspiracy of court pages against Alexander during his Asian campaign. Carney has offered a compelling analysis of common themes: an insecure system of primogeniture, a kingship based on personal (as opposed to institutional) power, and a court filled with intrigue resulting from institutional pederasty. If one adds the competition for marriage into the royal family and the use of royal children for political marriages, the result is an unstable mixture. When political and personal motives became virtually indistinguishable, conspiracy to commit murder could result.

The six years following the death of Archelaus saw what can best be

[36] Diod. 14.37.6. Craterus is variously known as Crataeus (Arist. *Pol.* 1311b.11), Crateas ([Plut.] *Amatorius* 368F), and Crateuas (Ael. *VH* 8.9.1). Hammond, who otherwise prefers Aristotle's account (*HM* 2: 166–67), gives the version of the name (Crateuas) found in Aelian. [Plato] *Alc.* 2.141d recounts the killing, but does not name the murderer.

[37] Carney ("Regicide in Macedonia," 262–63) rightly observes that, although the context of this passage is Aristotle's description of rulers killed for personal reasons, the motivation for Archelaus's murder is largely political. Carney cites additional bibliography on the matter. Hammond (note 36 above) is useful on matters of source criticism.

178 CHAPTER 7

described as a dynastic struggle.[38] The conflict raged between the branches of the Argeadae that descended from Perdiccas, Menelaus, and Amyntas, the sons of Alexander I (see genealogical table, p. xviii above). Two other lines failed to survive, those of Philip (wiped out by Perdiccas and Sitalces) and Alcetas (probably destroyed by Archelaus). Orestes, the son of Archelaus and Cleopatra (otherwise unknown, but a prominent female Macedonian name), succeeded to the throne at his father's death. As a minor, he ruled under a regent, Aeropus (his uncle?), who seems to have usurped the throne *ca.* 398/7. We know that Aeropus was still ruling in mid-summer 394, when he came into conflict with the Spartan commander Agesilaus. We have already seen that the Spartans had opposed Archelaus's intervention in Thessaly *ca.* 400 B.C. When the Spartans undertook their campaigns against the Persians in Asia and needed to move armies across the land route through Thessaly and Macedonia, they found Macedon unfriendly. Later, when Corinth revolted against Spartan hegemony, Aeropus sided with the rebels and confronted Agesilaus's army, but was outwitted and forced to make a treaty with Sparta.[39] There is no further evidence concerning Aeropus's policies, but it would seem that he and the Thessalians shared an effort to obstruct Agesilaus in their northern part of the world.

Aeropus is said (Diod. 14.84.6) to have died of disease sometime near the end of the year 395/4. The next year saw three kings rule. The succession shifted away from the line of Archelaus to Amyntas II (the "Little"), a son of Menelaus.[40] Amyntas was killed by one Derdas, who may have been a member of the household, and whose name is common in the royal house of Elimeia, into which the Argeadae had married.[41] If the assassination of Amyntas by Derdas was an Elimiote plot it was unsuccessful, as the throne returned to the line of Archelaus. The succession bypassed Philip, son of Amyntas, and returned to a son of Aeropus, Pausanias. Pausanias died shortly after his selection, probably assassinated (Diod. 14.89.2) by another Amyntas (who would rule as Amyntas III), the grandson of the Amyntas who was

[38] Discussion in Hammond, *HM* 2: 168–72 (whose reconstruction I follow in broad outline), with a description and bibliography of the usual chronological problems associated with the length of reigns. The best chronology of this period is only conjectural. Evidence in Diod. 14.37.6, 84.6, 89.2, and 15.60.3.

[39] Polyaenus 2.1.17 and 4.4.3; Xen. *Hell.* 4.3.3–8, 10, and *Ages.* 2.1–2.

[40] Here following Hammond, *HM* 2: 168–69. Errington (*Gesch. Make.* 233 n. 6) finds Hammond's view unacceptable, and makes Amyntas II a son of Archelaus.

[41] Evidence on the succession of the year 394/3 is collected in Hammond, *HM* 2: 169–70.

the son of Alexander I. The line of Perdiccas II and Archelaus had now probably died out, and most, if not all, kings of fourth-century Macedon—including Philip and Alexander—would descend from Alexander I through his son Amyntas, not through Perdiccas. The dynastic struggle of the 390s illustrates that primogeniture could play little role in the selection of Macedonian kings when strong natural heirs were lacking.

One of the interesting aspects of the competition was its effect on the further embellishment of the Argead foundation legend. We have seen that Euripides had replaced the founder Perdiccas with an Archelaus as the royal progenitor. Now, in the new struggle for the throne, Archelaus was replaced by a neutral Caranus (a Doric word for "lord" or "ruler"), thereby reducing the importance of Perdiccas and Archelaus.[42] Although there is no direct evidence, it is tempting to argue that the change to Caranus occurred under Amyntas II or Amyntas III, descendants of Menelaus and Amyntas. In either case, the struggle was won by Amyntas III, whose succession insured the adoption of the new king list, whether or not he invented it. The revised king list provides yet another example of the Argeads rewriting their own history as political propaganda.

[42] Persuasively argued by Greenwalt, "The Introduction of Caranus," with evidence cited. Additional early kings are added by later fourth-century writers. See p. 83 above.

The House of Amyntas III

The Reign of Amyntas

The events of the first half of the fourth century B.C. present a historiographical nightmare for the historian of Macedonia. There is no ancient narrative source for the careers of Archelaus and his successors. Chance references in Xenophon, Isocrates, Diodorus, Justin, Plutarch, and some Athenian orators, and a handful of fragments in late chronographers, provide a tantalizing but bare outline of events, and there is little archaeology for support. This remains one of the most obscure periods of Macedonian history, and any reconstruction of the era is problematic, made more so by several decades of scholarship more ingenious than persuasive. An understanding of Amyntas III's reign is made especially difficult by the possibility of a doublet existing in Diodorus (14.92.3–4 and 15.19.2–3; see Appendix C below, pp. 296–97). If one accepts that these passages form a doublet—that is, duplicate accounts of the same event intentionally or accidentally repeated—Amyntas was chased from his throne only once by an Illyrian invasion. If the passages are not a doublet, but accounts of two separate and similar events, Amyntas abandoned his kingdom twice in distress, once in 393 and again *ca.* 383/2. Whatever the case, Justin's comment (7.4.6) that Amyntas III's reign saw "formidable conflicts with the Illyrians and Olynthians" captures the spirit of the age.

Amyntas had barely seized the throne in 394/3 when he found his kingdom under attack by a powerful Illyrian force, probably led by Bardylis, king of the Dardanii.[1] The Illyrians were not a nation in any

---

[1] Hammond, *HM* 2: 172, and "The Kingdoms in Illyria," 248 and 252–53. There are few narrative accounts available to the reader who wishes to know more about the Illyrians. The most useful studies are those of Dell, "The Illyrian Frontier," and a work recently released by the Albanian Academy of Sciences by Islami et al. (*Les Illyriens*). While partly a political tract with transparent ideological content, the Albanian book nonetheless provides a readable narrative reflecting up-to-date scholarship and bibliography. Unfortunately, there are no notes. Stipčević's *The Illyrians* is deficient (e.g., see above, p. 75, n. 42).

strict sense, but rather a collection of tribes.[2] Individual tribal names were known by the Greeks, and it is unlikely that the tribes thought of themselves as part of any larger political entity. That they are grouped together is the result of Greek and Roman perceptions about them: they are barbarians, like Celts, Paeonians, and Thracians. Like many barbarians they kept no formal record of their activities, and we are entirely dependent upon foreign eyes in looking at them. Unlike the Thracians, who were more highly organized and had been influenced by their exposure to Persians and Greeks, the Illyrians are virtually silent archaeologically. Illyrian tribes moved about constantly, and there are no fixed land borders to the area known by the Greeks as "Illyris." Roughly speaking, Illyris consisted of the large region north of Epirus and western Macedonia from the Adriatic coast to the crest of the Dinaric Alps. From time to time the Illyrians spilled over into the fertile land in southeastern Serbia, Kosovo, and Yugoslav Macedonia.

If the evidence can be trusted (Just. 7.2.5–13), there were frontier skirmishes between Illyrian tribes and Macedonians as early as the later sixth century B.C., and much of what we know about Macedonian kings before Alexander I relates to their struggles against Illyrian incursions.[3] These Illyrian raids must have penetrated western Macedonia and threatened the Argead territory in the central plain. A century later, during the campaign of Brasidas and Perdiccas II against the Lyncestian chief Arrhabaeus, the Illyrians continued to press their claims against Macedon by joining Arrhabaeus.[4] Some Illyrians, individuals and tribes, played a peripheral role in the Peloponnesian War, especially in situations where their fearsome military reputation and proximity were exploited by Greeks in the struggle for control of the coastlines of Epirus and Acarnania. But the Illyrian invasions during the reign of Amyntas III had little to do with Greek politics. They must be seen rather in the context of the inland frontier struggles that marked Balkan history in antiquity.

[2] Hammond ("Kingdoms in Illyria," 239–42) is persuasive in opposing the view of Papazoglou ("Les origines et la destinée") that there existed an Illyrian confederation of which kings were members. Hammond correctly sees the Illyrians as independent tribes characterized by shifting balances of power.

[3] Dell, "The Illyrian Frontier," 32. Justin reports that after one Macedonian defeat, the infant king Aeropus was moved to the front to encourage the soldiers—the first instance of the Macedonian custom that the king should be physically present at military engagements.

[4] See above, p. 152. Dell, "The Illyrian Frontier," 37–38, persuasively discounts the claims that Arrhabaeus was an Illyrian.

The Illyrian invasion that followed shortly after Amyntas III's succession was severe enough to drive him off his throne and out of the country.[5] Desperate for aid, Amyntas offered to Olynthus some of his own territory bordering theirs, perhaps the same land in the Volvi-Koroneia Lake Corridor that Perdiccas II had temporarily granted the Olynthians in 432. There is no indication that Olynthus assisted the Macedonians, but eventually the Thessalians—who had been loyal since Archelaus's time—did help Amyntas regain his throne.[6] Whether Amyntas was briefly replaced on the throne in the late 390s by Argaeus is not clear.[7] What we know of these Illyrian incursions suggests that they were raids for booty, and not for political arrangements of the type suggested by the installation of puppet kings (*cui bono?*). Thus the evidence for Argaeus's kingship is so slim as to be almost invisible, and attempts to create a place for him in the Macedonian king list are too heavy a burden to place on a single afterthought in Diodorus. The interpretations that scholars have offered are irreconcilable. Prudence demands that we admit that we do not know for certain who Argaeus was, if he ever ruled, and if so, when.

It was about this time that Amyntas established an alliance with the Chalcidic cities led by Olynthus.[8] The surviving portions of the treaty, found on two sides of a stone at Olynthus, establish a military alliance between Amyntas and the Chalcidians and also provide some conditions for the export of forest products. The Chalcidians are permitted freely to export pitch and timber for construction and shipbuilding. The only restriction is that fir for ship timbers must be cleared with Amyntas, and the appropriate dues paid. Conditions regulating the export, transit, and dues of other commodities are established. Finally, both parties agree not to establish friendship, except by common consent, with Amphipolis, Acanthus, Mende, or the Bottiaeans. The

---

[5] Diod. 14.92.3–4 and, perhaps, 15.19.2–3. Isocrates (6.46), who recounts that Amyntas remained in Macedonia in a fortified place from which he recovered his kingdom in three months, cannot be reconciled with Diodorus. Moreover, for those who believe that the two passages in Diodorus refer to separate Illyrian invasions, there is disagreement about which incursion Isocrates—writing in the mid-360s—is referring to: that of 393/2 (Hammond, *HM* 2: 173), or of 383/2 (Ellis, "Amyntas III," 3–4).

[6] Amyntas's Thessalian friends were probably the Aleuadae of Larisa, led by Medius, who had managed to extend his control over a sizable part of the Thessalian plain and establish himself as a formidable power in the region; evidence cited in Hammond, *HM* 2: 172–73.

[7] On Argaeus's kingship, see Appendix C below, pp. 296–97.

[8] Tod *GHI*, no. 111, who dates the treaty to *ca.* 393. Translation and some commentary in Hornblower, *The Greek World*, 205, and Wickersham and Verbrugghe, *Greek Historical Documents*, no. 12.

treaty is one-sided, favoring Chalcidic interests, providing a nearly un-precedented freedom to trade in forest products traditionally under Macedonian control, and establishing the guidelines for isolating Olynthus's chief adversaries in the region.

The complexity and long-term arrangements of this treaty do not accord easily with the desperation of the newly elevated Amyntas on the eve of the Illyrian invasion, when he made a panic gift of land use to the Olynthians and abandoned his kingdom. Amyntas probably fled to Thessaly (not Chalcidice), where the Argeadae had long had friends who now helped restore him to the throne after a short period of time. It thus seems best to date this fifty-year treaty to the period following his restoration, as Amyntas set about establishing some long-term se-curity arrangements.[9] That it favored the Chalcidians shows how in-secure Amyntas was and what price he was willing to pay to ensure that he had allies along his eastern frontier.

The next few years saw the continued rise of the Chalcidians, led by Olynthus. And Amyntas's response was to seek additional allies, per-haps not only against the possibility of a new Illyrian attack, but also against his Chalcidian neighbors, now a formidable power in their own right. Sometime not long after 386, Amyntas may have established a connection with the ambitious, pleasure-loving Kotys, chief of the re-vived Thracian Odrysians. In the manner of his predecessors, Kotys had married his daughter to a prominent Athenian in the service of the Odrysians, the general Iphicrates. This Iphicrates was later adopted as a son by Amyntas, perhaps in recognition of a military link with the Thracians.[10]

By 385/4 the Illyrians were active again in the west, attacking Epirus in an attempt to restore an exiled Molossian king, Alcetas, to the Epi-rote throne. Some 15,000 Molossians were killed in battle, and the sit-uation was serious enough to provoke the Spartans into sending a force north to drive out the Illyrians.[11] Amyntas's position was precarious; he was threatened by the possibility of a renewed Illyrian attack

[9] Here I revise the date of the treaty I suggested in "Timber and Politics," 45, after Tod, GHI 2: 32–33. I cannot date the treaty precisely, except to put it after Amyntas's return. Hammond's date of ca. 391 (HM 2: 173) is as good as any, although I do not share his belief that the land around the Lake Volvi was returned (see below, note 12). The sources are silent on the matter.

[10] Aesch. 2.25, who speaks of Athenian friendship and service to Amyntas, and Athen. 4.131A–F, who tells of the legendary lavishness of Iphicrates's wedding to the Thracian princess. For modern bibliography, see Ellis, "Amyntas III," 7. Several of the Thracian inscribed silver vessels from the Rogozen hoard are from Kotys's reign; see Fol et al., The New Thracian Treasure, 11–12, 24 and nos. 28–31, 40–43, and 45–47.

[11] Diod. 15.13.1–3.

through the western Macedonian cantons, and wary of the ambitions of his Olynthian ally to the southeast. The Thessalians had proved friendly since Archelaus's time, and the new league with the Thracians—and, indirectly, with Athens—were Macedonian attempts to augment security. Although it is difficult to know why the Thracians agreed to a link with Macedon, the Thessalians may have seen in a strong Macedon a buffer against the troublesome Illyrians. Perhaps the Thracians saw Macedon the same way.

The possibility that the resurgence of Illyrian activity in the west actually spilled over into Macedon itself depends upon whether one accepts the validity of Diodorus's second entry (15.19.2–3), as we have seen. My own view is that the reference to the Illyrians may be a doublet of 14.92.3–4—essentially a reminder of the events of 393 B.C.—but that what follows is independent.[12] For we are told something new, that the Olynthians were enjoying Amyntas's land and its revenues, and were not about to return it, a situation that had obtained since 393. Indeed, the Olynthians had extended their control into Macedonia itself, by acquiring control first over the nearer towns, and then over those farther away, until, as Xenophon tells us, they possessed "many other Macedonian cities, including even Pella, the largest of the cities in Macedonia."[13] Amyntas's position was precarious, his kingdom reduced now probably to the confines of the Argead ancestral domain, the Pierian region around Aegae. Archelaus's new capital might have been strategically well placed for a state on a Balkan imperial path, but, under siege, Amyntas may have retired to the isolated citadels of his forebears.

At this crucial juncture, Amyntas regressed to the policy of his pre-Archelaus fifth-century predecessors: he sought the aid of a major Greek power. In the period following the Peloponnesian War, Sparta had developed a foreign policy that was active on several fronts—in Asia and East Greece, Sicily, Egypt, and the north.[14] While the Spartans under Agesilaus were off fighting in Asia, a concert of Greek states, including Athens, Thebes, and Corinth, led a rebellion against

[12] Diod. 15.19.2 has Amyntas again giving away a piece of borderland in return for Olynthian aid against the Illyrians. But there is no need for Amyntas to give away his land a second time: he now is tied to the Olynthians by the alliance of ca. 391, by which Olynthus pledges to give military aid, and there is no evidence that the first gift of land of 393 was ever returned. Again, the problem of the doublet is insolvable, and the present interpretation is tentative.

[13] *Hell.* 5.2.13, incidentally suggesting that Pella was already the capital.

[14] For an analysis of Spartan policy in this period (with sources and bibliography), see Hornblower, *The Greek World*, 181–91, and C. Hamilton, "Amyntas III and Agesilaus."

Spartan hegemony in Greece. This so-called Corinthian War (395–387) checked Spartan ambitions in the north, where Thrace, Macedonia, and Thessaly had been considered vital to Spartan military communications with Asia. The insurmountable difficulties faced by a small Greek city-state fighting a war on two continents forced the Spartans to abandon their Asian venture. The settlement with the Persians known as the King's Peace (387/6) favored Spartan interests in Greece and, by breaking up the hegemonies raised against them, freed the Spartans to renew an active Hellenic foreign policy. Thus the Spartans were able to send a force against the Illyrians in Epirus in 385/4, and thus in 383 they could listen to appeals from the north about the expanding power of Olynthus.

Apollonia and Acanthus (the latter was one of the Chalcidic cities excluded from friendship by the Macedonian-Olynthian alliance of 391) sent envoys to Sparta to plead for assistance against Olynthus. The Acanthian envoy, Cleigenes, put a strong case against Olynthian aggression in the region, and proferred the threat that the Athenians and Thebans might join Olynthus.[15] The spectre of a northern Olynthian empire supported by Athens and Thebes was intolerable to Sparta, especially if Olynthus's enemy were Macedon, who was not a party to the King's Peace. Macedonian policy had long been one of neutrality, even friendliness, to the southern Greeks, provided, of course, that Macedonian interests were not threatened. It may have seemed advantageous to Sparta to preserve a neutral and independent Macedonian state—both nonthreatening and nonthreatened—as the best assurance of freedom of passage for Spartan troops in the north, and perhaps as a continuing shield against Balkan barbarians. Thus when Amyntas of Macedon—having already gathered his own small forces against the Olynthian occupation of his kingdom—appealed to the Spartans for assistance, he found a ready ear.[16]

The Spartans wasted no time in responding to the appeals from Amyntas and the two Chalcidian cites, Apollonia and Acanthus. An allied advance force under Spartan leadership arrived in the north in spring 382 and took Potidaea.[17] The main force, under Teleutias, moved north, taking Thebes en route. Teleutias sent ahead to Amyntas, ordering him to enroll mercenaries and to gain the assistance of

[15] Xen. Hell. 5.2.11–20; also Seager, "The King's Peace," 41–42.

[16] Diod. 15.19.3. Amyntas may not have even been able to raise a national levy; his "personal force" (idian tē dynamin) probably consisted of the king's own men and mercenaries (after Hammond, HM 2: 177).

[17] For narrative and sources for the Spartan campaign in Chalcidice, see HM 2: 177–78.

nearby kings through the payment of money (Xen. *Hell.* 5.2.38–41; so much for Spartan confidence in Amyntas's army). Amyntas may have gotten hold of some Thracian mercenaries through his connection with Iphicrates. What is clear is that the "nearby kings" of Teleutias's instructions were the chiefs of western Macedonia. The Spartan commander contacted the Elimeian chief, Derdas, warning him that his realm was about to be overrun by the Olynthians, as the kingdom of Amyntas had been (ibid.). The well-trained cavalry of Derdas, admired and honored by the Spartans, distinguished themselves in battle against the Chalcidians, thereby offering a comparison with the lackluster performance of Amyntas's forces.

But Teleutias found himself hard-pressed in his campaigns against Olynthus in 382 and 381, and a dispatch of reinforcements from Sparta was necessary to save the day. The new Spartan commander, Agesipolis, managed to coordinate his northern allies, including Amyntas (Isoc. *Paneg.* 126), Derdas, and some Thessalians. Although we have no information about the Macedonian contribution to the final stages of the war, Olynthus surrendered in 379. The Chalcidian League was dissolved and forced to submit to Spartan leadership in matters dealing with foreign policy. Amyntas's former lands were restored, both his central kingdom and, presumably, the lands that he had entrusted to the Olynthians in 393.[18]

But fortunes changed quickly in the world of Greek antiquity. The collapse of Olynthus in 379 had deprived the restless Greeks of their rallying point of resistance against the Spartan hegemony. Within a year, the Athenians and several other cities had joined to form a new anti-Spartan alliance, which we know as the Second Athenian League.[19] With alacrity worthy of his Argead ancestors, Amyntas responded to the new situation and began to draw closer to Athens. The ties between Macedon and Athens are relatively well documented for the period of the 370s, and rest upon mutual interests. Amyntas continued to seek assistance against threats to Macedonian sovereignty, and the Athenians were as dependent upon Macedonian timber to meet their naval needs in the fourth century as they had been in the fifth.[20] Incidentally, Amyntas would also draw revenues from the sale of tim-

[18] Whether the territory in the corridor of Lakes Volvi and Koroneia, or in Anthemus (given in 383/2, as Hammond believes, ibid., 173 and 178).

[19] For which, now see Cargill's study of the league, *The Second Athenian League.*

[20] See the useful discussion in Cawkwell, "Athenian Naval Power." Earlier, when it appeared that Olynthus's fortunes were waxing *ca.* 383, the Athenians had pressed Olynthus for an alliance, probably to gain access to northern timber; see Tod *GHI*, no. 119, with commentary and bibliography on the disputed date for this treaty.

ber, although we have no information about an increase in wealth during his reign or the uses to which it might have been put.[21] It is clear that the Athenians were reliant upon Macedonian timber by the mid-370s (Xen. *Hell.* 6.1.11), and sometime shortly after, Amyntas and Athens made an alliance.[22] Although the two poor surviving fragments of the treaty make no specific reference to timber, the establishment of such an alliance was undoubtedly designed to formalize relations between the two states to ensure the continuation of the timber sales that had existed for some time. For example, about 370, Amyntas granted ship timber to the Athenian Timotheus for his naval enterprises. This was actually a private agreement between Amyntas and a foreigner, consistent with the prerogatives of Macedonian monarchs in their control over timber resources.[23] Although there is no evidence of any formal relationship between Amyntas and the Athenian League, the treaty with the Athenians and the private timber sales ultimately contributed to the strengthening of the league's power.

Part of the evidence for the renewal of Argead confidence toward the end of Amyntas's reign is the diplomatic involvement of Amyntas in the affairs of his neighbors. In Thessaly, the tyrant Jason of Pherae had overthrown the old Argead supporters, the Aleuadae of Larisa, but Amyntas found it convenient to reach an accommodation with the new ruler (Diod. 15.60.2). In western Macedonia, Amyntas served as an arbitrator in a frontier dispute between the Elimeians and the Perrhaebians.[24] And in 371, an envoy of Amyntas sat as a voting member in a conference called by the Athenians and Spartans to discuss a general peace (Aesch. 2.32). Macedon supported Athens's claim to Amphipolis, a reversal of the long-standing Macedonian position to encourage Amphipolis's independence. The Macedonian representative sat as an independent Athenian ally, perhaps set up by the Athenians to support their Amphipolitean policy. Athens's goal of recovering Amphipolis (with its access to the timber resources of the area) is a return to Athenian policy of the mid-fifth century, and would clearly

---

[21] Some striking silver didrachms appear in Amyntas's reign. Hammond (*HM* 2: 180), as usual, connects the enhanced quality of Macedonian coinage with the repossession of Bisaltic silver mines. This, however, neglects the possibility that silver may have come from another source, e.g., the sale of timber.

[22] Tod *GHI*, no. 129, usually dated to 375 or 373; see Cargill, *The Second Athenian League*, 85–87.

[23] Borza, "Timber and Politics," 40. The wood was sent from Macedon to Timotheus's house in Piraeus (Demos. 49.26–30). For Timotheus, his connection with Iphicrates, and the role of both in the politics of the north, see Kallet, "Iphikrates, Timotheos, and Athens."

[24] Hammond, *HM* 2: 178.

have been harmful to Macedonian economic and political interests. One wonders if Amyntas's fortunes had sunk so low as to require such a state of dependency upon Athenian wishes.[25] We are lacking information about Amyntas's motives, but if, as a true Argead, he was acting in a manner consistent with his predecessors, he was performing from a condition of weakness some short-term tactical maneuver that had no long-range significance. It seems unlikely (as events would eventually prove) that a Macedonian king was about to reverse a cornerstone of policy that had served the country well for more than half a century.

Amyntas's reign is a study in survival.[26] The death of Archelaus—who had been on the road to a greater Macedonian hegemony in the lower Balkans—and the dynastic struggles of the 390s had weakened Macedon rule. Unfortunately for the Argeads, this internal turmoil coincided with the pressure of the Illyrians under Bardylis and the expansion of Olynthian power. The former was unanticipated—it was part of the historical movement of Balkan tribes—but the latter had a basis unwittingly laid by Perdiccas II in his struggle against Athens. Part of Amyntas's reign saw the countryside under foreign attack and occupation. There was considerable devastation, and one awaits further excavation at places like Pella to confirm the extent of destruction. The Macedonian army, which had showed some promise under Archelaus, was reduced to inconsequence. Amyntas was forced into dependency upon Olynthians, Thessalians, Thracians, and eventually Athenians. Some had traditional ties with Macedon; others had correctly assessed Macedon's weak condition and were determined to exploit it for their own interests.

The situation illustrates how illusory were the superficial wealth and grandeur of Archelaus's reign and, even without direct evidence about Macedonian institutions, suggests strongly that the social, economic, and political infrastructure of the kingdom was still primitive and unable to withstand the onslaught of externally generated crises. Despite the facade of Hellenism that had accrued during the late fifth century, and the occasional appearance of Macedonians attempting to deal with Greek cities on a plane of equality, Macedon still functioned as a rather

[25] Argued by Hammond, ibid., 179, who also points out that Macedon was not regarded as a Greek state, and did not act on a par with Greek states in this panhellenic conference. Cargill (*The Second Athenian League*, 85–86) suggests that the Macedonians were not members of the Second Athenian League.

[26] There is a useful summation of his career and the condition of the kingdom (with sources) in Hammond, *HM* 2: 179–80.

backward Balkan kingdom, dependent almost entirely upon its sporadic military power and the luck and skills of its chiefs.

The Prelude to Philip II

Having survived so many dangers—including a conspiracy against him by his wife Eurydice and her lover, if Justin (7.4.7–8) is to be believed—Amyntas died at an advanced age and left the throne to his eldest son, Alexander. The year was 370/69, perhaps late in 370.[27] If it appeared that a succession based on primogeniture and the clear upswing in the fortunes of Amyntas during the last part of his reign portended well for Macedon, events proved otherwise. The decade of the 360s plunged the kingdom of Macedon into a new dynastic crisis, intensified by continuing external threats. Early in his reign, Alexander was forced to buy off the Illyrians, although it is problematic whether he also gave his younger brother, Philip (the future Philip II), over as a hostage.[28]

In Thessaly, the redoubtable Jason of Pherae, who, had he lived, might have anticipated Philip II's organization of the Balkans, was assassinated; his successor was also murdered.[29] The Aleuadae of Larisa saw an opportunity to regain their independence from Pherae and approached their traditional ally, the king of Macedon, for aid. Forestalling a move by Pherae, Alexander II of Macedon took Larisa and restored the Aleuadae. There was a movement of other Thessalians toward the Aleuadae, undoubtedly encouraged by Alexander's prom-

[27] Isoc. 6.46; Diod. 15.60.3; Just. 7.4.8. There is no evidence in the sources for Hammond's statement (HM 2: 181) that the "people elected" Alexander to the throne; Justin's *regno maximo ex filiis Alexandro tradito* can be taken figuratively as easily as literally. On Hammond's view that Tomb I at Vergina held the remains of Amyntas, see Appendix C below, pp. 297–98.

[28] Hammond (HM 2: 181) believes that Philip was an Illyrian hostage, preferring Just. 7.5.1 to Diod. 16.2.2, who emphasizes the initiative of the Illyrians in taking Philip hostage and later turning him over to the Thebans. Neither Diod. 15.67.3 nor Plut. *Pelop.* 26.4, both of whom mention Philip's Theban hostageship, refers to the Illyrian period. The chronology of events works against the matter. The new Illyrian campaign could not have begun until after the winter of 370/69 at the earliest, making Alexander's settlement with the Illyrians perhaps in the spring or summer of 369. Within a year (368, by Hammond's own chronology) Philip had been shipped off as a hostage to Thebes. It seems unlikely that Prince Philip would have been shunted around so (what prompted the Illyrians to give him up?), the chronology is too tight, and our best source for Philip, Diodorus, gives mixed signals on the matter of an Illyrian hostageship. Griffith (HM 2: 204 n. 5) also has some doubts about Philip in Illyris.

[29] For a review of Thessalian matters in this period see Westlake, *Thessaly in the Fourth Century B.C.*, 160–216, and Martin, *Sovereignty and Coinage*, 89–113.

ise of Thessalian self-rule, and from fear of Alexander of Pherae, one
of Jason's successors who threatened them. But Alexander of Macedon
reneged, betraying the long-standing goodwill between the Aleuads
and the Argeads by refusing to end his occupation of Thessalian towns.
At this juncture the Aleuadae called in the Theban Pelopidas, whose
Boeotian army freed Larisa from the Macedonians, while also confin-
ing Alexander of Pherae to his own city. Alexander II withdrew from
Thessaly, both because his forces were inadequate to hold it and because he was at war at home.

In Macedon the challenge to Alexander's rule came from Ptolemy
of Alorus, probably the same person mentioned as an envoy in the
inscription setting out the alliance of Amyntas III with Athens of *ca.*
375–373 (above, p. 187). His prominent place in the list of envoys suggests an important position in the Macedonian hierarchy, and Hammond has posited that he was the son of Amyntas II, and thereby descended from Menelaus, son of Alexander I.[30] If so, Ptolemy's
contention represents the final challenge by the house of Menelaus to
the line of Menelaus's brother, Amyntas. The evidence does not permit much understanding of Ptolemy's exact position as a member of
the royal family, his connection with Alorus, or the chronology of his
relationship with Eurydice, widow of Amyntas III.[31] We can only
guess at the reasons why the strong-willed Eurydice established a liaison with Ptolemy, whether to challenge Alexander's succession on
some political grounds unknown to us, or to overthrow the house of
Amyntas as part of a foreign plot (see below, p. 191), or to put Ptolemy on the throne as a feature of a simple lovers' plot. In any event,
Pelopidas was called in to arbitrate the dispute between the factions.[32]
He seems to have been successful, but the price of the settlement made
with Pelopidas in 368 included sending a number of leading Macedonian sons, including Alexander's brother, Philip, to Thebes as hostages. Philip, now thirteen or fourteen years of age, was installed in
the house of Pammenes, where he lived for three years, until 365.[33]

[30] *HM* 2: 181–83, also for what follows.
[31] Just. 7.4.7–8 and 7.5.4–8. If Justin is to be believed, Eurydice and Ptolemy were
lovers, even though Ptolemy was married to a daughter of Eurydice and Amyntas. The
lovers plotted to kill Amyntas, were found out, but remained unpunished in order to
save distress to Amyntas's daughter, to whom the king was deeply attached. See Hammond, *HM* 2: 183, who believes almost none of it, and Green, *Alexander of Macedon*, 14,
who believes a lot of it.
[32] Plut. *Pelop.* 26.3; Diod. 15.67.4.
[33] Plut. *Pelop.* 26.5; Diod. 16.2.2; Just. 7.5.3. The latter two—probably incorrectly—
have Philip living in the house of Epaminondas. Discussion in Griffith, *HM* 2: 204–6.

The hostages were intended to prevent a renewal of Macedonian activity in Thessaly.

Not long after, perhaps in the spring of 367, Alexander was assassinated during a festival that included the performance of the *telesias*, a war dance. Ptolemy is held responsible for the killing.[34] The conspiracy had succeeded, and Ptolemy now ruled the Macedonians, although whether as king or as regent in behalf of the young Perdiccas is a matter of debate. That Ptolemy succeeded to the throne is not proof that he had no part in the murder of Alexander II.[35] Even though one Apollophanes of Pella was executed for his part in the death of the king (Demos. 19.194–95), he could have been an agent in a conspiracy managed by others. Moreover, the throne was his who could take it and hold it, and Ptolemy was not a pretender. Whether the grandson of Menelaus or of Archelaus, he was the great-great-grandson of Alexander I—impeccable Argead credentials. As for the plots of Eurydice, it is difficult to know what to accept and what to deny. Clearly there was a considerable intrigue at the court, sufficient to attach her name to some of it, even though Plutarch and Diodorus fail to mention her as party to the conspiracies.

Until now Macedonian women have been mainly names—wives and daughters. They have been shown to be fit to bear children, provide legitimacy, and be married off to foreigners or collateral branches of the Argead clan for some political or diplomatic purpose. Eurydice, however, emerges as a person in her own right, strong and independent, if apparently improper. Her mother was the daughter of the Lyncestian king Arrhabaeus (against whom Perdiccas II and Brasidas had fought), and her father was an Illyrian chieftain, Sirrhas, who may have been a Lyncestian ally of Arrhabaeus or his son.[36] That Amyntas III should marry a woman of Lyncestian-Illyrian blood during a period in which the western frontier of Macedon was unstable is consistent with the Argead practice of making foreign marriages for political necessity. It is unfortunate that the evidence does not permit us to do more than speculate about a possible western connection in the conspiratorial attempts to overthrow Amyntas and Alexander II.

[34] Diod. 15.71.1 (Ptolemy personally); Marsyas Macedon, *FGrH* 135/6 F3 = Athen. 14.629D (Ptolemy's men).

[35] Hammond (*HM* 2: 183–84) believes that the Assembly met to investigate the killing of the king and choose a successor, although there is no evidence that there was a formal Assembly, what its powers were, or that it met on this occasion.

[36] Strabo 7.7.8 (C326); the name "Sirrhas" is now confirmed by the inscription discussed below. For Eurydice's family connections, see Hammond, *HM* 2: 14–16, and (better) Badian, "Eurydice," 103–4.

A recent discovery at the site of Aegae has provided us with our first, though imperfectly understood, material evidence for Eurydice. On the gentle slope down from the Hellenistic palace, in the area a little below the theatre, was excavated a small temple or shrine. Just outside the building itself are three statue bases, one of which bears the inscription *Euridika Sirra Eukleiai* ("Eurydice, daughter of Sirrhas, [erected this statue] to Eukleia").[37] The inscription was done by a skilled stonecutter, and the excavator dates it on the basis of letter forms to the last half of the fourth century.

Eucleia is a minor deity representing renown, good reputation, and honor, an abstraction, the worship of which sometimes had political significance.[38] Dedications to the goddess are well attested throughout Greece, including a temple in Athens.[39] Describing his walk through the Athenian agora, the second century A.D. traveller Pausanias (1.14.5) mentions the temple of Eucleia—probably located on the northwest slope of the Acropolis—as commemorating the battle of Marathon. On this analogy, Andronikos has suggested that the Eucleia temple at Aegae celebrated the Macedonian victory over the Greeks at Chaeronea in 338.[40] But the references to Eucleia in Athens are all to Eucleia Eunomia, and it seems more likely that the Eucleia at Aegae should be associated with Artemis Eucleia. Artemis Eucleia was widely worshipped in Boeotia, and the mid-fourth century was a period in Macedonian history during which, as we have seen, Boeotian connections were unusually close. Moreover, according to Plutarch (*Arist.* 20.6), Eucleia was thought by some persons to be the virgin daughter of Heracles (the Macedonian mythical progenitor) and Myrto. She received divine honors among the Boeotians and Locrians, and, Plutarch informs us, her altar and image were built in every marketplace, drawing sacrifices from those about to be married. One may therefore suggest that the monument dedicated by Eurydice not only reflects a Boeotian link and signifies the public liturgy of a prominent member of the royal house, but also helps mark the location of Aegae's agora.

Clearly this is not conclusive. Aside from the irony of the scandalous Eurydice dedicating a statue to the virgin Eucleia for the sake of sac-

---

[37] Description and photographs in Andronikos, *Vergina: The Royal Tombs,* 49–51, and *Ergon* (1983): 29–30.

[38] For other examples of such abstractions, see West, "Hellenic Homonoia," 308 n. 2.

[39] Testimonia in Wycherley, *The Athenian Agora,* 3: 58–59. Further discussion of the Athenian monuments in Culley, "The Restoration of Sacred Monuments," 187–92, and his epigraphical commentary, "The Restoration of Sanctuaries in Attica."

[40] *Vergina: The Royal Tombs,* 51, and *Ergon* (1983): 30.

rifices for successful marriages (although redemption is not impossible, as admirers of the Byzantine empress Theodora know), the date of the dedication is not precise enough to help determine its use. It stretches the imagination to think of Eurydice active at court for another three decades after the collapse of her own rule, still alive to erect a statue in commemoration of Chaeronea. If the construction of war memorials were a feature of Macedonian life, one would think that the king, as commander and victor, would do the honors. Moreover, the discovery of a second "Eurydice, daughter of Sirrhas" inscription in an early Christian church in the village of Vergina nearby complicates the issue.[41] One awaits the final excavation report on the Eucleia shrine to assist in dating the monument, and thereby perhaps to associate it with some aspect of Eurydice's career.

The uneasy reign of Ptolemy and Eurydice (for surely we must include her, even though "officially" a woman could not rule) was to last less than three years. The most serious continuing challenge came from Pausanias, whose origins are obscure, although he probably belonged to a collateral branch of the Argeadae.[42] Whatever his origins, Pausanias seems to have had considerable support within a kingdom still split over the matter of Alexander II's death and the elevation to the throne of Ptolemy. Ca. 367 Pausanias returned from an exile perhaps imposed by Amyntas III, and invaded Macedon with some Greek mercenaries. That he took Anthemus, Therme, and Strepsa among other places suggests a Chalcidic origin, and perhaps source of support, for his expedition. Eurydice appealed to Iphicrates of Athens, who was operating with a small fleet off Amphipolis.[43] It will be recalled that Ptolemy was mentioned as an envoy in the treaty binding Amyntas III and Athens at a period when Macedon had pledged to support Athens's attempts to recover Amphipolis. That Iphicrates should agree to assist Ptolemy and Eurydice against Pausanias not only reflects this earlier link, but enabled the Athenians to intervene in Macedonian affairs with the hope of continuing support in the north. With

[41] Reported briefly in *Ergon* (1983): 30. The excavator and author of the notice claimed that the discovery of the second inscription confirmed the earlier hypotheses concerning the Eucleia dedication. On the contrary, the second inscription raises new questions.

[42] Sources are: Aesch. 2.27–29; *Suda, s.v.* "*Karanos*"; and Diod. 16.2.4–6, although the latter's account is a hopeless conflation of the events of several years compressed into the year of Philip II's succession in 360/59. Hammond (*HM* 2: 184) makes Pausanias out to be a descendant of Archelaus.

[43] Hammond (see *HM* 2: 184) discounts Eurydice's tearful appeal to the Athenian commander (Aesch. 2.28–29, echoed in Nepos, *Iphicrates* 3) as so much of Aeschines's rhetoric and little more.

Iphicrates' help, Pausanias was driven from Macedon, although he would return briefly in 360/59 as one of Philip II's competitors for the throne.[44]

If the Athenians expected gratitude from Ptolemy for their having saved his rule, they had not accounted sufficiently for Macedonian self-interest, for Ptolemy simply returned to the strategic policy of his predecessors in working against Athenian interests at Amphipolis. Aeschines's rage (2.29–30) at Ptolemy's behavior is justified from the Athenian point of view, but it is also a curious appeal to honor from a city whose own relations with Macedon had been exploitative for nearly a century. At about the same time (367), the Theban Pelopidas invaded Macedon for the second time in less than two years, respond-ing to an appeal by a faction thought to be loyal to the dead Alexander and to Eurydice. Thebes was a major power and Ptolemy was forced to come to terms that were humiliating. An alliance was signed with Thebes, in which Macedon was pledged to support Theban policy, and hostages were taken to ensure Macedonian loyalty.[45] We cannot tell if Ptolemy's anti-Athenian policy in the matter of Amphipolis resulted from his being forced to adhere to the wishes of Thebes, Athens's en-emy, or whether it was a return to a traditional Macedonian position, as suggested above. The evidence does not offer an accurate enough sequence of events, although, in this case, Theban and Macedonian policy coalesced.

Ptolemy's death in 365 came at the hands of Amyntas III's second son, Perdiccas, for whom Ptolemy may have been serving as regent.[46] It is uncertain whether Ptolemy fell as the result of a plot against him

[44] M.C.J. Miller, "The Macedonian Pretender Pausanias and His Coinage," 23–25, has tried to show that Pausanias issued coinage in his own name during his rebellion against Amyntas. His argument rests on attributing to the pretender Pausanias a coin heretofore assigned to Pausanias the king (394–393 B.C.). Although I do not find Miller's position, based on such slim evidence, conclusive, he does raise the interesting possibility that all the pretenders of the period 367–360 issued coinage to help press their claims. More evidence is needed.

[45] Hammond, HM 2: 184–85 n. 3, rejects Geyer's view that this was the occasion of Philip II's hostageship in Thebes, an argument based on seeing Plut. Pelop. 26.4 and 27.3 as a doublet on Pelopidas's invasion(s) of Macedon. Hammond's reconstruction, which I follow, has two separate Theban invasions, in 368 and 367; Philip was made hostage on the occasion of the first of these. Whether the hostages of 367 were taken to ensure that Ptolemy would remain regent and not seize the throne from the young Perdiccas (whom the Thebans supported) depends upon whether one believes that Ptolemy served as regent or king. For the evidence, see Hammond, HM 2: 183, n. 2.

[46] Diod. 15.77.5, 16.2.4; Aesch. 2.29 (epitropos = "regent"). Discussion of Perdiccas in Hammond, HM 2: 185–88; Geyer, Makedonien, 134–39; and Errington, Gesch. Make., 41–42.

by Perdiccas, or whether Perdiccas came of age, achieved his kingship, and then disposed of his regent. What Eurydice's role was in all of this we cannot say, as our literary sources are henceforth silent about her. Perdiccas's younger brother, Philip, who was sixteen or seventeen at the time, was soon brought home from Thebes, where he had been a hostage for three years. The connection with the Boeotians was reaffirmed, and a recently discovered decree of the Theban league of about 365 honors the Macedonian Athenaeus as *proxenos* and *euergetēs*. It is not unlikely that Athenaeus was an advisor to the naval program of the Theban leader Epaminondas, and also served as the connection between the Boeotians and their timber source in Macedonia.[47]

In the period following Sparta's defeat by the Thebans under Epaminondas and Pelopidas at Leuctra in 371, Theban power continued to grow, and Epaminondas was on the verge of challenging the Athenians at sea. Macedonian timber was necessary, and, unlike the Athenians, the Boeotians sensibly recognized that diplomatic arrangements with the Argeadae were a more efficient means of securing timber than was the use of force. The alliance between Thebes and Macedon was natural: an exchange of timber for support against continuing Athenian threats in the north. It was a partial return to Macedonian foreign policy of the fifth century.

Timotheus, the Athenian commander in the north, was a formidable adversary. His fleet was strong, and it is not impossible that some of his ships had been outfitted with timber provided by Amyntas III in 370 (above, p. 187). The Athenian presence was established in the Thermaic Gulf, with Pydna, Methone, and Potidaea having been seized as bases to threaten both Macedon and Chalcidice. Moreover, alliances were made with inland princes on the borders of Macedon. Lacking the protection of the lower Macedonians against Illyrian attack, the Orestians had joined the Molossian kingdom, a member of Athens's alliance. North of Orestis, a Pelagonian chieftain provided assistance to Athens against the Chalcidians and Amphipolis, and it is possible that the Odrysian Thracians were involved through the old ties established by Iphicrates. Athens seemed on its way to recovering its old northern empire.[48]

By 364/3 Perdiccas was forced by overwhelming pressure to bend to

[47] Borza, "Timber and Politics," 46 and n. 59, and Roesch, "Un décret inédit." A useful review of Theban-Macedonian relations in the mid-fourth century can be found in Hatzopoulos, "La Béotie et la Macédoine."

[48] Details, with sources, in Hammond, *HM* 186–87. Other Thracians, perhaps the Bisaltae and the local Thracians who had usually supported an independent Amphipolis, joined in the defense of the city.

Athens's will, and for a brief time he provided assistance to Timotheus in his campaign against the Chalcidians. But Amphipolis remained elusive, even with Macedonian help; one wonders how effective Perdiccas could have been in supporting an Athenian drive against Amphipolis, the maintenance of whose independence from Athens had been a cardinal point of Macedonian policy since the days of Perdiccas II. In any case, the alliance with Athens was short-lived.[49] Perhaps encouraged now that Epaminondas seemed close to challenging Athens by sea, Perdiccas withdrew his support for the Athenians. But nothing came of Epaminondas's naval strategy, and his death shortly afterwards, in 362 at the battle of Mantinea, aborted the pretensions for establishing a Theban empire in Greece. Despite the collapse of Theban ambitions, Perdiccas maintained an anti-Athenian policy, sending troops to assist Amphipolis, and by 360, Timotheus abandoned the Athenian siege of the town. For nearly six decades Athens had attempted to recover its colony and failed. Within three more years, with Philip II on the throne, Amphipolis would be in Macedonian hands.

Macedonian fortunes in the late 360s appear to have been mixed. The kingdom's foreign policy was still hostage to the Great Powers, and one can describe Perdiccas's management of it only as walking the diplomatic and military tightrope that had marked the survival of his fifth-century Argead predecessors. Yet it was more than mere survival, for Macedon not only maintained sufficient independence to help thwart the Athenian recovery of Amphipolis, but also appeared to be rebuilding its internal structure. Certainly some revenue was realized from the sale of timber to Thebes, and a reorganization of finances by the exile Callistratus during Perdiccas's reign doubled from 20 to 40 talents the annual income from harbor dues.[50] The revenue may have enabled Perdiccas to organize, train, and equip his army, and to begin the process of recovery from the nadir of Amyntas III's reign. The cavalry performed well in Chalcidice in 363 (if Hammond is correct), Perdiccas sent a force to assist Amphipolis against Timotheus, a Macedonian garrison was installed in the city by 359 (Diod. 16.3.3), and, although Perdiccas lost 4,000 troops and his own life in a disastrous struggle against the Illyrians in 359 (Diod. 16.2.4–5), the fact that Macedon could put so many men into the field is significant.

The trouble in the west resulted from the renewal of activity by the

[49] Hatzopoulos, "La Béotie et la Macédoine," 255–56.

[50] [Arist.] Econ. 2.1350a. 22. See Borza, "Timber and Politics," 41, and Hammond, HM 2: 187 (as opposed to Geyer, Makedonien, 137).

Illyrian confederate chieftain, Bardylis.[51] This was more than a border raid, as evidenced by the size of the Macedonian force sent out. Perdiccas's campaign is significant, for it demonstrates that this Macedonian king, lacking the usual protective alliances in the western cantons, took a formidable military initiative. Had Perdiccas survived the Illyrian debacle, he might have anticipated much of what his younger brother and successor, Philip, actually effected. But his reign was cut too short to foretell any future accomplishments. Thus perished in battle the second son of Amyntas III. Although it appears that he had set the kingdom back on the path of reconstruction, the dangers were manifest as Balkan barbarians and Chalcidic and southern Greeks threatened Macedon on every side. At the time of Perdiccas's death in 360 or 359 no one could have foretold that the youngest son of Amyntas III would, in little more than two decades, vitalize Macedon, conquer Greece, and envisage an extension of Macedonian power even into Asia.

[51] See Dell, "The Illyrian Frontier," 59–61, and Hammond, *HM* 2: 188, both with sources and commentary. Like Dell, I discount the involvement of Eurydice (Just. 7.5.6–9) in causing Perdiccas's death through treachery. Our best sources recount that he fell in battle against the Illyrians, and we have no evidence to indicate what Eurydice's activities had been since the accession to the throne of Perdiccas.

$\bullet$ CHAPTER 9 $\bullet$

". . . The Greatest of the Kings in Europe . . ."

". . . THE greatest of the kings in Eu-
rope. . . ." Thus concludes Diodorus Siculus, in an encomium to the
man who conquered Greece, made Macedon a formidable power in
the Balkans, and planned to invade Asia.[1] Until recently, however,
Philip of Macedon has been more neglected by modern scholarship
than perhaps any other important person of classical antiquity. Some
of this disregard results from the overwhelming shadow cast by the
historical and romantic presence of Philip's son. For example, W. W.
Tarn, arguably the most influential (and wrong-headed) twentieth-
century exponent of Alexander the Great's achievements, virtually neglected Philip and the Macedonian background of Alexander. Moreover, it was Philip's ill fortune to be opposed by the most skilled orator
of his era, and most nineteenth- and twentieth-century classical scholarship, impressed by the power of Demosthenes's oratory, has seen
Philip as a barbarian determined to end the liberty of Greek city-states.
Demosthenes's ringing denunciations of the Macedonian have left a
highly Atheno-centric view of the events of the mid-fourth century
that has had little material evidence and few new interpretations of
literary sources to prompt a revisionist view.

In the late nineteenth century, David George Hogarth pioneered the
collection of Macedonian inscriptions and travelled in parts of the Balkans and Asia Minor that had witnessed the passage of Philip and Alexander. Producing in a single volume biographies of the royal pair,[2]
Hogarth rejected the sentimental pro-Athenian views of his predecessors. He praised Philip's statesmanship and generalship, thereby re-
calling Diodorus's commendation made nearly twenty centuries earlier. Hogarth's view, however, had little impact on subsequent
scholarship, either in altering the Demosthenic view of Macedonian
kings or in maintaining an interest in Philip. Except for a section in the

---

[1] Diod. 16.95.1.

[2] Hogarth, *Philip and Alexander*. For details on Hogarth, see Borza, "David George
Hogarth," and "Philip II and the Greeks," 236–39, a review of modern scholarship on
Philip.

Cambridge Ancient History and two books by European scholars, major studies of Philip languished in the first half of the twentieth century.[3]

The present intense interest in Philip II has sometimes been thought to stem from the fame of recent archaeological discoveries in Macedonia, especially those of Manolis Andronikos, who has claimed to have found Philip's tomb (see below, Chapter 11). Certainly the dramatic excavations of Greek archaeologists in the 1970s and 1980s have played a role in the current surge of enthusiasm to study Alexander's father, but the revival of studies of Philip has equally to do with the work of three scholars whose accounts of Philip were written before the earth of Macedonia began to yield its royal remains.[4] Much of the groundwork for this spate of recent learning was laid by Hammond in 1937–38 in his analysis of Diodorus's sixteenth book, our major source for Philip's career, and by the studies of Cloché somewhat later.[5] Now a small cottage industry on Philip has appeared, with the activity of scholars interested in his career matched perhaps only by those writing about his legendary son. One result of this flurry of attention is that the modern era has come to appreciate the significance of Diodorus's observation about the accomplishments of this extraordinary man. Another is that the modern commentator is less likely than his or her predecessors to take sides on the conflict between Athenians and Macedonians.[6] There can be no doubt that a more complex picture of the age of Philip II has begun to emerge, enhanced by archaeological discoveries annually so numerous and potentially important that their publication beyond the popular press has fallen far behind, leaving the historian with an imperfect understanding of their significance.

In such an unsettled situation, an attempt to review the accomplish-

[3] *CAH* 6 (1953), chs. 8–9; Momigliano, *Filippo il Macedone* (1934); and Wüst, *Philipp II* (1938).

[4] Ellis, *PMI* (1976); Cawkwell, *Philip of Macedon* (1978); and Griffith's account of Philip in *HM* vol. 2 (1979). For a critical evaluation of these three works (plus Hatzopoulos and Loukopoulos, *PM* [1980], a multiauthored volume of essays compiled after the discovery of the royal Macedonian cemetery at Vergina in 1977–78), see Errington, "Four Interpretations of Philip II." A new small-format biography of Philip by Wirth, *Philipp II* (1985), came into my hands too late for use in the present work. Wirth's is the first volume in a projected *Geschichte Makedoniens*; the second, written by Wolfgang Will and published in 1986, is about Alexander the Great. Thus in the mid-1980s in some quarters the history of Macedon still begins with biographies of Philip and Alexander.

[5] Hammond, "The Sources of Diodorus Siculus XVI," and Cloché, *Un fondateur d'empire*, and *Histoire de la Macédoine* (1955 and 1960, respectively).

[6] A residue of the old polemics remains; thus Cawkwell: "In so far as I have criticized Demosthenes as a defender of liberty, it is not because he sought to defend it, but because he did it badly. Likewise, I regard Philip as a great man and so a great menace to the liberty of Greece" (*Philip of Macedon*, 10).

ments of Philip II in these few pages may appear at first sight to be fruitless. Yet it might not be a misplaced effort to reflect on some aspects of Philip's reign that continue to be of particular interest or contention among modern scholars, and to place these matters in the context of the general flow of Macedonian history. Moreover, the amount and high quality of scholarship on his career in recent years make it unnecessary to repeat here what has been done well at length by others.[7]

Philip's Early Reign

The early years of Philip II's reign are imperfectly understood, and even the date of his accession to power is now in dispute. The generally accepted view places Perdiccas III's death and the commencement of Philip's rule in the summer of 359, but it has recently been proposed, on the basis of archaeological and literary evidence, that Philip succeeded Perdiccas in late summer or early autumn of 360.[8] The matter remains unsettled. A second problem attending Philip's rise to power is whether he assumed the throne immediately or acted as regent (*epitropos*) for a while. At Perdiccas III's death the most likely candidates for succession were Perdiccas's young son, Amyntas, and Perdiccas's brother, Philip. It is held by many scholars that Philip acted as Amyntas's regent for about three years, a view based upon an inscription from Levadeia in Boeotia (*IG* 7.3055, *ca.* 359/8) that can be read as "Amyntas, son of Perdiccas, king of the Macedonians," and on a passage in Justin (7.5.6–10) relating that Philip did not become king immediately, but acted as advisor to Amyntas for a short period of time. In his full analysis of the matter, Griffith rejects the notion that Philip ever acted as regent.[9] I am inclined to accept Griffith's view (although

[7] My debt to Griffith, Ellis, Cawkwell, et al. (see note 4 above) will be obvious to those familiar with their work. In what follows, source criticism will be minimal. Even to list all the evidence and appropriate commentary would make this chapter unnecessarily burdensome. I have limited myself to the most important and recent bibliography, trusting that any reader interested in pursuing matters in detail will eventually explore the full literature.

[8] Argued in detail by Hatzopoulos, "The Oleveni Inscription."

[9] Set out persuasively in *HM* 2: 208–9 and 702–4, where the validity as evidence of both the Boeotian inscription and Justin are questioned, and where we are reminded that, if Philip had ever served as regent, we are nowhere told how and when he became king. The strongest argument favoring a regency is offered by Tronson ("Satyrus the Peripatetic," 120–21), who recalls that Satyrus mentions Philip as having ruled 22 years, not the 24 years given by Diodorus (16.1.3 and 95.1). If, however, Philip, who was assassinated in 336, counted his rule as 24 years beginning with his actual exercise of

I do not regard the matter as settled) and have little to add to his exposition beyond a reinforcement of his suggestion that it seems quite improbable that, during a crisis of collapsing frontiers, the child Amyntas would be elected rather than a qualified adult member of the royal family. Moreover, Amyntas would go on to live a secure life at court and marry a daughter of Philip—hardly the stuff of royal competition, especially in light of the general Argead predilection to dispose of rivals, and in light of Philip's own activity in putting down contestants for the throne (see below). In the end, it is of little consequence beyond picking a historian's nit: from Perdiccas III's death, Macedonian policy was directed by Philip, whether as king or regent, and one would be hard pressed to tell the difference.

The details of the Macedonians's acceptance of Philip as king are not known,[10] but he wasted no time, either in putting down opposition or in raising support in the countryside. With Illyrians and Paeonians poised to invade, the Thracians supporting one pretender (Pausanias) and the Athenians another (Argaeus) as rival claimants to the throne,[11] the dangers to his position were manifest. Philip dealt directly with all issues, as Diodorus (16.2.6–3.6) makes clear. The Paeonians were bought off, along with the Thracian support for Pausanias. When Argaeus, backed by a contingent from Athens, arrived before Aegae and asked the citizens of that town for support, he was turned away and then set upon by Philip who had appeared suddenly with a small force. Nothing further is heard of either rival. Combining these bits of diplomacy with minor military action bought Philip time to prepare for the large battles ahead, and it surely must have stuck in the new king's mind that the first Greeks to oppose him at the moment of his accession were Athenian.

It is significant that Philip recognized at the outset that, like his Argead predecessors, he would have to deal with the never-ending Athenian attempt to stake a claim in the north. The prize, of course, was Amphipolis, which, as we have seen, had doggedly managed to retain its independence since the days of Brasidas. In a bold (and deceptive) stroke, Philip's envoys persuaded the Athenians to make peace on the grounds that he had no interest in Amphipolis. He thereby fore-

---

power (in 360, as Hatzopoulos argues ["The Oleveni Inscription," 42], using Antigonus Doson as a parallel), and acted as regent before assuming the actual kingship in 358, the sources can be reconciled: Diodorus was referring to the whole period of Philip's rule, while Satyrus cited only the years in which he held the kingship.

[10] On the royal succession among the Argeadae, see Chapter 10 below.

[11] According to Diodorus (16.3.3), this Argaeus had once served as king, although see Appendix C below, pp. 296–97.

stalled a major conflict with Athens in order to build his forces against the more serious perennial threat raised by the Illyrians.

By the spring of 358 Philip was prepared.[12] The recent death of the Paeonian king gave Philip an opportunity to test his army. A short campaign produced the capitulation of the Paeonians and an alliance along the northeastern Macedonian frontier. Philip now moved into the rugged mountains of the northwest, where the Illyrians had occupied a number of Macedonian towns, probably in Lyncus. The Illyrian king Bardylis offered peace based upon a status quo, but Philip insisted on an Illyrian withdrawal from the region. Bardylis refused, and warfare commenced. The antagonists were equally matched, each side fielding about 10,000 foot, with the Macedonians maintaining a slight edge in cavalry, 600 to 500.

The engagement of Philip and Bardylis is the first detailed description of the Macedonians in battle, an action culminating in an overwhelming victory for Philip. More than 7,000 Illyrians lay dead on the field, according to our source, Diodorus. Two significant points emerge from this engagement. First, the large number of troops mustered by the Macedonians far exceeded anything seen from them before.[13] Clearly Philip had been hard at work levying and training troops. Second, one wonders if his victory over Bardylis resulted from a major reorganization of the Macedonian army, or whether it was a skillful tactical adaptation of military resources already at hand. It seems unlikely that Philip would have been able to reform the army within a brief six or seven months over the winter of 358/7. Diodorus (16.4.4–6) makes it clear that the final successful Macedonian assault against the Illyrians was a coordinated use of cavalry and infantry, a hallmark of later armies led by Philip and Alexander. There is insufficient information to say whether the role of the king as a cavalry commander had yet evolved. Philip seems personally to have commanded a group of elite infantry on the right wing, as he would again nearly two decades later at Chaeronea, but, as at Chaeronea, this role may have been dictated by tactical considerations unique to the battle. The legendary role of the king as mounted cavalry commander may have more to do with Alexander and the plains of Asia than with fighting in the relatively close quarters common in the Balkans, where the infantry was a tactical arm and not primarily a defensive unit.

[12] For what follows, Diod. 16.4.2–7.

[13] The total of more than 21,000 soldiers on both sides, mainly infantry, strongly suggests a spacious battleground in the northern Lyncestian-Pelagonian plain, perhaps somewhere between modern Florina and Bitola, the corridor controlling the main passage between Illyria and Macedonia.

A main feature of Macedonian battlefield tactics in the age of Philip and Alexander was the use of cavalry as an assault force against an enemy line that was either extended (and thereby induced to open gaps) or held steady by the pikemen of the Macedonian infantry phalanx. In the battle against Bardylis, however, the cavalry provided a distracting attack on the Illyrian flank and rear, while the main assault was led by Philip's infantry.[14] Philip's use of coordinated cavalry and infantry reflects Theban strategy, even though the circumstances of the engagement with Bardylis required some tactics different from those which had prompted the Theban victory over Sparta at the battle of Leuctra (371 B.C.).[15] The extent to which Philip, as a hostage at Thebes, had studied Theban military innovations and then carried the lessons home to Macedon is, of course, a matter of opinion. The army that shocked Bardylis into submission was not the force that overwhelmed the Greeks at Chaeronea and then conquered Asia. The development of the cavalry as a swift shock unit would have to await the development of the cavalry pike (*sarissa*) and an increase in the number of horses and riders that depended upon access to the grazing lands of Chalcidice and Thessaly, which were not yet available to Philip.[16] We would do well to accept Griffith's suggestions that Philip's reorganization of the army occurred over a long period of time, and that the history of the army is a piece of social history as well; that is, the restructuring of the Macedonian army cannot be separated from a reshaping of the human and material resources of the Macedonian state.[17] The Macedonian army that cut down the Illyrians probably represented only the first tentative attempts at reform. Hastily recruited during the previous winter, it was larger and better trained than before. Dominated by infantry, the army sported a cavalry unit whose coordinated tactics reflect ideas that Philip had brought from Thebes. The touch of innovation is apparent, but it is only a forerunner of what was to follow. The fighting machine that we associate with Philip and

[14] For an analysis of the battle see Dell, "The Illyrian Frontier," 67–70, and Griffith, *HM* 2: 213–14.

[15] For Leuctra see, *inter alia*, Cawkwell, "Epaminondas and Thebes."

[16] Markle, "The Use of the Sarissa," 486, has suggested that the battle of Chaeronea (338 B.C.) may have marked the first use of the sarissa by the Macedonian cavalry. Markle's work in this essay and in the comprehensive articles upon which it is based ("The Macedonian Sarissa, Spear, and Related Armor," and "Macedonian Arms and Tactics under Alexander the Great") are informative for anyone interested in these matters. I am also indebted to J. R. Ellis, who, during our first trip together to northwest Chalcidice in 1973, pointed out the significance of the grazing lands of Anthemus and Crousis for a king intent on developing a formidable cavalry.

[17] *HM* 2: 406–8.

Alexander would require years to develop, and many of Philip's policies over the next decade or so must be viewed in light of his need to
acquire the resources and territory necessary to support such a force.

Detailed information about Philip's army depends mainly upon the
sources for Alexander's reign, as most authorities hold that, except for
specific reforms known to have been made by Alexander, his forces
were inherited from Philip. A summary follows:[18] The growth in size
of the army reflects not only a more efficient administration of men
and weapons, but also the incorporation into the greater Macedonian
confederation of additional territories, especially the cantons of western (upper) Macedonia, with a commensurate increase in the eligible
population capable of bearing arms. The heart of the army comprised
units of heavy and light infantry, organized by Philip (Diod. 16.3.1–3)
into a dense shock unit, or "phalanx." The troops were armed with an
unusually long pike (sarissa), a small shield, and little other protective
armor. The advantages of such infantryman over their heavily armed
Greek hoplite counterparts were several. In an age in which most levies
were expected to arm themselves, Macedonian financial (that is, property) requirements for service would have been far less than those for
most Greek city-states, thereby enabling Philip to draw upon huge
population reserves. The long sarissa (16–18 ft.) enabled the Macedonian infantryman to engage the enemy while still out of range of his
adversary's spear.

The amount of body armor was reduced, as was the size of the
shield, thereby freeing the soldier from the encumbering weight and
clumsiness of the hoplite's defensive equipment, and enabling him to
manipulate his main weapon with both hands. Indeed, the phalangites
may not have worn breastplates, which may have become largely unnecessary to soldiers who could engage their opponents at a distance.[19]
With intensive training and superb discipline these battalions of pikemen ultimately proved to be more effective on the field of battle than
their more heavily armed Greek counterparts. In Alexander's campaigns in the Balkans and Assyria, the tactical maneuverability of the
phalanx permitted it to open its ranks to permit enemy vehicles to pass

---

[18] This summary depends heavily on Griffith, *HM* 2: 405–49, the most comprehensive
recent analysis of the army, and J. R. Ellis, who kindly permitted me to see his chapters
on Philip in advance of their publication in the forthcoming new edition of *CAH*. In
common with both authors I hold that Philip, not his predecessors, was himself largely
responsible for organizing the military forces that conquered Greece and Persian Asia.
Griffith has presented a useful and well-illustrated essay on Philip's generalship ("Philip
as General") in *PM*, 58–77.

[19] See Appendix C below, pp. 298–99.

through.[20] The foot soldiers, whose individual units presented several variations on basic infantry weaponry and training for special duties, were mainly recruited as levies from a class of small landholders. They served as citizen-soldiers in an army that clarified their status through service to the king.

The cavalry included "heavy" and "light" units, distinguished by their weapons, arms, and tactics. An elite Companion cavalry was drawn from the barons and gentry, presumably large estate holders who, as in other ancient societies, could afford to equip themselves with horses and appropriate weapons.[21] They served the king personally, and eventually Alexander would form a special Royal Squadron as a status symbol. Otherwise, the major corps of cavalry was organized into squadrons armed with a somewhat lighter and shorter version of the infantry sarissa. They wore body armor and helmets, but the question of whether they carried shields is much debated. Archaeologically, the evidence is slim. We would not expect nonmetallic shields to be preserved, and thus far no metal battle shield has been uncovered (see Appendix C below, pp. 298–99). Neither the great mosaic preserved in the archaeological museum at Naples showing Alexander in battle against Darius nor the painting of an engaged cavalryman that once adorned "Kinch's Tomb" near Naousa depicts a cavalry shield.[22] The main purpose of the cavalry was to exploit a gap that had appeared or been induced in the enemy line. A cavalry squadron's speed against disorganized infantry was devastating, and accounted for the decisive tactics in Macedonian battles ranging from Philip's defeat of Bardylis in 358 to Alexander's final victory over Darius at Gaugamela 27 years later.

The new Macedonian army was marked by its great speed in movement, by versatility in tactics and weapons, and by the coordination of cavalry with infantry. Eventually Philip evolved a corps of engineers. Used with effect by both Philip and Alexander, the engineers developed many of those great engines which ushered in the age of siege machinery. Finally, there can be no doubt that unusual skills in per-

[20] Arr. 1.1.8–10, 3.13.5–6.

[21] On the development of the various contingents of cavalry, their weapons and armor, see Griffith, *HM* 2: 408–14, with abundant bibliography.

[22] See below, p. 275. Some battle shields are depicted on the panels of the so-called Alexander Sarcophagus in the archaeological museum at Istanbul, but it is unclear whether any of these belonged to cavalrymen. Macedonian shields from the Hellenistic period, bearing their characteristic designs of radiate suns (or stars), are well known from depictions on coins and in sculpture, e.g., *PM*, fig. 37 (Tomb of Lyson and Kallikles), and Price, *Coins*, no. 70 (a tetradrachm of Antigonus Gonatas).

sonal and military leadership created, reflected, and depended upon
excellence in the Macedonian army, as kings and men complemented
one another. Warfare in the West was irrevocably altered by Philip's
revolution in military science. The Macedonian army had become
both Philip's instrument of policy and the means by which a Macedonian expressed his identity with service to the king and, thereby, the
"national" will.

Philip thus early revealed skills in both military command and diplomacy. The rest of his life would be marked by an effort to balance
the use of force with tactful negotiation, as each situation required.[23]
If Philip stunned his frontiers into submission with a vitalized Macedonian army, he was equally successful in his use of marriages to secure
the border regions on a more permanent basis. We are fortunate that a
fragment of the Hellenistic biographer Satyrus, preserved in the work
of Athenaeus (3.557b–e), has given us a detailed list of Philip's marriages and their political implications. Whether these marriages should
be taken in the order given by Satyrus is problematic. Moreover, we
should keep in mind that Macedonian attitudes toward infidelity, romantic love, monogamy, and polygamy had nothing to do with modern middle-class notions about such matters.[24] Philip was notorious in
antiquity for (according to Satyrus) "marrying with each war." Although there may be grounds for quarreling over the order and legitimacy of Philip's several liaisons, ancient opinion had it right: the Argead predilection to marry foreigners for political reasons reached its
culmination in Philip's several marriages. I hold that all were legitimate marriages, both because of the validity of Satyrus's list and because they make historical sense in terms of Philip's policy aims.[25] The
evidence, however, does not permit us to determine the respective
status of legitimate wives within either monogamous or polygamous
relationships; in the case of Philip II, it would not appear to be an important issue beyond the intrigue caused by hurt feelings. Satyrus's list
of wives follows, in Tronson's useful translation:

> He married Audata the Illyrian and had from her a daughter,
> Cynna. And then he married Phila, the sister of Derdas and Ma-
> chatas. Then, as he wanted to appropriate the Thessalian people

[23] Diod. 16.95.3–4: "It is said that Philip himself was prouder of his skill in strategy
and his diplomatic achievements than of his bravery in actual battle."

[24] For more on the sexual and marital *mores* of the Argeadae, see Green, *Alexander of
Macedon*, 26–27.

[25] Following Griffith (*HM* 2: 214–15) and Tronson ("Satyrus the Peripatetic," esp.
121–22); the latter argues persuasively on the basis of the text that all seven women were
wives rather than mistresses or concubines.

as well, on grounds of kinship, he fathered children by two Thessalian women, one of whom was Nikesipolis of Pherae, who bore him Thessalonike, and the other, Philinna of Larisa, by whom he fathered Arrhidaeus. Then he acquired the kingdom of the Molossians as well, by marrying Olympias. From her he had Alexander and Cleopatra. And then, when he conquered Thrace, Cothelas, the King of the Thracians, came over to him bringing his daughter Meda and many gifts. Having married her too, he brought her into his household besides Olympias. Then, in addition to all these, he married Cleopatra, the sister of Hippostratus and niece of Attalus, having fallen in love with her. And when he brought her into his household beside Olympias, he threw his whole life into confusion. For immediately, during the actual wedding celebration, Attalus said, "Now surely there will be born for us legitimate kings and not bastards." Now Alexander, when he heard this, threw the cup, which he was holding in his hands, at Attalus; thereupon he too threw his goblet at Alexander. After this Olympias fled to the Molossians and Alexander to the Illyrians. And Cleopatra bore Philip the daughter named Europa.

A number of modern scholars, following a proposal made long ago by Beloch, have attempted to alter Satyrus's order.[26] While certainty is unlikely, it is not unreasonable to propose that either the Illyrian Audata or the Elimeian Phila could have headed the parade. If Philip's rule (as regent or king) commenced in 360, he might have soon thereafter married Phila, the sister of Derdas of Elimeia, in order to shore up the tottering western frontier threatened by the Illyrians (*all* such political marriages make more sense if they are with the king, not a regent). Then, after assuming the actual kingship in 358, he married the Illyrian as part of the peace settlement following his victory over Bardylis. But if the marriage to Audata were his first, and occurred in 358 (regardless of when Philip became king) for the reasons stated, there is no time for the production of a child and a second marriage to Phila before the Thessalian marriages in 358/7. This assumes, of course, that the marriages were serial, which does not seem to be the case: Satyrus-Athenaeus informs us that Philip brought home both the Thracian Meda and the Macedonian Cleopatra while still married to the Epirote princess Olympias. Thus it is not clear whether the Illyrian or Elimeian link was established first, that is, whether one should accept the word of our apparently reliable source (retaining the possibility of polygamy from the start), or attempt to alter the list to conform to more probable

[26] For bibliography, see Tronson, "Satyrus the Peripatetic," 116 nn. 5–7.

historical circumstances. Both marriages can be dated to the period in which Philip was consumed with western frontier problems.

Although our source does not give us an explicit reason for the marriages to Audata and Phila, the correspondence to Illyrian and Elimeian policy plus our information about Philip's subsequent marriages make them appear to be politically inspired. Except for his final liaison, Philip married foreign women as part of a policy to secure his Balkan and Greek frontiers: an Illyrian and Elimeian (or the reverse order), two Thessalians, a Molossian, and a Thracian. His final marriage, however, brewed trouble, as Philip married for love. Even so, one must not discount the value of a link to the house of the prominent Macedonian baron Attalus; after all, Philip had not yet married into the Macedonian heartland. Moreover, Philip was notoriously deficient in sons. Arrhidaeus seemed ill-suited for command,[27] and Alexander, though superbly fit for succession, was at constant risk as a front-line soldier. In an age in which it was not known that the chromosomes of the male parent determine the child's sex, kings sometimes abandoned one wife for another in an effort to increase the number of male offspring.[28] Thus, there may have been compelling reasons of state for Philip's marriage to Cleopatra. But Satyrus emphasizes that he married for love, and we must accept the likelihood that the middle-aged warrior was smitten by a girl of less than half his years. The politically sophisticated Olympias, who had admitted the Thracian Meda into the house without apparent conflict, now created a stir probably born of jealousy of the (much) younger woman, and matched only by the intrigue characterized by the uproar at Philip and Cleopatra's wedding celebration.[29] One wonders if Philip ever had second thoughts about combining politics with love.

Recent studies (above, note 4) have provided detailed discussions of the complex issues of the 350s and 340s, an era the investigation of which is marked by difficult methodological problems. In addition to Diodorus, our sole ancient narrative source, we are dependent upon an exiguous and widely scattered lot of evidence from a number of later writers, plus the published speeches of contemporary Athenian poli-

[27] Although he was not as inept as some have made him out to be; see below, Chapter 10.

[28] A practice not limited to the age of Philip of Macedon or Henry VIII of England, as certain modern Middle East rulers have demonstrated.

[29] See above, p. 207. One need not take the details of this scene as accurate while accepting that the underlying tradition of intrigue at the court of Philip is rooted in fact. For more elaborate accounts of the famous incident, see Plut. *Alex.* 9.3–5, Just. 9.7.3–5, and Ps.-Callisthenes 1.20; also Tronson's commentary, "Satyrus the Peripatetic," 124.

ticians. The latter are characterized by party propaganda, rhetoric, appeals to patriotism and to fear, obfuscation and alteration of facts, and attempts to manipulate public opinion on policy issues in a city in which relations with the Macedonian king were an obsession for nearly a quarter of a century.

Rather than retracing the steps of others through this historiographical morass, we shall proceed rather to examine the broad strokes of Philip's strategic policy as it has emerged from the body of recent competent scholarship. One underlying principle must be kept in mind: there is insufficient evidence to suggest that Philip's career followed a predestined or predetermined path leading to the conquest of Greece and the plan for an Asian expedition. It is seductive for the historian to make events of the past appear to be much more orderly and rational than they actually were. Thus, while it might appear at first sight that Philip dealt with the necessity to safeguard the frontiers before turning to the Greeks, in fact these are concurrent developments. It is clear that once Philip secured his position on the throne, he began to deal with both Greeks and his Balkan neighbors. Throughout the 350s and 340s, Philip's concerns included the continuing attempts to secure contiguous borders, expand his rule to include areas east of the Strymon, make favorable arrangements with the Greeks in Chalcidice and Thessaly, and establish some permanent settlement with the major Greek cities of the south that would permit him to take his army to Asia. But the coherent policy that appears to emerge from Philip's diversity of activity may be as much a construct of historical hindsight as it is a tribute to the unwavering vision of the king of Macedon.

In general, Philip preferred diplomacy to the use of force. Although never reluctant to commit troops to battle—occasionally even on a slight pretext—Philip was too competent a commander not to realize that unnecessary warfare wastes good soldiers. Campaigns against his Balkan neighbors, to whom the subtleties of diplomacy were probably not as refined as they were in the Greek world, were interspersed with marriage alliances into the Macedonian royal house. But ultimately it was the use of force that would shape Macedon's frontiers with the "barbarian" world. Perhaps Philip expected that. But his hopes that diplomacy might work with the Greeks foundered on the complexity of Greek internal and international politics and on the Greeks' general mistrust of Philip's intentions. In the end, it was the resort to Macedonian spears that ensured the success of Philip's policy among the Hellenic peoples with whom he had attempted to negotiate.

Philip and the Balkan Frontier

Philip managed to incorporate the cantons of western Macedonia into the Greater Macedonian kingdom on a permanent basis.[30] These mountainous regions had been virtually independent—and often hostile—until Philip's reign, and it was among his first necessities to stabilize the frontier. It was a matter of continuing concern to Philip for some eighteen years, and to Alexander after him. Philip established Argead control west of Eordaea in the cantons of Orestis and Lyncus, and created a new frontier along the high Pindus running up to the Prespa lakes and Lake Ohrid following his defeat of Bardylis in 358 (Diod. 16.8.1). This region included the basin of the upper Haliacmon and the rich Lyncestian and Pelagonian plains that form the main corridor from the northwestern Balkans into western Macedonia. Philip now controlled the high, forested Pisoderi Pass connecting Little Lake Prespa with the Lyncestian plain, and the low pass between pretty Lake Ohrid and Bitola that took the route of the Via Egnatia from the Adriatic into the Pelagonian plain. Just south of Bitola is the magnificent and barely excavated site of Heracleia Lyncestis, probably founded by Philip as a garrison town guarding his northwest frontier. All traffic moving toward Macedon from coastal Illyria and the north had to pass Heracleia. The new territories gave Philip both their concomitant human and natural resources and also control over the major routes leading from the northwest Balkans into Macedonia.

The result of Philip's efforts was the creation of a permanent western borderland, which the Hellenistic successors of the Argeadae attempted to protect. By the addition of these western cantons Philip added to his kingdom an important new source of recruits, some of whom probably included those very folk chastized by Alexander at Opis in 324 B.C. as having been brought down out of the mountains by Philip, clothed decently, and made into a civilized people and respected army.[31] It is one of the tragedies of Macedonian history that the relatively large population resources upon which Philip and Alexander depended for their military operations were ruthlessly exploited

[30] Dell, "The Illyrian Frontier," 62–99; Hammond, *HM* 2: 14–31 and 650–56; and Hammond "The Western Frontier," esp. 212–17.

[31] Arr. 7.9.2–3 (cf. Just. 8.5), taking into account exaggeration in a speech designed to quell a mutiny. For a recent evaluation of the speech, including some doubts about its value on grounds of both historiography and content, see Montgomery, "The Economic Revolution," 38–39. Several of these western Macedonians were incorporated into the service of the king at the highest levels. One of them, the royal bodyguard Pausanias of Orestis, was Philip's assassin (Diod. 16.93.3).

by the latter. Tens of thousands of men were sent to fight and die in remote Asia. Macedon suffered a severe manpower shortage in the following generations, as Alexander's continuing appetite for new recruits from home resulted in what has been called "a never ending dance of death."[32]

If Philip incorporated the mountain cantons of western Macedonia as a source of recruits and as a buffer against the tribes who lived beyond, he, like his royal predecessors, never had as an objective the annexation of Illyrian territory, aside from the new frontier around Lake Ohrid. Macedonian policy in the west was defensive.[33] Bardylis, seen by Dell as the prototype of a national Illyrian leader, disappears from history shortly after his defeat by Philip in 358, but the Illyrians found new warlords in the following decades.[34] The Macedonians would continue to campaign against the Illyrians virtually until the end of Philip's reign, and it is symptomatic of the unsettled nature of things that among Alexander's first necessities was to fight against the Illyrians who had rebelled following news of Philip's death in 336.

Epirus had also suffered from Illyrian raids. An anti-Illyrian alliance was struck in 357 between Philip and the Molossian chief Arybbas, sealed in part by Philip's marriage to Arybbas's niece, Olympias. The canton of Orestis, which had had long ties with the Molossian tribes, again came under Macedonian rule about this time; whether the recovery of Orestis by the Argeadae was part of the Molossian-Macedonian alliance is unclear.[35] Philip strengthened the Epirote link by taking Olympias's brother, Alexander, into the Macedonian court. In 342, Arybbas was replaced by Alexander, thereby reinforcing Philip's control over Epirus through this client king.

The geopolitical importance of Epirus can hardly be overemphasized.[36] Not only did Epirus block the southern frontier of the Illyrians, but it gave Philip access to the main passage across the snowy Pindus from the Adriatic into the Thessalian plain. The modern traveller may follow this route by taking the spectacular highway from Ioannina in Epirus up the gorge of the Mesovitikos River, past the charming Vlach alpine village of Metzovo to the high Katara Pass, before dropping down into the Thessalian plain near Kalabaka. Control

[32] See Bosworth, "Alexander the Great and the Decline of Macedon," 1–12 (quotation from p. 12).
[33] Shown by Dell and Hammond (note 30 above), although Hammond ("The Western Frontier," 216–17) emphasizes Philip's economic and social reorganization of the area.
[34] Dell, "The Illyrian Frontier," 72.
[35] Discussed by Griffith, *HM* 2: 215.
[36] For which see the basic regional study by Hammond, *Epirus*.

of Epirus also provided Philip with parallel north-south routes on both sides of the Pindus, essential for access to western Greece. But Philip never seems to have exploited the Molossians beyond this strategic security. Molossians were not much recruited for Macedonian military service, a fact perhaps partly explained by the unsteady personal relationship between Philip and his Epirote queen, and partly by the necessity to maintain an Epirote home guard against the Illyrians.

Philip's Balkan neighbors were not insensitive to the strategic implications of Macedonian activity. Unable individually to curb what they regarded as a threat, the Illyrians, Paeonians, and Thracians sought assistance from outside, and—in what must be regarded as an unusual development—joined among themselves to oppose Philip (Diod. 16.22.3). The Balkan motives were mixed. Without a doubt, some felt their freedom to raid jeopardized by the New Order being imposed by Macedon, and others may have believed that Philip's military activity was the prelude to annexation of their territories. At least one Thracian chief, Cersebleptes, seemed intent on reuniting the old kingdom of Cotys under his own rule, an effort being blocked by Macedonian expansion into the region east of the Strymon River. Athens, whose allies' rebellion in the northern Aegean (the so-called Social War) endangered its grain routes to the Black Sea, made alliances with the Balkan powers in 357 and again in 356, although it was able to do little in the way of sending military assistance in the wars against Philip.[37]

In his military activity Philip seemed content to secure defensible frontiers, in particular the long mountain wall that separated Macedonia from the main body of the Balkans to the north. This roughly corresponds to the modern Greek border with Yugoslavia and Bulgaria. The gaps in this formidable barrier (notably the gorges of the Axios and Strymon rivers) were fortified, and most campaigning north of the Rhodopi was intended to put down disorder and establish a few military outposts. In these northern and eastern regions, as in Illyria, there was no attempt to annex territory to the Macedonian kingdom. Philip's conception of Macedon was hardly different from that of his forebears, except for the incorporation into the realm of the region between the Strymon and the Nestos rivers, an area heretofore regarded as Thracian. What Philip accomplished was the organization and defense of lands tenuously controlled by Alexander I and Arche-

[37] Fragments of the inscriptions recording the alliances are in Tod *GHI*, nos. 151 and 157, with commentary and additional bibliography.

laus, plus the annexation of the territory immediately east of the Strymon River.

In the east, Philip had appeared shortly after his accession to abandon Macedonian support of Amphipolis's independence, but this was done mainly as a device to soothe the Athenians while he dealt with the more immediate threat to the Illyrian frontier.[38] He now changed course and attacked the old Athenian outpost. In 357, after breaking through the walls with his siege engines (Diod. 16.8.2), he took Amphipolis, thereby accomplishing in a few weeks what the Athenians had failed to achieve for more than sixty years.[39] Amphipolis retained its democratic constitution, although probably under the supervision of Macedonian overseers. Utilizing an existing economic and political infrastructure that controlled the lower Strymon basin, the city became a garrison town and the provincial capital of eastern (trans-Strymon) Macedonia. Amphipolis is gradually being recovered by Greek archaeologists. Their excavations reveal a prosperous and elegant Greek city with some Macedonian features, notably a series of vaulted chamber tombs. Although Amphipolis preserved most of its local institutions, it paid taxes to the king and had no autonomy in foreign relations. The population of the town remained largely Greek, but included some prominent native Macedonians or Greeks who had been given Macedonian citizenship. They are identified as "Macedonians from Amphipolis," paralleling such nomenclature from other cities.[40] Amphipolis had in effect become a Greek city incorporated into the Macedonian kingdom. What is significant about Amphipolis is that, after thirteen years of Athenian rule, it had retained its independence against all odds in a turbulent and dangerous part of the world for two-thirds of a century, until Philip's annexation in 357.

For the first time, Macedon, led by an energetic twenty-five-year-old king, was installed as a power in the Strymon valley, and the repercussions were felt in several quarters. The Athenians, faced with a rebellion among their own northern allies, were uncertain how to react. Exploiting Athenian confusion, Philip moved with speed to seize Athens's outpost at Pydna in late 357. He followed up in 354 with a

[38] Diod. 16.3.3–4; Polyaenus *Strat.* 4.2.17.

[39] An inscription (Tod *GHI,* no. 150) found on the site provides details of the exile of Philip's opponents from Amphipolis following his capture of the city. For a full discussion of Philip's acquisition and reorganization of Amphipolis, see Griffith, *HM* 2: 230–42 (including an analysis of the now-discredited story that Philip invested Amphipolis under the pretext of exchanging it for Pydna) and 351–56.

[40] A convenient list of such "Macedonians" is given by Griffith, *HM* 2: 359–60. The evidence is largely epigraphical.

successful siege of Methone (Diod. 16.31.6 and 34.4–5). The whole
Thermaic Gulf coast of Macedonia was now in Philip's hands, but
there was a personal price: at Methone an arrow shot cost him the sight
in one eye.[41] With the Macedonians firmly entrenched in the coastal
areas on both sides of Chalcidice, and Athens's own cities in disarray,
the Athenians could vacillate no longer. They declared war on Philip
(winter of 357/6), although, as Griffith has pointed out, they may have
seen the conflict with Philip as part of the larger Social War.[42]

As stated above, Philip's activity had driven Athens into an alliance
of mutual interest with three Illyrian, Paeonian, and Thracian kings.
The Thracian chief, Cetriporis, ruled over the westernmost Thracian
realm, roughly the area between the Strymon and the Nestos, but it
was not Philip's capture of Amphipolis that was the primary concern
to him. Rather, it was Philip's interest in Crenides, the mining center
at the head of the Angitis River basin. Refounded by the Thasians not
long before, Crenides served as a processing headquarters for the gold
mines in its hinterland as well as for those of nearby Mt. Pangaion. It
was important not only as a source of revenue, but also as a potential
strategic outpost in the easternmost part of Philip's expanded kingdom. The situation was complicated by the fact that Crenides, while
technically in Cetriporis's kingdom, was also the goal of the eastern
Thracian chief, Cersebleptes,[43] who was intent on reunifying the
Thracians at Cetriporis's expense. Philip intruded into this Thracian
rivalry, and took Crenides in mid-356, whether saving it from an attack by Cersebleptes is unclear. Eventually Philip refounded the city
as Philippi (the first known instance in the greater Greek world of a
founder naming a city after himself), and derived a huge revenue from
its gold mining and processing facilities.[44] He made the region a show-
case for royal development through the draining of the nearby marshland, an increase in the productivity of the mines, the importation of

[41] The right eye, if one is to believe the report of one group of pathologists who examined the skull fragments from the main burial in Tomb 2 at Vergina. For some
doubts, see Borza, "A Macedonian Skull," and "The Royal Macedonian Tombs and
Paraphernalia," 106 and n. 5.

[42] HM 2: 242–44, with sensible judgments and review of evidence.

[43] Spelled Kersobleptes by (inter alia) Diod. 16.34.4 and Dem. 19.174, 181, 334; 23.107,
followed by Griffith, HM, vol. 2, and Cawkwell, Philip of Macedon. The correct Kerse-
bleptes (Tod GHI, no. 151, ll. 10, 19, and 21) is now confirmed by the discovery of a
Thracian silver cup with his name inscribed; see Fol et al., The New Thracian Treasure,
no. 44.

[44] According to Diod. 16.8.6–7, over 1000 talents annually, probably including the
revenue from the whole Angitis valley-Mt. Pangaion region. Discussion of Philippi's
status under the Macedonians is found in Griffith, HM 2: 358–61.

settlers, and the construction of a fine town. Virtually nothing remains of Philip's settlements, but the magnificent ruins of Roman Philippi are testimony to the continued vitality of the city and its hinterland.

Undaunted by Philip's preemptive move into the region of Crenides, Cersebleptes, an ally of Athens, continued his attempt to unify the Thracians in the eastern Balkans, sometimes at the expense of local Greek cities. Rarely missing an opportunity to intervene in response to pleas for assistance from beleaguered towns, Philip would campaign against Cersebleptes as far east as Byzantium and Perinthus as late as 352. By the autumn of that year, the Thracian chief was detached from his Athenian alliance and forced to pay homage to the king of the Macedonians. Whether Philip's campaigns in the Chersonese and Propontis were part of an effort to protect the eastern marches of Macedonia, or whether they represented a signal to the Athenians that Macedon was now in position to choke the Athenian grain routes through control over the northwest Aegean, is unknown from our scant evidence.[45] Philip did not follow up on his campaigns in this region, but returned instead to matters closer to home, in particular, Chalcidice. But the loss of their Thracian ally in the area of the Hellespont must have caused some Athenians to be uneasy about the security of their shipping lanes into the Black Sea.

Philip's expansion into the east brought under full Argead control for the first time the whole Strymon basin and the area stretching virtually to the Nestos River, including the rich mining regions of Mt. Pangaion and Crenides/Philippi. Diodorus (16.8.6–7) states clearly that the revenues from this region's mines made Philip a wealthy man. The new fortune also permitted Philip to hire mercenaries to join the Macedonian troops, whose service to the king was part of their obligation, and who could be rewarded only with grants of land. The settlement of veterans required land, and it must be thought that at least part of Philip's motive to expand into Chalcidice and eastern Macedonia was to increase the amount of arable land available for this use (see below, p. 219).

That Philip produced an agricultural revolution should not be doubted, but that it contributed in a major way to an enlarged prosperity in his kingdom is a matter that should be treated with caution.[46]

[45] The matter is discussed in some detail by Griffith, *HM* 2: 281–85.

[46] On this issue, those who believe that Philip's economic revolution made possible the underlying prosperity for his military program include Hammond, *HM* 2: 657–62, and Cawkwell, *Philip of Macedon*, 17–18. The major dissenter is Montgomery ("The Economic Revolution"), who offers some compelling criticisms. Also see Borza, "Natural Resources," 16–17, on land reclamation in the plains of Emathia and Philippi.

CHAPTER 9

Economic reforms of the type attributed to Philip (the draining of marshes, deforestation, the resettlement of populations, and the founding of towns) are in themselves expensive projects and, even if successful, take years to produce a marked increase in material prosperity. Thus, while the reforms undertaken by Philip may have had a dramatic long-term effect on the economic and social stability of the Macedonian nation, the results may not have directly affected his immediate military program beyond providing more land for raising horses and settling veterans.

As for the impact of the gold and silver mines of eastern Macedonia, the evidence is contradictory. Diodorus (16.8.7) informs us that the revenues from these mines were used to buy mercenaries and bribe Greeks. Whatever the value of the bribery charge, there is no doubt about the increase in Philip's silver coinage and the introduction of his gold coins (*Philippeioi*). But the most exhaustive study of Philip's coins dates the *Philippeioi* to no earlier than the late 340s and the marked increase in silver coins to the mid-340s.[47] Of course, gold and silver were used for other purposes, as the abundant quantity of precious metal objects from Macedonian tombs testify. But here, too, the dates of these grave goods are late in Philip's reign, post-Philip, or in dispute. That is, it is not clear how Philip financed the early stages of his military operations. Certainly the addition of new territory increased considerably the size of the human population upon which he could depend, and it may have been true—though now unprovable—that major agricultural resources had long existed in the form of estates (see below, p. 219). Moreover, there can be no doubt about the continuing source of revenue from the sale of Macedonian timber under royal control. Although one cannot be precise about the economic underpinnings for Philip's policies, he was able to build a formidable military force,[48] and the lavish festival he organized at Aegae in 336 supports the notion that he had at hand considerable resources.

Philip and the Northern Greeks

Philip's activities from the start had been of concern both to those Greeks who were his neighbors in Chalcidice and Thessaly and to those who lived at some distance in the city-states of the south. Not

[47] Le Rider, *Le monnayage d'argent et d'or*, 435; also Kraay, *Archaic and Classical Greek Coins*, 138–47.

[48] Philip fielded 30,000 foot and 2000 cavalry at Chaeronea (Diod. 16.85.5), a threefold growth over the Macedonian forces assembled to meet the Illyrian Bardylis in 358; his Argead predecessors' armies were meagre by comparison.

long after the conqueror of Amphipolis had taken Pydna and then staked his claim in the area east of the Strymon, an alliance was formed between him and the Chalcidians (winter of 357/6). We are fortunate that this period is, epigraphically speaking, the richest in Argead history, and an inscription discovered by excavators near Olynthus reveals further testimony to Philip's diplomacy.[49] Although the inscription itself is fragmentary and deals mainly with procedural matters, it nonetheless suggests that this was a military alliance of sufficient importance to require elaborate diplomatic and religious consultation, including an appeal to Delphi. This treaty was Philip's response to the Athenian alliance with the three Balkan kings. He exploited traditional Chalcidic apprehensions about Athens, and promised to turn over to the Chalcidians the Athenian outpost at Potidaea. After a difficult siege in summer 356, Potidaea fell to Philip, who then made good on his pledge.

Within a decade, however, Philip's position in the north was consolidated, and the Chalcidic alliance had become less useful. In the meanwhile, the leading Chalcidic center at Olynthus—to judge from its ruins, perhaps the greatest Greek city in the north—had drifted toward Athens.[50] It is perhaps inevitable that Olynthus, long a competitor of Macedon in the north and occasional ally of Athens, would become an obstacle to Philip's need to complete the circle of security deemed necessary for his kingdom's border. This is not to say that compromise and a political settlement were not possible, and it appears that opinion was divided among the Chalcidians themselves about the proper course of action. Would survival be better assured by being Philip's friend or Philip's enemy? In the late 350s Philip began to test his Chalcidic alliance by some small interventions in the region, but the impoverished nature of our sources does not permit us to reconstruct the events of the period leading up to Olynthus's fall.[51]

In 349, on a pretext that can hardly be credible (that Olynthus had refused to return to Philip his two half-brothers, who had taken refuge there during an earlier campaign [Just. 8.3.10]), Philip invaded Chalcidic territory. Faced with a league of Chalcidic towns crumbling before Philip's advance, the Olynthians sought assistance from Athens. Led by the power of Demosthenes's oratory in his *Olynthiacs*, the

---

[49] Tod *GHI*, no. 158 (with commentary); Diod. 16.8.3–5; Dem. 23.107–8, 2.7, 2.14, 6.20. Also see Griffith, *HM* 2: 243–46, for discussion.

[50] For details, Griffith, *HM* 2: 296–304, and Cawkwell, *Philip of Macedon*, 69–90, with considerable ancient evidence from the anti-Macedonian speeches of Demosthenes.

[51] As Griffith (*HM* 2: 319) pointed out, our main narrative source, Diodorus 16.52.9–10, covers all the events in mainland Greece for the year 349/8 in only two sentences.

Athenians voted to send aid, but only a token force was dispatched. Olynthus was briefly spared the full onslaught of the Macedonian army, as Philip's attention was temporarily diverted to Thessalian affairs. The respite from Philip's Chalcidic campaign was not, however, used to bolster Olynthus's defenses, as the Athenians found themselves militarily occupied closer to home. Despite the fact that two further Athenian forces would find their way to assist the Olynthians against Philip, Athens's commitment to its Chalcidic ally was sporadic and ineffective. One cannot but feel the same sympathy for the Olynthians that one feels for the Thebans in their rebellion against Alexander the Great in 335. Both cities had resisted Macedon for their own reasons, but were encouraged to do so with the promise of Athenian assistance that never fully materialized. Athens always seemed willing to challenge the Macedonians to the last drop of its allies' blood.

In the spring of 348, Philip returned to Olynthus, and the city came under intense siege, to judge by the large number of Macedonian arrow points and sling bullets inscribed with Philip's name discovered in the modern excavation of the ruins.[52] Our sources do not provide many details about Olynthus's last moments (e.g., Diod. 16.53.2–3), but it appears that, although some Olynthians surrendered to the Macedonian king, the remainder held out in a desperate and vain stand. The walls were breached and the city fell in the early autumn.[53]

What followed the collapse of Olynthian resistance was perhaps unexpected. Not only was the city sacked, but its population was sold into slavery and the site leveled. Olynthus, the grand city of the northern Greeks, ceased to exist. A brutal ending, to be sure, but in an age when the rights of the victor over the vanquished were absolute, anything could happen, and often did. Few important Greek cities could claim to have always exercised leniency when it came to dealing with conquered peoples. In this regard the Macedonians behaved no worse, and often better, than their contemporaries. Griffith has argued that Philip's motives in obliterating Olynthus were mixed (Diod. 16.53.3).

[52] The fall of Olynthus is discussed by Griffith, *HM* 2: 321–28 (with useful source analysis), and by Cawkwell, *Philip of Macedon*, 82–90, and "The Defence of Olynthus," a lucid account of Demosthenes' policy. The site is well published in the excavation reports of D. M. Robinson (*Excavations at Olynthus*); see p. 15 above. For the missiles bearing Philip's name, see Appendix C, p. 299 below.

[53] For a discussion of the precise date, either September or October 348 B.C., see Griffith, *HM* 2: 327 n. 4. Incidentally, the fall of Olynthus in 348 provides us with one of the few fixed dates in Greek archaeology, thereby establishing an essential chronological base for the dating of Greek pottery. But, as it has been recently determined that the city was reoccupied, the year 348 as the *terminus ante quem* for the types of materials found at Olynthus must be used with caution.

He both derived revenue from the sale of booty and inhabitants, and served notice to the Chalcidic Greeks about the nature of their alliance. But the intimidation was directed elsewhere as well. Olynthus had been a large and important city, and its utter devastation was a telling event. All the more so if the agent of that destruction was the man who continually offered political settlements, and acted the role of the witty and rational hellenized king. That such a person could encompass both civil and ruthless behavior with equanimity might well keep potential adversaries off balance. Whatever the other benefits to the Macedonians accruing from Olynthus's extinction, the lesson might not, Philip hoped, be lost on Athens.

The extent to which Philip reorganized and exploited Chalcidic territory is problematic.[54] The northern, hilly half of Chalcidice is rich in wood and mineral resources, whereas the southern half—a broad plain gently sloping from the Cholomon hills down to the sea—is excellent farm and grazing land. There is no doubt that it was the practice of both Philip and Alexander to provide estates to Macedonians and Greeks, and some of these lands were Chalcidic.[55] If, however, Griffith's analysis is correct, there was neither a significant distribution of Chalcidic land to the king's men nor any mass resettlement of the region by Macedonians. There was probably some use of captured territory, especially from destroyed sites like Olynthus, to raise horses and to support ranking Macedonians through gifts of estates, but these practices would barely alter the character of the general Greek population. With Olynthus now extinct, there was no rallying point for renewed Chalcidic opposition to Macedon, and Philip could afford to leave most of the area unaltered, both for the sake of his own exploitation of the resources of the region—its inhabitants and cities—as future allies, and as an act of public relations directed toward the Greeks in the south.

We have seen that Argead kings since the time of Alexander I recognized the importance of the Thessalian frontier for the security of Macedonia. As early in his reign as 358, Philip reaffirmed the traditional Argead alliance with the Aleuadae of Larisa, supporting them against the tyrant of Pherae. His marriage at this time to the Aleuad

---

[54] Extensively and well discussed by Griffith, *HM* 2: 365–79.

[55] E.g., Theopomp. *FGrH* 115, F 225b = Athen. 260d–61a; Plut. *Alex.* 15.3; Dem. 19.145; Just. 11.5.5, although it is unlikely that the king gave away all of the royal land to his men, and the passages in Plutarch and Justin (above) are suspiciously close to suggest a doublet. The discovery in 1982 of an inscription near the northern Chalcidic community of Kalamoto partly confirms the practice of royal land grants by Alexander (confirming Plutarch 15.3); see Vokotopoulou, "I Epigraphi tōn Kalindōn."

Philinna was a sign that Philip intended to continue the Thessalian policies of his predecessors to use his connections with the Thessalians to protect his southern border.[56]

But there was a new twist. With Thessaly acting as a springboard between Macedon and the entangled world of Greek cities and alliances, Philip could be selective in supporting his Thessalian allies in their relations with the southern Greeks. Thus Philip could establish himself as a force in central Greek politics without the necessity of either abandoning his efforts to consolidate his position in the north or mounting a full military intervention in the south. During much of the 350s and 340s Philip maintained this delicate balance with a high degree of success, also contriving to emerge as the de facto leader (*tagos*) of the Thessalian cities by *ca.* 352, and fighting successfully on behalf of the Thessalians against the perennially rebellious city of Pherae. Probably as part of the settlement ending the war against Pherae, Philip married a local woman of prominence, Nicesipolis. Their daughter, who would be the half-sister of Alexander the Great and, later, the wife of Cassander, was appropriately named Thessalonikē, to commemorate Philip's victory in Thessaly. In 315 Cassander founded at or near the site of ancient Therme the great city that still bears her name.[57]

When, in the course of his campaigns, Philip seized the port town of Pagasae (near modern Volos) and established a garrison there, it probably seemed to many Greeks that the Macedonian occupation of this strategic site on the vital Gulf of Pagasae transcended the mere bounds of alliance. But Philip brought peace and stability to the fractious Thessalians, something that may have been valued by most of them.[58] He also derived profit from his Thessalian venture. The buffer protecting southern Macedonia now extended nearly to central Greece. Philip gained revenues from some Thessalian territory, and his position as Thessalian *tagos*, along with the geographical proximity of Thessaly to central Greece, made the Macedonian king a power to be

[56] On the Macedonians and Thessalians in this period, see Griffith, "Philip of Macedon's Early Interventions in Thessaly." Also see *HM* 2: 218–30 and 259–95. Philinna would produce a son, Arrhidaeus, who succeeded Alexander the Great as Philip III (323–317).

[57] The 2300th anniversary of the foundation of Thessaloniki was deservedly celebrated by the Greek nation, but in the incorrect year (1985), thereby replicating the arithmetical error embodied in the national commemoration of the 2300th anniversary of the death of Alexander the Great in 1977, instead of the correct 1978. In figuring chronology back from the Christian/Common Era to the pre-Christian, one must keep in mind that there is no Year 0.

[58] Here I follow Griffith, *HM* 2: 295.

reckoned with in the region. Finally, he incorporated into the Macedonian army a substantial number of Thessalian allies. During Alexander's expedition the Thessalian cavalry serving under Parmenio's command distinguished itself as the most important Greek allied unit until its dismissal after the collapse of Persian resistance.

By 348 Philip controlled through direct annexation or alliances virtually everything north of the Lamian Gulf. Among the major Greek cities, Athens had lost the most, although not as much in actual territory, population, and resources as in the thwarting of its traditional expansionist interests in the northern Aegean. Moreover, the collapse of Athenian alliances in the Chersonese and Propontis represented a potential threat to its grain ships. It is no wonder that some Athenians saw Philip as a force that threatened the very independence of the city.

Philip and the Southern Greeks

Thus far the Macedonian presence had been some hundreds of miles and several mountain ranges removed from Thebes and Athens. But events in central Greece would bring the Macedonians to the doorstep of Boeotia and Attica. The Amphictyonic League was an ancient and mainly religious association of central Greek peoples, centered on the sacred panhellenic site at Delphi. The Amphictyony, whose primary responsibility was to ensure the neutrality of the sacred precinct, was, however, not without politics, and was sometimes used by neighboring states to further their individual schemes. In 356 a dispute broke out resulting in the occupation of Delphi by local Phocian forces. The following year saw an Amphictyonic declaration of war against Phocis. By 354 a number of Greek states had, for their own reasons, joined the Phocians. Thus many of the most prominent states were lined up on opposite sides of what is known as the "Sacred" War; in particular, Thebes opposed Phocis, while Athens supported it. Philip became involved through his leadership of the Thessalians, also opposed to the Phocians. The Sacred War continued sporadically over the next few years, largely without Macedonian intervention.

But by 348 nothing stood between Philip's armies and Thermopylae, which was both the gateway to central Greece and the Amphictyonic center while Delphi was occupied by rebels. The Phocians seemed to be on the verge of collapse, but Thebes was too exhausted to exploit the situation. A Theban appeal to Philip for assistance was greeted with uncharacteristic Macedonian vacillation. Philip's irresolution, however, was not based on fear or on interest elsewhere. As events would prove, Philip was not hesitant to intervene in central Greece, but it was necessary to do so in such a way as to keep Athens and Thebes off balance. Neither city alone was dangerous to Macedon, but allied—itself a rare prospect for these ancient adversaries—Athens and Thebes could thwart Philip's plan to invade Asia Minor (see below), not by threatening an attack on Macedon, but by offering continuing troublesome resistance in central Greece and the Aegean. It was therefore Philip's wish to avoid a wasteful military confrontation against an anti-Macedonian coalition of Athens and Thebes. Desiring to retain his existing alliance with Thebes, he hoped also to win a union with Athens as the price of intervening against the Phocians.[59]

But little or none of this was known in Athens, where Philip's expected imminent intervention in central Greece was viewed with alarm. The Athenians took a series of countersteps, including renewing their old links with Cersebleptes and reaffirming ties with the Phocians. By doing so Athens was edging toward what Philip hoped to avoid: war between the Athenians and Macedonians. Yet prudence prevailed for awhile, and in the spring of 346 an Athenian embassy arrived at Pella to present Athens's position and learn Philip's terms.[60] The envoys' meeting with Philip was without rancor, and they returned to Athens mainly persuaded that Philip wished peace and was willing not only to forego any ambitions in the Chersonese beyond reducing the now rebellious Cersebleptes but also to guarantee Athenian hegemony in several areas near Attica. Philip insisted only that the details of his proposals not be broadcast widely, so as to avoid arousing the opposition of Thebes. In mid-April the Athenian people began to debate Philip's offer, formulated as a matter of public business under the name of Philocrates, who had urged negotiations with the Macedonians. Not without difficulty, Philocrates's proposal was accepted, gaining even the support of Demosthenes. A second embassy was sent to Pella to ease a number of disagreements over interpretations of the first proposals and to consider some important matters overlooked in the earlier negotiations. Again with difficulty, agreements were reached and oaths were given, and then Philip accompanied the embassy as far south as Pherae on its return home to Athens.

But matters began to go wrong. Thebes was aroused at the prospect

[59] In this summary I follow the scheme of Ellis, *PMI*. Also see Griffith, *HM* vol. 2, whose account does not differ markedly from Ellis's and is much more detailed. One must keep in mind, however, that what seems so strategically simple to us who have the advantage of historical hindsight may have been less so to Philip.

[60] Details in Aesch. 2.15–39.

of a settlement that seemed both to exclude it and to let off the Phocians if they would relinquish Delphi to the Amphictyony. Philip marched to Thermopylae, the passage to fortified central Greece, and prepared to carry out his part of the bargain. Demosthenes, who thus far had not appeared to oppose the proposals, turned against further negotiations, declining a place on a third embassy to Philip at Thermopylae. Instead, he vigorously began to rouse public opinion against Macedon, effectively preying upon the deep-rooted Athenian suspicions of Philip that lay just beneath the surface. With the Thebans now raising their military levy and the Athenians backtracking on their commitments to their Macedonian ally, Philip turned to the Amphictyonic Council in order to avoid war. Meeting at Thermopylae in late summer, the council voted to disbar the Phocians from Amphictyonic participation, and to replace them with the king of the Macedonians. The Phocians were punished severely for their anti-Amphictyonic activity, but the most ruthless excesses of which their neighbors—especially the Thebans—were capable were restrained by the presence of Macedonian soldiers. In the face of impending war, Philip had turned to diplomacy. The Phocian rebellion was ended, the Amphictyony had prevailed, warfare with Thebes was averted, Athens was allied with Macedon, and Philip was now a voting member of the Amphictyonic League. These arrangements must be considered a diplomatic victory for Philip, but the larger and more permanent settlement he sought still eluded him.

The proposals agreed to by Philip and the Athenian envoys, and ratified by the Athenian Assembly, are known as the Peace of Philocrates.[61] As well as peace, there was to be a mutual, permanent defense alliance between the parties, also binding on their allies. Each party was to recognize the other's rights in territories held at the moment, and both parties pledged to concern themselves with the safety of the seas and to control piracy. Despite Demosthenes's opposition, an underlying Athenian uneasiness about Philip, and a disappointment that the settlement of the Sacred Wars was not entirely to Athenian satisfaction, there still remained some support for the peace proposal, especially among the envoys who had negotiated it. But as public opinion turned more and more toward the Demosthenic position, the peace became a dead issue and the Athenians drifted toward war.

Having achieved an equal seat in the council of Greek powers in the Amphictyony, Philip now returned to Pella, perhaps to commence

[61] Details in Griffith, *HM* 2: 338–39, with evidence. The sources on the Peace of Philocrates are collected in Bengtson, *Staatsvertrage*, vol. 2, no. 329.

preparations for an invasion of Asia, although the absence of a general framework to ensure stability in Greece was still a matter of priority for him. Continuing to portray himself as the guardian of weaker states, Philip in 344 made alliances with some Peloponnesian cities hostile to Sparta. It would thus seem that if Philip were denied the general settlement he proposed in the Peace of Philocrates, he would attempt to accomplish it piecemeal through a large number of bilateral arrangements.[62] When objections were raised about the growing number of treaties between Greek states and Macedon, Philip renewed his offer of 346, that a Common Peace (*koinē eirēnē*) be arranged, which would be a substitute for the existing bilateral alliances and be open to all who wished to join. The Athenians amended the proposal in ways to ensure that it would be unacceptable to Philip. Politics in Athens seemed now to turn on an obsession with Philip of Macedon. Aeschines argued that Athens should exploit the Peace of Philocrates to its own advantage, while Demosthenes proposed that it should be used as a license to subvert Philip. In the background, the Athenian speechwriter and essayist Isocrates, who for four decades had urged the Greeks to abandon their perennial conflicts and unite in a panhellenic crusade against the Persians, urged in his oration *Philip* and in his two letters to the Macedonian king that Philip offered the most favorable opportunity to unite the city-states.[63] The fierce quality of the debate was marked by character assassination, obfuscation of facts, and the deliberate misreading of both the local opposition and Macedonian intentions.

By 340 the apparent resistance to his offers had begun to make Philip doubt that an accommodation with Athens was possible, especially after the Athenians had begun to support the formation of anti-Macedonian factions in the northern Aegean. Philip was forced again to campaign in the Chersonese and Propontis, and, in the course of protecting his hard-won northern hegemony, he seized the Athenian grain fleet in the late summer of 340. The drift toward war was now complete. Under Demosthenes' leadership, the Athenians persuaded the Thebans to join them against Philip, and the weaker or uncommitted states were compelled to join their coalition in what had become what

---

[62] Philip's Peloponnesian policy is dealt with in some detail by Hamilton, "Philip II and Archidamus."

[63] The quality of support for Philip is analyzed by Markle, "Support of Athenian Intellectuals for Philip." Markle concludes that Isocrates's adherents—themselves no democrats—saw their own material well-being and philosophical interests best served by Philip's policies, even if it meant sacrificing some of Athens's autonomy in foreign affairs.

Philip had attempted to avoid: a military confrontation between Greece and Macedon. The matter was settled in late summer 338 in the shallow Cephisus River valley near the sleepy village of Chaeronea on the road to Thebes. In a battle that must be regarded as a culmination of Philip's military reforms, the Macedonian army soundedly thrashed the allied forces of Athens and Thebes. The battle ushered in a new age of warfare, as the Macedonians, commanded by the king and seconded by the eighteen-year-old Alexander, taught the Greeks a hard lesson about the value of precise coordination between flexible aggressive cavalry and a formidable disciplined infantry.[64]

The Aftermath of Chaeronea

Immediately following his victory, Philip set about making arrangements for the settlement he had long hoped for. Avoiding retribution in favor of reconciliation, he dealt individually with a number of Greek cities. With cities (such as Athens) that had been allied with him until their defection in the recent war, he simply renewed the old alliances.[65] He may have made new treaties with some others, while in the case of yet others it may have been necessary to ensure through political pressure the institution of governing factions friendly to his interests. All of these maneuvers were preparatory to the establishment of his general peace.

A grand peace conference was called over the winter of 338/7 at Corinth, or perhaps at the panhellenic center nearby at Isthmia, a site more in keeping with the spirit of Philip's avowed panhellenic policies. Notably, only Sparta among the major states refused to attend, but Philip did not press the point. To invade Laconia and invest even a Sparta in decline would have been, for the cautious commander, an unnecessary waste of good men, especially when the same end—the neutralization of the Spartans—could be accomplished by isolating them inside a ring of states tied to the common peace. It seemed a prudent decision at the time, and it can be only a matter of speculation that the later rebellion

---

[64] On Chaeronea see Diod. 16.85.5–86.6; Just. 9.3; Plut. *Alex.* 9.3; Polyaenus *Strat.* 4.2.2 and 7. Griffith, *HM* 2: 596–603, provides a useful summary of the main problems faced in reconstructing this battle, a turning point in western history, but very poorly documented by the ancient writers. Markle, "The Use of the Sarissa," 486–97, argues that Alexander's cavalry may have been equipped with sarissas, but that Philip's right-wing infantry probably could not have effected their tactical withdrawal armed with long spears. It is not known whether any infantry in the center carried sarissas.

[65] In these matters I follow Griffith, *HM* 2: 608–9.

of the Spartans against Macedonian rule in 331 might have been prevented had Philip subdued Sparta in 338.

With the grim reminder that a Macedonian garrison was entrenched atop the imposing slopes of Acrocorinth nearby, the Greek delegates at the Isthmus went about their business of formulating the common peace so long sought after by the king of the Macedonians. Fortunately, two fragments of a copy of this alliance, known in modern times as the "League of Corinth," have been preserved.[66] The settlement was both a common peace and a military alliance of Greek city-states. It provided that no state should make war upon another, and that no party should alter the constitutions existing in the cities at the time that the oaths were sworn (the carefully installed governments loyal to Philip). Any attempt to subvert the kingship of Philip and his descendants (*tēn basileian tēn Philippou kai tōn ekgonōn*) was prohibited, as was aid to any party that attempted to violate the provisions of the alliance. Philip was to act as guarantor of the treaty; that is, it was an alliance among the Greeks and an alliance between the Greeks and the king of the Macedonians. A council (*synedrion*) was established, with a proportional representation the basis of which is unclear due to the broken nature of the stones. It was a "normal" alliance, both in its conception of equality among a number of lesser states looking to a major power as the guarantor, and in its personification of Macedon in the form of the king and his descendants, not successors. Later, the league met to elect Philip as commander-in-chief of the Asian expeditionary force.

The peace imposed on the Greeks by force of arms in 338/7 was not unlike what Philip had first offered the Greeks through diplomacy beginning nearly a decade before. This fact remains the most important single argument favoring the sincerity of those earlier proposals. If the settlement at the Isthmus was not exactly what Philip had envisioned in 346 or 344, he had mainly Athens to blame. In the end the delay may have postponed the Asian expedition for up to a decade, depending upon when Philip first conceived the idea for a Persian war. When the Asian crusade was finally taken up, it was under command of a much younger and, in many respects, different sort of man.

Philip returned to Macedon and, probably confident that Greek affairs were settled more or less to his liking, turned to preparations for the Asian venture. Advance parties had been sent into Asia Minor, di-

[66] Tod *GHI*, no. 177, for text and commentary. The settlement has been intensively studied by modern scholarship, *inter alia*, Roebuck, "The Settlements of Philip II with the Greek States in 338 B.C.," and Griffith, *HM* 2: 623–46. Also see Wilcken, *Alexander*, 42–49.

plomacy with local rulers initiated,[67] and arrangements were made to
commence the eastern offensive in the spring of 335. Philip married
out of love the young Macedonian Cleopatra, who bore him a female
child. In autumn 336, Philip celebrated his exalted status with a lavish
festival at Aegae. Representatives from the Greek world were invited
to share in games and a religious festival and to witness the marriage
of the king's daughter (Cleopatra, by Olympias) to Alexander of Epirus. After more than two decades of war and diplomacy, Philip now
seemed prepared to enjoy some of the ritual benefits of having conquered and organized most of the Balkans south of the Danube.

During a procession in the theatre at Aegae a member of the royal
bodyguard, Pausanias, struck Philip dead with a dagger thrust. The
assassin attempted to escape to horses stationed nearby, but was caught
and dispatched on the spot. It would be an understatement to suggest
that the assassination of Philip was unexpected and untimely, and considerable attention has been lavished on the event by modern scholarship. Attempts to attribute the king's murder to some internal political
conspiracy or foreign plot have, in my view, been unsuccessful. The
ancient sources give us a perfectly plausible motive, a personal grudge
against Philip long held by the assassin. Moreover, the very public nature of the execution among a people who, had anyone wished to be
rid of a king for political reasons, were experienced in a variety of subtle and secret techniques of assassination, supports the notion that the
murder results from the rage of Pausanias's private grievance.[68] No
wider conspiracy seems warranted, beyond the possibility that Pausanias may have intended more than a single victim and that he may have
had help.[69] Without delay Alexander was presented to the army and
acclaimed king. There never could have been any doubt that Philip had
intended Alexander as his heir. Everything in the young man's career
to this moment—even taking into account the anger that sometimes

[67] On the growing independence of local rulers in the western satrapies, see the survey
by Burn, "Persia and the Greeks," 368–91.

[68] Months or even years earlier, Pausanias had been mocked at court and abused by
some of Attalus's men. When Pausanias complained to the king, Philip did nothing,
perhaps not wishing to alienate Attalus, an important Macedonian baron. Apparently
Pausanias nurtured a bitterness at the king of the Macedonians not having redressed this
grievance. In these matters I share many of the views of Ellis, "The Assassination of
Philip II," and Hammond, *HM* 2: 684–91, supported by a reliable contemporary source
(Arist. *Pol.* 1311b.2–4). The main narrative account of Philip's murder is Diod. 16.91.4–
94.4.

[69] Two of our sources (Diod. 16.94.4 and Just. 9.7.9) are explicit: *horses* (plural) are
mentioned, suggesting more than a single assassin or at least someone on the outside
who was to assist with the escape.

marred the relationship between the careful Philip and the more impetuous and impatient Alexander—pointed to Philip's preparation of
his son for the task of rule. Alexander was probably better trained for
kingship than any figure in Macedonian history. And in many respects
he proved to be a worthy successor.

Whatever Philip's skills as a statesman and diplomat—and they were
considerable (Diod. 16.95.2–4)—he established Macedon for the first
time as an international military power. Unlike some of his predecessors, who, lacking the military resources necessary to enforce their
diplomacy, survived mainly by their wits and duplicity, Philip could
reinforce his diplomatic gestures with the threat of a formidable army.
He could thus afford to be more direct in his dealings with Greeks, and
one wonders if part of the mistrust that characterized Greek-Macedonian relations in this period arose from Greek—particularly Athenian—disbelief that a Macedonian king could keep his word.

Philip's panhellenic aspirations were genuine, but not based on any
need to prove his Hellenism to the Greek world. It was essentially a
practical matter: His desire to protect Delphi from the ravages of the
local Phocians was as much—if not more—a device to cloak his entry
into the Amphictyonic League, and thus central Greek politics, as it
was an act of devotion on behalf of the gods. The commissioning of
the Philippeion at Olympia and his entry into the horse races at the
Games was a further statement that the king of Macedon would now
be treated on the basis of equality. And the formation of his panhellenic
league in the settlement of 338/7 was a testament to the need for security and stability in Greece under the watchful eyes of Macedonian garrisons.

For it appears that Greece was for Philip of Macedon a way-station
to the Orient.[70] The Greeks were incidental to his long-term ambition.
Despite the cultural attraction, Greece was too poor to be the goal of a
Macedonian king for whom the wealth of Asia was the prize—too
poor in everything but the quality of its men. For Greek soldiers were,
after Philip's own, the most skilled anywhere, and Greek deviousness
in diplomacy might continue to test Macedonian responses. The prudent adventurer, bent on Asia, hardly wanted Greek adversaries on his
rear. The necessity to achieve security and coalition in Greece was a
precondition for the ultimate objectives: the military goals and wealth
of the East. The Greeks—Demosthenes in particular—may have seen

[70] Here I adopt a modification of a thesis proposed by Ellis, *PMI*, more than a decade
ago. Errington's recent challenge ("Four Interpretations of Philip II," 73–83), while not
entirely persuasive, has sufficient merit to make one wish that he would address the
problem of Philip's strategic objectives more fully.

Philip's diplomacy and military activity as the vehicle for Philip's entry into Greece, whereas Philip was also preparing for the Macedonian exit from Europe into Asia. It may have been one of the ironies of the age that the Athenians, burdened by their own insular pride and checkered past relations with the Argeadae, could not conceive of the Macedonians not being interested in *them*. The "barbarian" from the north had developed a foreign policy so consistent and pragmatic as to be utterly alien to the Hellenic mind.

Whence the attraction to Asia? It is certain that Philip intended a major military campaign in Asia. But it is a matter of speculation whether he envisaged an all-out attack on the Persian empire (in the manner actually accomplished by Alexander) or only an expedition in Asia Minor, where many local satraps and tyrants were already virtually independent from weak central Persian authority.[71] And it is not clear just when the plan for an Asian expedition was formulated and what the relationship of that future Asian policy was to Philip's activities in Greece. The views of Ellis and Cawkwell—that Philip had conceived of a campaign against the Persians by the early 340s, which then served as the backdrop for his Greek policy—have been challenged by Errington.[72] Although Errington rightly points out that the evidence for an "early" Asian plan is not as conclusive as first appearance suggests, it is also clear that by the time of the battle of Chaeronea and its consequent panhellenic diplomatic and military settlement in 338/7, events were moving toward an Asian expedition. It is Errington's view that the plan for a Persian campaign was formulated as the result of Philip's failed policy in central Greece, and that the adoption of a presumably popular crusade against the common Persian enemy was a gesture to secure the neutrality of several leading central Greek states.

Yet, as Errington admits, there is no confirmation in the sources for his hypothesis. Moreover, the degree to which Philip's central Greek policy was a failure is a matter of interpretation. One could as easily suggest that, although Philip did not achieve in the mid-340s the common peace he desired, he still managed to construct a settlement that worked tolerably well under difficult circumstances. The only "failure" may have been to delay the Asian campaign by a decade, but this is a judgment entirely from historical hindsight, as other factors unrelated to the southern Greeks might also have altered his plans. It may

[71] On the Persian context of Philip's activities, see Burn, "Persia and the Greeks," 368–91, and Griffith, *HM* 2: 458–63 and 517–22, plus Errington, "Four Interpretations of Philip II," 77–84.

[72] Errington, "Four Interpretations of Philip II," 77–84. Errington's views on this matter are more in accord with those of Griffith than with those of Ellis and Cawkwell.

well be impossible to know just when Philip's scheme for an attack on the Persians was first expressed. It is not a matter that we would expect our contemporary Greek sources to be well informed about, or, even if they knew about it, to be open in reporting.[73]

It is difficult to imagine that Philip's policy toward Greece was an end in itself. Once his Balkan borders had been secured, his general course seems to have been directed toward the establishment of stability in Greece, not conquest. Philip normally attempted diplomacy as a first resort, although the threat of Macedonian spears loomed conspicuously in the background. Ever the careful general, he knew better than to sacrifice good soldiers if his aim could be achieved by nonmilitary means. The policy from the beginning is consistent: to achieve security in Greece. Since there is no evidence that Greece was the *object* of his policy—he drew no wealth from Greece and committed few troops as garrisons there—there must have been some other object in mind. This hypothesis is not proof, but it is consistent with, and may even explain, Philip's activities in Greece in the 440s and 430s.

It is equally troublesome to measure the effect on Philip of Isocrates' long-time denunciations of Greek instability and promotion of a panhellenic effort directed at the ancient and common Persian enemy. Philip may have found Isocrates' views a convenient bolster in a city whose support Philip valued for a policy he had already formulated for other reasons. One suspects that the petty ambitions and politics of Greek city-states had no attraction for a Macedonian king bent on empire. Moreover, for a monarchy that itself had developed many of the trappings and institutions of the Orient—along with its Hellenic adornments—Asia may have seemed the more natural outlet for an expression of the military skills of a Philip of Macedon. He was the first Macedonian king with ambitions outside the Balkans. It is a pity that we shall never know how Philip, so successful in Europe, would have fared in Asia.

---

[73] Diod. 16.60.4–5 first refers to Philip's Persian ambitions in his account of the king's central Greek settlement of 346, but perhaps with the authority of hindsight. And, although Isocrates's *Letter to Philip* (ll.9 and 83–84, written in 346) refers to an Asian expedition, it does not show knowledge of Philip's plans, nor do we know when or if Philip read it.

Political Institutions in the Age of Philip
and Alexander

PHILIP II inherited a weak and frag-
mented Balkan kingdom and, as we have seen, transformed it into a
major European power that would confront, challenge, defeat, and organize the unruly Greek city-states. His son Alexander, the story of
whose conquests are outside the scope of the present work, took the
Macedonian army into Asia and terminated 2½ centuries of Persian
hegemony, thereby permitting the introduction of some features of
Greek civilization into the eastern rim of the Mediterranean. What
these two men accomplished in the third of a century encompassed by
their reigns could hardly have been foretold at the start of Philip's rule.

One wonders to what extent the extraordinary accomplishments of
these two most famous sons of Macedon rested upon traditional Macedonian institutions, to what extent they resulted from the changes
these kings wrought, and to what extent they reflected their individual
personalities. The study of their personal qualities I leave to others. But
it might useful here to review the political institutions that are attributed to their era, to attempt to put these into the context of an emerging Macedon, and to examine some innovative features of their respective reigns.

We have seen that there is precious little information concerning either the internal structure or the material goods of Macedon before the
reign of Philip II. Thus far the sources for Macedonian affairs have
been external and either uninterested in or ignorant of Macedonian
institutions beyond court gossip. The reign of Philip II marks the first
time that there is anything like contemporary, even eyewitness, evidence that has survived in the accounts of later writers. There are, for
example, rich, though often highly prejudiced, Athenian documents,
as Philip was a public issue in that city.

But the emergence of a relative abundance of information brings
with it a danger, for it is tempting to read back into an earlier age the
features of the later fourth century. The consequent anachronisms can

present a false impression of Macedonian life before Philip's time. Methodologically it is essential to ensure that any picture of early Macedon reflects contemporaneous evidence. If the following reconstruction of Macedonian institutions appears conservative—even minimalist—it results from the rejection of several interpretations that may reflect the ideas (and hopes) of their proponents more than they describe how the ancient Macedonians themselves actually lived. We would do well to accept the caution of one modern critic, who, in response to an elaborate recent reconstruction of the Macedonian political and juridical system, wrote: ". . . the manner of systematic legalized thinking about the Macedonian state is not an ancient but a modern phenomenon."[1]

The rise of Macedon's power under its two pre-eminent fourth-century monarchs has inevitably drawn a number of modern scholars to investigate the institutions of the kingdom. Like so much else that touches on the history of a people who are mainly silent about themselves, the reconstruction of those institutions has often been more ingenious than persuasive. Nowhere has invention been more manifest than in the analyses of Macedonian "constitutionalism." It is natural for historians to seek order (and occasionally even reason) in the chaos of events, and the fragmentary evidence for internal Macedonian history has provided a challenge for those who have desired to know whereby these people rose to such historical greatness. Unfortunately, the ancient Macedonians lacked a Polybius, who illuminated the institutions that made Rome famous. Those who mention Macedonian customs were the enemies of Macedon or later biographers of Philip and Alexander or dilettante collectors of gossip and exotica. Any attempt to reconstruct the inner history of Macedon from such fragmentary material is difficult in the extreme.

There are two basic schools of thought about the Macedonian "constitution," if by the use of that term we mean a description of the customs and institutions by which a society was regulated—the German *Staatsrecht*. One holds that the Macedonian kingdom was run according to a generally accepted set of traditions, within which various groups held and exercised customary rights that the king oversaw and guaranteed. This is the "constitutionalist" position. The other school believes that the kingdom was centered on the autocracy of the monarch himself, who did precisely what he wanted, or—more exactly— what he could get away with.

It is not my intention here to argue the question anew: a brief review

[1] Errington, "Historiographical Origins," 101.

will suffice. The various positions have been abundantly laid out by their respective advocates, and there is no telling new evidence that bears on the subject. Nearly all of the information about Macedonian political and social institutions comes from the age of Philip and Alexander—famous kings whose reigns are relatively well documented—and any attempt to read back into earlier Macedonian history requires assumptions (if not a leap of faith) about the continuity of institutions from the fifth and early fourth centuries into the later fourth century and Hellenistic era. If the advocates of constitutionalism use this evolution or continuity as an operating methodological assumption, they should also be able to trace the continuation of these institutions into the Hellenistic period, or, if not, to posit why there was a break.

The constitutionalist position was laid out forcefully more than half a century ago by Friedrich Granier, and much of the discussion since has evolved in support, modification, or rejection of his views.[2] Using evidence mainly from the Hellenistic period, Granier believed that the Macedonian kingship evolved from a primitive chieftainship, like that of the Homeric Greeks or the ancient Germans described in Tacitus's *Germania*, in which the king was a first among equals, chosen by his fellow warriors. As Macedonian institutions became more formal, an organization of Macedonian men-at-arms came into existence, marking a transition to something akin to a sovereign military assembly.[3] As the population became more settled and the Macedonians were transformed from a warrior society into a landed aristocracy, the nobility usurped popular sovereignty. In the fourth century, however, the assembly was revived to provide the monarchy with support against the nobility. The army assembly acquired some judicial functions and even selected the king or regent. All parties were aware of their rights, although practically the king ruled as an autocrat. Nonetheless, the relationship between king and people was regulated by two constituent functions of the army assembly: the right to elect the king and the right to sit as judge and jury. Granier's book had an immediate and enor-

[2] Basic bibliography on this issue, listed alphabetically: W. L. Adams, "Macedonian Kingship"; Anson, "Macedonia's Alleged Constitutionalism"; Aymard, "Sur l'assemblée macédonienne," and "*Basileus Makedonōn*"; Briant, *Antigone le Borgne*; de Francisci, *Arcana Imperii*, 2: 345–91; Errington, "Macedonian 'Royal Style,' " "Historiographical Origins," and "The Nature of the Macedonian State"; Granier, *Die makedonische Heeresversammlung*; Lock, "The Macedonian Army Assembly"; plus appropriate sections in Errington, *Gesch. Make.* (196–212), and Hammond and Griffith, *HM* 2: 150–65 and 383–404.

[3] One wonders how much influence Mommsen's *Römisches Staatsrecht* had on Granier's work; see Errington, "The Nature of the Macedonian State," 77.

mous impact, and, although small parts of it were soon found flawed, the basic thesis that the Macedonians lived according to traditional customs long remained unchallenged.

In 1950, nearly two decades following the appearance of Granier's work, André Aymard modified it by suggesting that the Macedonians also had the right of free speech and appeal to the king. The kingship itself was an organ of state, subject to customs and traditions, a view based upon evidence from the court of Alexander the Great and the Hellenistic period. If there is little evidence that the army assembly actually played a role in determining policy, it is because it consciously refrained from using its powers. A further extension of Granier's views was made by Pierre Briant in 1973, who posited that a second, popular assembly existed alongside the army assembly. Hammond (*HM* 2: 160–62), while rejecting Briant's view that there was a civilian assembly, accepted that the "Macedonians" were "Macedones under arms," and that an assembly of the Macedonians possessed the right to elect the king or regent, speak freely, sit in judgment, determine the manner of execution in capital cases, and exercise a variety of other minor discretionary functions.

This constitutionalist view is an attractive hypothesis, despite the fact that there is no evidence from antiquity to support the kind of political evolution that Granier offered. Moreover, the fragments that have been used to prove the existence of an assembly at any period have been drawn from late authors far removed from the scene or have referred to events in the Hellenistic era. The major challenge to the constitutionalist position has been led by Malcolm Errington,[4] who has received some support from Robert Lock and Edward Anson. The critics' position may be summarized: (1) Granier et al. have constructed a theoretical model based upon an unacceptable assumption that peoples' rights were recognized by Macedonian kings but not realized in practice; (2) the evidence used to support the model comes mainly from the Hellenistic period, and the assumption that there was an institutional continuity from early Macedon to the Hellenistic period is unproven; (3) the evidence from the reign of Alexander the Great that shows occasional meetings of the army for some judicial or forensic purpose describes a special situation—an exception to the rule, not the rule itself; and (4) there is no supporting evidence from reliable contemporary writers (e.g., Aristotle). The sources centuries removed are

---

[4] See especially "The Nature of the Macedonian State" and "Historiographical Origins." Errington was anticipated somewhat by Pietro de Francisci's attack on Granier, but de Francisci's views remained largely unnoticed until they were revived and enlarged by Errington.

mainly ignorant about early Macedonian institutions and anachronistic in describing institutional terms and procedures.

One might add that the existence of an "aristocracy" in Macedon—if by that is meant a class whose status is based on land and birth—is virtually without evidence in the early period. Any model that posits a conflict between royalty and aristocracy, however valid an interpretation for other early societies or for Europe in the late Middle Ages and early modern period, has rather little to do with the ancient Macedonians. Moreover, the external ancient sources saw Macedonian events in terms of the kingship pure and simple, and in this respect the descriptions of Macedonian activities as an extension of the royal will is more akin to the reports of Asian states than to accounts of societies (e.g., the Greek city-states) where complex institutional arrangements were influential. That the ancient writers should emphasize the personal character of the Macedonian monarchy to the virtual exclusion of a description of other institutions must reflect more than ignorance of those institutions; it must also suggest something of the truth.

It would appear that the modern critics have thus far struck a telling blow at the constitutionalist position, which must remain what it has always been, a theoretical construction unsupported by evidence from antiquity. Now it could be argued that it is not methodologically incorrect to develop a theoretical model by extending a body of information from a relatively well-documented period into an era lacking sources. That is, if one could show that there was a constitutional structure in the Hellenistic period like that in the age of Philip and Alexander, it would not be unreasonable to suspect that its origin lay back in the earlier period of Macedonian history for which there is no evidence. But the critics have shown that these institutions did not exist under the autocracy of the Antigonid dynasty of Hellenistic Macedon. Assuming that they had existed earlier, what made them to cease to exist? The only possible answer lies in the reigns of Philip and Alexander; the latter's autocracy was legendary and probably strangled whatever constitutional arrangements may have existed. But this is the very monarch whose reign is said to have provided us with much of our information about the rights of the Macedonians. We are thus driven to the improbable conclusion that the constitutional arrangements of the Macedonian monarchy collapsed under the absolutism of that very king whose reign provides evidence of their existence. This simply will not do. The more probable alternative is that the interaction between Alexander, his commanders, and assembled soldiers was a unique situation resulting from the extraordinary circumstances of a Macedonian army operating far from home and lacking the normal

forms of support and references. We shall return to this point a little
later.

To present a minimalist picture of Macedonian institutions by denying the validity of constitutionalism without providing a substitute
may not be very satisfying. All one can offer—lacking evidence—is a
theoretical model. But what model? The "Homeric" model is attractive, but it, too, is fraught with problems of evidence and method that
are part of the ongoing struggle to understand Dark Age Greece.
Moreover, we lack information about the social and economic support
of Macedonian kings to match what we know about the support of
Homeric chieftains and their relationships with other members of the
community. And, clearly, the Macedonian king was more autocratic.
There is no contemporary Greek model, certainly not the constitutionally constrained monarchies of the Spartans and, perhaps, the Molossians. Illyrian and Thracian models come to mind, but these appear
to be too tribal, and are imperfectly understood. Fifth- and fourth-
century Macedon may have been influenced by the Persians, but no
serious analysis can be offered until there is a clearer notion of Persian-
Macedonian relations of the fourth century before the age of Philip and
Alexander.[5] We are thus left without the theoretical model that Granier
sought to create as an aid to understanding the development of Macedonian institutions, and we are forced by the lack of evidence to describe in an impressionistic manner how things worked among the
Macedonians.

The Kingship

That the Macedonian monarchy remained in the hands of a single family from its early Archaic origins down to the death of Alexander IV
(son of the Conqueror) *ca.* 310 B.C., and again in the hands of another
family throughout most of the Hellenistic era, is remarkable and puzzling. Hammond[6] has suggested that the Hellenic ancestry of the Argeadae (Hammond's Temenidae) made them sufficiently distinct to
rise above the feuds that might have plagued other Macedonian noble
families. That is, the longevity of the Argeadae resulted partly from
their special ethnic character: Greeks ruling Macedonians. Moreover,
Hammond continues, the royal family was held in reverence by the
people, and the "cohesion" of the state was a result of this reverence.
But we have seen that the traditions of Hellenic origins for the Ar-

[5] Although see below, p. 249.
[6] *HM* 2: 152.

geadae can in all likelihood be traced back no further than the propaganda of Alexander I, and thus cannot account for the Argead continuity of the earliest kings. Moreover, a theory of Hellenic origins cannot explain the stability of the Macedonian Antigonid family in the Hellenistic period. As for the rivalries among Macedonian families, these are unclear until the time of Philip II, and even here most of the evidence points to a hostility between the houses of western Macedonia and the Argeadae. If Hammond's view were correct, one would be hard pressed to explain the longevity of the Capetians and Bourbons in France, or comparable royalty in England and central and eastern Europe, where families ruled for centuries even while ethnically similar to other noble (and highly competitive) families.

The reason for Argead longevity probably lies beyond our understanding, although I would suggest that there is a lack of evidence for a well-developed aristocracy that might threaten the throne. (And here I make no comparisons with modern royal families, as the evolution of modern European monarchy grew out of conditions of land ownership, feudal allegiances, and Roman, canon, and common law that are not analogous to those of ancient Macedon.) This apparent absence of a "nobility" itself makes the evolution of primitive Macedonian society quite different from the experience of most Greek and many Italian communities in antiquity, and therefore probably deprives us of a range of theoretical models that could be used for comparison (see below). The only serious challenge to the Macedonian royal family occurred in the aftermath of Alexander the Great's death, when weak Argead successors were set upon by a group of experienced military commanders who had tasted empire during the campaigns of Alexander, and who had at their disposal for the first time in Macedonian history sufficient military power to usurp the throne. It was a unique situation, and when the dust settled after the struggles among Alexander's successors, a new single family occupied the throne until Macedon was crushed by Rome. Finally, there is no evidence of any sort about what the Macedonian "people" thought about their kings (or anything else), beyond the respect that soldiers have for good commanders.

The monarchy seems to have been personal; that is, the king represented himself, not the Macedonians as a nation. He seems to have enjoyed personal powers largely unrestricted. A summary of these powers follows:

(1) The king controlled the natural resources of the country. We have seen abundant evidence of the throne's right to allot the har-

vest, sale, and export of timber, thereby providing the king with a source of wealth and with one of the most effective weapons in his diplomatic arsenal. With the advent of Philip II's reign, the precious-metal mines of eastern Macedonia were almost certainly also under royal control.

(2) To the extent that the king participated in panhellenic events—doubtful before the time of Philip II—he did so as an individual, not as a representative of a people.

(3) All the surviving evidence points to foreign alliances made directly with the king, who is named specifically. Under such an arrangement it is problematic whether any foreign alliance—except for those which also referred to the king's descendants—was made in perpetuity. The only other principal persons named in surviving treaties are members of the royal family.

(4) The king served as commander-in-chief of the army, and perhaps in no other area was his power so absolute. This may have included the right to make war and peace.

(5) The king appears to have exercised the power of a judge; whether or not others were involved in the judicial process was a matter for the king's discretion.

(6) The king supervised rituals and festivals. These consisted both of sacrificing to the gods and of celebrating the Heracleidae, the family ancestors.[7]

(7) The king determined foreign policy.

(8) The king appointed his successor, although the evidence is not conclusive on this point.[8]

In short, the restrictions on the king's power were not institutional, but situational. That is, the king's ability to act depended upon a number of factors, including the force of his own personality; the balance of power that existed between himself, other Argeadae, barons, and soldiers; the constraints of the external situation in which the king found himself; and a rather vague set of *mores* concerning tradition. The king could do exactly what he could get away with. The burden of proof that there were institutional limits on the king's powers lies with the advocates of constitutionalism, and they have failed to prove their case.[9]

---

[7] Here especially see the evidence (all from the age of Philip and Alexander) gathered by Hammond, *HM* 2: 155–56.

[8] See Anson ("Macedonia's Alleged Constitutionalism," 312), who gathers the evidence for the Hellenistic period and also shows the influence of important barons; but also see Hatzopoulos, "Succession and Regency."

[9] The nonconstitutionalist view, as most forcefully represented by Errington, has had its recent critics. While accepting much of the correction of Granier et al., there are those

Macedon was not subject to the law of the jungle, but neither was it a city-state—like Athens or early Rome—that evolved constitutional forms to protect the power and property of a landed elite against the rise of rural or urban middle and lower classes. Such states developed their constitutional order when one group acquired sufficient social or economic cohesion to challenge another group. The resultant "constitution" is the formalization of a balance of power among competing groups to ensure each group a share in the political process sufficient to maintain the mutual need for order. Hence the formalization of the rights and powers of landed gentry in Athens under the "constitutions" of Draco and Solon with a gradual movement toward incorporating the poorer (lower) classes into a more equitable system of justice and political opportunity. In the case of Rome, it was the gradual acquisition of some citizen-rights by some plebeians without the aristocracy sacrificing the hold on government that was their traditional prerogative.

But where was the cohesion in Macedonian society? Who were the "people"? Who were the "aristocrats," if by this we mean a landed gentry who, as a collective interest, claim power as a birthright? Where is the evidence of a struggle among such groups, the result of which is a "constitutional" arrangement? Clearly there is insufficient evidence to describe the relationships between the king and others in terms that derive from the analysis of the historical development of city-states. A better model would be the feudal proto-states of medieval Europe,[10] or even the absolutist states of some European monarchies in the age of Louis XIV. But even these are insufficient as analogs for Macedon. It will do neither to follow a "noble savage" model, nor to describe Macedon in terms of Greek and Italian city-states, with which Macedon had little in common.

In constitutional arrangements the actual power of the monarch rests with a balance established between that monarch and the other competing factions: rival aristocratic groups, a religious establishment, assemblies, popular opinion, law, custom, etc. The actual exercise of power by the monarch (or emperor, chancellor, president,

---

who, believing that Errington's views are too extreme, prefer a middle ground. See the discussion of Mooren, "Hellenistic Monarchy," esp. 210–32, supported by W. L. Adams, "Macedonian Kingship," 44–45.

[10] In a stimulating article confirming this suggestion, Alan E. Samuel ("Philip and Alexander as Kings") argues that what bound the king and the Macedonians was the winning of land. The king was a "leader more like a Viking king than a settled Oriental despot" (1286), and the king's path of conquest was followed by his people in expectation of the fulfillment of mutual benefit. Recently discovered inscriptions in Macedonia deal with the king's land-grants to his veterans (above, p. 219).

prime minister, etc.) normally depends upon his or her ability to interact with the other forces within the society. The extent to which personal power can be exercised determines who is "strong" and who is "weak," even within elaborate constitutional frameworks. But in Macedon, these other forces seem ill-defined. There were no Macedonian aristocratic groups that could challenge the royal family (in the manner of the later European model), only rival branches of the Argeadae and their occasional allies—including western Macedonians, whose ties to the Argeadae, at least through the reign of Philip II, were tenuous at best—who were perfectly prepared to use murder as a weapon of expressing opposition. The other factors that determined the strength of the king were external to constitutionalism: his own personality, the physical setting (home or abroad), external challenges, and wealth generated from mines and forests. There is no evidence even that the king was economically supported by the barons. Our conclusion must be to agree with those who advocate the highly personal nature of the Macedonian monarchy, where the power of the king to act rested upon nonconstitutional factors.

A wise monarch recognized the limits to which his power could be put, and he exercised self-restraint in order to avoid abuses that might cause his demise. But what seems prudent in theory often did not work out in practice. Despite the apparent stability of rule by a single family, about half of the Argead kings of the fifth and fourth centuries fell to assassins: Archelaus was killed by a lover, Amyntas II by Derdas, Pausanias (probably) by Amyntas III, Alexander II by Ptolemy, Ptolemy by Perdiccas III, Philip II by Pausanias, Philip III by Olympias, and Alexander IV by Cassander. Moreover, there were additional conspiracies against at least Amyntas III and Alexander III, and a number of potential rivals were dispatched in the struggles for succession of Archelaus, Philip II, and Alexander the Great. Indeed, the matter of succession was one of the most chaotic aspects of the Argead monarchy, with primogeniture playing only a minor role.[11] If we knew nothing of Macedonian history beyond the violent history of its kingship, we would believe that the law of the jungle prevailed. However one wishes to characterize the monarchy, constitutionalism is hardly applicable to the history of royal succession. Macedonian kings, even

---

[11] In a recent paper ("Regency and Succession"), Hatzopoulos has argued that in the succession priority was given to the first son born (or conceived) after the king's accession to the throne. While Hatzopoulos raises some valuable questions about succession and regency, I am not persuaded that the Macedonians themselves were aware of all the subtle niceties that Hatzopoulos proposes. For a recent response to Hatzopoulos, see Greenwalt, "Polygamy and Succession."

successful ones like Archelaus, had to exercise caution, not only against external threats, but against enemies from within. It is no wonder that among the Greeks of the Classical period—organized with relative internal stability in their city-states—the Macedonians appeared to be barbarians.

Council and People

Hammond believes that the king was advised by a council consisting of his Companions (*hetairoi*) and Friends (*philoi*).[12] There is, however, no evidence, either literary or archaeological, to suggest the existence of a formal council. What would have formed the basis for membership in such a council? Age? Birth? Wealth? Military status? We know of no group of advisors existing before the reign of Alexander the Great.[13] For Alexander's rule there is considerable evidence about advice and opinion being traded by individuals and groups. It is self-evident that the Companions were the king's comrades, chosen to accompany the king in war. They rode, fought, and drank together, and undoubtedly consulted one another about military and political matters. But none of this suggests a formal council. All of the evidence cited by Hammond concerning the king's companions, friends, and commanders points to soldiers' camaraderie, made more intense, perhaps, by the enormous distance from home. The distinctions made by our sources between "companions" and "friends" should not be pressed, as there is rather little understanding and consistency in the use of such terms by the ancient writers.[14]

What existed in Alexander's camp, and probably in Philip's as well, was the symposium—the drinking party—where a group of the king's closest associates met socially. Between 65 and 70 names can be identified as Alexander's Companions, and there were other friends who

[12] *HM* 2: 158–60.

[13] Hammond, ibid., 158, strains a passage in Herodotus (8.138.1) to prove the existence of a formal council in the early fifth century, but the passage only makes a very general comment about advice given the king. Herodotus, who, as a Greek, knew about councils, failed to use the precise vocabulary that one might expect had he been describing a procedural institution. Griffith, *HM* 2: 397–98, recognizes that the deliberative and consultative process was informal.

[14] Stagakis, "Observations on the *Hetairoi*" (with citations to earlier literature), argues that the *hetairia* involved a reciprocal relationship among men, which the king himself shared as a *hetairos*. Griffith's discussion of the relationship between king and Companions is sensible: *HM* 2: 395–404. Also see Borza, "The Symposium at Alexander's Court," esp. 53.

also were symposiasts.[15] They ate heartily, drank hard,[16] shared enter-
tainment, contested with one another, and sometimes conspired.
Lacking a formal council, it was the means by which a man was identified as part of the king's inner circle. The symposium was no less
important than a council, but it was not institutionalized. It was a social forum in which one competed for the king's attention and defined
one's status at court. Advice was given and sometimes taken, but one
had to be wary about what was said and apprehended in an alcoholic
haze. The symposium was the arena in which were played out the
sometimes deadly political games of the Macedonians.

Any discussion of the symposium's existence before the reigns of
Philip and Alexander is speculative, although it would not be unreasonable to expect that it evolved as a traditional soldiers' event modified by exposure to the Greek symposium. Excavations at both Pella
and the Hellenistic palace at Vergina reveal the existence of drinking
and dining chambers not unlike those at Olynthus and Athens, and it
is certain that this social aspect of life at home was carried into Asia.[17]
Alexander used the symposium as a relief from the rigors of the road,
but also as a testing ground for policy. Individuals and ideas were pit-
ted against one another—as in the case of introducing Eastern rituals
into the Macedonian court—thereby providing the king with an opportunity to sound out opinion and identify potential supporters and
detractors. In this sense the symposium served many of the deliberative functions of a formal council, but without the restrictions of a
constitutional framework. That is, it was useful for both parties, but
the king was not required to adhere to any consensus.

There were other situations in which the consultative process is evident, but, as usual, most of the information concerns the reign of Alexander. The king conferred with his leading generals and advisors
about military and other policy matters (e.g., Plut. *Alex.* 11.2); Parmenio, Eumenes, Callisthenes, and others are associated with Alexander in this capacity. And on the occasion of Alexander's final illness,
a small group of men met to hear the king's last wishes about the suc-

[15] Berve, *Das Alexanderreich*, 1: 31, identified the names of sixty-four *hetairoi*, and
J. R. Hamilton (*Plutarch. Alexander: A Commentary*, 37) added another. Undoubtedly
there are several others as yet unknown to us.

[16] For the traditions about Macedonian drinking habits, see Borza, "The Symposium
at Alexander's Court," 47–50.

[17] Ibid., 46. Diodorus (17.16.4) and Athenaeus (12.538c and 539d) tell of the "Tent of
a Hundred Couches" that served as the scene of Alexander's celebration at Dion on the
eve of the Asian expedition, and was used on at least two other occasions in Asia. Symposia were held in several other settings as well.

cession.[18] When asked to whom he left his rule, the dying Alexander answered, "To the strongest" (or "the most able"). That may or may not have been a popular answer, depending upon one's point of view. Our sources use imprecise words—*basileia* (Diodorus and Arrian), *regnum* (Curtius), and *imperium* (Justin), meaning "kingdom," "realm," "authority," or "area ruled by a king"—a vocabulary whose significance is difficult to determine. Does the *empire* go to the strongest, but the Macedonian *kingship* (a different matter) stay with the Argeadae, of whom there were two possible candidates, Alexander's less-than-competent stepbrother, Arrhidaeus, and the as-yet-unborn child of his wife, Roxane? It is difficult to know whether the use of the word "kingdom" (*basileia*) suggests that the Asian territory acquired by conquest was now considered annexed to the old Macedonian kingdom, or whether the distinction between the empire and the kingdom was maintained, as suggested above. Or are we in fact faced with the prospect of attempting to draw distinctions that are too fine from sources who were either ignorant or themselves unclear about any such significance in the final question and answer, and in any case had the advantage of writing with hindsight? The problem begs a solution.

The king's ring was given to Perdiccas, who was not an Argead, but this does not signify succession as far as we can tell, unless one believes the unlikely event that Alexander intended that the throne pass out of Argead hands. The decision to arrange a succession by Arrhidaeus, and to await the birth of Alexander's child by Roxane (as it turned out, a son who would eventually co-rule as Alexander IV), was made by the leading commanders, who took into account the volatility of an army confused by the circumstances. This is the only evidence we have of a group of Macedonians determining the succession. If the "army assembly" was constituted to elect a king (as some have argued), why did it not function in June 323? And why (if one accepts the story of the king's last words) did a small group of generals ask the dying Alexander about *his* choice of successor? Who would enforce such a decision? In the course of the confusion, Perdiccas held the ring (whatever that signified), Ptolemy proposed rule by a *junta*, and a throng of soldiers pushed for Arrhidaeus.[19] It was an extraordinary scene, and, while not all of the details have been accepted as historically accurate, the general sense of what went on is undeniable. It all boils down to this: For the whole history of the Argeadae there is preserved a detailed

[18] Diod. 17.117.4 and 18.1.4; Arr. 7.26.3; Curt. 10.5.5; Just. 12.15.8.

[19] The most detailed account is in Curtius 10.5–10. For an analysis, see Martin, "Quintus Curtius' Presentation." There is a useful discussion of the Argead succession in Greenwalt, "Studies in the Development of Royal Authority," 73–118.

account of only this one scene of succession, characterized by chaos, ambition, fear, and political maneuvering. If there were constitutional procedures for selecting a king, they were not in evidence at this moment.[20] These were extraordinary circumstances made more difficult both by Alexander's irresponsible last words (if true as reported) and by the fact that the army found itself leaderless far from home. It was a situation made unique in Argead history by the special character of Alexander's career and personality and by his death abroad. No constitutional procedures for selecting Alexander's successor appear to have been operating; the circumstances of that succession cannot be taken as a model for anything else. But the generals, despite the divisiveness of their individual ambitions, were more cohesive and in a better position to influence events than was the army. Taking into account the popular feelings of troops upon whose cooperation their own schemes depended, they presented their compromised decision to the army as a fait accompli, along with a version of Alexander's last will and testament.[21]

There exist in varying degrees of detail accounts of three Argead successions of the later fourth century, those of Philip II, Alexander the Great, and Arrhidaeus. Insofar as limited evidence permits us to say, the procedures used in all three differ. Some sort of assembly may have participated in the choice of Philip; at least Philip was addressing an assembly as part of the process.[22] Further, Philip's accession was quickly challenged by Argaeus, who marched on Aegae to secure the support of the local population, a move forestalled by Philip.[23] No assembly is mentioned in the case of Alexander's succession, even though he is portrayed as courting and winning support through tactful statements.[24] The circumstances of Arrhidaeus's succession are described above.

The evidence for these mid- to late fourth-century successions permits the following conclusion: Groups of persons participated in the

[20] See Appendix C below, p. 298.

[21] Whatever Perdiccas read to the troops as Alexander's last wishes was done not to subject it to their free decision, but deliberately to court the army's rejection of a series of unpopular, expensive, and vainglorious schemes. The generals, after all, had better things to do. See Badian, "A King's Notebooks."

[22] Diod. 16.3.1. I follow Griffith, *HM* 2: 208–10 and 702–4, in accepting that Philip was selected as king immediately and did not serve a regency for Amyntas IV. Also see above, pp. 200–201.

[23] Diod. 16.3.5 and Griffith, *HM* 2: 211–12.

[24] Diod. 17.2.2. Justin (11.1.8) mentions a *contio*, the same word used by Curtius (10.7.13) to describe the crowd assembled at the time of Arrhidaeus's selection, but this is not to be taken as meaning a formal electoral assembly (*pace* Griffith, *HM* 2: 391).

selection of a king, probably (but not necessarily always) including members of the royal family, important barons, and military chiefs, and parts of the army and civilian population. The evidence strongly suggests that the selection was not fixed according to an established constitutional procedure, but was circumstantial, depending upon the political and military conditions existing at the time. The king, as autocratic as he might be, nevertheless needed the support of important individuals and perhaps also the army, some troops of which might be consulted if the situation demanded military support, as in the cases of Philip II and Arrhidaeus. Acclamation by the army, which may have been a usual part of the process, is not the same as election by the army. Acclamation represented a publicly demonstrative expression of support for a candidate whose actual selection had already been determined by political agreements and compromises made on a higher level. There is no evidence showing that the sovereign power to elect a king rested with any group of persons. Succession appears rather to have been the result of a series of political and military decisions made by those in a position to do so, and the manner in which they conducted themselves depended upon circumstances at hand.

Once selected, the king maintained a relationship with the army that was something more than just a general's relationship with his troops. A shrewd general, as Field Marshal Montgomery observed, mixes with his soldiers, keeps them informed, exhorts them on the eve of battle, and praises them in victory. But Montgomery by no means suggested that a commander should consult with his troops about military and political decisions: a soldier's duty is to carry out orders and fight well. The Macedonian king as general maintained contact with soldiers in order to promote efficiency in the army. But as king of the Macedonians in a multinational force, Alexander had a special relationship with the Macedonian core, who may have looked to him for assurances in an alien environment.

One aspect of this relationship was the right of a Macedonian to address his king. There can be little doubt that, at least in the fourth and third centuries, some Macedonians felt they had the right to petition the king for redress of grievances.[25] But there is insufficient evidence to prove that the king was obliged to render judgments in accord with a formal body of law, or that he was restricted in his verdicts by human institutions, such as assemblies or councils. He heard petitions in the manner of a Solomon, a Roman emperor, or a modern sheik. A vast effort has been expended interpreting a passage in Arrian (4.11.6)

[25] Evidence collected in W. L. Adams, "Macedonian Kingship."

that describes a debate between two of Alexander's courtiers, Callisthenes and Anaxarchus, over the matter of introducing *proskynēsis* into Macedonian court ritual.[26] The considerable amount of scholarship on the matter has concentrated on whether Callisthenes had in fact raised a constitutional question: should Alexander force the Macedonians, accustomed to their own manner of approaching the king, to engage in this Oriental ritual obeisance? Amid the learned debates the end of the story has been overlooked: Alexander attempted to introduce a custom deemed alien by the Macedonians, and after considerable opposition was raised, he abandoned the effort. This scheme to address the king with Oriental obsequiousness was not put before any constituent deliberative body, empowered with the right to accept or reject the practice. Rather it was a matter proposed by the king and some of his staff, debated in symposiac and other informal settings, and withdrawn when the opposition appeared severe. It was a situation in which the *mos maiorum* prevailed—unwritten, but spoken—and served as a restriction on the king's power to act. The incident probably goes a long way toward explaining how the consultative relationship between the king and his men actually worked without the necessity of formal constitutional procedures.

If the evidence for an electoral assembly and a legislative assembly is wanting, there is reason to believe in the existence of a judicial assembly, at least for capital crimes. The argument rests on one slim passage in Curtius (6.8.23–25), who is a repository for bits of information about Macedonian customs and internal procedures. At the treason trial of his commander Philotas, son of Parmenio, Alexander called an assembly of both armed men and civilian aides and servants, of whom there were a large number in the expeditionary train.[27] In keeping with ancient custom, the king conducted the investigation in such criminal cases, and the army rendered a verdict—in peacetime the prerogative of the common people—and the power of the king carried no weight, unless he had earlier influenced them.[28] If Curtius is to be trusted on this point, a civilian judicial assembly tried capital cases in normal

---

[26] On the conflicts between Anaxarchus and Callisthenes, see Borza, "Anaxarchus and Callisthenes."

[27] Griffith, *HM* 2: 390.

[28] Curt. 6.8.25: *De capitalibus rebus vetusto Macedonum modo inquirebat rex, iudicabat exercitus—in pace erat vulgi—et nihil potestas regum valebat, nisi prius valuisset auctoritas.* The words *rex* and *iudicabat* are the restoration of a modern editor; if their omission reflects what Curtius actually wrote, the king played a diminished role in criminal proceedings, and depended mainly upon his *auctoritas* to influence the outcome of events. Useful analysis of the passage in Griffith, *HM* 2: 389 n. 3.

times ("peacetime"); and it is interesting to note that Alexander made sure that those civilians who were part of the expedition were called to sit along with the army. We may conclude that, by custom, the "people"—whether army in the field as in this special situation, or civilian population at home—could sit in capital cases. But it is also apparent that the king announced the conditions of the trial, including (in this case) who could attend. And one might suggest that he could also choose not to call a trial, or to make a political show trial, as in the case of Callisthenes and the Royal Pages who were charged with plotting against the king.[29] Among our sources, both Arrian and Curtius charge Alexander with violating due process; this suggests both that there was due process and that this king ignored it.[30]

Unfortunately, we are faced with the old methodological problem: the most detailed information about constitutional procedures comes from the age of Alexander, whose reign was exceptional on many counts. Otherwise we are ill-informed about legal procedures, but would do well to attribute our ignorance to a lack of evidence. Macedon was a large land, and the Macedonians were accustomed to regulating their internal affairs and to dealing with foreigners.[31] While the king was expected to act as a judge in some cases, an appropriate amount of judicial authority necessarily had to have been delegated, but whether these were resident or circuit judges is not known.

Indeed, we are pressed to know whether there was anything like a "government" in Macedon, even judging by the relatively simple standards of Greek city-states. The king was solely in charge of foreign policy. All treaties are with the king personally, and the only other Macedonians mentioned as cosignatories are members of the royal family.[32] Trusted persons were appointed to accomplish specific tasks, such as the Macedonian advisor who was honored by the Thebans *ca.* 365.[33] The high level of Macedonian diplomatic intercourse with (at various times) Athens, the Chalcidian cities, Sparta, Thessaly, and the Balkan kingdoms involved representatives of the king. And the exploitation of Macedonia's rich forest lands for revenues and diplomacy certainly required a staff of overseers to supervise the cutting of tim-

[29] Plut. *Alex.* 55.2–5; Arr. 4.14.1–4; and Curt. 8.6.1–8.23.

[30] By contrast, Philip II was thought to have been a good judge; for evidence and commentary, see Griffith, *HM* 2: 394.

[31] E.g., there were provisions in some treaty arrangements with Athens for the judicial redress of contractual disputes; see Borza, "Timber and Politics," 41 and n. 38, for evidence.

[32] As in *IG* I³.89 and Tod *GHI*, no. 177; see pp. 153 and 226 above.

[33] See Borza, "Timber and Politics," 46 n. 59.

ber, its shipment under conditions of contractual or treaty arrangements, and the assessment and collection of revenues.[34] Military affairs—the levy, training, supply, and disposition of troops—were
entirely under the control of the king as commander-in-chief. There
are tantalizing glimpses of public servants at work, but it is quite unlikely that there existed anything remotely like a ministerial system.
Necessary bureaucratic tasks were probably done by persons appointed by the king and responsible directly to him, and this would
seem to be true both at home and on the march. Neither the literary
nor the archaeological evidence has yet to support any other conclusion.

Continuing excavations at Pella and Aegae may in time reveal more
information about the physical accommodations of "government," although one is tempted to guess that a richer source of information
resides in epigraphy. Thus far, the Macedonians seem not much inclined to commit their official procedures and records to stone (excepting, of course, religious and funerary dedications), and the few
inscriptions we possess are "royal," that is, they speak of arrangements
made with and by the king. The best hope for more details of internal
organization may lie in the age of Philip II, as Philip's organization of
his kingdom may have required some arrangements for administration, especially in the eastern and western marches. One would hope
that the monarch who stamped his name into the terracotta roof tiles
now on display in the archaeological museum at Pella and (perhaps)
into the arrow points that showered onto Olynthus might have also
left posterity some inscriptions that speak of how he managed his
realm.

Some Innovations of Philip and Alexander

Thus far, we have described a monarchy that had at its core a kind of
military chief or warlord, the representative of a single ruling family.
The Macedonian king may have adhered to some time-honored customs that characterized his relationships with subordinates, but the
monarchy remained uncomplicated and highly personal. If one were
to theorize about the evolution of such a kingship, one could suggest—
using historical models from several eras—that the chieftainship would
lose some of its authoritarian character to a more "constitutionally"
ordered society, in which the relationships between king and others

---

[34] We are reminded that in the 360s Callistratus overhauled the revenue system for
Perdiccas III; [Arist.] *Econ.* 2.1350a.22.

would become more regulated by customs and laws. One might also posit that this primitive kingship could evolve into something more autocratic.

Kienast has offered a compelling thesis suggesting that Persian influence in the Macedonian court increased during the fourth century.[35] Under Philip, there was an intensification, if not invention, of a number of institutions associated with the Achaemenid monarchy. These include the formation of a corps of Royal Pages, the taking of multiple wives and titles, the establishment of a Royal Secretary and Archive, the creation of a Royal Bodyguard, and the elevation of the religious role of the king. Perhaps the most important of these innovations was Philip's move toward divine honors, and the best evidence emerges from the most reliable account of Philip's last days.[36] In either August or October 336 Philip sponsored a huge festival to the gods at which he celebrated the wedding of his daughter Cleopatra to Alexander, king of the Molossians.[37] The festival was also intended to include banquets, contests, the receipt of honors from Greek cities, and a general display of Philip's generosity designed to impress the Greeks and provide a suitable backdrop for the man who was about to lead a panhellenic crusade into Asia. At sunrise of the fateful day a lavish parade included ostentatiously adorned statues of the twelve gods, along with a thirteenth—likewise suitable for a god—of Philip himself, enthroned among the twelve gods.[38] This was the splendid scene that was cut short by the assassin's dagger ending Philip's life.

The significance of Philip's godlike statue being enthroned among the twelve gods is a matter of some dispute. Fredricksmeyer has developed a vigorous case for Philip having planned to achieve divine honors, including the establishment of a ruler cult to his family.[39] This was part of a scheme to establish an absolute monarchy, the means by which Philip intended to rule his European and Asian empire, and the deification of the kingship would provide a theoretical support for this innovation in Argead rule. In a compelling criticism of this view, Bad-

[35] Kienast, *Philipp II. von Makedonien* esp. 7–37.

[36] What follows is from Diod. 16.91.4–92.5.

[37] August is the most commonly accepted date, but there is an attractive October alternative offered by Hatzopoulos, "The Oleveni Inscription," 37–42. Hatzopoulos connects the festivities at Aegae with the Olympia, which was celebrated each year during the Macedonian month of Dios (October, roughly). This is supported by Arrian's statement (*Anab.* 1.11.1) that the Olympian games were held at Aegae. For the more traditional view, see Chapter 7 above.

[38] Diod. 16.92.5: *synthronon eauton . . . tois dodeka theois.*

[39] Fredricksmeyer, "Divine Honors for Philip II," "On the Background of the Ruler Cult," and "On the Final Aims of Philip II."

ian has shown that there is no valid evidence of an attested deification of the Macedonian king during Philip's lifetime, and indeed not until the first cults to Alexander were established during the last four years of his reign.[40]

That Philip was aiming at something beyond mortal aspirations is clear, as shown in part by the unusual religious procession at Aegae. Whether he actually had gained divine recognition during his life-time—I think it unlikely that he did—is not as important as the fact that he was headed toward a new conception of the Macedonian mon-archy that intended to elevate his kingship beyond what was tradi-tional in the world of Greeks and Macedonians. It is only a matter of modern opinion whether Philip wished for himself some special form of homage or actual worship.[41]

Thus, while one might quarrel with some of the details of what Kienast and Fredricksmeyer have proposed, the main thrust of their views must be taken seriously. For example, sometime between the battle of Chaeronea and his death, Philip ordered the construction of a round peristyle building within the sacred precinct at Olympia, designed to display statues of his family (Paus. 5.20.9–10).[42] The architecture of the monument is of no known Asian or Greek style, but something peculiarly "Macedonian," utilizing elements of both, suggesting the employment of a Macedonian architect. The building was completed during the reign of Alexander, who commissioned the Athenian sculptor Leochares to create the chryselephantine statues of Alexander as a central figure, flanked by his parents, Philip and Olym-pias, and Philip's parents, Amyntas III and Eurydice. Chryselephan-tine was normally used for cult statues, but there is no evidence that this building was intended or used as a cult shrine. The use of chrys-elephantine (whosoever idea it was) does call attention to Pheidias's great chryselephantine statue of Zeus within the god's own temple barely one hundred meters away. We may see in this monument at Olympia the tangible expression of a new conception of monarchy, elevating and celebrating the Argeadae in forms novel to the Greek world, and amalgamating European and Asian influences.

[40] Badian, "The Deification of Alexander the Great," esp. 67–71.

[41] See Griffith, *HM* 2: 695. On the background for the ruler cult in the Greek world, with a suggestion that, had circumstances been somewhat different half a century earlier, divine honors might have been held by an Argead as early as 394, see Flower, "Agesilaus of Sparta," 134.

[42] For what follows, see the study of S. G. Miller, "The Philippeion and Hellenistic Macedonian Architecture," and Griffith, *HM* 2: 691–95, who thinks that the building had a secular use.

At the time of his assassination, Philip was in the process of transforming the Macedonian kingship into a monarchy possessing some of the attributes of Asian absolutism. The intervention of his death prevents us from knowing the final direction of his intentions, but it is clear that the simple Argead kingship of an earlier day had metamorphosized into something more complex. This is not to suggest that the traditional idea of the king as commander and fellow warrior would be replaced by new institutions. As far as we know from the evidence available for the reigns of Philip and Alexander, the customary role of king as soldier and personification of the Macedonian nation would remain central to their rule. Indeed, it could be argued that these traditional military and "national" values accounted for their considerable success in diplomacy and military affairs, for it enabled two talented individuals to shape a coherent policy utilizing the human resources of the Macedonian population. But the notion of a Macedonian monarchy elevated to something approaching divine status did not outlive Philip and Alexander. Among the monarchies of the Hellenistic world that had their origins among Alexander's generals, the Antigonids in Macedon alone reverted to something similar to the traditional Argead conception of the kingship.

Neither Philip nor Alexander was successful in providing permanent arrangements outside Macedon itself. However clever Philip's settlement of the Greeks appeared to be, it failed to prevent Greek rebellions at his death, during the reign of Alexander, and after Alexander's death. In his intercontinental empire Alexander never advanced beyond the role of a military conqueror, and there is no good evidence that he ever intended anything different.

One wonders what was to be achieved by the transformation of the Macedonian court under Philip, except perhaps the enhancement of the status of the kingship itself to provide more effective rule of a multiethnic empire. That is, Philip and Alexander attempted to rule Greater Macedon through the trappings of a more exalted monarchy. The other component necessary for successful imperial rule along the lines of the Persian and Roman empires was a dependence upon an efficient administrative bureaucracy. We cannot know Philip's plans about this, and Alexander made rather few changes in existing Asian administration. But the kingship itself was modified. In this sense it was a new Argead kingship, and probably Alexander I and Archelaus would have been surprised at what their descendants had wrought.

Philip and Alexander appear to be as much a conjunction of their own personalities with the circumstances at hand as an outgrowth of their heritage. When the world recovered from the rush of events that marked their reigns, and the Macedonians settled down under a new dynasty in the Hellenistic period, the region in Olympus's shadow still seemed a lot like old Macedon. This makes us wonder about the transitory nature of their reigns, and suggests that, if we wish to discover some striking long-term effects of their accomplishments, we would do well to look outside Macedon.

· C H A P T E R   1 1 ·

Material Culture in the Age of Philip
and Alexander

The Excavations at Vergina: The Monuments of Aegae

The heart of the Macedonian kingdom was the Emathian plain. In antiquity this region consisted of a sea inlet and barren marsh bordered by a piedmont rising to meet the hills of the Pierian Mountains on the south, Mt. Vermion on the west, and Mt. Paiko on the north. The east end was open to the Axios valley and the Thermaic Gulf. The twentieth century has transformed Emathia. The marshes have been drained and the rivers Haliacmon and Loudias rechanneled by Greek and American engineers in order to control malaria and recover agricultural land. It is now one of the richest farming regions of Europe, devoted to cotton, tobacco, grain, orchards, and vineyards.

The Haliacmon emerges from its awesome gorge at the southwestern corner of plain and for awhile runs close to the southern edge, its course marked by tree-lined banks. Not far away the ground begins to rise gently to form the Pierian piedmont, and at the juncture of the plain and these slopes lies the village of Vergina.[1] With its scattered low, stuccoed houses, it is undistinguished in appearance, like so many Macedonian villages that owe their modern history to the settlement of refugee Greeks during the population exchanges of the 1920s. Behind the village the ground rises more steeply, culminating in a series of wooded hills that are the outliers of the Pierian Mountains. In the 1860s the French traveller Léon Heuzey discovered and described a huge monument situated less than a mile above the village, about halfway up a hill. Measuring 104.50 m by 88.50 m, it is one of the largest structures known in the Greco-Macedonian world, and may well have

[1] For matters relating to the various monuments at Vergina I owe much to several discussions both on and off the site with Professor Manolis Andronikos and with Dr. Chrysoula Saatsoglou-Paliadeli, both of whose generosity over the past few years is gratefully acknowledged and whose publications have helped illuminate the discoveries at Vergina.

been a palace of the Hellenistic kings of Macedon.[2] Its position on the hill overlooking the plain must have made it visible from afar, presenting a most imposing sight. The date is problematic, and has been placed in a range encompassing the late fourth and first half of the third centuries, its construction being attributed both to the period of Cassander's pre-eminence (*ca.* 315–297) and the reign of King Antigonus Gonatas (276–239). The location of the fifth-century royal residence, however, is unknown. Explorations of the foundations of the later palace in order to recover information about the earlier have yielded little, partly because an insufficient area has been surveyed, and partly because the instability of the slope and the large amount of ancient fill have made stratigraphical analysis difficult. We are even hard pressed to know what to look for, as there is no clue to the scale on which the early Argead kings built, or in what form.

Of the later palace only foundations survive, along with a jumble of collapsed Doric entablatures and roof tiles, but its plan is clear. The two-story building consisted of a series of ceremonial, dining, and ritual chambers surrounding and facing a large open inner courtyard. The north side included what appears to be a huge veranda overlooking the plain. Today one can sit midst its ruins, enjoy a picnic lunch, and savor the quiet beauty of the place. Behind rises the steep woodland of the Pierian Mountains. To the west are a ravine and a series of hills separating Vergina from the Haliacmon Gorge. The east presents a gentle rolling piedmont where hills meet plain, and where the village of Palatitsia is only the closest of a dozen settlements.[3] Beneath the rich fields and orchards is a treasure of Macedonian antiquities awaiting the excavators' spades. And to the front lies the great plain itself, stretching away for two dozen miles. If the air is clear (an increasingly uncommon event), Mt. Paiko looms as the northern boundary of plain, and occasionally one can even see beyond to the forbidding snow-capped peaks of the Greek-Yugoslav border.

Some things have changed since Macedonian royalty occupied the

---

[2] Described by Heuzey in Heuzey and Daumet, *Mission Archéologique*. The "palace" is fully discussed by Andronikos in *Vergina: The Prehistoric Necropolis and the Hellenistic Palace*, brought up to date in *Vergina: The Royal Tombs*, 38–46 (with a good recent plan). Discussion of the architectural details can be found in S. G. Miller, "Hellenistic Macedonian Architecture." Miller (98) dates the palace to the early part of the last third of the fourth century.

[3] *Palatitsia* is to be preferred to the less common *Palatitsa* in accord with most Greek maps and local usage. Manolis Andronikos, the excavator of the site, once assured me that *Palatitsia* (neut. pl. for "little palaces") is the correct form, and that is the form he uses in his excavation reports; e.g., *Vergina: The Royal Tombs*, 31, etc., and "Some Reflections on the Macedonian Tombs," 9, passim.

veranda. Instead of seeing fertile fields in the plain they gazed upon marshes, and perhaps the open water of the sea inlet, which in those days intruded quite far inland. But the appearance of the distant mountains was the same, as may have been the symbiosis of nearby villages and fields. This site was no longer the "capital" after Archelaus developed Pella as an administrative center *ca.* 400 B.C. But Aegae remained a place for refuge, royal ceremonies, burials, and recreation. The purpose of this great building must have been pleasure. Its rooms were designed for eating and drinking, ceremonial greeting, relaxation, and athletics. It was a kind of royal resort, elevated above the humidity and discomfort of the marshes, removed from the dust and heat of Pella, and overlooking much of the kingdom. In the late afternoon, the view is one of the most pleasant prospects in Macedonia.

Directly below the palace is a theatre, excavated in 1981.[4] It has been dated by Andronikos to the fourth century, but the evidence for that chronology (pottery, stratigraphy, architectural style) has not been presented, and there are some features of the structure that may point to both earlier and later dates. The cavea of the theatre is rather small, even primitive, in comparison with fourth-century Greek theatres. Built stone seats exist for only the first row, most of the audience presumably having sat either on the hillside or on wooden bleachers long since disappeared. There are no seats specially designated for priests or the king, but there is no reason to accept the excavator's assumption that the deficiency was made up by the installation of a temporary wooden throne. Indeed, the single row of fixed seats could hold about 100 persons, almost exactly the number who may have made up the king's inner circle (Friends and Companions) in the age of Alexander, and the number of the Tent of a Hundred Couches used by Alexander both in Macedon and Asia.

What is remarkable about the theatre is the size of its orchestra, some 28.50 m in diameter, by far the largest known for this type of structure.[5] The area of the orchestra is far in excess of the needs of formal dramatic performances, and our evidence suggests that a variety of rituals were held in such places, that is, the theatre acted as an amphitheatre. For example, the festival at which Philip II was assassinated celebrated the marriage of his daughter Cleopatra to Alexander, king of the Molossians. The wedding festivities included dramatic and musical performances and a great religious procession.[6] We may assume that

[4] Description in Andronikos, *Vergina: The Royal Tombs,* 46–49.

[5] By comparison, the diameter of the orchestra at Epidaurus is about 19.50 m, average for a mainland Greek theatre.

[6] Diod. 16.91.4–94.4.

the large size of this orchestra was intended to provide space for pageantry, parades, and rituals consistent with the displays of royal—that is, national—significance. It is thus different from Classical and early Hellenistic Greek theatres in the size of its cavea and orchestra and the arrangement of its seats. It appears to have been designed for needs appropriate to the Macedonians, but our understanding of it as a structure is limited both by a lack of parallels with other theatres on the fringes of the Greek world and by the difficulty of dating it. If this theatre belongs to the middle of the fourth century, we have the actual setting of Philip II's assassination.

Otherwise, the slopes above Vergina have revealed a number of other aspects of ancient Aegae, including the walls of its acropolis that snake up the hill behind the great palace. Future excavations will reveal additional features of these ramparts, but the outlines of town walls— not unexpectedly following natural topographical features—have now been determined on the south, east, and west sides. Continuing surveys seek the north wall while magnetometer soundings and trial trenches attempt to determine something of the city plan and additional monuments requiring systematic excavation. The location of the Eucleia monument described earlier (above, pp. 192–93) may provide a clue to the site of the agora, and a small edifice located hard up against the western wall may be the remains of an administrative or commercial building. If so, it is the first structure discovered that does not have either a recreational or a religious function. The whole slope has been declared an archaeological zone, and there seems little doubt that the next few years will gradually reveal the form of the ancient town, and thereby provide important information about life in fifth- and fourth-century Aegae.

The Royal Cemetery

Below the village of Vergina toward the east is a large area of grazing land marked by dozens of small burial tumuli. It was here that the archaeologist Manolis Andronikos labored for years, patiently recovering grave goods and human remains, and establishing a chronology for the Iron Age inhabitants of the area.[7] Throughout this period the archaeologist's eye was attracted to a huge tumulus (110 m in diameter and 12 m high) near the center of the village. By 1976 the conditions were favorable for excavation and, with considerable support from the

---

[7] Published in Andronikos, *Vergina*, vol. 1, *To nekrotapheion tōn tymvōn*, and summarized in "Vergina, the Prehistoric Necropolis and the Hellenistic Palace," 3–5, and *Vergina: The Royal Tombs*, 25–30.

Aristotelean University of Thessaloniki and the Greek government, digging commenced. The result is one of the most important archaeological discoveries in Greece of the past half-century. The recovery in 1977 and 1978 of three fourth-century tombs, two of which were unlooted, produced a variety of rich grave goods the extravagance of which was matched by the extraordinary public interest in their discovery. The normal excitement attending a discovery of so many gold and silver objects was augmented in this case by an initial identification of one of the tombs and its human remains as the burial of Philip II. The Vergina excavations have been richly documented and do not require a detailed presentation here.[8] We shall consider two aspects of this extraordinary excavation: the controversy surrounding the identification of the tombs, and the contribution to our understanding of ancient Macedon made by these discoveries.

Four structures were recovered from the great tumulus at Vergina. One of these was a small building of which only the foundations survive, identified as a *heroon,* or a shrine dedicated to the worship of the dead (Philip II?, although see below, p. 265). Nearby was a simple cist tomb (Tomb 1) covered with stone slabs, enclosing a single interior space 3.50 m long, 2.09 m wide and 3 m high. The tomb had been robbed of its contents save for some scattered bones, identified as those of a mature male, a somewhat younger female, and an infant.[9] Three of the interior walls were covered with extraordinary paintings, the most impressive of which was a monumental composition showing a famous mythological scene, the Rape of Persephone.[10] It is a masterwork and a major contribution to our understanding of fourth-century painting. The excavator suggests that it may be attributed to the famous artist Nichomachus, who was said by Pliny (*NH* 35.109) to have executed a painting on that subject. If so, it continues the tradition of Macedonian royalty commissioning work by prominent Greeks, and one wonders what persons interred here should command such an important project.

Tomb 2 is quite different. It is a chamber tomb—a rectangular structure roofed with a barrel vault, divided into an antechamber and a somewhat larger main chamber, and decorated with a facade designed

---

[8] The most recent descriptions by the excavator are in *Vergina: The Royal Tombs* (with selective bibliography) and "Vergina: Archaiologia kai Istoria." The most extensive bibliography can be found in Borza, "Macedonian Royal Tombs at Vergina," 84, and "Those Vergina Tombs Again," 9.

[9] Andronikos, *Vergina: The Royal Tombs,* 87.

[10] Illustrated in ibid., 86–95, with discussion by the excavator. There are useful comments by von Blanckenhagen, "Painting in the Time of Alexander and Later," 257.

to give the impression of a small Doric building—what has come to be known as a "Macedonian-style" tomb. A doorway led through the facade into the antechamber, and doors connected the two interior rooms. Both sets of doors were sealed before the tomb was buried within its tumulus. The antechamber in such vaulted (or "Macedonian") tombs was normally a repository for grave goods, while the burial itself was placed in the main chamber. Tomb 2 at Vergina is unique among tombs discovered thus far in that interments were made in *both* chambers, a situation that leads to some interesting historical speculation, as we shall see. The roughly finished main chamber held an elaborate gold casket containing the burned bones of the deceased (a middle-aged male). Nearby was a rich assortment of grave goods, including a panoply and numerous silver and bronze vessels. Richly decorated furniture and a number of what appear to be personal possessions make up the remainder of the items placed in the main chamber. Most of the burial goods are to be associated with a Macedonian warrior: weapons, armor, and wine-drinking vessels. The diverse and rich jumble of objects that were presumably the personal property of the deceased is more reminiscent of Egyptian or Etruscan burials than of anything known from the Greek world.

The more highly decorated antechamber held a second burial in a somewhat simpler, but similarly designed, gold casket. The burned bones are identified as those of a young woman, and the deceased's sex is confirmed by the absence of symposiast items and military paraphernalia, except for a few pieces deliberately set up against the sealed doors leading into the main chamber and clearly intended to be associated with the burial therein. These include a pair of gilded bronze greaves, an embossed gold cover for a *gorytos* (a flat quiver that held a bow and arrows), and a large number of arrow points, all that has survived of the arrows and the leather quiver. It is noteworthy that the antechamber is, relative to the main chamber, much larger than in any other Macedonian tomb whose dimensions are known to me.[11]

The facade of the tomb is dominated by an extraordinary painted frieze extending virtually the full width of the structure (5.56 m) and standing more than a meter high. The subject of the well-executed composition is a hunting scene, most of which has survived in general

---

[11] The antechamber measures 14.65 m², the main chamber 19.89 m², making an antechamber-main chamber ratio of 1:1.28; that is, the antechamber is nearly three-quarters as large as the main chamber. For statistics comparing the interior dimensions and ratios of nearby two-chambered tombs of the later fourth and early third centuries, see Borza, "The Royal Macedonian Tombs and Paraphernalia," 121.

outline if not in detail.[12] It is a royal hunt, featuring three mounted figures and seven on foot. The hunters and their dogs are involved in several stages of stalking, confronting, and killing wild animals, among which are two deer, a wild boar, a bear, and a lion. The focal point is a mounted figure about to spear the lion. The composition is full of energy, but it cannot have been intended to be a depiction of an actual hunt.[13] It is highly impressionistic—four different types of animals being hunted in a single scene—with a variety of hunting activities all conducted in a confined space. Indeed, it is a declaration of the painter's skills to have successfully illustrated so many events within this limited area. While the frieze remains a splendid testimony to the vigor of Macedonian court life, the identification of any of the figures as real persons is problematic.

The third tomb is similar to the second, a two-chambered "Macedonian" type, also unlooted.[14] The single burial in the main chamber consists of the bones of a teenaged male interred in a silver vessel. A magnificent assemblage of silver vessels and ivory reliefs bears witness to the wealth and taste of the royal family. For there can be little doubt that this is an Argead burial tumulus. Although no inscription testifies to the names of the deceased in any of the three tombs, the site is Aegae, well known as the royal burial place of the royal family.[15] More-

[12] Its long burial has caused some deterioration, and photographs cannot do justice to the exceptional draftsmanship and sensitivity of the surviving details. The best illustrations accompany the excavator's analysis of the frieze, in Andronikos, *Vergina: The Royal Tombs*, 101–19; also see von Blanckenhagen, "Painting in the Time of Alexander and Later," 257–58.

[13] Unlike the excavator, I am not confident suggesting that any of the figures can be assigned as portraits of known persons, such as Philip and Alexander. The identification of a mounted figure about to spear the lion as Philip II on the basis of facial features (Andronikos, *Vergina: The Royal Tombs*, pl. 71) both reads too much into the poor condition of the paint in this part of the frieze and relies too heavily on the accuracy of known "portraits" of Philip. Likewise, to identify Alexander as the central horseman is a leap of faith akin to that of similarly identifying one of the tiny ivory heads discovered midst the burial goods inside the tomb. Moreover, what are portraits of Alexander, the living king, doing adorning the tomb of his father? For a sensible analysis of the painting see Carroll-Spillecke, *Landscape Depictions*, 151–55.

[14] The tomb and its contents are discussed and well illustrated in Andronikos, *Vergina: The Royal Tombs*, 198–217.

[15] Just. 7.2.2–5 informs us that the first king, Perdiccas, called in his successor, Argaeus, and directed that his bones and those of all the kings who followed be deposited at Aegae, saying that as long as this practice continued, their family would retain the throne. Justin continues by relating that some people think that the Argeadae lost the crown because Alexander the Great was buried elsewhere (in Alexandria). That Justin's observation about the Argead loss of the crown is *post factum*, and the details about Per-

over, while many of the objects in the Vergina tombs are only richer and more elaborate versions of what is found in tombs throughout Macedonia, certain aspects suggest uniqueness to royalty: a diadem, the unusual luxuriousness of much of the material, the arms and armor, and a royal hunt as decoration. The tombs at Vergina reflect a common Macedonian burial culture, but exhibit some features that accord with the accepted view of the status of the royal family within the society.

The identification of the royalty buried within these three tombs has been one of the most hotly debated issues in the recent annals of archaeological inquiry. The excavator, many of his Greek colleagues, the Greek government, and a few foreign scholars hold that Tomb 2 is the burial place of Philip II. Some Greek scholars and a number of foreign archaeologists and historians are more sceptical. Following the chronology suggested by the excavator—that all tombs belong to the last third of the fourth century B.C.—only a few royal personages were eligible by birth, status, or marriage for burial at Aegae in that period.[16] If the identification of the bones in Tomb 3 as a teenaged male is correct, the structure must be the final resting place of Alexander IV, son of the Conqueror and of the Bactrian princess, Roxane. He was the last Argead, and his murder by Cassander *ca.* 310 marks the end of the dynasty. When the debris of battle over Tomb 2 is cleared, two sets of candidates for this unique double burial survive: Philip II and his last wife, Cleopatra, and Philip III Arrhidaeus and his wife, Eurydice.

Following Philip's II's assassination at Aegae in 336, Alexander was declared king. He soon left Aegae and set about putting down frontier rebellions. In his absence, Olympias, Alexander's mother and Philip's estranged wife, returned to Aegae and murdered Philip's widow, Cleopatra, and her small child. When Alexander returned he was outraged at Olympias's act. It is likely that he interred the young queen at Aegae.[17] Nearly two decades later (317), during a fierce Macedonian civil war, Arrhidaeus and Eurydice were taken prisoner and murdered on Olympias's orders. By 316, however, Cassander had eliminated Olympias and interred the royal couple with formal honors at Aegae.[18]

The arguments for identifying the deceased of Tomb 2 as Philip II and Cleopatra may be summarized: Tomb 2 was built in two distinct

---

diccas and Argaeus are myth, does not reduce the validity of the main point of the story, that Aegae was the resting place for the Argeadae.

[16] See Green, "The Royal Tombs of Vergina," with a summary table at 140–41.

[17] Evidence for these events gathered in Borza, "Macedonian Royal Tombs at Vergina," 76–77.

[18] Evidence set out by W. L. Adams, "The Royal Macedonian Tomb."

stages, with the main chamber showing signs of hasty construction and rough decoration. This accords well with the known historical circumstances surrounding the hurried aftermath of Philip's assassination, as Alexander probably supervised his father's burial and the sealing of the main chamber before rushing off to settle rebellion. The antechamber was left for a more leisurely completion. Upon his return and discovery of the murder of Philip's wife and baby, he modified the plan for burial to accommodate a second, unique, interment in an antechamber normally used for ceremonial purposes. Cleopatra's relationship to powerful Macedonian barons whose support Alexander would need may have motivated him to bury her with her husband in a manner befitting a queen.

The initial examination of the bones of both occupants suggests ages consistent with those of Philip and Cleopatra at the time of their deaths—46 or 47 and *ca.* 20, respectively.[19] Another independent examination of the bones from the main chamber reveals trauma and healing in the eye socket and cheekbone of the male's skull consistent with a major eye injury suffered by Philip during his siege of Methone in 354.[20]

Support for the interments of Arrhidaeus and Eurydice in Tomb 2 rests on a complex analysis of several kinds of evidence. First, the tomb contained ceramic objects that have been identified as Athenian and securely dated on stylistic and numismatic grounds to the late fourth century, at least a generation after the death of Philip II.[21] The existence of late fourth-century materials would make it virtually impossible that the tomb belonged to Philip and Cleopatra, who were buried in 336 B.C. If the proposed date of about 315 B.C. or later for the ceramic materials is correct, the possibility that this is the tomb of Arrhidaeus and Eurydice, who were interred in 316, is enhanced. Moreover, the existence of an antechamber nearly as large as the main chamber points more to the interment of Eurydice as part of a planned double burial, rather than to that of Cleopatra, whose interment in what had been designed as a ceremonial room was unanticipated.

[19] Consistent also with the ages of Arrhidaeus (early 40s) and Eurydice (early 20s) at the time of their deaths. Phyllis W. Lehmann was the first to challenge the excavator's identification of Tomb 2 as the burial place of Philip II, preferring instead an attribution to Arrhidaeus and Eurydice; see Lehmann, "The So-Called Tomb of Philip II: A Different Interpretation."

[20] Argued by Musgrave, Neave, and Prag, "The Skull from Tomb II." 60–78. For more on the bones, see Appendix C, pp. 299–300.

[21] Rotroff, "Royal Saltcellars from the Athenian Agora," and "Spool Saltcellars in the Athenian Agora"; J. Kroll, "Nailing Down the Archaeological Chronology"; Borza, "The Royal Macedonian Tombs and Paraphernalia," 107 n. 6.

There are a number of stylistic features of Tomb 2 that might be best associated with the period following Alexander's invasion of Asia.[22] The barrel-vault roof is an architectural feature that may have been introduced into Macedonia and Greece only with Alexander's expedition or after. The lion hunt that forms part of the hunting scene portrayed on the exterior frieze was a theme absent from Greek art from the end of the orientalizing period in the seventh century B.C. until its revival and sudden popularity after Alexander's expedition.[23] The lion hunt was depicted as the sport of Asian kings, whether they actually hunted lions or not, and the lion hunt on the frieze of Tomb 2 is a central feature of the composition. The grove of trees providing background for the scene also features a tall pillar, suggesting a hunt in a formal game park (*paradeisos*), in the Persian manner. And in some respects the impressionistic quality of the painting is reminiscent of the great Hellenistic mosaic from the archaeological museum in Naples showing Alexander and Darius engaged in battle. The mosaic probably copied a painting done by Philoxenus of Eretria, who was said (Pliny *NH* 35.110) to have painted for Cassander a picture on this theme.[24] Moreover, the armor from the main chamber may suggest a later fourth-century date. The restored iron and gold cuirass from the main chamber is similar to that worn by Alexander in the Naples mosaic.[25] Moreover, an iron helmet—unique in Macedonian archaeology—found in the main chamber accords with Plutarch's description (*Alex.* 32.5) of the helmet worn by Alexander at the battle of Gaugamela, and is similar to the type of helmet depicted on a contemporary coin as worn by Alexander.[26]

Thus there are both archaeological and stylistic arguments suggesting that Tomb 2 belongs to a period following Alexander's Asian expedition. It may also be possible to identify the provenance of some of

[22] For details of what follows, see Borza, "The Royal Macedonian Tombs and Paraphernalia," 107–10.

[23] M. Robertson, "Early Greek Mosaic," 246, and Pollitt, *Art in the Hellenistic Age*, 38 and 40. A lion hunt is the subject of one of the large mosaics at Pella, dated to the late fourth or early third century.

[24] Details in Borza, "The Royal Macedonian Tombs and Paraphernalia," 109–110 and 117, with notes.

[25] Cuirass illustrated in Andronikos, *Vergina: The Royal Tombs*, 138–39. Discussion of the mosaic copy of Philoxenus's painting in Pollitt, *Art in the Hellenistic Age*, 45–46, and (with illustrations) in Maiuri, *Museo nazionale Napoli*, 70–74, and Charbonneaux, Martin, and Villard, *Hellenistic Art*, 114–18.

[26] Helmet illustrated in Andronikos, *Vergina: The Royal Tombs*, 140–41, with discussion at 144, where the excavator acknowledges the similarity between the helmet of Tomb 2 and the helmet described by Plutarch. More details in Borza, "The Royal Macedonian Tombs and Paraphernalia," 112–14; see also note 33 below for additional references to the coin.

the burial goods in light of evidence that some of Alexander's personal equipment survived into the wars of his successors.

According to Quintus Curtius, during the turmoil immediately following Alexander's death at Babylon in June 323, which saw the king's commanders and the army divided on the matter of succession, Perdiccas displayed the king's throne, draped with Alexander's diadem, robe, and arms.[27] Not long after, Arrhidaeus was nominated for the succession, and he put on the robe of his brother, the very one that had been placed on the throne.[28] Whether Arrhidaeus also took the diadem and arms, however likely that appears, is not mentioned in our sources. The only further reference in Curtius to Alexander's personal accessories occurs in the account of the preparation of his body for burial, where we are told, somewhat enigmatically, that the emblem of his rank (*fortunae eius insignia*) was placed on his head.[29] If these details are to be trusted, Arrhidaeus alleviated his initial insecurity as successor by taking at least the king's garment, which may have been his right as the sole surviving Argead and son of Philip II.

Preserved in Diodorus is the account of an incident that sheds further light on the disposition of some of Alexander's paraphernalia.[30] Eumenes of Cardia was representative of that group of skilled Greeks who had come into the employ of the Macedonian court. He had served Philip, was Alexander's secretary, and was one of the few Greeks to have achieved prominence in the king's staff. During the struggle following Alexander's death he emerged as an Argead loyalist. As an ethnic Greek, he was denied a claim to power in the struggle among Macedonians, and he pledged his services to the surviving members of the royal family.[31] In an attempt to retain Argead continuity, Eumenes endeavored to mediate among the competing Mace-

---

[27] Curt. 10.6.4: *in qua diadema vestisque Alexandri cum armis erant.* On the validity of Curtius as a source for these events see Martin, "Quintus Curtius' Presentation," and Borza, "The Royal Macedonian Tombs and Paraphernalia," 110.

[28] Curt. 10.7.13: . . . *vestem fratris, eam ipsam quae in sella posita fuerat induitur.*

[29] Curt. 10.10.13, a passage that must be used with caution, as it also narrates that the king's unattended corpse lay for seven days without putrefaction in his coffin in the mid-June Babylonian heat.

[30] Diod. 18.60.3–61.3, based on Hieronymus of Cardia, who was probably an eyewitness. There are less detailed versions in Diod. 19.15.3–4; Plut. *Eum.* 13.3–4; Nepos *Eum.* 7.2–3; and Polyae. *Strat.* 4.8.2; and an echo in Curt. 10.6.15 (Ptolemy's proposal that a *junta* of commanders rule); although all accounts save, perhaps, Curtius's seem to go back to the same source used by Diodorus. The "Alexander-Tent" has drawn considerable attention; for a recent discussion and bibliography see Mooren, "Hellenistic Monarchy," 238 and n. 146; Errington, "Alexander in the Hellenistic World," 140–41; and Borza, "The Royal Macedonian Tombs and Paraphernalia," 111 n. 20.

[31] The ethnic prejudice against Eumenes is manifest; e.g., Plut. *Eum.* 3.1, 8.1, 18.1; Diod. 18.60.1–3, 62.7, and 19.13.1–2.

donian generals by holding a council under the following strategem: Eumenes took materials from the royal treasury, and set within a fine tent a throne, Alexander's own diadem (*diadēma*), sceptre (*skēptron*), and armor (*hopla*). With these materials at hand, Eumenes joined the other commanders in earnest discussions, as if in the presence of Alexander.

Thus we have literary evidence that some of Alexander's personal paraphernalia did not accompany the king's funeral train (hijacked to Egypt by Ptolemy), and that these items were in the hands of the Argead loyalist Eumenes. Moreover, except for the throne, examples of all the items mentioned by Diodorus as being used by Eumenes are found in Tomb 2 at Vergina: a cuirass similar to the one shown on the Pompeii mosaic depicting Alexander in battle, an iron helmet similar to that described by Plutarch as Alexander's, and a splendid gilded silver diadem, fashioned to be worn either on the head directly or to adorn the traditional Macedonian hat, or *kausia*, in the manner of Alexander as described by Athenaeus (12.537e–f).

There were also early published reports, including some by the excavator, of the discovery of a two-meter-long gold-sheathed sceptre.[32] The sceptre, however, has disappeared from the recent literature without explanation, and no further description of the object itself can be offered. The possibility that a sceptre was found in Tomb 2 may nonetheless have some bearing on the date and identity of the burials within. It is difficult to account for a sceptre if this is the tomb of Philip II, as this instrument of royal authority was, one assumes, normally passed down from king to king, and it seems likely that Philip's sceptre would have been inherited by Alexander. Indeed we have a confirmation that Alexander had a sceptre. The same coin—a rare silver decadrachm called "the Porus medallion"—that depicts Alexander wearing a helmet of the type found in Tomb 2 also portrays him holding a rodlike object in his left hand. Judging from the height of the king himself, the rod is about two meters long, consistent with the length of the object from Tomb 2 thought at one time by the excavator to be a sceptre.[33] One might suggest that when Cassander interred Arrhidaeus he buried not only the elder son of Philip II, but also the personal para-

[32] Bibliography and details in Borza, "The Royal Macedonian Tombs and Paraphernalia," 115–16 and n. 38.

[33] The Porus medallion, issued to commemorate Alexander's victory over the Indian king Porus, is generally considered to be a life issue, and as such is the only surviving life portrait of the Macedonian. There is a specialists' literature on the subject, for which see Borza, "The Royal Macedonian Tombs and Paraphernalia," nn. 29 and 39, but the coin is also illustrated in Davis and Kraay, *The Hellenistic Kingdoms*, nos. 10–12, and *The Search for Alexander: An Exhibition*, no. 21.

phernalia of Alexander, including the sceptre of the Argeadae. It was a sign that the Old Order was finished; within a few years the son and wife of Alexander would be dispatched, and the Argeadae were no more.[34]

The main chamber of Tomb 2 also yielded an elaborate ceremonial shield, finely wrought of ivory, gold, glass, and wood. Concentric bands of decoration encircle the central composition, which consists of the ivory figures of a reclining, submissive female and a dominant male. When the excavators first came upon this object it had collapsed into thousands of fragments of material, but, thanks to the extraordinary skills of the restorers, this elaborate work of art is now on display in the Archaeological Museum of Thessaloniki. The shield, which is a very great work of ancient art, is unique, and we are reminded by reliable sources from antiquity that Alexander owned a ceremonial shield, taken by him from the temple of Athena at Ilium, and cared for by one of his ranking officers, Peucestas.[35]

We thus have the *possibility* that some of the magnificent armor and royal emblems in Tomb 2—which on other grounds might be suited to a date later than Philip II—are in fact those of Alexander the Great. This is not proof that the very objects in Tomb 2 are Alexander's, but several of the objects are unique in archaeology and are of the type that our ancient sources relate as belonging to the Macedonian king. Moreover, the small "heroön," the ruins of which stand on the perimeter of the tumulus containing the royal tombs, might thus be interpreted as pointing to a heroic figure nearby, perhaps not Philip II (who, as we have seen, was headed for his own divine tendencies), but perhaps him whose personal possessions were interred in Tomb 2.

There is little or no direct evidence that identifies the tomb as that of Arrhidaeus and Eurydice, but indirectly we have specific literary evidence that they were interred at Aegae together, and the tomb itself and some of its contents appear to be from the age of Alexander and a little later. The process of elimination points to Arrhidaeus and Eurydice.

Where was Philip II buried? No anthropologist's analysis of the remains found in Tomb 1 has been published, and the tomb was otherwise robbed. Stylistically, this cist tomb is similar to Tomb B discov-

[34] For additional details and analysis of the decoration of Tomb 2 and of the grave goods that might be associated with Alexander, plus some speculation about how they got there, see Borza, "The Royal Macedonian Tombs and Paraphernalia," 116–18.

[35] Arr. 6.9.3, 10.2; Curt. 9.5.14–18; Plut. *Alex.* 63.4. The fullest description of the shield from Tomb 2 is Andronikos, *Vergina: The Royal Tombs*, 136–40, with figs. 91–94. Some of the decoration on the shield grip suggests Asian origin; see Borza, "The Royal Macedonian Tombs and Paraphernalia," 115 and n. 37.

ered at Derveni, north of Salonica, which has been dated to the 330s.[36] We thus have in the Argead royal cemetery a tomb dating from the era of Philip II and containing the remains of a mature male, younger female, and infant. We are reminded of the relative ages of Philip and Cleopatra and the fact that Olympias killed Cleopatra only after forcing the young queen to watch the murder of her young child.[37] Moreover, the fine interior painting of this tomb depicting the Rape of Persephone is worthy of a royal patron.

I would thus offer the possibility that these three tombs be taken in their natural order: Tomb 1 belongs to Philip II, his queen, Cleopatra, and their infant; Tomb 2 belongs to Philip III Arrhidaeus and his queen, Eurydice, and contains as well some of the royal paraphernalia of Alexander the Great; and Tomb 3 belongs to Alexander IV, the last of the Argeadae.

This hypothesis is limited by problematic and incomplete evidence. Some questions may be resolved with the full publication of the final excavation reports and by additional archaeological discoveries that every year provide impressive new information. Other questions will continue unanswered because of the incomplete documentary record of Macedonian royal burial practices. To that extent, every attempt to explain the contextual circumstances of Macedonian grave goods will remain at least partly conjectural. We have from Vergina a full range of materials: architecture, painting, human remains, weapons and armor, jewelry, metal and ceramic vessels, and a variety of other practical and ceremonial items. The materials are rich enough and important enough to provide a possible scene for a historical drama we know just barely through literary sources. We are tantalized by the proximity of material remains and documentary evidence, and risk the temptation to associate this extraordinary array of goods with events in the lives (and deaths) of some of the most important people of the era. But, as always in a field of scholarship in which new discoveries are forthcoming, caution must be exercised in proposing any interpretation that cannot be firmly rooted in an environment of immutable evidence.

Excavations Outside Vergina

The Vergina discoveries are only part of a larger picture. Encouraged by Andronikos's work, earlier sporadic excavation throughout Macedonia has been intensified and made more systematic. Macedonian ar-

---

[36] Ninou, *Treasures of Ancient Macedonia*, no. 184, and *The Search for Alexander: An Exhibition*, no. 127. The existence in Tomb 1 of a few sherds of mid-fourth-century pottery (Andronikos, *Vergina: The Royal Tombs*, 86) supports a date in the 330s.

[37] Paus. 8.7.7; Just. 9.7.12–14.

chaeology today benefits from both a larger infusion of financial support and a considerable public interest, exemplified by an exhibition of a number of Macedonian objects that toured North American museums, the installation of a new wing in the archaeological museum in Salonica, and a series of lavishly illustrated books. The result has been a virtual explosion of material from the soil of Macedonia. The number of chamber tombs has increased so rapidly that, lacking publication for most of them beyond newspaper announcements, no one knows precisely how many tombs have been recovered. Indeed, one of the most important desiderata for a historian of Macedon is the production of an up-to-date catalog of tombs and grave goods, as the quality of analysis rests now upon the quantity of materials available for study.[38] Unfortunately, an inflexible bureaucracy, the difficulty of publication, and the penchant among some excavators (though not those at Vergina) to retain total personal control over objects have prevented knowledge about these discoveries from being disseminated in a rational manner. It thus does not seem likely that many of these objects will find their way into the scientific literature in the foreseeable future, if ever. Yet the interested observer only need visit the archaeological museums of Macedonia—those in Salonica, Dion, Pella, and Kavalla, in particular—to examine many of these items, which have been proudly displayed. Moreover, there are available a number of well-produced, richly illustrated books whose purpose is to trumpet these discoveries.[39]

What has been learned about the Macedonians from these recent archaeological excavations? First, we know very little more about ordinary Macedonian life than we did before. The tombs are those of a wealthy elite, including the royal family. The extraordinary moveable wealth from their tombs tells us virtually nothing about the underlying economic system and social relationships of the Macedonians beyond the obvious, that there was considerable wealth close at hand, that the grave goods appear to be personal items that would accompany the deceased into the afterworld, and that there was a highly refined tradition of metalworking nearby, with all that that implies in the way of mining resources and skilled artisans. The graves of Macedonian farm-

[38] One useful comprehensive description of the tombs is Gossel, *Makedonische Kammergräber* (1980), but this work is somewhat uneven in quality because of erroneous or incomplete data provided by excavators; in any case, it is now out of date.

[39] Especially Ninou, *Treasures of Ancient Macedonia*, produced by the Archaeological Museum of Thessaloniki; Hatzopoulos and Loukopoulos, *Philip of Macedon*; Barr-Sharrar and Borza, *Macedonia and Greece*; and *The Search for Alexander: An Exhibition*, the catalog of the exhibition of Macedonian antiquities that travelled throughout the United States and Canada in 1980–83.

ers and herders, like those of common folk in many such cultures, have
yielded little in the way of objects. We may also suggest that literacy
was too rare to illuminate the lives of ordinary persons to the extent
accomplished, for example, by inscriptions on some Greek and many
Roman funerary monuments. Even the tombs of the rich are virtually
barren of inscriptions until the Hellenistic period. Thus the evidence
from the tombs sheds light on only a segment of Macedonian life,
while the future awaits the recovery of more information and a consequently finer analysis of the infrastructure of Macedonian society. We
thus eagerly await the continuing publication of inscriptions by scholars from the Greek archaeological services and universities and the National Hellenic Research Foundation.[40]

What the tombs and their contents have provided is an insight into
the wealth, taste, and burial customs of the Macedonian gentry and,
of course, the royal family. Some of the burial goods from Vergina are
unique, as has been pointed out: the diadem, the ceremonial shield, the
unusual weapons and armor, and other items identified as royal paraphernalia. But most of the grave goods are similar—though richer or
more finely wrought—to those found in burials throughout Macedonia. Silver and bronze vessels, ossuaries for the remains of the deceased, greaves, jewelry, decorative plaques, and a variety of small implements provide a picture of a common burial culture through the
land. The culture owes much to Greek, especially Athenian, inspiration, but it is also clear that some vessel shapes are Balkan—especially
Thracian—whereas others are influenced by material from the Persian
empire, perhaps directly, but probably through East Greek interme-
diaries.[41] The hoard of Thracian vessels discovered in 1986 provides an
enlarged data base for analyzing the connections between Macedonian
metal objects and those of the neighboring Balkan regions.[42]

Indeed, one is impressed with the eclecticism of Macedonian taste.

[40] The presentation by Saatsoglou-Paliadeli (*Ta epitaphia mnimeia, q.v.*) of the mainly
fourth-century grave stelae from the tumulus at Vergina marks an important contribution to our understanding of some ordinary Macedonian proper names, although I cannot share Andronikos's conclusion (*Vergina: The Royal Tombs*, 83–84) that the existence
of Greek-sounding names written in Greek is proof that the Macedonians were a Greek
tribe (see Chapter 4 above).

[41] Foreign influence on Macedonian metal vessels has been analyzed by Barr-Sharrar
in "Eastern Influence on the Toreutic Art of Macedonia." For a survey of Macedonian
toreutic ware, see Barr-Sharrar's "Macedonian Metal Vases in Perspective," to which
my own presentation owes a great deal. I am also deeply indebted to Dr. Barr-Sharrar
for numerous discussions and a joint examination of many of the objects themselves,
although she may not share all of my views.

[42] Cf. Ninou, *Treasures of Ancient Macedonia*, and Fol et al., *The New Thracian Treasure*.

Objects known from other places are widely seen in Macedonian tombs, but Macedonian craftsmen were free not to imitate slavishly the details, shapes, or materials of foreign models. The extent to which local craftsmen were itinerant or established in ateliers is still an open question, but it is clear that they were masters of metalwork, especially in silver and gold. The ultimate origins of some of the precious-metal objects were other mediums. The antecedents of the gold ossuary caskets from Vergina Tomb 2 were probably wood,[43] and the gilded silver diadem imitates a cloth fillet. The analysis of these objects has only begun, and it remains for specialists to establish a more precise chronology of their stylistic evolution both within Macedonia and with reference to external cultural influences.

Grave goods, of course, are evidence of burial practices, and presumably reveal something of Macedonian religious beliefs found at all levels of the society. We have already seen that the Macedonians worshipped many of the same gods that the Greeks venerated, but it is also clear that the expressions of worship were markedly different. For example, there has yet to be discovered from the Argead period anything like a Greek temple, that is, a major public religious monument. This is not to suggest that the Macedonians did not celebrate the gods in a public way, for there is abundant evidence from the age of Philip and Alexander concerning festivals and rituals. Perhaps the recent discovery at Vergina of a shrine to Eucleia (pp. 192–93 above) may be only the forerunner of other such monuments. But thus far we are lacking the great religious edifices that characterized public expression among so many of the Greeks.

So, too, the burial customs as evidenced by the tombs suggest something quite different from contemporary Greece. The Macedonians who have left us evidence of their funerary practices clearly believed in depositing with the deceased a variety of goods associated with their activities in life, in particular, arms and armor, and drinking vessels. Burial chambers sometimes held a ceremonial couch (klinē) of stone, often carved in relief or painted with Dionysiac or symposiast scenes. At Vergina, the couch in Tomb 2 was of wood, long since disintegrated, but preserving some of its applied decoration, including ivory figures.[44] The ivory figures from Tomb 2 are not unique. Small human

---

[43] J. P. Adams, "The *Larnakes* from Tomb II at Vergina." The closest Macedonian parallel is a large, fourth-century silver ossuary from a tomb at Amphipolis, now on display in the Kavalla archaeological museum, illustrated in Ninou, *Treasures of Ancient Macedonia*, no. 396 (pl. 55).

[44] There are couches to be seen in the archaeological museums in Salonica and Kavalla, and a tentative reconstruction of the disintegrated couch from Tomb 2 at Vergina ap-

heads and limbs were found in the "Tomb of the Palmettes" at Lefkadia, and similar figures from a tomb at Dion are on display in the archaeological museum at that site.[45] Occasionally a marble throne was
placed in the burial chamber, as at the tomb of the warrior at Palatitsia,
or as in the case of the enormous, larger-than-life throne in the Romaios tomb at Vergina.[46]

Some tombs, of both the cist and chambered types, seem to have
been lavishly furnished, as if they were small symposium chambers,
with all the appropriate accoutrements.[47] But what is most impressive
is the extraordinary variety of drinking vessels, mostly of metal. These
cups, buckets, bowls, jugs, ladles, and sediment strainers constitute an
astonishing display of silver craftsmanship. Known drinking implements are abundant, save the krater, a vessel designed to mix water
with wine. For, unlike the Greeks, the Macedonians were accustomed
to drink their wine *akratos* ("unmixed"), a practice that may have contributed to the suspicion among some Greeks that the Macedonians
were little better than barbarians.[48] Only five kraters have been recovered from Macedonian tombs, and certainly one (and perhaps others)
may not have been intended as an actual mixing bowl.[49] Only the recovery of a much larger number of wine accessories will determine if
the rarity of the krater relative to other vessels will continue; thus far,
the archaeological evidence seems to support the notion that the Macedonian gentry was a hard-drinking lot.

Instruments for hunting, warfare, and drinking thus testify to what
the Macedonians of our tombs thought were important in life, and
what they wished to accompany them into death.[50] That they consid-

---

pears in Andronikos, *Vergina: The Royal Tombs*, 122. For illustrations of the couch-
sarcophagus in the largest tomb at Palatitsia, see ibid., 34.

[45] For the Lefkadia figures, see Rhomiopoulou, "A New Monumental Chamber
Tomb." For those from Dion, see illustrations in the unpaginated guidebook to the site
by Pandermalis, *Dion: The Sacred City of the Macedonians at the Foothills of Mt. Olympus*,
and in *I Archaiologi Miloun yia tin Pieria*, pl. 1.

[46] Palatitsia: Andronikos, *Vergina: The Royal Tombs*, 32–33 and 36; Romaios tomb:
S. G. Miller, "Macedonian Tombs," 157, fig. 9.

[47] E.g., a silver four-legged stool was recovered from a cist tomb at Stavroupolis; see
Ninou, *Treasures of Ancient Macedonia*, no. 292 (pl. 39).

[48] E.g., Diod. 16.87.1 and Athen. 12.537d. For a description of Macedonian drinking
habits, see Borza, "The Symposium of Alexander's Court," 47–49.

[49] Ninou, *Treasures of Ancient Macedonia*, nos. 157 (pl. 25) and 174 (Derveni, Tomb
A), 184 (pl. 27) and 223 (pl. 36) (Derveni, Tomb B), and 270 (pl. 40) (Stavroupolis). Of
course, there is no reason why Macedonians could not have mixed water and wine in
other vessels, such as their finely wrought silver situlas, vessel types that are found in
abundance.

[50] In death, they "preferred to drink from containers of silver rather than clay": Barr-
Sharrar, "Eastern Influence on the Toreutic Art of Macedonia," 4.

ered death a passage into the afterlife is clear from the painting on the facade of the huge early Hellenistic tomb recovered by Petsas at Lefkadia.[51] Four life-size figures are painted on the facade of the tomb, two on each side of the entrance. At the far left (as one faces the tomb) is the warrior-figure of the deceased. Next is Hermes, guide to the underworld. The figures to the right of the entrance are Aeacus and Rhadamanthys, judges of the dead. Thus the observer's eye is drawn from the deceased warrior—believed by the excavator to be one of Alexander's veterans—through the guide toward the judges. Not only is this one of the most technically proficient examples of painting to survive from the period, but it is a dramatic statement of the passage from this world into the next.[52]

One of the most interesting ideas to grow out of the recent interest in Macedonian chamber tombs is the recognition that the architectural design and decoration are illusory.[53] The architectural facade is often that of a small Doric or Ionic building, sometimes with a pediment. It looks like a monument from the front, but not from any other perspective. Its architectural facade is not structural (as in Greek architecture), but strictly ornamental. It is designed to imitate Greek architecture, but hides completely what lies behind: normally a simple barrel vault with one or two chambers. The main architectural principle is to create an illusion. There is little need to conform to the canons of architectural or decorative integrity, especially since the facade is not an essential structural component of the building.

Not only did the Macedonians develop illusory facades, but they also employed a wide range of polychromatic painting, both to highlight architectural features and to cover walls and ceilings with designs.[54] The painting is often of high quality, using vivid colors, delicate shading, and foreshortening. Painting also contributes to the illusory principles, as a number of decorative architectural features that would be molded or carved in relief on Greek buildings are painted

[51] Illustrated in Petsas, *O Taphos tōn Lefkadiōn*, plates *Z-I* and 5–10; reconstructions in Touratsoglou, *Lefkadia*, 9, and S. G. Miller, "Macedonian Tombs," 152, fig. 3.

[52] This Macedonian theme of transition can be matched visually, perhaps, only in Egyptian tomb decoration. For a comment on the quality of the painting, see Pollitt, *Art in the Hellenistic Age*, 188; unfortunately, the figures have badly deteriorated.

[53] The pioneering study was by S. G. Miller, "Hellenistic Macedonian Architecture." For the thesis of illusory design, see Miller, "Macedonian Tombs."

[54] The richest and most lavish of the painted tombs is the "Tomb of the Palmettes" at Lefkadia; some illustrations are in Rhomiopoulou, "A New Monumental Chamber Tomb." Unfortunately, this most exquisitely painted of all Macedonian tombs is still unpublished (beyond the early brief notice), now nearly two decades after its discovery. What is more tragic is that the poor environment of its preservation is contributing to a dramatic deterioration of this fine monument.

onto stucco in Macedonian tombs. Moreover, at the "Tomb of the Palmettes" at Lefkadia, the wide lower register below the painted vault of the antechamber is stucco, subtly painted to look like variegated marble, a technique that also can be seen on a stucco wall painted to look like expensive stone that is exhibited in the galleries of the archaeological museum at Pella. The Lefkadia tomb, with its highlighted Ionic facade, contains in the pediment nearly life-sized painted portraits of a man and a woman, presumably the deceased. As the surviving contents of this tomb, which was robbed in antiquity, have not been fully published, it is difficult to say more about its date and its burial(s).

So little is known about ancient Greek painting from this period that one is hard pressed to put the use of decorative painting in Macedonian tombs into context. But the use of paint should probably not be separated from the illusory architectural principles, also a form of decoration. Both are relatively inexpensive ways to create for the deceased a sufficiently impressive monument as an appropriate repository for considerable moveable wealth. For the tomb is more than just a secure container for human remains and grave goods. Were it merely that, the decorated facade would be unnecessary; security for bones and goods requires only a sturdy structure and burial, either by tunneling into a hillside or by placement beneath a tumulus. The decorated tomb—sometimes possessing a built entrance path, or *dromos*—should probably be seen as an abode for the deceased, as well as a statement of wealth displayed as part of an elaborate funeral ceremony.

We are still ignorant of the origin of this form of interment, as the chronological development of Macedonian tombs—both cist and chamber—is not yet clear. If one postulates that the cist tomb as a type preceded the chamber tomb—and continued to co-exist with it at a later time—there is evidence that very simple cist tombs, such as those at Derveni, already contained rich grave goods as early as the 340s or 330s B.C. But we do not know when the Macedonians began to build chamber tombs, and to what extent chamber tombs began to replace cist tombs. The rich quality of the goods in the cist tombs at Derveni suggests that the deceased were wealthy. But there is an insufficient number of cist tombs from the later fourth century to know whether or not chamber tombs replaced cist tombs entirely, or whether cist tombs continued to be used by those who could not afford chamber tombs.[55]

Some have suggested that the barrel-vaulted chamber tomb was in-

[55] See Appendix C below, p. 300.

troduced only with Alexander's Asian expedition, as there is no early history of the evolution of the barrel vault in Greek architecture, and the device arrives quite suddenly in Greece and Macedonia, after the Macedonians' exposure to the concept in Asia.[56] If it could be shown that Tomb 2 at Vergina contained the remains of Philip II, we would have a secure date (336 B.C.) for the existence of such a built tomb, but the verification of that tomb as Philip's is uncertain, as we have seen.

The arguments concerning a late (that is, post-Philip) date for the introduction of the built tomb have concentrated on the barrel vault[57] and have largely neglected the development or introduction of decorated illusory architectural facades. Asia Minor was replete with small tombs with architectural facades.[58] The use of rock-cut chamber tombs had been widespread in Asia for centuries, but in southern Anatolia they took an altered form with the addition of Greek—usually Ionic—architectural facades. The facades were often stuccoed and the architectural details painted. The dates of these tombs are much debated, for many of them were built or reused for later burials down into the period of the Roman Empire. The facades of Greek monuments were most likely combined with the customary rock-cut tombs when Greek culture was introduced into the region in the second quarter of the fourth century.

There are many such tombs in Caria and Lycia, in particular, both of which areas saw Alexander's passage. And we know that Alexander himself visited Pasargadae, near Persepolis, where he saw Cyrus's tomb, an isolated built chamber tomb.[59] It is thus possible that the transition in Macedonian burial practices from simple cist graves to built tombs with architectural facades might have resulted from ideas imported by those who accompanied Alexander.[60] The suggestion that

[56] Detailed arguments and bibliography in Borza, "Macedonian Royal Tombs at Vergina," 75–77.

[57] E.g., Tomlinson, "Vaulting Techniques," and Boyd, "The Arch and Vault." The work of both Tomlinson and Boyd was in press before the announcement of Andronikos's discoveries at Vergina, and is thus unconnected with the ensuing controversy over the identification of Tomb 2.

[58] For an overview of the evolution of Anatolian rock-cut tombs, see Kurtz and Boardman, *Greek Burial Customs*, 283–97, with illustrations. For details, see Roos, *The Rock-Cut Tombs of Caunus*, and *Survey of Rock-Cut Chamber Tombs in Caria*. The six groups of tombs at Caunus alone number 166 individual monuments.

[59] Curt. 5.6.10; Strabo 15.3.7; Arr. 3.18.10, 6.29.4–11. The tomb is illustrated, *inter alia*, in Ghirshman, *Persia*, pl. 185, and Huot, *Persia*, vol. 1, pl. 68.

[60] This was first hinted at by Kurtz and Boardman (*Greek Burial Customs*, 288), who tentatively suggested that the Greek architectural facades of Anatolian rock-cut tombs may have "played some role in determining this feature in Macedonia." See Borza, "The

this development was an imported idea is supported by the absence of archaeological evidence in Macedonia and mainland Greece of the evolution of both the barrel vault and the architectural facade.[61] Both appear rather suddenly in the later fourth century, full blown. Many of the veterans who survived the Asian expedition and the following wars of succession had acquired considerable wealth, some of which was used for more ostentatious burial places. The rich grave goods that had long been a feature of Macedonian burials were now enhanced by a monument that imitated elements of both Greek and Asian architecture, and which was adapted, as was the Macedonian manner in some of the minor arts, for local tastes and uses. If this hypothesis has merit, it provides yet another example of the Macedonians borrowing and adapting from foreign cultures to suit their own needs.

The plains and hills of Macedonia provide an exciting prospect for excavation. The discoveries of the past decade or so seem to offer a tantalizing vision of the future, but they also raise questions unknown to earlier generations of scholars. For example, although we have learned much about Macedonian burials, especially those of the more wealthy segments of society, we continue to be puzzled about the placement of tombs. The normal practice in the Classical Greek world was to bury the dead outside the city walls, everything within the town precinct being considered sacred to the local deities. That is, the ancients seem to have made a clear distinction between the city of the living and the city of the dead. Thus, it is common to find cemeteries grouped outside the walls of Greek towns; indeed, in some Mediterranean communities, the distribution of such burial grounds assists in tracing the growth of urban settlement boundaries over a long period of time.

But Macedonia presents a somewhat more complex situation. Although the northern boundary walls of Aegae, for example, have not been precisely determined, there is little doubt that the royal cemetery lay outside—in the familiar manner. Yet the great "Romaios" tomb—a fine, chambered, vaulted tomb of the late fourth or early third century—lies rather close to a number of public monuments already excavated: the shrine of Eucleia, the theatre, and the small administrative structure, which buildings may help define the public area, or agora,

Royal Macedonian Tombs and Paraphernalia," 108–9, for the use of this interpretation to help date Tomb 2 at Vergina.

[61] Rock-cut tombs also exist in Macedonia, notably at Veria and Siderokastro, but the former are securely dated to the late third and early second centuries, and the latter—probably an analogy with the former—should be dated to the same period. See Drougou and Touratsoglou, *Hellinistiki Laksefti*, 187–90.

of that city. It is not unusual for a tomb to be discovered within the sacred precinct of a town, but normally it is an early tomb that had been constructed outside the walls when the community was smaller, and later, when the town expanded, became incorporated within the walls. This is not the case at Aegae, where both the tomb and nearby monuments belong, roughly speaking, to the same period.

Four major tombs have been recovered around Lefkadia among the fruit orchards below Naousa. Two—those excavated by Petsas and Rhomiopoulou—are within two hundred meters of one another. "Kinch's" tomb lies further distant, as does the Tomb of Lyson and Kallikles.[62] The tombs do not seem to be part of a group, and they cannot be associated with the necropolis of a town. As far as we know, there was no town nearby. Mieza, where Aristotle tutored Alexander, was more than a mile away on the slope leading to modern Naousa, but it is problematic whether or not Mieza was a proper town. The probability is that these were estate burials, that is, interments on estates and/or in proximity to local sanctuaries.

Moreover, a number of individual chamber tombs of the late fourth and third centuries have been recovered along the main roads leading out of Therme/Thessaloniki. Isolated tombs have also been recovered, among many places, at Kerdylion, near the crossing of the Strymon, near Pydna, and along the banks of the Haliacmon on the road between Veria and Vergina. Groups of tombs are found both at Palatitsia and at Derveni—which sites have no known ancient town equivalents—but also in association with Greek cities at Pydna, Amphipolis, and Olynthus. The eclecticism of fourth-century and early Hellenistic Macedonian burial practices and tomb placement is more reminiscent of Roman practices in Latium in the middle and late Republic than of anything in the contemporary Greek world. Thus both the placement and the large size of many Macedonian tombs are at odds with Greek burials, which tend to be modest and clustered in cemeteries.

This diversity of expression in fourth-century and early Hellenistic material culture precludes our establishing any single convention by which to measure future discoveries. It is clear that in many respects Macedonians in the age of Philip and Alexander (and shortly after) were not bound by the canons of Greek practices. Indeed, one of the pleasures of studying the materials of this period is the impression of Macedonian openness in exploiting a variety of influences. The predominant influence is, of course, Greek, especially Athenian. But one

---

[62] For bibliography and descriptions for these and other tombs, see Gossel, *Makedonische Kammergräber*, and S. G. Miller, "Macedonian Tombs."

276CHAPTER 11

sees the mark of the Thracians and the Asians as well. Macedonian material culture, like Macedonian political and military institutions, appears to be an amalgam of the diverse historical experience of a people who developed self-sufficiency at a geopolitical crossroads.

The foregoing reconstructions must remain tentative as we await further excavation and the publication of materials already recovered. For example, the analysis of the amphora stamps at Macedonian sites like Pella will provide information about trade. New inscriptions will certainly yield data about internal economic and political organization from at least the fourth century on, and may reveal more about contacts with the Greek world. Perhaps the most promising prospect lies in the new excavations of Greek settlements in Chalcidice, on the frontier of the kingdom of the Macedonians. Continuing archaeological investigation of Pella, Aegae, and Dion will enable us to understand better how Macedonians in the Argead kingdom developed towns that were indigenous, as opposed to those taken over from the Greeks. More graves of common Macedonians need recovery to illuminate an area of Macedonian life still largely unknown. Field surveys in the corridors and passes of western Macedonia, only now commencing, will provide the first pieces of information about local culture and the gradual incorporation of those regions into the greater Macedonian kingdom.

And, with the continuing recovery of new materials from Macedonian tombs (there may be hundreds yet undiscovered in the countryside), we can continue to describe the development of native and borrowed tastes. Ultimately, we will come to appreciate Macedonia as a region that assimilated foreign influences, and Macedonians as a people some of whose material culture provided inspiration to their contemporary Greek neighbors and, eventually, their Roman conquerors.

The Emergence of Macedon

If MACEDONIAN relations with the Greek world have commanded our attention, it is because the surviving literary evidence is derived almost entirely from Hellenic sources. Indeed, it is one of the restrictions of writing about early Macedonian history that we are dependent upon what Greek authors and politicians knew about the vast area lying to the north, and especially how that region impinged upon their own historical experience. We know very little about Macedon's Balkan neighbors, in particular the Thracians and Illyrians, beyond their occasional contacts with the Greek world and conflicts with the Macedonians. Moreover, the Macedonians made their mark on history through the Greeks—first by hellenizing their own royal house, then by conquering and organizing the Greek city-states, and finally by providing the vehicle for the spread of some aspects of Greek civilization into large parts of western Asia. Thus Macedon emerged from the half-light of Balkan prehistory into a world dominated and defined by the activities and perceptions of Greek states.

As far as the ancient Greeks were concerned, the Macedonians were not Greeks. Some Greeks apparently accepted the Macedonian tradition that the Argead family had Hellenic antecedents in Argos, but the overwhelming evidence is that the Macedonians as a people were considered non-Greek. I have tried to show that the evidence for the Hellenic origins of the Argeadae goes back to a single fifth-century source: Alexander I's propaganda as related by Herodotus. It is more likely that the royal house was indigenous, risen from some early tribal leadership through a natural evolutionary process.

Once the myth of Argive origins for the royal house is recognized for what it was, we can concentrate on the Macedonians themselves. Here we have seen that their early history is still largely an open question. They may have had Greek origins: whatever process produced the Greek-speakers (if that is how one defines "Greek") who lived south of Olympus may have also produced the Makedones who wandered out of the western mountains to establish a home and a kingdom in Pieria. Unfortunately, there is insufficient linguistic and archaeological evidence to corroborate this view.

Perhaps the greatest single desideratum of evidence is fifth-century Macedonian archaeology. The internal development of the Macedonians, at least as far as their political and social institutions were concerned, was considerably different from that of the Greeks, who evolved the city-state. The relatively richer archaeological evidence for the last half of the fourth century shows a royal and baronial material culture heavily indebted to the Greeks, with Asian and Thracian influences. But these monuments and grave goods derive largely from a later period, in which connections with Greece were emphasized. Thus we have in the later fourth century a political and social system that is little like anything in contemporary Greece, but is adorned with the outward manifestations of Greek culture.

The fifth century B.C. was a period that saw the emergence of important Macedonian connections with the Greeks. This era is the key to understanding how deeply Greek culture permeated Macedon—to the extent that archaeology permits an answer to such a problem. Our literary sources provide little insight, but the grave goods and public monuments of the Macedonians, if available, could offer some understanding of the indigenous culture before the advent of formal hellenization. The excavations in nearby Greek Chalcidic cities or Greek colonies in Thrace and Pieria might provide the controls by which to evaluate the native culture. The major excavations at Sindos in the lower Axios basin reveal a culture that is—its imported Greek objects aside—in many respects alien to the Greek world. But, as we have seen, it is still not clear whether this site is Macedonian or belongs to some other local Balkan people. Until there is considerably more excavation from this crucial period, and until the results are disseminated among scholars, the matter of the ethnic character of the Macedonians will remain an open question.

Given the paucity of evidence, one cannot measure the impact of Greece on Macedon until the time of Alexander I. Alexander's reign marks the earliest known attempt to connect the two cultures, manifested by the introduction of a tradition that the Argeadae were a Greek family from Argos, descended from Heracles. We have seen that this story emerges as part of Alexander's prohellenic policy, and there is little doubt that it was part of his effort to establish himself—and his kingdom—as a power in a world increasingly dominated by the activities of Greek city-states. We are, unfortunately, denied a look at the crucial last part of Alexander I's rule, as well as the early reign of Perdiccas II. The mid-fifth century B.C. is virtually lost to us, falling as it does in the gap between the end of Herodotus's account and the start of Thucydides' interest in Macedon as a participant in the events of the Peloponnesian War. When Perdiccas eventually appears on the scene, he does so as a manipulative character, possessing a relatively weak military force, very long borders, and the need to protect the integrity of his kingdom against attacks from without and within. The perfidy that appears to mark his rule was Perdiccas's attempt to survive.

Archelaus's ostensible and superficial adoption of Greek culture was, as Hammond has pointed out, his means of entry into the Greek world. By Archelaus's time the Macedonian royal family seems to have irrevocably joined the Greek sphere. The Argead goal was not to become Greek, but to bend Hellenism to pragmatic Macedonian interests. In foreign relations, Archelaus and his successors adopted a policy that treated the Greeks—in hostility, neutrality, or friendship—as a concern more primary than Balkan interests. But this foreign policy was mutable, as evidenced by the continuing struggle against Illyrian incursions and Philip II's view of Greece as a stepping-stone to Asia. On the cultural level, Macedonian interests with Greece were more firmly forged. For example, an examination of mid-fourth-century graves reveals that—whatever Balkan influences still existed, especially in some kinds of metalware—Greek objects set the standards for taste. That is, along with the political links established by the Argeadae, there developed a concurrent desire for Greek goods among the Macedonian gentry.

The Macedonian monarchy that had emerged by the mid-fourth century was marked by two distinct characteristics. One of these is philhellenism or panhellenism. This was perhaps the natural outgrowth of the cultural and political pattern that had evolved from the time of Archelaus, if not earlier. There is no evidence suggesting that Macedonians wanted to be Greek. Rather, there was an attempt by Macedonian kings to be recognized on a plane of equality with the Greeks, in order that matters of state, war, and peace might be dealt with on the basis of mutual advantage. The prohellenic policy might have been the means used by the Argeadae to press their advantage in a precarious world in which the ambitions of Greek city-states were an important continuing threat.

Yet in outlook, sympathy, and practice Macedon was a Balkan monarchy (befitting its genesis) increasingly influenced by the absolutism of the East. In this respect it was dissimilar to the institutions of the Greek world. The view that Macedon's political life became more constitutional rests on shaky ground. The period about which we have most information is the era of Philip and Alexander, and in the case of both kings there is an increase in at least the superficial characteristics of an orientalized monarchy. Moreover, archaeology has revealed a splendor that begs the descriptive vocabulary of Asian studies. Thus the later fourth century reveals a monarchy *sui generis*, with many of the cultural appurtenances of Classical Greece laid over a core partly Balkan and newly Eastern.

Yet one of the curious aspects of this multicultural phenomenon was its lack of ideological and sentimental attachment to a New Order. Macedonians—and here we mean more than just the Argeadae—assimilated foreign practices, tastes, and personnel for pragmatic ends, without foresaking their traditional Macedonian identity. Alexander's imperial administration is a case in point. In the early part of his reign he reinforced Philip's panhellenic policies, maintained the settlements his father had imposed on Greece, and incorporated into his army contingents of Greek troops. As the expedition wound its way to India and back, Asian (mainly Persian) administrators were added to the train. But by the time of his death, virtually all Greek soldiers except for mercenaries had been sent home, and Asians were gradually replaced with Macedonians in vital military and administrative posts. Ethnic Greeks never held more than a handful of important posts, and for the most part their acknowledged skills in a number of administrative, athletic, and artistic endeavors were exploited by Alexander in about the same manner as they had been by Darius and Xerxes. Under the most absolute monarchy in their history, the Macedonians in Asia turned out to be terribly ethnocentric, without even the tolerance exhibited by their Persian predecessors. The train of Alexander is replete with examples of prejudice and tension between Macedonians and both Greeks and Persians, undoubtedly a response to an alien environment. In the period of political instability immediately following Alexander's death, one of the Conqueror's most capable administrators, the Greek Eumenes, was denied an opportunity to compete for the throne, not because he was unrelated to the Argeadae, but because he was not Macedonian.

Yet we have seen that the Macedonians were perfectly capable of both borrowing from and modifying foreign influences in order to suit their own needs. The use of Hellenism and Orientalism by Philip may have been designed to accomplish a specific end: to rule both Greeks and Asians while retaining the traditional hold on the Macedonians themselves. If so, some of what Alexander attempted no longer appears so innovative. But in the end Alexander may have lost the support of the Macedonians who were the core of his army, both because he had used up so many of them in his dream of conquest and because they were not as willing to adopt foreign traits—whether Hellenic or Oriental—as were their kings. However one wishes to describe the elusive character of the Macedonians, it constantly asserted itself before their most famous king, and in the post-Argead period there was a return to more traditional ways.

The Macedonians emerged from a Balkan milieu that had long witnessed competition among a number of non-Hellenic peoples: Thracians, Paeonians, Illyrians, and others. The Macedonian rise to a position of pre-eminence among these folk is due to a complex series of factors. Clearly the Macedonians' prolonged exposure to the Greeks who lived along the northern littoral of the Aegean enabled them to absorb some of the higher culture of the Hellenes. Moreover, Macedon was blessed with abundant natural resources and access to the sea that made it both economically self-sufficient and close to the lively activity of the Aegean world. But, as these factors were more or less constant, we must look elsewhere to explain the uneven quality of Macedonian fortunes, and the variable factor—in addition to some external events over which the Macedonians had little control—was the fluctuating abilities of the Argead kings. Unlike Rome, which was able to survive the vicissitudes of a turbulent monarchy because of the stability of its imperial administrative institutions, Macedon's fortunes seemed to rest heavily upon the abilities of its kings to survive internal upset and promote the national will.

Thus it is to the highly personal monarchy that one returns in an assessment of Macedonian history. It is not that we are compelled to adopt a preoccupation with Macedonian kings only because there is rather little evidence about other aspects of Macedonian life. It is that the ancients themselves—or at least those whose information and opinions about the Macedonians have survived—apparently recognized that any expression of Macedonian policy was a reflection of the activities and personalities of kings. The absence of evidence about institutions is not just another case of the loss of knowledge about antiquity; it probably reflects the reality of Macedonian life, suggesting that a reason for the dearth of references to Macedonian institutions is that they were not very highly developed.

The emergence of the kingdom of the Macedonians from the obscurity of Balkan tribal life made a telling impression upon foreigners, from the earliest Persian kings and Greek politicians who discovered the importance of those northern regions to the Roman senators who, correctly or not, perceived Macedon to be a threat, and thereby ended Macedonian independence.

I once wondered whether Macedon was Europe's earliest national

282

CHAPTER 12

state. That the Macedonians were an ethnic group derived from their predecessors, the Makedones, and defined in historical times by their service to the king, has been demonstrated by Hammond and others. In this sense they were a people, or *ethnos*, with a common set of loyalties and a shared historical experience. And, although their customs still remain largely elusive to us, one must posit that some set of generally accepted *mores* bound them together, as the alternative could only be a totalitarian monarchy guiding a repressive administration, and there is no evidence for that. Perhaps it was the very simplicity of the Macedonian kingship that enabled the Argeadae to maintain such continuity of monarchical rule for so many centuries. But there is little evidence that other institutions grew in prestige and authority sufficient to cause a growth in the moral authority of an impersonal state. The apparent lack of complex institutional arrangements suggests strongly that, while the Macedonians were a nation, their continuing dependence upon a simple and personal monarchy prevented them from achieving statehood.

The Macedonian nation served as a buffer to protect the Greeks from the inroads of non-Hellenic Balkan peoples—an important factor contributing to the growth of Greek civilization. Macedon's very existence as a formidable Balkan power made a deep impression on the course of Roman history in the third and second centuries B.C. The conquests of Macedon's most famous kings altered the history of Greece and the eastern Mediterranean-western Asian world in a most profound manner. And innovations in the conduct of warfare made by Philip and Alexander were lessons not lost on those who followed, although it can be plausibly argued that some of the military reforms had already begun among the Greeks. Of course Macedonian kings after Alexander were agents for the spread of general Greek culture and institutions throughout the eastern Mediterranean, while also maintaining monarchical rule in those areas in which they were dominant. But aside from a few innovations in painting, metalware, and architecture, the Macedonians left little in the way of a unique cultural imprint on the world. Perhaps this was to be expected from a people whose outstanding personalities were warrior-chiefs, whose indigenous institutions remained simple in Macedonia itself, and whose society, when galvanized by a forceful monarch, spoke most effectively with its spears.

Some Bibliographical Notes

$$T$$HERE follows an attempt to alleviate the burden of footnotes already cumbersome. I have endeavored, wherever possible, to provide bibliography in the footnotes as a means of conveniently directing the reader to the literature on the topic at hand. But it has also seemed appropriate to collect in one place a basic bibliography on subjects that are not covered in detail in the narrative, which the reader might find useful for continuing reference to matters outside the scope of the present work. The works listed below are also included as full citations in the general bibliography at the end of the volume.

Prehistoric Macedonia

The primary reports concerning this still imperfectly known period lie in the technical journals. The section on Macedonian prehistory in this volume owes much to the following works: Wardle, "The Northern Frontier of Mycenaean Greece"; Hammond, *HM*, vol. 1, chs. 7–17, in which appropriate debt is acknowledged to Heurtley's pioneering work in *Prehistoric Macedonia*; Rodden, "Excavations at Nea Nikomedeia"; Caskey, "Greece, Crete and the Aegean Islands," esp. 771–75; Crossland, "Immigrants from the North," esp. 845–50; Caskey, "Greece and the Aegean Islands," esp. 135–40; Hammond, "The End of Mycenaean Civilization and the Dark Age," esp. 681–89 and 702–12; Chadwick, "The Prehistory of the Greek Language"; Hammond, *Migrations*, chs. 4–6; and Desborough, *The Last Mycenaeans and Their Successors*. Anyone interested in this early period would do well to remember Geyer's comment, made nearly half a century ago, that the "time for a Macedonian prehistory has not yet come" (*Makedonien*, 19).

Archaeological Reports

The continuing progress of archaeology in Macedonia (and other regions of Greece) can be followed through the annual *Archaeological*

Reports published jointly by the Society for the Promotion of Hellenic Studies and the British School at Athens, the "Chronique des fouilles et decouvertes archéologiques en Grèce," in *BCH*, the *Ergon* of the Archaeological Society of Athens, and the *Chronika* of *Archaiologikon Deltion*. There is also a useful review of post-World War II Macedonian studies by Petsas, "Chronika Archaiologika 1966–67." An important annual review of Macedonian archaeology has just commenced publication, too late for its material to be included in the present book. The first volume has appeared as *To Archaiologiko Ergo sti Makedonia kai Thraki* for 1987. Many of the most active excavators in Macedonia have contributed up-to-date reports on several of the sites mentioned in the present book. The volume is a joint undertaking of the Ministry of Macedonia and Thrace, the Ministry of Culture, and the Aristotelean University of Thessaloniki.

International Scholarly Cooperation

Frequent colloquia such as the Greek international symposia on ancient Macedonia (proceedings published as *Archaia Makedonia*) and the Bulgarian congress "Terra Antiqua Balcanica" attempt to ease scholarly isolation. But old habits persist: the recent Greek publication of the inscriptions of western Macedonia (Rizakis and Touratsoglou, *Epigraphes Anō Makedonias*; see below) has collected the epigraphical materials from the ancient western Macedonian cantons, including "southern" Lyncus. "Northern" Lyncus lies within Yugoslavia, and it is unfortunate that the inscriptions from the important ancient region of Lyncus should be divided by an arbitrary modern political boundary, and only those discovered south of the Yugoslav-Greek frontier be published in this volume.

Hellenistic Kings

For further information on the Hellenistic kings, see especially Fortina, *Cassandro, re di Macedonia*; Manni, *Demetrio Poliorcete*; Mueller, *Antigonus Monophthalmus*; Wehrli, *Antigone et Démétrios*; Tarn, *Antigonus Gonatas*; Walbank, *Philip V of Macedon*; and Briant, *Antigone le Borgne*, in which is found a very useful bibliography of materials on the Hellenistic period. The most recent materials can be found in the relevant chapters in Edouard Will, *Histoire politique du monde hellénistique*, and *CAH*, 2nd ed., vol. 7, pt. 1 (1984), and, on the Antigonids, the chapters by Walbank and Hammond in *HM*, vol. 3.

Special Topics

On institutional matters, including military and political topics, the following works are useful: F. Geyer, *Makedonien*; F. Hampl, *Der König der Makedonen*; (Weida 1934); Charles F. Edson, "Early Macedonia"; F. Granier, *Die makedonische Heeresversammlung*; Errington, "The Nature of the Macedonian State"; Aymard, "Sur l'assemblée macédonienne"; and Engels, *Alexander the Great and the Logistics of the Macedonian Army*.

Inscriptions

The first volume of Macedonian inscriptions in the series *Inscriptiones Graecae* was edited by Charles F. Edson (*IG*, vol. 10. pt. 2, fasc. 1), and includes only the region around Salonica, with no materials earlier than the early third century B.C. Now the premiere volume of a new series has recently appeared: Rizakis and Touratsoglou, eds., *Epigraphes Anō Makedonias*. In addition, individual collections arranged by site are occasionally published as adjuncts to excavation reports.

Literary Sources

In general, we are deficient in ancient literary sources on the Macedonians. For those which exist, the following commentaries are indispensable: F. W. Walbank, *A Historical Commentary on Polybius* (indispensable for the career of Philip V); Hammond, Griffith, and Walbank in *HM*, vols. 1–3 (where the sources are carefully presented and analyzed for all periods); and the commentaries on Herodotus (How and Wells, *A Commentary on Herodotus*), Thucydides (Gomme et al., *Comm. Thuc.*), Plutarch's *Alexander* (Hamilton, *Plutarch. Alexander: A Commentary*), and Arrian (Bosworth, *Historical Commentary on Arrian*).

Coins

The original classification and description of Thraco-Macedonian and Macedonian coins was done in 1919 by the then-director of the Numismatic Museum at Athens, J. N. Svoronos (*L'hellénisme primitif*). Although marked by considerable contemporary political propaganda, and although some of Svoronos's attributions are no longer accepted, the work remains fundamental for the study of the tribes. Of more use is Doris Raymond's *Macedonian Regal Coinage*. Raymond is especially effective in tracing several tribal and civic motifs through the coinages from the preregnal period into the early kingdom, thereby showing the coinage links between the fifth-century Macedonian kings and their predecessors. The work covers issues only through the reign of Perdiccas II, since the coins of Archelaus and the fourth-century kings down to Philip II had not been much studied.

Martin Price's *Coins of the Macedonians*, a British Museum handbook, provides an excellent brief treatment of the major types, and is marked by sound historical insights. Like Raymond, Price traces common Macedonian themes through the tribal and early regnal periods. A new catalog of the Macedonian coins in the British Museum is eagerly awaited, to replace the out-of-date (though well-produced) *A Catalogue of the Greek Coins of the British Museum: Macedonia, etc.*, by B. V. Head and R. S. Poole. An important gap in the literature has recently been filled by Martin Price's *The Coinage in the Name of Alexander the Great and Philip Arrhidaeus*, British Museum (London 1991). Among the well-presented major collections of Macedonian coins is that of the Ashmolean Museum, Oxford, published in *Sylloge Nummorum Graecorum*, vol. 5, pt. 3, supervised by Colin Kraay. Kraay's excellent *Archaic and Classical Greek Coins*, 131–47, has a useful summary of Macedonian coins.

Two other older standard works are: Head, *Historia numorum*, with a section on Macedon (192–244, with an instructive classification scheme and useful summary of coin types); and Gaebler, *Die antiken Münzen Nord-Griechenlands*, vol. 3 and pt. 2, *Makedonia und Paionia*.

The coinage of Philip II (life issues and posthumous) are treated by Le Rider, *Le monnayage d'argent et d'or*, with the cautionary review-article by Martin Price, "The Coinage of Philip II," *The Numismatic Chronicle* 139 (1979), 230–41. As might be expected from their series and sheer number, the coins of Alexander the Great offer innumerable problems. No one has yet undertaken the formidable task of a comprehensive study. The main problems are thoughtfully presented by Bellinger, *Essays on the Coinage of Alexander the Great*, with good bibliography. The complexity of the Alexander-issues are illustrated by the debate published in *The Numismatic Chronicle* 142 (1982), "The Earliest Coins of Alexander the Great," between Orestes Zervos, "1. Notes on a Book by Gerhard Kleiner" (pp. 166–79), and M. J. Price, "2. Alexander's Reform of Macedonian Regal Coinage" (pp. 180–90).

Some Topographical Notes

The Orestian-Tymphaean Border

Hammond wrote (*HM* 1: 110): "The limit of Orestis downstream is set by the march of Alexander when he passed from Eordaea to Elimiotis through the pass of Siatista [Arr. *Anab.* 1.7.5]. The probable boundary *just north of the exit of this pass is set by the watershed between the Pramoritsa River and Grevenitikos River*" (my italics). But the watershed between these two tributaries of the Haliacmon is west-southwest of the Siatista Pass exit, not north as Hammond suggests. The watershed is in fact an east-west ridge some 500–1000 ft. above the level of the river plain, 4–5 miles north and northwest of Grevena. After Alexander's exit from the Siatista Pass he turned directly *south* into Elimiotis (Elimeia). Had he gone directly west (the implication of Hammond's view), he would have been in Orestis (*contra* Arrian). After proceeding south for a while, Alexander turned west toward the site of Grevena, but by this time he was below Orestis and thus had crossed over into Tymphaea.

The Location of Aegae

Hammond's thesis that the site of Aegae is near the modern villages of Vergina and Palatitsia was introduced in 1968 in a paper presented to the First International Symposium on Ancient Macedonia, published as "The Archaeological Background to the Macedonian Kingdom" (see esp. 65–67), and more fully in *HM* 1: 156–58. There were two steps in Hammond's argument. The first showed from ancient literary and epigraphical sources that Aegae and Edessa (previously thought to be the site of Aegae) were in fact two different places. Additional support came from Huxley, "Baanes the Notary on 'Old Edessa,' " 253–55. Second, Hammond put Aegae near Vergina on the basis of literary evidence relating specific characteristics: on the slopes of Olympus-Pieria, facing the plain, steep country behind, closer to Thessaly than is Edessa, and the object of a mercenaries' strike in 359 B.C. that had to occur no further than one day from a base at Methone (see Griffith in *HM* 2: 211–12).

Archaeological confirmation was provided by Manolis Andronikos's discoveries, beginning in 1977, of fourth-century B.C. royal tombs, a theatre, walls, and an acropolis at Vergina. In the same area are the extensive Hellenistic remains explored in the nineteenth century by Léon Heuzey; all are monuments well suited to Aegae.

Mieza and "Borboros"

According to Plutarch (*De exil.* 603C), Theocritus of Chios chided Aristotle for preferring to live in the "outflow of mud [or slime]" (*borborou en prochoais*) rather than in the Academy. Plutarch explains this outflow by saying that there was a river "Borboros" near Pella. No such river is otherwise known, but Hammond (*HM* 1: 148) suggests that this was a muddy branch of the Axios that in those days emptied into Lake Loudias below Pella. I offer here a different interpretation: Aristotle is usually associated with Mieza, not Pella. Might this not be a reference to the streams flowing around Naousa? The text is corrupt, and the reading *Pella* is uncertain. Moreover, perhaps it is a pun—*borboros* for *barbaros*—which Plutarch missed. Thus Theocritus's play on words becomes clear: an outflowing stream (the otherwise unknown Borboros) near Mieza, and the image of the great thinker choosing to live in the outflow of barbarians.

The Sea Level in Antiquity

Hammond's view that the sea level has risen several feet since ancient times is based on opinions of local Greek seamen, changes in *North Sea* levels, and the existence of a half-dozen archaeological sites off the western coast of Greece that are consistently 5–6 feet below the surface. Nowhere does he accept that such submergence is often the result of local land subsidence, a frequent phenomenon in a region as geologically active as the Mediterranean.

Moreover, it is virtually impossible to find an ancient stable geological formation to serve as a reference point against which to measure eustatic (general) sea-level variations. The remains of classical shipsheds at Cape Sounion and in Piraeus suggest a virtually unchanged sea level, as do the underlying assumptions of Hammond's own study of the battle of Marathon ("The Campaign and Battle of Marathon"). And the remains of the canal dug by Xerxes across the narrow neck of the Athos peninsula are now several feet *above* the present level of the sea. There is a considerable scientific literature on this problem (none of it cited by Hammond), which points to a general sea-level rise of only about 30 cm in historical times, all other relative differences between land and sea being due to local phenomena.

See Shackleton et al., "Coastal Paleogeography"; Scarre, "Archaeology and Sea-Level"; and Kraft et al., "Geological Studies of Coastal Change." For a more detailed analysis of the evidence, with earlier relevant scientific literature cited, see Borza, "Some Observations on Malaria," 110–11.

Lake Loudias through the Centuries

A 1:75,000 Greek army map of the 1920s (just prior to the draining) shows Lake Loudias only 4–5 miles north of the Haliacmon, with a length measuring over 15 miles—half the length of the plain. Leake (*Travels in Northern Greece*, 3: 436) described Lake Loudias in 1806 as occupying the greater part of the plain. The British GSGS 1:250,000 map shows the lake and its marshes as taking up about a third of the plain, yet, as Hammond pointed out (*HM* 1: 144), a traveller in 1869 saw mainly swamp from a vantage at Yiannitsa. Several nineteenth- and early twentieth-century guidebooks show a variety of lake sizes. Whereas the drained lake bed is now one of the richest agricultural areas of Greece (with abundant orchards and tobacco and cotton fields), the last few miles of the plain, where the Haliacmon, Loudias, and Axios nearly join to empty into the gulf, are still mainly marshland. At some places within a few hundred yards of the vehicular traffic rushing along the National Highway, there are untracked swamps. In general, the plain has been desolate throughout historical times; see Borza, "Natural Resources," 3–7.

Darius's Route into Macedonia

Hammond (*HM* 2: 58) claims that there is "no doubt about the route" used by the Persians into Macedonia *ca.* 510, based in part on his placement of Lake Prasias in the northern part of the Strymon basin. Herodotus (5.17) says that the way from Lake Prasias into Macedonia is a "short route." The short route from the lower Strymon is through the corridor formed by Lakes Koroneia and Volvi. This is the "short inland" route mentioned by Herodotus (9.89) in his description of the hurried Persian withdrawal from Greece after Plataea, as confirmed by Aeschylus (*Persae* 494). The short route from the upper Strymon is the corridor that runs under Mt. Kerkini to the headwaters of the Echedorus (modern Gallikos) river. Unlike Hammond, I find it impossible to place Lake Prasias with certainty (Borza, "Some Toponym Problems," 60–61). And Herodotus's accounts of Persian movements from the Strymon into Macedonia are fraught with difficulties; e.g., Hdt. 7.124, which makes no geographical sense. Whatever the truth of the matter, Hammond's view of the swampiness of the Lake Corridor militating against the use of such a route by a small party is vitiated by the fact that this was the very route used by the Persian army during its withdrawal from Greece several years later.

Xerxes' Route around Tempe

Much has been made of Herodotus's references (7.128 and 173) to Gonnus as a place of exit behind Tempe. The goat paths around Gonnus along the gorge of Tempe are impossible for a huge army to traverse, and the fact that Xerxes' army spent some time constructing a road militates against a Thermopylae-style circumvention.

Pritchett, "Xerxes' Route over Mount Olympos," offers a plausible alternative to the Petra Pass. There is a modern route that leaves the southern part of the Pierian coastal plain at Leptokaria (near ancient Heracleion) and ascends the Ziliana Gorge between Olympus and Lower (Kato) Olympus. About 15 miles inland, a track cuts south through the upland basin of the drained Lake Nezero and along the western flank of Lower Olympus before descending easily to modern Gonni, thereby bypassing Tempe. This route is without major obstacles and may have been used by a Roman army in 191 B.C. (Livy 36.10.11). It was the scene of a World War II campaign involving heavy German motorized vehicles. Like the Petra Pass route, it has the advantage of being supported by Herodotus's comment (7.131) that Xerxes waited in Pieria for several days while the army's route was being prepared.

Pritchett's route is easier topographically, but the Petra route fits Herodotus somewhat better. It is likely that Gonnus was the nearest landmark for Herodotus as he described the route through the Petra circling Olympus and entering the Thessalian plain about ten miles to the west of modern Gonni: the language of 7.128 (*Perraibous para Gonnon polin*) and 7.173 (*kata Gonnon polin*) can mean "beyond" and "nearby" Gonnus. Moreover, the Petra Pass was known as a military route; e.g., it may have been used by Brasidas in 424 when he entered Macedonia from Perrhaebia to Dion (Thuc. 4.78.6), and its importance was recognized in the Roman campaign against King Perseus in 169 B.C. (Livy 44.6.5–17, where there is a succinct and knowledgeable description of the passes, including Tempe, that lead from Thessaly into Macedonia).

A route from central Macedonia into Thessaly via the Haliacmon Gorge and the Volustana Pass is unsuitable (see Hammond, *HM* 2: 100 n. 2), as the Haliacmon Gorge is impassable. For a review of the scholarship on Xerxes' bypass of Tempe, see N. Robertson, "The Thessalian Expedition of 480 B.C.," 111–16; and Pritchett, "Xerxes' Route over Mount Olympos."

Some Diverse Endnotes

Hesiod Cat. Gyn., *frag. 4*

The obscure *Aiolos hippiocharmēs* in Hesiod, *Cat. Gyn.*, frag. 4, was rendered by Hammond (*HM* 1: 272) as "Aeolus who fought from a chariot." Cf. Hesiod *Cat. Gyn.*, frag. 3 (Loeb edition), where *hippi-ocharmēn* is also difficult to understand, but in my view does not refer to fighting from a chariot, but rather (as in frag. 4) to one who takes joy in horses. Whatever the realities of warfare in the Greek Bronze Age, it was the epic literary tradition to give heroes chariots (a vestigial memory of Heroic splendor) for transport to the scene of battle—a kind of primitive military taxi service—but not for platforms from which to fight. See Greenhalgh, *Early Greek Warfare*, chs. 1–3. The topography of Greece is generally not well suited for the mass chariot attacks used widely in the Near East. In any case, chariots were never part of the later military traditions of the Macedonians, insofar as we know. See also Liddell-Scott-Jones, *Greek-English Lexicon*, 9th ed., *s.v. charma* and *charmē*.

The Reliability of Strabo on Macedonia

I take exception to Hammond's interpretation (*HM* 1: 421) of Strabo 7, frag. 11. The failure of Strabo to mention the Makedones in his description of the Illyrian expansion into Emathia certainly refers to the period before *ca.* 650 B.C., but does not necessarily, as Hammond believes, restrict the settlement of the Makedones to the coastal areas of Macedonia. The absence of reference to the Makedones in the frag- ment might mean either that they had not yet made their way out of the western mountains into Emathia, or that Strabo (or his medieval epitomizer) got his information wrong. Indeed, the more one consults Strabo—especially the fragments—on Macedonian matters, the less confident one becomes about making finely drawn interpretations.

The fragments of Strabo's seventh book are quite uneven in value, and to cite Strabo for anything Macedonian is risky. For example, what are we to make of an author (or his source) who puts the western boundary of Macedonia at the coast of the Adriatic (frag. 10), places its southern boundary at the Via Egnatia (frag. 10), and has the mouth of the Haliacmon separating Dion from Pydna and Methone (frags. 20 and 22)? I accept Hammond's reconstruction of early Macedonian expansion (above, p. 87) on the grounds of general strategic and geographic probability rather than because of his use of Strabo as evidence.

The Persian Satrapy in Europe

The question of whether the Persians organized a satrapy in Europe has been a subject of considerable debate. Fundamental reading includes Balcer, "The Persian Occupation of Thrace" and "Persian Occupied Thrace"; and Castritius, "Die Okkupation Thrakiens." Hammond ("The Extent of Persian Occupation in Thrace") argues that the Persians established a large European satrapy in Thrace—called "Skudra"—including not only the Aegean coastal regions, but also the interior lands north of the Rhodopi Mountains. This view is not shared by Balcer ("Persian Occupied Thrace") and two writers in the second volume of the *Cambridge History of Iran* (1985): Cook ("Rise of the Achaemenids," 266–67) points out that there is no archaeological evidence of Persian occupation in the Thracian interior, and the freedom of movement of Greeks and Thracians alike in the coastal regions makes it uncertain whether even southern Thrace was occupied by the Persians until the eve of the invasion of Greece. For Burn ("Persia and the Greeks," 306), there was "no military occupation beyond the sea."

I am inclined toward the arguments of Balcer ("Persian Occupied Thrace") and Isaac, *Greek Settlements in Thrace*, 17–18, the latter of whom suggests that the main aim of the Persians in Thrace (presumably before Xerxes' invasion) was to control the coastal routes. This is supported by the Persian lack of interest in exploiting the mineral resources of the Strymon-Pangaion area, and in the generally pacific relationship among the various parties in the region. There was a Persian presence, to be sure, but, beyond some garrisons at strategic points, it was not heavy-handed, and the Greeks and Thracians in the region carried on pretty much as usual.

Aristeus's Expedition to Potidaea

Gomme (*Comm. Thuc.*, 1: 215) wondered how Aristeus's march could avoid Pydna, which was besieged by the Athenians, and Therme, now in the hands of Philip's faction. The lack of a satisfactory answer to this problem results from the wrong question having been asked. No land route is possible, not only because much of the Macedonian part of it was in enemy hands, but also because 40 days is insufficient time for: (here following Thuc. 1.60) news of the revolt of Potidaea to reach Corinth, troops from several parts of the Peloponnesus to be gathered and an army assembled, and a march made to Potidaea in Chalcidice. Common sense requires that this force arrived at Potidaea by ship, if we are to keep Thucydides' 40-day chronology. Although Thucydides fails to mentions ships at 1.60, they are mentioned at 1.65.1–2, where they are used by Aristeus to escape from besieged Potidaea. The problem disappears: Aristeus arrived at and departed from Chalcidice by ship.

The Athenian Movement from Pydna to Potidaea

From Pydna, Thucydides (1.61.4–5) has the Athenians march to Beroea (mod. Veria) and Strepsa (if one accepts a textual emendation; see Gomme's commentary on this passage) at the head of the Thermaic Gulf, which they attacked without success. Then they returned to their route, and moved by land to Potidaea, their ships coasting in accompaniment. Thucydides' text presents some insurmountable problems that no amount of emendation or ingenuity can resolve. First, if the object of the Athenians' departure was to move on Potidaea, why did they not simply board ship for the easy crossing(s) of the gulf to Chalcidice? If, however, their object was to attack some Macedonian center—thereby immediately breaking their recent alliance with Perdiccas—why attack Beroea? Why not Aegae, which they had to pass en route to Beroea? Or did Thucydides get it wrong, and was there really an unsuccessful attack on Aegae? But an attack on a Macedonian town lying in exactly the opposite direction of the goal of the Athenian expedition (Potidaea) seems unlikely, especially in light of the urgency that the Athenians seemed to have felt about Aristeus's arrival at Potidaea. Moreover, the first part of this Athenian odyssey may have been by ship, if we are to take seriously Thucydides' reference that, after the attack on Beroea (and Strepsa), they moved by land (*kata gēn*), in three slow marches to Gigonus in the northwest Chalcidice with 70 ships coasting in support. But Beroea was never accessible by ship, although Strepsa may have been. Now, this Emathian itinerary makes sense only if one believes that the Athenian strategy after leaving Pydna was to harrass central Macedonian towns. But that is *not* what Thucydides says. Potidaea was the cause of abandoning Pydna, and it was, in fact, to Potidaea that Perdiccas himself was headed with a force of cavalry.

In short, the passage defies reason, and is the product of Thucydides' confusion about events. For some ingenious attempts to resolve the difficulties (all with additional bibliography), see Gomme, *Comm. Thuc.*, 1: 215–18; Hammond, *HM* 2: 123; and Hatzopoulos, "Strepsa: A Reconsideration," 54–60, who reasonably suggests that part of the difficulty is resolved by the recognition of the fact that a road ran from Pydna to Beroea, before turning north and east to cross the northern part of the plain toward the Axios basin.

The date of IG I³.89

My date of about 423 B.C. for a Macedonian-Athenian alliance is opposed to that of Hammond (*HM* 2: 135), who argues that the internal situation in Macedonia in 423 was not suitable, partly because Perdiccas's power was "almost at its lowest ebb." This assumes, of course, that one seeks alliances only from a position of power and not from weakness, when in fact alliances can be sought by any party believing that it is to its advantage to do so. In reality, despite his failure to add Lyncus to his domain, Perdiccas was as secure as he had ever been, and, although a treaty with Athens would produce the loss of some Chalcidic and Peloponnesian allies, the Macedonian king would gain the support of Athens. The remainder of Hammond's argument favoring a date of *ca.* 415 rests on an analysis of the names in the list in *IG* I³.89—both those surviving and his own restorations—and, in my view, can support a date as early as 423/2 as well.

Macedon as Part of the Athenian Empire?

Hammond (*HM* 1: 133) has suggested that, in the period 423–417 B.C., Macedon was in fact part of the Athenian Empire. This suggestion is attractive, but not conclusive. Hammond sees Perdiccas as much weaker and more subject to Athens in this period than I do. Part of the difference of interpretation rests on my belief that Athenian-Macedonian relations in 423–417 were regulated and limited in part by the treaty of 423/2, which Hammond assigns to a later date (see above). As far as we know, Perdiccas supplied only oars to Athens (not "timber for naval construction," as Hammond suggests), Perdiccas provided no other military assistance, and the king could be satisfied with maintaining the arrangement until an external change in the general military/diplomatic situation caused him to rebel from it. One must

concede, however, that Hammond's argument that the failure of Perdiccas to issue coins in this period is compelling, although, as we have
seen earlier, any argument based on the statistics of numismatic sur-
vivals may be tenuous.

Excavations at Pella

I am deeply indebted to Maria Siganidou, the Ephor of Antiquities for
the Pella region and director of excavations at the site, and her associates, who, on several occasions, generously shared their knowledge of
the area and the results of their continuing work. Photios Petsas,
whose early excavations at Pella revealed much of the lower city, has
discussed at length with me both the history and difficulty of excavating the town, and has helped put the city into a historical context. My
own interpretations of the site are necessarily tentative, and are subject
to the amplification and correction of the excavation's formal publication. Recent developments in the excavation of Pella are summarized
in *AR* (1986–87): 39–40, (1987–88): 50–51. One should also note the
recent view of Hatzopoulos ("Strepsa: A Reconsideration," 41–44),
who has argued that the evidence favors the capital having been moved
to Pella not by Archelaus, but by Amyntas III—a suggestion that I find
attractive, but not entirely convincing.

The Supposed Kingship of Argaeus

Diod. 14.92.3–4, after recounting Amyntas's restoration to the throne
and giving the length of his reign as 24 years, adds that "some say"
that after Amyntas's expulsion, Argaeus ruled the Macedonians for
two years, after which Amyntas recovered his kingship. This is the
only reference to Argaeus. Islami (*Les Illyriens*, 57–58) makes Argaeus
a Lyncestian, set up on the throne by the Illyrians. Hammond (*HM* 2:
172) argues that Argaeus was a son of King Archelaus (no direct evidence; arguments inferential) and was installed by the Illyrians as a
puppet-king for part of the two-year period 393/2–392/1. This appears
to conflict with Hammond's view (*HM* 2: 175) that Amyntas was de-
posed from his kingship by the Macedonians, with Argaeus elected to
replace him. Even if we accept the dubious proposition that such "constitutional" procedures were operative among the Macedonians, one
wonders how and why such legal niceties would occur during the Illyrian occupation. Hammond's elaborate reconstruction without a
reconciliation of or explanation for the differences in the sources raises
more questions than the slim evidence will permit answers.

Ellis ("Amyntas III," 5–8) believes that Diodorus and Isocrates' chronology of events does not permit sufficient time for Argaeus's two-year reign during the aftermath of the Illyrian invasion of 393. By a process of elimination, Ellis offers the period 385–383 for Argaeus's reign, making him a puppet-king of the Olynthians; this agrees with Geyer's view (*Makedonien*, 116–18), but for different reasons. Ellis's argument is attractive because it coincides with the Olynthian occupation of much of central Macedonia, including Pella (Xen. *Hell.* 5.2.13).

Ellis asked the right question: "Did [Argaeus] reign, and, if so, when?" Unfortunately, without linking the two components, he attempted to answer the second part of the question without considering the first. Placing Argaeus in the 380s also violates the clear sequence of Diodorus, who connected Argaeus with Amyntas's loss of kingship during the Illyrian invasion of 393. Hammond's chronology is preferable, although it infers far more about the events of 393–391 than the evidence will permit.

Both Hammond and Ellis have challenged the older view that Diod. 14.92.3 and 15.19.2–3 form a doublet. Hammond's argument (*HM* 2: 174) that the doublet in Diodorus should be attacked on principle is unsatisfactory; there is a clear doublet where Diodorus's description of the Dead Sea at 19.48 is almost a verbatim repetition of what he had written at 2.48.6–9. See Simpson, "Abbreviation of Hieronymus," 376, on the matter of reduplication, with additional examples. The point is that Diodorus was sometimes not in control of his material, and each situation must be judged on its own merit. Both Hammond and Ellis ("Amyntas III," 2) see sufficient differences between the two passages to warrant considering them as accounts of separate events— two Illyrian invasions—but there are as many similarities (perhaps more) to warrant considering them a doublet: two versions of the same event. Neither rejection nor acceptance of the doublet is conclusive, but I am inclined toward acceptance.

Amyntas's Tomb at Vergina?

Hammond's view ("The Evidence for the Identity of the Royal Tombs at Vergina," 115–16) that the painted cist tomb (Tomb 1) in the great tumulus at Vergina (Aegae) was the burial place of Amyntas is guesswork. The scattering of bone fragments found on the floor of the tomb were of a large man, a young female, and an infant or fetus (evidence cited in Borza, "Macedonian Royal Tombs at Vergina," 81 and n. 54). Presumably the remains of the deceased, they cannot be connected with Amyntas. Moreover, both the architecture of the tomb and its splendid interior painting have been associated with a date well after Amyntas's death. (The painting has been connected with the school of the painter Nicomachus, who was active in the late 330s and early 320s; see Andronikos, *Vergina: The Royal Tombs*, 90–91, and Chapter 11 above.) Finally, Hammond's view ("The Evidence for the Identity of the Royal Tombs at Vergina," 120) that two of the miniature ivory heads found in Tomb 2 were portraits of Amyntas and Eurydice cannot be sustained. Dozens of such heads have been recovered from Macedonian tombs, and almost none are representational portraits. Even the excavator has backed away from his initial suggestion that the parents of Philip II are to be identified among the heads in Tomb 2. See Borza, "Macedonian Royal Tombs at Vergina," 79–81 (with bibliography), and Andronikos, *Vergina: The Royal Tombs*, 130–32. In brief, nothing yet found in the royal burials at Vergina can be connected with Amyntas and Eurydice.

Royal Succession and the Constitutional Order

Chaos reigned in 326/5, when Alexander lay seriously wounded from the siege of a Mallian city (Arr. 6.12.1–3). The army, fearing the king was dead, was in distress, wondering who would lead them home. The uncertainty of the troops in this situation hints not only at anxiety over the loss of a leader, but also at a lack of procedure to select his successor.

Note, however, the different view of Hatzopoulos ("Succession and Regency," 291), who argues that the succession was "not effective until it had been solemnly ratified by the Macedonian assembly." I do not find sufficient evidence to indicate that such a procedure existed, nor can I accept Hatzopoulos's view that a "moral contract" bound the Macedonian people with the Argeadae. Moreover, the quality of the instability both within Macedon and in the remnants of the empire in the period between Alexander's death and the settlements that shaped the future Hellenistic political order (323–297 B.C.) suggests an unsteady constitutional arrangement.

Macedonian Body Armor

For the scant literary and archaeological evidence on body armor, see Griffith, *HM* 2: 422–23, and Markle, "The Macedonian Sarissa, Spear and Related Armor," 326–29. Macedonian excavations have been notably deficient in yielding breastplates and shields, and it may be that only officers wore body armor. I have personally seen only one battle shield—an unpublished bronze example from the Hellenistic period—shown to me by a curator in a museum storeroom. Even allowing for the fact that large metal objects—which are so attractive to looters for the intrinsic value of the metal itself—tend not to survive, the unusual paucity of body armor from Macedonian tombs suggests a rather small incidence of use in antiquity.

The "Philip" Missiles from Olynthus

It is generally accepted that the bronze arrow points found at Olynthus inscribed *Philippo* are Macedonian (Robinson, *Excavations at Olynthus*, 10: 382–83, nos. 1907–11; also illustrated in *The Search for Alexander: An Exhibition*, no. 104 and color plate 16). But the numerous Macedonian sling bullets from Olynthus (Robinson, *Excavations at Olynthus*, 10: 418–43, nos. 2176–2380) that are inscribed with Philip's name (nos. 2228–40) bear *Philippou*, the normal genitive, meaning "of Philip" or "Philip's." Likewise other sling bullets bear the names of some of Philip's commanders, also in the genitive. One wonders if the Philip arrow points are in fact Olynthian, inscribed in a local dative form ("for Philip"). Yet it might be argued that *Philippo* is not a shortened genitive (*Philippo[u]*), but rather a shortened nominative (*Philippo[s]*), in the manner of some sling bullets found inscribed *aischro[n] doro[n]* ("an unpleasant gift"); for the latter see Robinson, "New Inscriptions from Olynthus and Environs," 56. The find spots of the Philip arrow points on the west slope of Olynthus's North Hill outside the walls, as well as inside an Olynthian house, may also be significant. There is much more to this problem, and I hope to consider it fully in the near future.

The Bones in Tomb 2 at Vergina

See my criticism of Musgrave et al., "The Skull from Tomb II," in Borza, "A Macedonian Skull." The initial anthropologists' report found no evidence of either injury or healing in the skull of the male buried in Tomb 2; see Xirotiris and Langenscheidt, "Cremation."

Andronikos has continued to believe (most recently in *Vergina: The Royal Tombs*, 186, 189, and 231) that a pair of mismatched gilded greaves from the antechamber point to the identity of the deceased warrior as Philip II, who suffered severe leg and thigh wounds. The *left* greave is considerably shorter and smaller in diameter. Yet I pointed out long ago ("Macedonian Royal Tombs at Vergina," 78–79) that not only are all Macedonian greaves for which I found measurements of unequal length—although the dimensions of this pair are unusually mismatched—but it is generally conceded that a severe thigh wound (Philip was pinned to his horse by a spear) in an adult male would not shorten the lower leg. Moreover, Green ("The Royal Tombs of Vergina," 135–36) showed on the basis of the ancient evidence that Philip's wounds were in the *right* leg. Unfortunately, the leg bones have not been subjected to the anthropological scrutiny that has characterized the skull bones. Beyond determining the age and sex of the deceased, the bones from the tomb are of little use in establishing their identities.

A Transitional Cist/Chamber Tomb?

An interesting—and puzzling—tomb that might shed light on the matter of tomb development was discovered near Katerini, at the Pierian opening of the Petra Pass. It is a small cist tomb, complete with a slab roof, but the interior contains two chambers of nearly equal size, with a dividing wall and doors. It lacks only the barrel vault and front entrance of a proper Macedonian tomb. The tomb is dated to the second quarter of the fourth century, based on some incidental pottery and a coin of Amyntas III found within. It would at first sight appear to be a transition between cist and chamber tombs, but it is the only example, and in fact predates many of the existing cist tombs. This single tomb, which lacks exterior architectural decoration, is insufficient evidence on which to base any theory about transitional forms. See the reports of its excavator, Despini, "O taphos tis Katerinis," in *AAA*, and "O taphos tis Katerinis," *I Archaiologi Miloun yia tin Pieria*.

Addenda to the Paperback Edition

WHEN presented with the opportunity to produce a revised edition of this work, I contacted a number of scholars active in Macedonian studies, asking them to identify errors and lapses and to offer suggestions concerning new and different interpretations of the issues raised herein. I am grateful to colleagues both in this country and abroad who responded with their customary courtesy and generosity, and am pleased to acknowledge their contributions: W. Lindsay Adams, Manolis Andronikos, Ernst Badian, William Biers, Kostas Buraselis, Stanley M. Burstein, Elizabeth Carney, J. R. Ellis, Malcolm Errington, Peter M. Green, William Greenwalt, Nicholas Hammond, Kenneth W. Harl, Waldemar Heckel, Charles A. Hersh, Frank L. Holt, Simon Hornblower, Jonathan Musgrave, and Olga Palagia.

Corrections have been made to the original text and notes. Where appropriate, some bits of information were added to text, notes, and appendices, but only insofar as preserving the original pagination permitted. The bibliography and index remain unaltered. This appendix thus serves as the means to introduce new material. I have not attempted to include all the scholarly literature that has appeared in the five years since I completed the research for the original edition. To have been comprehensive would have necessitated either rewriting large sections of the book or producing an appendix that would be cumbersome. I have instead selected items that would reflect some new trends and enable the serious reader to initiate the pursuit of matters in detail.

Some of the archaeological information is taken from newspaper reports and from papers and lectures presented at various conferences, none of which can be considered a satisfactory substitute for the scholarly publication of excavations. Perhaps the easiest way to keep abreast is to read the annual summary of excavations and surveys in the Macedonian sections of *Archaeological Reports*.

Following a brief introduction to new books on Macedonia, the additional material is organized under the rubrics of the original chapter headings. The reader is therefore advised to use these new notes in conjunction with the original chapters. In this way one can be introduced to fresh ideas and discoveries and mark how quickly interpretations (including some of the author's), can change as a response to new evidence and challenges to old ideas.

Some Recent Publications

Three new books on Macedonian history have appeared recently. English-language readers are pleased to welcome a translation of R. Malcolm Errington's *Geschichte Makedoniens* (Munich, 1986), *A History of Macedonia*, trans. Catherine Errington (Berkeley and Los Angeles, 1990). The work is unrevised except for corrections.

The pen of the indefatigable Nicholas Hammond has produced two new volumes. *The Macedonian State: Origins, Institutions, and History* (Oxford, 1989) is succinctly described by its title. In it Hammond describes in detail and with useful references to the ancient evidence and some modern literature many of the views set forth in his *A History of Macedonia* (3 vols., Oxford, 1972–1988). The author has not changed his mind in any major way on the main issues of the origins and institutions of the Macedonians. *The Miracle That Was Macedonia* (London and New York, 1991) was written for Sidgwick & Jackson's "Great Civilizations" series. The book is too detailed and formal for the general readership for which it is presumably intended and, lacking notes and new interpretations, it is not suitable for a specialist audience. Errington's history is still the better introduction to the life and times of the ancient Macedonians. A comprehensive review essay comparing Hammond's *Macedonian State*, Errington's *A History of Macedonia*, and the present volume was written by Elizabeth Carney, "Review Essay on Macedonian History," *AHB* 5 (1991): 179–89.

Peter Green's *Alexander of Macedon*, originally published in 1974 by Penguin in the Pelican Biography series, has been reprinted by the University of California Press (Berkeley and Los Angeles, 1991), and will remain in print until Green completes a new edition of the work. Although out-of-date on some issues, it remains one of the most comprehensive and lively biographies of Alexander ever written, and deserves attention by anyone interested in this most legendary king of the Macedonians.

And, although its main themes lie outside the limits of the present work, an important study has appeared covering the career of one of the most important transitional figures between the age of Philip and Alexander and the Wars of the Successors: Richard A. Billows, *Antig-*

onos the One-Eyed and the Creation of the Hellenistic State (Berkeley and Los Angeles, 1989).

Chapter 1
Toward a History of Ancient Macedonia

BALKAN POLITICS

The faint hope I had originally expressed concerning peace and international cooperation in the Balkans has been dashed by recent events. The end of the Soviet empire in Eastern Europe and the apparent dissolution of the Yugoslav state—or at least a reduction in its size following the declared sovereignty of several republics—casts the Macedonian Question in new form. Yugoslav Macedonia has announced a partial independence, although its status as one of the poorest of the republics makes true autonomy from Yugoslavia problematic.

The Greek reaction to the possibility of a Slavic "Macedonia" has been hostile. The Greek position is that in modern times "Macedonia" has only geographical significance, and that, as there is no Macedonian ethnicity, there can be no Macedonian nation-state. (Greek newspapers regularly refer to the Macedonian republic as "The republic of Skopje.") The citizens of Yugoslav Macedonia consider themselves to be ethnic Macedonians, as do some western Bulgarians. The Bulgarian government has thus been ambivalent, although Bulgarian interests would probably be affected by the creation of a sovereign Macedonian state on their western border. The matter continues to be provocative, not only in the Balkans proper, but in Balkan immigrant communities throughout the world. Long-suppressed ethnic hostility has been released, as we witness a tension reminiscent of 1912–1913, just after the collapse of Turkish rule and prior to the new political order created by World War I. The chilling effect of recent events on earnest scholarship about the ancient Balkans is self-evident and bodes ill for the future. A lucid exposition of the contemporary Macedonian Question by Robert D. Kaplan appeared recently: "History's Cauldron," *Atlantic Monthly* (June 1991): 92–104.

Chapter 2
The Land of Macedonia

THE GREVENA REGION

One of the least-studied regions of western Macedonia is the area around Grevena. A comprehensive geographical, archaeological, and historical survey of the region conducted by a joint Greek-American team supervised by Professor Nancy Wilkie had (as of 1989) located 267 sites ranging from the prehistoric to the modern periods. *AR* 36 (1990): 49–50.

THE SITE OF METHONE

For an exhaustive study of the location(s) of Methone, including the possibility of the city's refounding, now see M. B. Hatzopoulos, D. Knoepfler, and V. Marigo-Papadopoulos, "Deux sites pour Methone de Macédoine," *BCH* 94 (1990): 639–68. In any case, the site of Methone in the Classical period should be moved two or three miles further north than shown on the maps in this book.

Chapter 3
Prehistoric Macedonia

NEW PREHISTORIC DISCOVERY

Archanthropos petraloniensis may have a much earlier relative. In a widely heralded discovery in the summer of 1991, Curtis Runnels of Boston University uncovered a flint hand ax from a paleolithic lake bed in western Greece, in the region of Nikopolis near the Bay of Actium. The tool, which has parallels in western Europe, is thought to have been fashioned between 200,000 and 500,000 years ago.

THE ARCHAEOLOGY OF ALBANIA

The difficulty of securing information about early Albania is partly relieved by the work of F. Prendi, "The Prehistory of Albania," *CAH*, 2d ed., 3 (1982): 187–237.

MYCENAEANS IN MACEDONIA

Continuing excavations in the Pierian coastal plain between the Vale of Tempe and the Mt. Olympus region reveal the possible existence of several Mycenaean cemeteries, according to the reports of archaeologist E. Poulaki-Pandermali. It is not yet clear the extent to which these Mycenaean remains are *settlements* (with all that that implies), as opposed to collections of imported Mycenaean ware. Any detailed assessment must await the full publication of this material.

NEW SCHOLARSHIP

Some useful work on the historical, linguistic, and archaeological problems of the late Bronze Age through the Archaic periods in Macedonia was published in *Magna Grecia, Epiro, e Macedonia*. Atti del Ventiquattresimo Convegno di Studi sulla Magna Grecia, Taranto, 5–10 Ottobre 1984 (Taranto, 1985). See especially the papers of J. Vokotopoulou, "La Macédoine de la Protohistorie a l'époque Archaique," pp. 133–66, and Klaus Kilian, "Magna Grecia, Epiro e Macedonia durante l'eta del Ferro," pp. 237–88.

Chapter 4
Who Were the Macedonians?

IRON AGE ARCHAEOLOGY

For an overview see N.G.L. Hammond, "Illyris, Epirus and Macedonia in the Early Iron Age," *CAH*, 2d ed., 3 (1982): 619–56, esp. 642ff. for Macedonia, although much of this period is now being reevaluated because of a rapid increase in information resulting from new excavations.

ETHNICITY

In the original edition I had hoped to put to rest the tangled question of the ethnicity of the ancient Macedonians by (1) establishing some reasonable standards by which one could address the nationality of an ancient people, and (2) attempting to disconnect the issue from modern politics. While I maintain the principles of my first point, I admit failure on the second. Nothing will deter many Greeks from linking their modern history to a Hellenic Macedonian past; it remains a vital political issue in Greece today.

The only new evidence that bears on the issue of ancient Macedonian ethnicity is epigraphical. For example, G. Akamatis reported at the Second International Congress for Macedonian Studies in Melbourne (1991) that the discovery of a late fifth-century B.C. Greek-language lead curse tablet from a "common" burial at Pella strengthens the case that the use of Greek was not necessarily limited to a hellenized upper class. The publication of the tablet—and the analysis of its dialect—will be a contribution to the continuing issue of the language of the Macedonians.

It now appears that the use of the written Greek language may have been more widespread at an earlier date than previously known. Nevertheless, my basic view has not changed: evidence of an appropriate quality is still insufficient to permit a precise identification of the ethnicity of the Macedonians on the basis of language alone. It is essential that there be a closer study of the Greek dialect(s) in use in Macedonia during any given period. Thus far, forms of Ionic, Doric, Aeolic, plus standard Attic Greek have been reported. As a question of method: why would an area three hundred miles north of Athens—not colonized by Athens—use an Attic dialect, unless it were imported? That is, the Attic dialect could hardly be native, and its use is likely part of the process of hellenization. To put the question differently: if the native language of the Macedonians is Greek, what is its *Macedonian* dialect?

The Macedonians may or may not have been connected with other known ethnic groups, such as the Greeks who lived to the south. It remains clear that, although their monarchs and barons were quite highly hellenized in many respects, they made their mark in antiquity as *Macedonians*, not as a tribe of some other people.

SINDOS

Many of the items recovered from the cemetery at Sindos (ancient Anchialos)—e.g., plaques, granulated jewelry, and iron "toys"—once regarded as unusual for Macedonian burials (thus, were the inhabitants of this site Macedonians?) now have parallels at places as widely separated as Aiani (in Upper Macedonia near modern Kozani) and Aegae in the central plain.

Chapter 5
Alexander I

THRACIAN STUDIES

For more on the Thracians, a knowledge of whose history and culture requires more archaeological investigation, see the useful commentary on our best surviving written evidence by David Asheri, "Herodotus on Thracian Society and History," *Hérodote et les peuples non Grecs*, Fondation Hardt, Entretiens 35 (Vandoervres-Geneve, 1990): 131–69.

HELLENISM IN WESTERN MACEDONIA

The discovery of a well-developed site identified as ancient Aiani, in the region of Kozani, including public and private buildings, tombs (both chambered and cist types) ranging from the sixth century B.C. down to the Hellenistic period, pottery, and statuary, suggests that Elimeia was hardly an isolated and poor outpost. The site provides important information about the hellenizing process in western Macedonia. The material is unusually eclectic, and we await full publication and discussion of the architecture, the tombs, and the grave goods. The unexpected richness of Aiani is indicative of the surprises that have marked archaeology in Macedonia in recent years, and confirms the view that we are only on the threshold of understanding this remarkable region. *AR* 33 (1986–1987): 40; 34 (1987–1988): 49–50; 35 (1988–1989): 74–75; and 36 (1989–1990): 56.

Chapter 6
Perdiccas II

NEW COIN EVIDENCE

In 1989 a large hoard of tetrobols, including 197 pieces of royal Macedonian silver, was unearthed. The hoard includes virtually the entire range of Macedonian fifth-century royal light tetrobols, doubling the known number of this type struck by Alexander I, and nearly trebling those of Perdiccas II. The weights and alloys of the light tetrobols do not show any severe reduction between the stable rule of Alexander and the fragile reign of Perdiccas, thereby confirming my view that one cannot judge the success of reigns solely by examining the quality of coins. I am indebted to Charles A. Hersh for informing me of this important numismatic discovery through an offprint of his article, "A Fifth-Century Circulation Hoard of Macedonian Tetrobols," *Mnemata: Papers in Memory of Nancy M. Waggoner*, American Numismatic Society (New York, 1991), 3–19, with plates 1–8.

Chapter 7
Archelaus

PELLA

William S. Greenwalt suggests to me that Archelaus, who engaged in a major monetary reform, may have also seen in the development of Pella an important economic innovation. Certainly Pella was in a splendid position, together with its port of Phacus, to exploit the resources of the Axios valley. The continuing archaeological investigation of the city might provide material evidence of Pella's economic position. Excavations at the site continue at rapid speed, although nothing of the palace dating to Archelaus's era has yet been recovered, the oldest palace part being mid-fourth century B.C.

Chapter 8
The House of Amyntas III

EURYDICE

In a compelling new interpretation, "Eurydice: Demonic or Devoted Mother?" (*AHB*, forthcoming), Kate Mortensen argues that the un-flattering portrait of Eurydice in the ancient sources, especially Justin (7.4.5–5.8), is a piece of ancient propaganda reflecting mistrust of an accomplished and strong woman (one is reminded of similar hostility expressed toward Olympias and Cleopatra VII). Mortensen suggests that Eurydice's efforts were directed at safeguarding the throne for her sons, and that the portraits of her in Aeschines (*On the Embassy* 25–27) and Plutarch (*On the Education of Children* 14A–C) are closer to the mark.

For additional recent work on Macedonian royal women in general and Eurydice in particular see Elizabeth Carney, " 'What's in a Name?': The Emergence of a Title for Royal Women in the Hellenistic Period," *Women's History and Ancient History*, ed. S. B. Pomeroy (Chapel Hill, 1991), 154–72, and "The Career of Adea-Eurydice," *Historia* 36 (1987): 496–502.

In 1987 Manolis Andronikos uncovered a large vaulted two-chambered tomb at Vergina near the "Rhomaios" tomb (described by Andronikos in "Some Reflections on Macedonian Tombs," *BSA* 82 [1987]: 1ff). Although the tomb had been looted, remains of burial offerings point to a female interment, and the richness of decoration and offerings suggest someone prominent. Andronikos believes that this is the tomb of Eurydice, and that it can be dated to the late 340s (followed by N.G.L. Hammond in "The Royal Tombs at Vergina: Evolution and Identities," *BSA* 86 [1991]: 70–71). The date of the tomb is based on some Attic red-figured sherds and on a pan-Athenaic amphora bearing the name of the Athenian archon for 344/3 B.C. Professor William Biers reminds me that such a vessel normally belongs to the "heirloom" class of objects that tend to be passed down; that is, their use as evidence to date burials is problematic. Andronikos has used the existence of this amphora to date his vaulted tomb to the 340s (followed by Hammond), but I remain cautious. Moreover, Andronikos believes that the monument dedicated to Eucleia by Eurydice commemorates the Macedonian victory at Chaeronea in 338 (see p. 192 above). One cannot have it both ways: a woman interred in 343–340 dedicating a monument commemorating an event of 338! Clearly this whole matter needs further thought.

Two recent articles of interest on the Argeadae of the mid-fourth century by William S. Greenwalt: "Amyntas III and the Political Stability of Argead Macedonia," *AncW* 18 (1988): 35–44, and "The Marriageability Age at the Argead Court: 360–17 B.C.," *Classical World* 82 (1988): 93–97.

METHONE

The chronology of Athens's renewed presence in the region of the Thermaic Gulf and the seizure of Methone is uncertain. Errington argues that it cannot have occurred before ca. 360 B.C.; see his *A History of Macedonia*, pp. 36–37 and 271 n. 5 (with sources).

Chapter 9
"... *The Greatest of the Kings of Europe* ..."

DATE OF PHILIP'S ACCESSION

E. Badian, "History from 'Square Brackets'," *ZPE* 79 (1989): 59–70, remains skeptical (p. 68 n. 24) that the Oleveni inscription, which Hatzopoulos uses to date Philip's accession to 360 (rather than 359), actually refers to Philip II, rather than a viable alternative, Philip V. Otherwise Badian cogently blends an analysis of two additional inscriptions (the "letter" from Alexander concerning forests [p. 56 above], and the Kalindon decree [p. 219 n. 55 above]) to show how tenuous it is to use epigraphical restorations to argue about Macedonian royal titles. It is a lesson that every student of ancient history should take to heart.

THE MOLOSSIAN KING ARYBBAS

For more on Arybbas see Julia Heskel, "The Political Background of the Arybbas Decree," *GRBS* 29 (1988): 185–96. Heskel correctly emphasizes the effect of Arybbas's own ambitions on Philip II during the formative years of Philip's reign.

PHILIP'S MILITARY REFORMS

The extent to which Philip's military reforms were truly innovative (as opposed to being part of an evolving style of fourth-century warfare) is presently a theme of scholarly discussion. The old interpretation—that the Theban battle plan at Leuctra in which the coordinated offen-

sive use of Theban cavalry and infantry defeated the rigid Spartan phalanx was a revolution in warfare—must be reevaluated. Now see the
interpretations of Victor David Hanson, "The Leuctra Miracle," *Military History Quarterly* 2 (1990): 54–59.

POLITICAL INSTABILITY IN PERSIAN ANATOLIA

One of the most important (and frequently neglected) aspects of Philip
II's plans for an intervention in Asia is the instability of Persian rule in
Asia Minor. In an outgrowth of his University of California disserta-
tion, *The So-Called "Great Satraps' Revolt," 366–60 B.C.: Concerning
Local Instability in the Achaemenid Far West*, Historia Einzelschriften,
Heft 63 (Stuttgart, 1989), Michael Weiskopf argues that the ancient
sources incorrectly describe a general, well-organized threat to Achae-
menid rule. He sees instead an instability resulting from a series of local
Anatolian satrapal squabbles. (One wonders, of course, how *Philip*
saw it.) For a counter to Weiskopf's thesis, see Robert A. Moysey,
"Diodoros, the Satraps and the Decline of the Persian Empire," *AHB*
5 (1991): 113–22.

The remarkable city of Olynthus continues to draw scholarly interest. E.g., see the discussion of Olynthus's Hypodamian urban plan
and construction techniques by Ernst-Ludwig Schwander, "Sull'ar-
chitettura ed urbanistica Epirotica nel IV secolo," *Magna Grecia, Epiro,
e Macedonia*, Atti del Ventiquattresimo Convegno di Studi sulla Magna
Grecia, Taranto, 5–10 Ottobre 1984 (Taranto, 1985), 447–76, esp. 447–
59.

THE PEACE OF PHILOCRATES

As to whether the Peace of Philocrates was a *koine eirene*, see the con-
text developed by E. Badian, "The King's Peace," *Georgica: Greek
Studies in Honour of George Cawkwell*, Institute of Classical Studies,
Bulletin Supplement 58 (1991): 25–48, esp. 70–71.

Chapter 10
Political Institutions in the Age of Philip and Alexander

THE ARMY ASSEMBLY

In a recent study ("The Evolution of the Macedonian Army Assembly," *Historia* 40 [1991]: 230–47), Edward M. Anson augments his earlier views about the lack of formal constitutional arrangements by arguing that the special circumstances of Alexander's expedition resulted
in a transformation of the army assembly. While heretofore it had

served mainly as a sounding board for kings, it evolved during the Asian expedition as a policy-making body whose voice could not be ignored in the selection of a new monarch (e.g., the selection of Arrhidaeus), although Anson (noting Curtius' comment [10.7.11] on the novelty of the situation) sees this development as the expression of an army that had become less "national" and more "personal" during the eastern campaigns far from home. Anson's view, if correct, has important implications for the role of Alexander as a watershed between the political history of the Macedonians in the Balkans and their later activities abroad.

Chapter 11
Material Culture in the Age of Philip and Alexander

NEW LITERATURE ON MACEDONIAN TOMBS

In *Monumental Tombs of the Hellenistic Age* (Toronto, 1990), Janos Fedak provides an exhaustive synthesis of Hellenistic funerary monuments throughout the Mediterranean and western Asia regions. While his sections on Macedonian tombs (104–9 and 165–67) offer no new insights, they provide a fair summary of style and development. Fedak expresses conditional reservations about the date of Tomb II (and therefore its occupant) at Vergina, and connects that tomb's frieze to the age of Alexander (213–14 n. 19). The value of Fedak's well-illustrated volume is that it puts the development of Macedonian tombs in a larger cultural and geographical context.

My views (p. 262 above) on the post–Philip II date of Tomb II at Vergina are partially confirmed by Aristides Stamatiou, "Alexander the Great as a Lion Hunter," *Praktika* of the Twelfth International Congress of Classical Archaeology, Athens, 4–10 September 1983, II (Athens, 1988), 209–17. Stamatiou cites the literature on the absence of lion hunts in Macedonia before the age of Alexander, and dates the hunting frieze on the tomb to the period 320–10 B.C. (see especially his p. 210 n. 2). It is the boar hunt, of course, that is the traditional sport in Macedonian life. One might point out that the appearance of both a lion and a boar (along with other animals) in the Vergina hunting frieze points to a significant meld of the new Asian and traditional Macedonian themes.

In 1979 a site excavated on the southern shore of Cape Megalo Karaburnu on the eastern shore of the Thermaic Gulf revealed a number of fourth-century tombs, mostly of the cist type. The site has been identified by the excavators as ancient Aenea, in the fifth century a tribute-paying member of the Athenian Empire, and in the fourth century a member of the Chalcidic League until its conquest by Philip II about the time of his campaign against Olynthus. The tombs contained not only skeletal materials and a rich assortment of fifth- and fourth-century grave goods, but some quite sophisticated wall painting, now strikingly illustrated in color by Julia Vokotopoulou, *I Taphiki Tymvi tis Aineias* (Athens, 1990).

One eagerly awaits the imminent publication of Stella G. Miller, *The Tomb of Lyson and Kallikles: A Painted Macedonian Tomb* (Mainz, 1992), with its introductory section on the development of Macedonian tombs.

The level of archaeological activity in Macedonia is so high, and the rate of discovery increasing at such a rapid pace, it is likely that no one knows how many tombs of both the cist and chambered types have been recovered in recent years. It is now essential that the present chaos of reporting be altered in favor of some type of continuously updated catalog that would undertake to describe these discoveries. The quality of interpretation rests to a considerable extent on the availability of evidence. One hopes that some agency or authority in Greece will develop a data-gathering center which would make available to all scholars information about this rapidly growing body of Macedonian burials.

Appendix C
Some Diverse Endnotes

THE BONES IN TOMB II AT VERGINA

The skeletal materials from Vergina continue to excite interest. In "Reconstructing King Philip II: The 'Nice' Version," *AJA* 94 (1990): 237–47, A.J.N.W. Prag describes the use of an ancient medical implement, the "spoon of Diocles," which may have been used to extract the arrow point from Philip's eye wound suffered at the siege of Methone. Philip's face would thus have suffered considerably less disfigurement than previously envisioned. Prag, however, adds nothing new to the issue of whether the bones from Tomb II's main burial are actually those of Philip, and he depends for some of his information and interpretations upon an obscure and out-of-date eighteenth-century biography of Philip II.

For a full discussion of the tradition of Philip's eye, leg, and collarbone wounds, with ancient testimonies cited and an analysis of the fictitious literary traditions that grew out of the story of his injuries, see A. Swift Riginos, "The Wounding of Philip II of Macedon: Fact and Fabrication" (forthcoming). Any future discussion of Philip's several injuries will have to take Riginos's study into account, including her contention that it is impossible to tell from the ancient sources which of Philip's legs suffered the blow that was severe enough to fell the king's horse.

Recently recovered Macedonian skeletal materials, including the bones from Vergina, have been examined by Jonathan Musgrave of the Department of Anatomy, Medical School, Bristol University. Musgrave holds that the bones from the main chamber of Tomb II are those of Philip II. A colloquium on the Vergina tombs was held at the 1990 annual meeting of the Archaeological Institute of America. The papers presented there by Musgrave on the bones, Beryl Barr-Sharrar on silver vessel chronologies, Elizabeth Carney on the burials of Macedonian royal women, and W. Lindsay Adams on the possibility of the reburial of Alexander IV as part of Cassander's policy, with a commentary by this author, have been published in *AncW* 22 (1991). Musgrave's examination of the bones from Tomb I concludes that the deceased were a middle-aged male, a much younger female, and a neonate.

One of the most promising avenues for future investigation is the plan to establish a data base that provides information about all Macedonian skeletal materials. Musgrave hints at the possibility of learning a great deal more about the circumstances of inhumation, cremation, and reburials through such an analysis. This would be a welcome study.

On 30 March 1992 the renowned Greek excavator of the royal Macedonian cemetery at Vergina, Manolis Andronikos, died after a long illness. Professor Andronikos's archaeological contributions to Macedonian studies were marked by energetic presentations of his discoveries, both in print and lectures. He was unusually generous in sharing his discoveries, even before their formal scientific publication, with his foreign colleagues. Even though I came to hold interpretations that were at variance with his own, Andronikos always remained courteous and helpful to me. He served his nation and scholarship well, and one hopes that those who succeed him will follow the course he set.

· BIBLIOGRAPHY ·

T̲HE following bibliography in-
cludes only works consulted in the preparation of this volume. Under
each author heading, books precede articles, and each category is arranged alphabetically.

*Acta of the Second International Symposium on Aegean Prehistory: The First Arrival
of the Indo-Europeans in Greece.* Athens, 1972.

Adams, John Paul. "The *Larnakes* of Tomb II at Vergina." *ArchNews* 12 (1983):
1–7.

Adams, W. Lindsay. "Macedonian Kingship and the Right of Petition." *AM* 4
(1986): 43–52.

———. "The Royal Macedonian Tomb at Vergina: An Historical Interpretation." *AncW* 3 (1980): 67–72.

Adams, W. Lindsay, and Eugene N. Borza, eds. *Philip II, Alexander the Great
and the Macedonian Heritage.* Washington, D.C., 1982.

Andriotes, N. P. "History of the Name 'Macedonia.' " *BalkSt* 1 (1960): 143–
48.

Andronikos, Manolis. *Vergina: The Prehistoric Necropolis and the Hellenistic Palace.* Lund, 1964.

———. [Andronicos]. *Vergina: The Royal Tombs and the Ancient City.* Athens,
1984.

———. *Vergina.* Vol. 1. *To nekrotapheion tōn tymvōn.* Athens, 1969.

———. "Excavations at Vergina." *AM* 1 (1970): 168–71.

———. "Regal Treasures from a Macedonian Tomb." *National Geographic* 154
(1978): 54–77.

———. "The Royal Tomb of Philip II." *Archaeology* 31 (Sept.–Oct. 1978): 33–
41.

———. "Some Reflections on the Macedonian Tombs." *BSA* 82 (1987): 1–16.

———. "Vergina: Archaiologia kai Istoria." In *Philia Epe eis Georgion E. My-
lonan,* vol. 1, pp. 19–37 Athens, 1986.

———. "Vergina, the Prehistoric Necropolis and the Hellenistic Palace." *Studies in Mediterranean Archaeology* 13 (1964): 3–11.

———. "Vergina: The Royal Graves in the Great Tumulus." *AAA* 10 (1977):
1–72.

Anson, Edward M. "Macedonia's Alleged Constitutionalism." *CJ* 80 (1985):
303–16.

Anson, Edward M. "The Meaning of the Term *Makedones*." *AncW* 10 (1984): 67–68.

I Archaiologi Miloun yia tin Pieria. Thessaloniki, 1985.

To Archaiologiko Ergo sti Makedonia kai Thraki. Vol. 1, 1987. Thessaloniki, 1988.

The Athenian Tribute Lists. Ed. B. D. Meritt, H. T. Wade-Gery, and M. F. McGregor. 4 vols. Cambridge, Mass. and Princeton, 1939–53.

Aymard, André. *Études d'histoire ancienne*. Paris, 1967.

——. "*Basileus Makedonōn*." *RIDA* 4 (1950): 61–97. Reprinted in Aymard, *Études*, 100–122.

——. "Sur l'assemblée macédonienne." *REA* 52 (1950): 115–37. Reprinted in Aymard, *Études*, 143–63.

Badian, E. "A King's Notebooks." *HSCP* 72 (1968): 183–204.

——. "Alexander the Great, 1948–1967." *CW* 65 (1971): 37–56 and 77–83.

——. "Eurydice." In W. Lindsay Adams and Eugene N. Borza, eds., *Philip II, Alexander the Great and the Macedonian Heritage*, pp. 99–110. Washington, D.C., 1982.

——. "Greeks and Macedonians." In Beryl Barr-Sharrar and Eugene N. Borza, eds., *Macedonia and Greece in Late Classical and Early Hellenistic Times*, pp. 33–51. Studies in the History of Art 10. Washington, D.C., 1982.

——. "Some Recent Interpretations of Alexander." In *Alexandre le Grand: Image et réalité*, pp. 279–303. Fondation Hardt, Entretiens 22. Vandoeuvres-Genève, 1976.

——. "The Deification of Alexander the Great." In *Macedonian Studies in Honor of Charles F. Edson*, pp. 27–71. Thessaloniki, 1981.

Baege, Werner. *De Macedonium Sacris*. Dissertationes Philologicae Halenses 22. 1913.

Balcer, Jack M. "The Date of Herodotus IV.1: Darius' Scythian Expedition," *HSCP* 76 (1972): 99–132.

——. "Persian Occupied Thrace (Skudra)." *Historia* 37 (1988): 1–21.

——. "The Persian Occupation of Thrace, 519–491 B.C.: The Economic Effects." *Actes de IIe Congres International des études du sud-est europeen* 2 (1972): 241–58.

Barr-Sharrar, Beryl. "Eastern Influence on the Toreutic Art of Macedonia before the Conquest of Alexander the Great." *ArchNews* 13 (1984): 1–12. [Revised version in *AM* 4 (1986): 71–82.]

——. "Macedonian Metal Vases in Perspective: Some Observations on Context and Tradition." In Beryl Barr-Sharrar and Eugene N. Borza, eds., *Macedonia and Greece in Late Classical and Early Hellenistic Times*, pp. 122–39. Studies in the History of Art 10. Washington, D.C., 1982.

Barr-Sharrar, Beryl, and Eugene N. Borza, eds. *Macedonia and Greece in Late Classical and Early Hellenistic Times*. Studies in the History of Art 10. Washington, D.C., 1982.

Beaumont, R. L. "Corinth, Ambracia, Apollonia." *JHS* 72 (1952): 62–73.

Bellinger, A. R. *Essays on the Coinage of Alexander the Great*. American Numismatic Society, Numismatic Studies 11. New York, 1963.

Bengtson, H., ed. *Die Staatsvertrage des Altertums*. Vol. 2. Munich and Berlin, 1962.

―――. *Die Strategie in der hellenistischen Zeit*. 3 vols. Munich, 1937–52.

Berve, H. *Das Alexanderreich auf prosopographischer Grundlage*. Vol. 1. Munich, 1926.

Best, J.G.P. *Thracian Peltasts and Their Influence on Greek Warfare*. Groningen, 1969.

Betancourt, Philip P. "The End of the Greek Bronze Age." *Antiquity* 50 (1976): 40–47.

Bevan, E. R. *The House of Seleucus*. 2 vols. London, 1902.

Bintliff, J. "The Plain of Western Macedonia and the Neolithic Site of Nea Nikomedia," *PPS* 42 (1976): 241–62.

Borza, Eugene N. "Anaxarchus and Callisthenes: Academic Intrigue at Alexander's Court." In *Ancient Macedonian Studies in Honor of Charles F. Edson*, pp. 73–86. Thessaloniki, 1981.

―――. "Athenians, Macedonians, and the Origins of the Macedonian Royal House." *Studies in Attic Epigraphy, History and Topography Presented to Eugene Vanderpool*. *Hesperia*, suppl. 19 (1982): 7–13.

―――. "David George Hogarth: Eighty Years After." *AncW* 1 (1978): 97–101.

―――. "The Macedonian Royal Tombs at Vergina: Some Cautionary Notes." *ArchNews* 10 (1981): 73–87.

―――. "A Macedonian Skull." *Association of Ancient Historians Newsletter* 36 (April 1985).

―――. "The Natural Resources of Early Macedonia." In W. Lindsay Adams and Eugene N. Borza, eds., *Philip II, Alexander the Great and the Macedonian Heritage*, pp. 1–20. Washington, D.C., 1982.

―――. "Philip II and the Greeks." *CP* 73 (1978): 236–43.

―――. "The Royal Macedonian Tombs and the Paraphernalia of Alexander the Great." *Phoenix* 41 (1987): 105–21.

―――. "Some Observations on Malaria and the Ecology of Central Macedonia in Antiquity." *AJAH* 4 (1979): 102–24.

―――. "Some Toponym Problems in Eastern Macedonia." *AHB* 3 (1989): 60–69.

―――. "The Symposium at Alexander's Court." *AM* 3 (1983): 45–55.

―――. "Those Vergina Tombs Again." *ArchNews* 11 (1982): 8–10.

―――. "Timber and Politics in the Ancient World: Macedon and the Greeks." *PAPS* 131 (1987): 32–52.

Bosworth, A. B. *Conquest and Empire: The Reign of Alexander the Great*. Cambridge, 1988.

―――. *From Arrian to Alexander: Studies in Historical Interpretation*. Oxford, 1988.

―――. *A Historical Commentary on Arrian's History of Alexander the Great*. Vol. 1. Oxford, 1980.

―――. "Alexander the Great and the Decline of Macedon." *JHS* 106 (1986): 1–12.

Bosworth, A. B. "*ASTHETAIROI.*" *CQ*, n.s. 23 (1973): 245–53.

———. "Errors in Arrian." *CQ*, n.s. 26 (1976): 117–39.

———. "Eumenes, Neoptolemus and *PSI* XII.1284." *GRBS* 19 (1978): 227–37.

———. "Macedonian Manpower under Alexander the Great." *AM* 4 (1986): 115–22.

———. "Philip II and Upper Macedonia." *CQ*, n.s. 21 (1971): 93–105.

Bouché-Leclerq, A. *Histoire des Lagides.* 4 vols. Paris, 1903–7.

———. *Histoire des Séleucides.* 2 vols. Paris, 1913.

Bouzek, Jan. "Macedonia and Thrace in the Early Bronze Age." *AM* 4 (1986): 123–32.

Boyd, Thomas. "The Arch and Vault in Greek Architecture." *AJA* 82 (1978): 83–100.

Brailsford, H. N. *Macedonia: Its Races and Their Future.* London, 1906.

Briant, Pierre. *Antigone le Borgne: Les débuts de sa carrière et les problèmes de l'assemblée macédonienne.* Paris, 1973.

Bridge, F. R., ed. *Austro-Hungarian Documents Relating to the Macedonian Struggle, 1896–1912.* Thessaloniki, 1976.

Broekhuizen, S., ed. *Agro-Ecological Atlas of Cereal Growing in Europe.* Vol. 1. *Atlas of Cereal Growing Areas of Europe.* Wageningen, New York, London and Amsterdam, 1969.

Brunt, P. A. "Anaximenes and King Alexander I of Macedon." *JHS* 96 (1976): 151–53.

Bryson, R. A., H. H. Lamb, and D. L. Donley. "Drought and the Decline of Mycenae." *Antiquity* 48 (1974): 46–50 and 228–30.

Burn, A. R. "Persia and the Greeks." In *Cambridge History of Iran*, vol. 2, *The Median and Achaemenian Periods*, ch. 6. Cambridge 1985.

Bursian, Conrad. *Geographie von Griechenland.* 2 vols. Leipzig, 1862–72.

Cargill, Jack. *The Second Athenian League.* Berkeley, Los Angeles and London, 1981.

Carney, Elizabeth. "Olympias." *Ancient Society* 18 (1987): 35–62.

———. "Regicide in Macedonia." *PP* 38 (1983): 260–72.

Carpenter, Rhys. *Discontinuity in Greek Civilization.* Cambridge, 1966.

Carroll-Spillecke, Maureen. *Landscape Depictions in Greek Relief Sculpture: Development and Conventionalization.* European University Studies, Archaeology (series 38), vol. 11. Frankfurt am Main, Bern and New York, 1985.

Carter, F. W., ed. *An Historical Geography of the Balkans.* London, San Francisco and New York, 1977.

Cary, M. *The Geographic Background of Greek and Roman History.* Oxford, 1949.

Caskey, J. L. "Greece and the Aegean Islands in the Middle Bronze Age." *CAH*, 3rd ed., vol. 2, pt. 2, ch. 4a. 1973.

———. "Greece, Crete and the Aegean Islands in the Early Bronze Age." *CAH*, 3rd ed., vol. 1, pt. 2, ch. 26a. 1971.

Casson, S. *Macedonia, Thrace and Illyria.* Oxford, 1926.

———. "Note on the Ancient Sites in the Area Occupied by the British Salonika Force during the Campaign 1916–1918." *BCH* 40 (1916): 293–97.

Castritius, H. "Die Okkupation Thrakiens durch die Perser und der Sturz des athenischen Tyrannen Hippias." *Chiron* 2 (1972): 1–15.

Cawkwell, G. L. *Philip of Macedon*. London, 1978.

———. "Athenian Naval Power in the Fourth Century." *CQ*, n.s. 34 (1984): 334–45.

———. "The Defense of Olynthus." *CQ*, n.s. 12 (1962): 122–40.

———. "Epaminondas and Thebes." *CQ*, n.s. 22 (1972): 254–78.

———. "The Peace of Philocrates Again." *CQ*, n.s. 22 (1978): 93–104.

Chadwick, John. *The Mycenaean World*. Cambridge, 1976.

———. "The Prehistory of the Greek Language." *CAH*, 3rd ed., vol. 2, pt. 2, ch. 39a. 1975.

———. "Who Were the Dorians?" *PP* 31 (1976): 103–17.

Charbonneaux, J., R. Martin, and F. Villard. *Hellenistic Art (330–50 B.C.)*. Trans. Peter Green. New York, 1973.

Childe, V. Gordon. *The Danube in Prehistory*. Oxford, 1929.

Cloché, Paul. *Histoire de la Macédoine jusqu'à l'avènement d'Alexandre le Grand*. Paris, 1960.

———. *Un fondateur d'empire: Philippe II, roi de Macedoine*. St. Etienne, 1955.

Cole, J. W. "Alexander Philhellene and Themistocles." *L'Antiquite Classique* 47 (1978): 37–49.

———. "Not Alexander But Perdikkas (Dem. 23.200 and 13.24)." *GRBS* 18 (1977): 25–32.

———. "Peisistratus on the Strymon." *G&R* 22 (1975): 42–44.

———. "Perdiccas and Athens." *Phoenix* 28 (1974): 55–72.

Collart, Paul. *Philippes, ville de Macédoine*. 2 vols. Paris, 1937.

Cook, J. M. "The Rise of the Achaemenids and the Establishment of Their Empire." *CHI*, vol. 2, *The Median and Achaemenian Periods*, ch. 5. Cambridge, 1985.

Cousinery, M.E.M. *Voyage dans la Macédoine*. Vol. 1. London, 1831.

Crossland, R. A. "Immigrants from the North." *CAH*, 3rd ed., vol. 1, pt. 2, ch. 27. 1971.

———. "Linguistic Problems of the Balkan Area in the Late Prehistoric and Early Classical Periods." *CAH*, 2nd ed., vol. 3, pt. 1, ch. 20c. 1982.

Crossland, R. A., and A. Birchall, eds. *Bronze Age Migrations in the Aegean: Archaeological and Linguistic Problems in Greek Prehistory*. London, 1973.

Culley, Gerald Ray. "The Restoration of Sacred Monuments in Augustan Athens (*IG* II/III² 1035)." Dissertation, University of North Carolina, 1973.

———. "The Restoration of Sanctuaries in Attica: *I.G.*, II², 1035." *Hesperia* 44 (1975): 207–23.

Curtius, E. *Griechische Geschichte*, 6th ed. 3 vols. Berlin, 1887–89.

Cvijić, J. *La péninsule balkanique: Géographie humaine*. Paris, 1918.

Daskalakis, Ap. [Dascalakis]. *The Hellenism of the Ancient Macedonians*. Thessaloniki, 1965.

Davis, N., and C. M. Kraay. *The Hellenistic Kingdoms: Portrait Coins and History.* London, 1973.

de Francisci, Pietro. *Arcana Imperii.* Vol. 2. Milan 1948.

Dell, Harry J. "The Illyrian Frontier to 229 B.C." Dissertation, University of Wisconsin, 1963.

———. "The Western Frontier of the Macedonian Monarchy." *AM* 1 (1970): 115–26.

Desborough, V. R. d'A. *The Greek Dark Ages.* London, 1972.

———. *The Last Mycenaeans and Their Successors.* Oxford, 1964.

Despini, Aik. "O taphos tis Katerinis." *AAA* 13 (1980): 198–209.

———. "O taphos tis Katerinis." In *I Archaiologi Miloun yia tin Pieria,* pp. 43–46. Thessaloniki, 1985.

Dodds, E. R., ed. *Plato. Gorgias: A Revised Text and Commentary.* Oxford, 1979.

Drougou, Stella, and I. Touratsoglou. *Hellinistiki Laksefti taphi Verias.* Athens, 1980.

Droysen, J. G. *Geschichte des Hellenismus.* 2nd ed. 3 vols. Gotha, 1877–78.

Dusing, K.A.S. "The Athenians and the North in Archaic Times." Dissertation, University of Cincinnati, 1979.

École Française d'Athènes. *Études Thasiennes.* 10 vols. Paris, 1944–.

———. *Guide de Thasos.* Paris, 1968.

Eddy, Charles B. *Greece and the Greek Refugees.* London, 1931.

Edson, Charles F. "Early Macedonia." *AM* 1 (1970): 17–44.

———. "Notes on the Thracian *Phoros.*" *CP* 42 (1947): 88–105.

———. "Strepsa (Thucydides 1.61.4)." *CP* 50 (1955): 169–90.

Ehrenberg, V. "Early Athenian Colonies." In *Aspects of the Ancient World,* pp. 116–43. Oxford, 1946.

Ellis, J. R. *Philip II and Macedonian Imperialism.* London, 1976.

———. "Amyntas III, Illyria and Olynthos, 393/2–380/79." *Makedonika* 9 (1969): 1–8.

———. "The Assassination of Philip II." In *Ancient Macedonian Studies in Honor of Charles F. Edson,* pp. 99–137. Thessaloniki, 1981.

Engels, Donald W. *Alexander the Great and the Logistics of the Macedonian Army.* Berkeley and Los Angeles, 1978.

Errington, R. M. *Geschichte Makedoniens.* Munich, 1986.

———. "Alexander in the Hellenistic World." In *Alexandre le Grand. Image et réalité,* pp. 137–79. Fondation Hardt, Entretiens 22. Vandoeuvres-Genève, 1976.

———. "Alexander the Philhellene and Persia." In *Ancient Macedonian Studies in Honor of Charles F. Edson,* pp. 139–43. Thessaloniki, 1981.

———. "Macedonian 'Royal Style' and Its Historical Significance." *JHS* 94 (1974): 20–37.

———. "Review-Discussion: Four Interpretations of Philip II." *AJAH* 6 (1981): 69–88.

———. "The Historiographical Origins of Macedonian 'Staatsrecht,' " *AM* 3 (1983): 89–101.

———. "The Nature of the Macedonian State under the Monarchy." *Chiron* 8 (1978): 77–133.

Ferguson, W. S. "Orgeonika," *Commemorative Studies in Honor of Theodore Leslie Shear. Hesperia*, suppl. 8 (1949): 130–63.

Feuer, Bryan. *The Northern Mycenaean Border in Thessaly.* BAR International Series 176. Oxford, 1983.

Flower, Michael A. "Agesilaus of Sparta and the Origins of the Ruler Cult." *CQ*, n.s. 38 (1988): 123–34.

Fol, A., B. Nikolov, and R. F. Hoddinott. *The New Thracian Treasure from Rogozen, Bulgaria.* British Museum Publications. London, 1986.

Fortina, M. *Cassandro, re di Macedonia.* Turin, 1965.

Fredricksmeyer, E. A. "Alexander, Midas and the Oracle at Gordium." *CP* 56 (1961): 160–68.

———. "Divine Honors for Philip II." *TAPA* 109 (1979): 39–61.

———. "On the Background of the Ruler Cult." In *Macedonian Studies in Honor of Charles F. Edson*, pp. 145–56. Thessaloniki, 1981.

———. "On the Final Aims of Philip II." In W. Lindsay Adams and Eugene N. Borza, eds., *Philip II, Alexander the Great and the Macedonian Heritage*, pp. 85–98. Washington, D.C., 1982.

French, D. H. *Index of Prehistoric Sites in Central Macedonia.* Athens, 1967.

Gaebler, Hugo. *Die antiken Münzen Nord-Griechenlands*, vol. 3. Part 2, *Makedonia und Paionia.* Berlin, 1906 and 1935.

Gardner, E. A., and S. Casson. "Macedonia II: Antiquities Found in the British Zone, 1915–19." *BSA* 23 (1918–19): 10–43.

Gerolymatos, Andre S. "The *proxenia* of Alexandros I of Makedonia." *LCM* 11, no. 5 (May 1986): 75–76.

Geyer, F. *Makedonien bis zur Thronbesteigung Philipps II.* Munich and Berlin, 1930.

———. "Makedonia." *RE* 14.1, pp. 638–771. 1928.

Ghirshman, Roman. *Persia from the Origins to Alexander the Great.* Trans. Stuart Gilbert and James Emmons. London, 1964.

Gomme, A. W., A. Andrewes, and K. J. Dover. *A Historical Commentary on Thucydides.* 5 vols. Oxford, 1945–70.

Gossel, B. *Makedonische Kammergräber.* Berlin, 1980.

Granier, F. *Die makedonische Heeresversammlung: Ein Beitrag zum antiken Staatsrecht.* Munich, 1931.

Great Britain Admiralty, Naval Intelligence Division, Geographical Section. *A Handbook of Macedonia and Surrounding Territories.* London, 1920.

———. *Greece.* 3 vols. Cambridge, 1944–45.

Great Britain Admiralty, Naval Staff, Geographical Section. *Notes on Climate and Other Subjects in the Eastern Mediterranean.* London, 1916.

Green, Peter. *Alexander of Macedon.* Harmondsworth, 1974.

Green, Peter. "The Royal Tombs of Vergina: A Historical Analysis." in W. Lindsay Adams and Eugene N. Borza, eds., *Philip II, Alexander the Great and the Macedonian Heritage*, pp. 129–51. Washington, D.C., 1982.

Greenhalgh, P.A.L. *Early Greek Warfare: Horsemen and Chariots in the Homeric and Archaic Ages.* Cambridge, 1973.

Greenwalt, William S. "Studies in the Development of Royal Authority in Argead Macedonia." Dissertation, University of Virginia, 1985.

———. "The Introduction of Caranus into the Argead King List." *GRBS* 26 (1985): 43–49.

———. "Polygamy and Succession in Argead Macedonia." *Arethusa* 22 (1989): 19–43.

Grieg, J.R.A., and J. Turner. "Some Pollen Diagrams from Greece, and Their Archaeological Significance." *JAS* 1 (1974): 177–94.

Griffith, G. T. "Philip as General and the Macedonian Army." In M. B. Hatzopoulos and L. D. Loukopoulos, eds., *Philip of Macedon*, pp. 58–77. Athens, 1980.

———. "Philip of Macedon's Early Interventions in Thessaly (358–352 B.C.)." *CQ*, n.s. 20 (1970): 67–80.

Gruen, Erich S. "Macedonia and the Settlement of 167 B.C." In W. Lindsay Adams and Eugene N. Borza, eds., *Philip II, Alexander the Great and the Macedonian Heritage*, pp. 257–67. Washington, D.C., 1982.

Habicht, C. *Gottmenschentum und griechische Städte*, 2nd ed. *Zetemata* 14. Munich, 1970.

Hamilton, Charles D. "Amyntas III and Agesilaus: Macedon and Sparta in the Fourth Century." *AM* 4 (1986): 239–45.

———. "Philip II and Archidamus." In W. Lindsay Adams and Eugene N. Borza, eds., *Philip II, Alexander the Great and the Macedonian Heritage*, pp. 61–83. Washington, D.C., 1982.

Hamilton, J. R. *Plutarch. Alexander: A Commentary.* Oxford, 1969.

Hammond, N.G.L. *Epirus.* Oxford, 1967.

———. *A History of Greece to 322 B.C.* 3rd ed. Oxford, 1986.

———. *A History of Macedonia.* Vol. 1, *Historical Geography and Prehistory.* Oxford, 1972.

———. *Migrations and Invasions in Greece and Adjacent Areas.* Park Ridge, N.J., 1976.

———. *Three Historians of Alexander the Great.* Cambridge, 1983.

———. *Venture into Greece with the Guerrillas, 1943–44.* London, 1983.

———. "The Archaeological Background to the Macedonian Kingdom." *AM* 1 (1970): 53–67.

———. "The Campaign and Battle of Marathon." *JHS* 88 (1968): 13–57.

———. "The End of Mycenaean Civilization and the Dark Age: (b) The Literary Tradition for the Migrations." *CAH*, 3rd ed., vol. 2, pt. 2, ch. 36b. 1975.

———. "The Evidence for the Identity of the Royal Tombs at Vergina." In

W. Lindsay Adams and Eugene N. Borza, eds., *Philip II, Alexander the Great and the Macedonian Heritage*, pp. 111–27. Washington, D.C., 1982.

———. "The Extent of Persian Occupation in Thrace." *Chiron* 10 (1980): 53–61.

———. "Grave Circles in Albania and Macedonia." In R. A. Crossland and A. Birchall, eds., *Bronze Age Migrations in the Aegean. Archaeological and Linguistic Problems in Greek Prehistory*, pp. 189–97. London, 1973.

———. "The Kingdom of Asia and the Persian Throne." *Antichthon* 20 (1986): 73–85.

———. "The Kingdoms in Illyria *circa* 400–167 B.C." *BSA* 61 (1966): 239–53.

———. " 'Philip's Tomb' in Historical Context." *GRBS* 19 (1978): 331–50.

———. "Prehistoric Epirus and the Dorian Invasion." *BSA* 32 (1931–32): 131–79.

———. "The Sources of Diodorus Siculus XVI." *CQ* 31 (1937): 79–91; 32 (1938): 137–51.

———. "The Western Frontier of Macedonia in the Reign of Philip II." In *Ancient Macedonian Studies in Honor of Charles F. Edson*, pp. 199–217. Thessaloniki, 1981.

Hammond, N.G.L., and G. T. Griffith. *A History of Macedonia*. Vol. 2, *550–336 B.C.* Oxford, 1979.

Hammond, N.G.L., and F. W. Walbank *A History of Macedonia*. Vol. 3, *336–167 B.C.* Oxford, 1988.

Hampl, F. *Der König der Makedonen*. Weida, 1934.

Hankey, V., and P. Warren. "The Absolute Chronology of the Aegean Late Bronze Age." *BICS* 21 (1974): 142–52.

Hansel, Bernhard. *Kastanas: Ausgraben in einem Siedlungshugel der Bronze-und Eisenzeit Makedoniens 1975–1979*. 3 vols. Berlin, 1983–84.

Harder, Annette. *Euripides' Kresphontes and Archelaos*. Mnemosyne, suppl. 87. Leiden, 1985.

Harmatta, Janos, ed. *Proceedings of the VIIth Congress of the International Federation of the Societies of Classical Studies*. Vol. 2. Budapest, 1984.

Hatzopoulos, M. B. "La Béotie et la Macédoine a l'époque de l'hégémonie thébaine: le point de vue macédonien." *Colloques internationaux du CNRS, "La Béotie antique,"* pp. 247–57. Paris, 1985.

———. "Les limites de l'expansion macédonienne en Illyrie sous Philippe II." *L'Illyrie méridionale et l'Épire dans l'Antiquité*. Actes du colloque international de Clermont-Ferrand (22–25 octobre 1984) réunis par Pierre Cabanes. Clermont-Ferrand, 1987.

———. "The Oleveni Inscription and the Dates of Philip II's Reign." In W. Lindsay Adams and Eugene N. Borza, eds., *Philip II, Alexander the Great and the Macedonian Heritage*, pp. 21–42. Washington, D.C., 1982.

———. "Strepsa: A Reconsideration, or New Evidence on the Road System of Lower Macedonia." In *Two Studies in Ancient Macedonian Topography*, Meletimata 3. Athens, 1987.

Hatzopoulos, M. B. "Succession and Regency in Classical Macedonia." *AM* 4 (1986): 279–92.

Hatzopoulos, M. B., and L. D. Loukopoulos, eds. *Philip of Macedon.* Athens, 1980.

Head, B. V. *Historia numorum: A manual of Greek numismatics.* 2nd ed. Oxford, 1911.

Head, B. V., and R. S. Poole. *A Catalogue of the Greek Coins in the British Museum: Macedonia, etc.* London, 1879.

Herrin, Judith. "Aspects of the Process of Hellenization in the Early Middle Ages." *BSA* 68 (1973): 113–26.

Heurtley, W. A. *Prehistoric Macedonia.* Cambridge, 1939.

Heuzey, Léon, and H. Daumet. *Mission Archéologique de Macédoine.* 2 vols. Paris, 1876.

Hill, G. F., R. Meiggs, and A. Andrewes, eds. *Sources for Greek History between the Persian and Peloponnesian Wars.* Oxford, 1962.

History of the Hellenic World. Vol. 1: *Prehistory and Protohistory.* Athens and London, 1974.

Hoddinott, R. F. *The Thracians.* London, 1981.

Hodlofski, Leo C. "Macedonian Relations with Athens to 413 B.C." Thesis, The Pennsylvania State University, 1979.

Hoffman, Richard J. "Perdikkas and the Outbreak of the Peloponnesian War." *GRBS* 16 (1975): 359–77.

Hogarth, D. G. *Philip and Alexander of Macedon.* London, 1897.

———. "In Macedonia." *Macmillans Magazine* (August 1889): 281–88.

Hooker, J. T. *Mycenaean Greece.* London, Henley, and Boston, 1976.

Hornblower, Simon. *The Greek World, 479–323 B.C.* London and New York, 1983.

How, W. W., and J. Wells. *A Commentary on Herodotus.* 2 vols. Oxford, 1928.

Huot, Jean-Louis. *Persia.* Vol. 1. *From Its Origins to the Achaemenids.* Trans. H.S.B. Harrison. London, 1967.

Huxley, George. "Baanes the Notary on 'Old Edessa,' " *GRBS* 24 (1983): 253–57.

———. "On the Erudition of George the Synkellos." *Proceedings of the Royal Irish Academy* 81, C, no. 6 (1981): 207–17.

Inscriptiones Graecae. Vol. 1, *Inscriptiones Atticae Euclidis anno anteriores,* 3rd ed. David Lewis, ed. Berlin, 1961.

———. Vol. 10, *Epiri, Macedoniae, Thraciae, Scythiae.* Pars 2, *Inscriptiones Macedoniae,* fasc. 1, *Inscriptiones Thessalonicae et Viciniae.* Charles F. Edson, ed. Berlin, 1972.

Isaac, Benjamin. *The Greek Settlements in Thrace until the Macedonian Conquest.* Studies of the Dutch Archaeological and Historical Society 10. Leiden, 1986.

Islami, Selim, Skënder Anamali, Muzafer Korkuti, and Franco Prendi. *Les Illyriens.* Tirane, 1985.

Johnson, A. C. "Ancient Forests and Navies." *TAPA* 58 (1927): 199–210.

Kaerst, Julius. *Geschichte des Hellenismus.* Vol. 1 (3rd ed.), vol. 2 (2nd ed.). Berlin and Leipzig, 1926–27.

Kagan, Donald. *The Outbreak of the Peloponnesian War.* Ithaca and London, 1969.

Kalléris, J. N. *Les anciens Macédoniens: Étude linguistique et historique.* 2 vols. Athens, 1954–76.

Kallet, Lisa. "Iphikrates, Timotheos, and Athens, 371–360." *GRBS* 24 (1983): 239–52.

Kelly, Thomas. *A History of Argos to 500 B.C.* Minneapolis, 1976.

Kienast, Dietmar. *Philipp II. von Makedonien und das Reich der Achaimeniden.* Abhandlungen der Marburger Gelehrten Gesellschaft, 1971, no. 6. Munich, 1973.

Knoch, K. *Klima-Karten von Europa.* Bad Kissengen, 1951.

Kofos, Evangelos. *Nationalism and Communism in Macedonia.* Thessaloniki, 1964.

Kokkoros, P., and A. Kanellis. "Découverte d'un crâne d'homme paléolithique dans la péninsule chalcidique." *L'Anthropologie* 64 (1960): 438–46.

Kraay, Colin. *Archaic and Classical Greek Coins.* London, 1976.

Kraft, John C., Ilhan Kayan, and Stanley E. Aschenbrenner. "Geological Studies of Coastal Change Applied to Archaeological Settings." In George Rapp, Jr. and John A. Gifford, eds., *Archaeology Geology*, pp. 57–84. New Haven and London, 1985.

Kroll, Helmut. "Bronze Age and Iron Age Agriculture in Kastanas, Macedonia." In W. Van Zeist and W. A. Casparie, eds., *Plants and Ancient Man: Studies in Paleoethnobotany*, pp. 243–46. Rotterdam and Boston, 1984.

Kroll, John H. "Nailing Down the Archaeological Chronology of Early Hellenistic Athens." *AJA* 87 (1983): 241–42. [Abstract.]

Kurtz, Donna C., and John Boardman. *Greek Burial Customs.* London, 1971.

Lauffer, Siegfried. *Alexander der Grosse.* 2nd ed. Munich, 1981.

Lazaridis, Demitrios. *Amphipolis kai Argilos.* Ancient Greek Cities 13. Athens, 1972.

———. *Thasos and Its Peraia.* Ancient Greek Cities 5. Athens, 1971.

Leake, William M. *Numismatica Hellenica.* London, 1856–59.

———. *Topography of Athens.* 2nd ed. London, 1841.

———. *Travels in Northern Greece.* 4 vols. London, 1835.

———. *Travels in the Morea.* 3 vols. London, 1830.

Lefkowitz, Mary R. *The Lives of the Greek Poets.* Baltimore, 1981.

Lehmann, Phyllis W. "The So-Called Tomb of Philip II: A Different Interpretation." *AJA* 84 (1980): 527–31.

———. "The So-Called Tomb of Philip II: an Addendum." *AJA* 86 (1982): 437–42.

Le Rider, Georges. *Le monnayage d'argent et d'or de Philippe II frappé en Macédoine de 359 à 294.* Paris, 1977.

Liritzis, Yannis. "A Critical Dating Re-evaluation of Petralona Hominid: A Caution for Patience." *AAA* 15 (1982): 285–96.

Lock, Robert. "The Macedonian Army Assembly in the Time of Alexander the Great." *CP* 72 (1977): 91–107.

Macan, R. W. *Herodotus: The Fourth, Fifth and Sixth Books.* 2 vols. London, 1895.

Maiuri, Bianca Teolato. *Museo nazionale Napoli.* Novara, 1971.

Manni, E. *Demetrio Poliorcete.* Rome, 1951.

Markle, Minor M., III. "Macedonian Arms and Tactics under Alexander the Great." In Beryl Barr-Sharrar and Eugene N. Borza, eds., *Macedonia and Greece in Late Classical and Early Hellenistic Times,* pp. 87–111. Studies in the History of Art 10. Washington, D.C., 1982.

———. "Support of Athenian Intellectuals for Philip: A Study of Isocrates' *Philippus* and Speusippus' *Letter to Philip.*" *JHS* 96 (1976): 80–99.

———. "The Macedonian Sarissa, Spear and Related Armor." *AJA* 81 (1977): 323–39.

———. "The Use of the Sarissa by Philip and Alexander of Macedon." *AJA* 82 (1978): 483–97.

Marsden, John H. *A Brief Memoir of the Life and Writings of the Late Lt-Col. William Martin Leake.* London, 1864.

Martin, Thomas R. *Sovereignty and Coinage in Classical Greece.* Princeton, 1985.

———. "Quintus Curtius' Presentation of Philip Arrhidaeus and Josephus' Accounts of the Accession of Claudius." *AJAH* 8 (1983): 161–90.

Martis, Nicolaos K. *The Falsification of Macedonian History.* Trans. John Philip Smith. Athens, 1984.

Mattingly, H. B. "The Methone Decrees." *CQ,* n.s. 11 (1961): 154–65.

Meiggs, Russell. *The Athenian Empire.* Oxford, 1972.

———. *Trees and Timber in the Ancient Mediterranean World.* Oxford, 1982.

Meiggs, R., and D. Lewis. *A Selection of Greek Historical Inscriptions.* Oxford, 1969.

Mendel, G. "Les travaux du Service archéologique de l'armée française d'orient." *Academie des inscriptions et belles-lettres, Comptes rendus* (1918): 9–17.

Meritt, Benjamin D. "Archelaos and the Decelean War." In *Classical Studies Presented to Edward Capps on his Seventieth Birthday,* pp. 246–52. Princeton, 1936.

Michell, H. *The Economics of Ancient Greece.* Cambridge, 1940.

Mihailov, Georgi. "La Thrace et la Macédoine jusqu'à l'invasion des Celtes." *AM* 1 (1970): 76–85.

Miller, M.C.J. "The Macedonian Pretender Pausanias and His Coinage." *AncW* 13 (1986): 23–27.

Miller, Stella G. "Hellenistic Macedonian Architecture: Its Style and Painted Decoration." Dissertation, Bryn Mawr College, 1972.

———. "Macedonian Tombs: Their Architecture and Architectural Decoration." In Beryl Barr-Sharrar and Eugene N. Borza, eds., *Macedonia and Greece in Late Classical and Early Hellenistic Times,* pp. 152–69. Studies in the History of Art 10. Washington, D.C., 1982.

———. "The Philippeion and Hellenistic Macedonian Architecture." *AthMitt* 88 (1973): 189–218.

Missitzis, Lambros. "A Royal Decree of Alexander the Great on the Lands of Philippi." *AncW* 12 (1985): 3–14.

Momigliano, A. *Filippo il Macedone*. Florence, 1934.

Montgomery, Hugo. "The Economic Revolution of Philip II—Myth or Reality?" *SO* 60 (1985): 37–47.

Mooren, Leon. "The Nature of the Hellenistic Monarchy." In *Egypt and the Hellenistic World. Proceedings of the International Colloquium. Leuven, 24–26 May 1982*, pp. 205–40. Louvain, 1983.

Moretti, Luigi. *Olympionikai, i vinctiori negli antichi agoni Olimpici*. Rome, 1957.

Mueller, O. *Antigonus Monophthalmus und "Das Jahr der Könige."* Saarbrucker Beitrage zur Altertumskunde 11. Bonn, 1973.

Musgrave, Jonathan H., R.A.H. Neave, and A.J.N.W. Prag. "The Skull from Tomb II at Vergina: King Philip II of Macedon." *JHS* 104 (1984): 60–78.

Ninou, K., ed. *Treasures of Ancient Macedonia*. Athens, 1980.

Oost, S. I. "The Alexander Historians and Asia." In *Macedonian Studies in Honor of Charles F. Edson*, pp. 265–82. Thessaloniki, 1981.

Palagia, Olga. "Imitation of Herakles in Ruler Portraiture: A Survey, from Alexander to Maximinus Daza." *Boreas* 9 (1986): 137–51.

Pandermalis, Dimitris. *Dion: The Sacred City of the Macedonians at the Foothills of Mt. Olympus*. Thessaloniki, n.d.

Papakonstantinou-Diamantourou, D. *Pella*. Vol. 1. Athens 1971.

Papangelos, I. A. *Chalkidiki*. Thessaloniki, 1982.

Papastavrou, I. *Amphipolis: Geschichte und Prosopographie*. Klio Beiheft 37. Leipzig, 1936.

Papazoglou, Fanoula. "Les origines et la destinée de l'Etat illyrien: *Illyrii proprie dicti*." *Historia* 14 (1965): 143–79.

Petsas, Ph. *Pella, Alexander the Great's Capital*. Thessaloniki, 1978.

———. *O Taphos tōn Lefkadiōn*. Athens, 1966.

———. "Chronika Archaiologika 1966–67." *Makedonika* 9 (1969): 101–223.

Picard, Ch. "Les recherches archéologiques de l'armée française en Macédoine, 1916–19." *BSA* 23 (1918–19): 1–9.

Pollitt, J. J. *Art in the Hellenistic Age*. Cambridge, 1986.

Poulianos, Aris N. "Petralona: A Middle Pleistocene Cave in Greece." *Archaeology* 24 (1971): 6–11.

Price, Martin. *Coins of the Macedonians*. British Museum Publications. London, 1974.

Price, Martin, and Nancy Waggoner. *Archaic Greek Coinage: The Asyut Hoard*. London, 1975.

Pritchett, W. Kendrick. "Amphipolis Restudied." In *Studies in Ancient Greek Topography*, vol. 3, pp. 298–346. University of California Publications in Classical Studies 22. 1980.

———. "Chimney Corner Topography." In *Studies in Ancient Greek Topogra-*

phy, vol. 3, pp. 347–69. University of California Publications in Classical Studies 22. 1980.

———. "Xerxes' Route over Mount Olympos." *AJA* 65 (1961): 369–75.

Rapp, George, Jr., and John A. Gifford, eds. *Archaeological Geology*. New Haven and London, 1985.

Raubitschek, A. E. "Theophrastos on Ostracism." *C&M* 19 (1958): 73–109.

Raymond, Doris. *Macedonian Regal Coinage to 413 B.C.* American Numismatic Society, Numismatic Notes and Monographs 126. New York, 1953.

Renfrew, A. C. "Problems in the General Correlation of Archaeological and Linguistic Strata in Prehistoric Greece: The Model of Autochthonous Origin." In R. A. Crossland and A. Birchall, eds., *Bronze Age Migrations in the Aegean: Archaeological and Linguistic Problems in Greek Prehistory*, pp. 263–76. London, 1973.

———. *Archaeology and Language: The Puzzle of the Indo-European Origins*. New York, 1988.

Rey, Léon. "Observations sur les premiers habitats de la Macédoine: Recueilles par le Service archéologique de l'Armée d'Orient, 1916–19." *BCH* 41–43 (1917–19). Published as a monograph, Paris, 1921.

———. "Observations sur les sites préhistoriques et protohistoriques de la Macédoine." *BCH* 40 (1916): 257–92.

Rhomiopoulou, Katerina. "A New Monumental Chamber Tomb with Paintings of the Hellenistic Period near Lefkadia (West Macedonia)." *AAA* 6 (1973): 87–92.

Rizakis, Athanasios, and John Touratsoglou, eds. *Epigraphes Anō Makedonias*. Vol. 1, *Catalog of Texts*. Athens, 1985.

Robertson, Martin. "Early Greek Mosaic." In Beryl Barr-Sharrar and Eugene N. Borza, eds., *Macedonia and Greece in Late Classical and Early Hellenistic Times*, pp. 240–49. Studies in the History of Art 10. Washington, D.C., 1982.

Robertson, N. "The Thessalian Expedition of 480 B.C." *JHS* 96 (1976): 100–120.

Robinson, David M. "New Inscriptions from Olynthus and Environs." *TAPA* 62 (1931): 40–56.

Robinson, David M., G. E. Mylonas, J. W. Graham, P. A. Clement, F. P. Albright, and J. L. Angel. *Excavations at Olynthus*. 14 vols. Baltimore, 1929–52.

Rodden, R. J. "Excavations at the Early Neolithic Site at Nea Nikomedeia, Greek Macedonia (1961 season)." *PPS* 28 (1962): 267–88.

Roebuck, Carl. "The Settlements of Philip II with the Greek States in 338 B.C." *CP* 43 (1948): 73–92.

Roesch, Paul. "Un décret inédit de la Ligue thébaine et la flotte d'Épaminondas." *REG* 97 (1984): 45–60.

Roos, Paavo. *The Rock-Cut Tombs of Caunus*. Vol. 1, *The Architecture*. Studies in Mediterranean Archaeology 34, part 1. Göteborg, 1972.

———. *Survey of Rock-Cut Chamber Tombs in Caria.* Studies in Mediterranean Archaeology 72, part 1. Göteborg, 1985.

———. "Alexander I in Olympia." *Eranos* 83 (1985): 162–68.

Rotroff, Susan I. "Royal Saltcellars from the Athenian Agora." *AJA* 86 (1982): 283. [Abstract.]

———. "Spool Saltcellars in the Athenian Agora." *Hesperia* 53 (1984): 343–54.

Ruiperez, M. S. "The Mycenaean Dialects." In Janos Harmatta, ed., *Proceedings of the VIIth Congress of the International Federation of the Societies of Classical Studies*, vol. 2, pp. 461–67. Budapest, 1984.

Saatsoglou-Paliadeli, Chrysoula. *Ta epitaphia mnimeia apo ti megali toumba tis Verginas.* Thessaloniki, 1984.

Sakellariou, M. B., ed. *Macedonia: 4000 Years of Greek History and Civilization.* Athens, 1983.

Samsaris, Demetrios. *Istoriki Geographia tis Anatolikis Makedonias kata tin Archaiotita.* Thessaloniki, 1976.

Samuel, Alan E. *From Athens to Alexandria: Hellenism and Social Goals in Ptolemaic Egypt.* Louvain, 1983.

———. "Philip and Alexander as Kings: Macedonian and Merovingian Parallels." *AHR* 93, no. 5 (1988): 1270–86.

Scarre, C. "Archaeology and Sea-level in West-central France." *WA* 16 (1984): 98–107.

Schweigert, Eugene. "Epigraphical Notes." *Hesperia* 8 (1939): 170–76.

Seager, Robin. "The King's Peace and the Balance of Power in Greece, 386–362 B.C." *Athenaeum* 52 (1974): 36–63.

The Search for Alexander: An Exhibition. New York, 1980.

Seibert, Jakob. *Alexander der Grosse.* Erträge der Forschung 10. Darmstadt, 1972.

Semple, Ellen C. *The Geography of the Mediterranean Region: Its Relation to Ancient History.* London, 1932.

Shackleton, J. C., T. H. van Andel, and C. N. Runnels. "Coastal Paleogeography of the Central and Western Mediterranean during the Last 125,000 Years and Its Archaeological Implications." *JFA* 11 (1984): 307–14.

Simpson, R. H. "Abbreviation of Hieronymus in Diodorus." *AJP* 80 (1959): 370–79.

Snodgrass, A. M. "Climatic Changes and the Fall of Mycenaean Civilization." *BICS* 22 (1975): 213–14.

———. "Metal-work as Evidence for Immigration in the Late Bronze Age." In R. A. Crossland and A. Birchall, eds., *Bronze Age Migrations in the Aegean: Archaeological and Linguistic Problems in Greek Prehistory*, pp. 209–14. London, 1973.

Stagakis, George S. "Observations on the *Hetairoi* of Alexander the Great." *AM* 1 (1970): 86–102.

Stipčević, Aleksander. *The Illyrians: History and Culture.* Trans. S. C. Burton. Park Ridge, N.J., 1977.

Stringer, C. B., F. C. Howell, and J. K. Melentis. "The Significance of the Fossil Hominid Skull from Petralona, Greece." *JAS* 6 (1979): 235–53.

Svoronos, J. *L'hellénisme primitif de la Macédoine.* Paris, 1919.

Sylloge Nummorum Graecorum. Vol. 5, *Ashmolean Museum*, part 3, *Macedonia.* London, 1976.

Tarn, W. W. *Antigonus Gonatas.* Oxford, 1913.

Tataki, Argyro B. *Ancient Beroea: Prosopography and Society.* Meletimata 8. Athens, 1988.

Tod, M. N. *A Selection of Greek Historical Inscriptions.* 2 vols. Oxford, 1946–48.

Tomlinson, R. A. "The Architectural Context of the Macedonian Vaulted Tombs." *BSA* 82 (1987): 1–16.

———. "Vaulting Techniques of Macedonian Tombs." *AM* 2 (1977): 473–79.

Touratsoglou, John. *Lefkadia.* Keramos Guides. Athens, 1973.

Triantaphyllides, H. "Macedonian Customs." *BSA* 3 (1896–97): 207–14.

Tripodi, Bruno. "Sulla morte di Alessandro I di Macedonia." *AnnPisa*, Cl. Let. e Fil., ser. 3, vol. 14, no. 4 (1984): 1263–68.

Tritsch, F. J. "The 'Sackers of Cities' and the 'Movement of Populations,' " In R. A. Crossland and A. Birchall, eds., *Bronze Age Migrations in the Aegean: Archaeological and Linguistic Problems in Greek Prehistory*, pp. 234–38. London, 1973.

Tronson, Adrian. "Satyrus the Peripatetic and the Marriages of Philip II." *JHS* 104 (1984): 116–26.

Turrill, W. B. *The Plant-life of the Balkan Peninsula: A Phytogeographical Study.* Oxford, 1929.

Van Zeist, W., and W. A. Casparie, eds. *Plants and Ancient Man: Studies in Paleoethnobotany.* Rotterdam and Boston, 1984.

Vartsos, A. "The Foundation of Brea." *AM* 2 (1977): 13–16.

Vickers, Michael. "Therme and Thessaloniki." In *Ancient Macedonian Studies in Honor of Charles F. Edson*, pp. 327–33. Thessaloniki, 1981.

Vokotopoulou, I. "I Epigraphi tōn Kalindōn." *AM* 4 (1986): 87–114.

Vokotopoulou, I., Aik. Despini, Vasiliki Misailidou, and Michalis Tiverios, eds. *Sindos: Katalogos tis ekthesis.* Athens, 1985.

Von Blanckenhagen, P. H. "Painting in the Time of Alexander and Later." In Beryl Barr-Sharrar and Eugene N. Borza, eds., *Macedonia and Greece in Late Classical and Early Hellenistic Times*, pp. 251–60. Studies in the History of Art 10. Washington, D.C., 1982.

Wace, A.J.B. "North Greek Festivals and the Worship of Dionysos." *BSA* 16 (1909–10): 232–53.

———. "The Mounds of Macedonia." *BSA* 20 (1913–14): 123–32.

———. "The Site of Olynthus." *BSA* 21 (1914–15/1915–16): 11–15.

Wace, A.J.B., and A. M. Woodward. "Inscriptions from Upper Macedonia." *BSA* 18 (1911–12): 166–88.

Wade-Gery, H. T. "Kritias and Herodes." *CQ* 39 (1945): 19–33.

Walbank, F. W. *A Historical Commentary on Polybius.* 3 vols. Oxford, 1957–79.

————. *Philip V of Macedon*. Cambridge, 1940.

Walbank, Michael B. *Athenian Proxenies of the Fifth Century B.C.* Toronto and Sarasota, 1978.

Wallace, M. B. "Early Greek *Proxenoi*." *Phoenix* 24 (1970): 189–208.

Walker, E. M. "The Confederacy of Delos, 478–463 B.C." In *CAH* 5 (1927), ch. 2.

Walker, Susan. "Women and Housing in Classical Greece." In Averil Cameron and Amelie Kuhrt, eds., *Images of Women in Antiquity*, pp. 81–91. Detroit, 1983.

Wardle, K. A. "Assiros: A Macedonian Settlement of the Late Bronze Age and Early Iron Age." *AM* 3 (1983): 291–305.

————. "Assiros Toumba." *ArchDelt* 31 (1976): 251–54.

————. "The Northern Frontier of Mycenaean Greece." *BICS* 22 (1975): 206–12.

Wehrli, Cl. *Antigone et Démétrios*. Geneva, 1968.

Weinberg, Saul S. "The Stone Age in the Aegean." *CAH*, 3rd ed., vol. 1, pt. 1, ch. 10. 1970.

West, William C. "Hellenic Homonoia and the New Decree from Plataea." *GRBS* 18 (1977): 307–19.

Westlake, H. D. *Thessaly in the Fourth Century B.C.* London, 1935.

————. "The Medism of Thessaly." *JHS* 56 (1936): 12–24.

Wickersham, John, and Gerald Verbrugghe, eds. *Greek Historical Documents: The Fourth Century B.C.* Toronto, 1973.

Wilamowitz-Moellendorff, Ulrich von. "Die Thukydideslegende." *Hermes* 12 (1877): 326–67.

Wilcken, Ulrich. *Alexander the Great*. Trans. G. C. Richards, ed. Eugene N. Borza. New York, 1967.

————. "Philip II von Makedonien und die panhellenische Idee." *Sitz. preuss. Akad. Wiss. zu Berlin*, Philo.-hist. Kl. 28 (1929): 291–318.

Will, Edouard. *Histoire politique de monde hellénistique (323–30 av. J.-C.)*. 2nd ed. 2 vols. Nancy, 1979–82.

Will, Wolfgang. *Alexander der Grosse*. Geschichte Makedoniens 2. Stuttgart, Berlin, Köln, and Mainz, 1986.

Wirth, Gerhard. *Philipp II*. Geschichte Makedoniens 1. Stuttgart, Berlin, Köln, and Mainz, 1985.

Woodhouse, C. M. *The Struggle for Greece, 1941–1949*. London, 1976.

Wüst, F. R. *Philipp II von Makedonien und Griechenland in den Jahren 346 bis 338*. Munich, 1938.

Wycherley, R. E. *The Athenian Agora*. Vol. 3, *Literary and Epigraphical Testimonia*. Princeton, 1957.

Xirotiris, N. I., and F. Langenscheidt. "The Cremation from the Royal Macedonian Tombs at Vergina." *ArchEph* (1981): 142–60.

Youri, Evgenia. *O krateras tou Derveniou*. Vivliothiki tis en Athinais Archaiologikis Hetairias, no. 89. Athens, 1978.

· INDEX ·

The names of modern scholars and ancient writers are mentioned in the index only when there is some special significance to their work beyond bibliographical references. This general index also incorporates map references for place names, citing the individual map(s). **(I, II, III, IV**, and **End)** and coordinates in boldface.